Stoner to Seeker:
1970s Asian Hippie Trail

Gordon Schwerzmann

Stoner to Seeker - 1970s Asian Hippie Trail

Copyrights © 2024 by Gordon Schwerzmann

All Rights Reserved

No part of this book may be reproduced or transmitted in any form or by any means, electronic or mechanical, including photocopying, recording, or by any information storage and retrieval system without the written permission of the author, except where permitted by law.

Dedication

To my son Nils who bravely journeyed to China to discover his own world and meaning in life, teaching, mastering Mandarin Chinese, and becoming a virtuoso on the Chinese violin, erhu.

Acknowledgements

I am deeply indebted to Fanny Lee for her "tough love," criticism, and professional editing. "Good night, Mrs. Calabash, wherever you are." Arden Gallagher for her indefatigable help in getting this book ready for publication. Without her advice, help, and understanding, this book would have remained a crinkled photograph in an unsorted dusty box in the attic of my imagination.

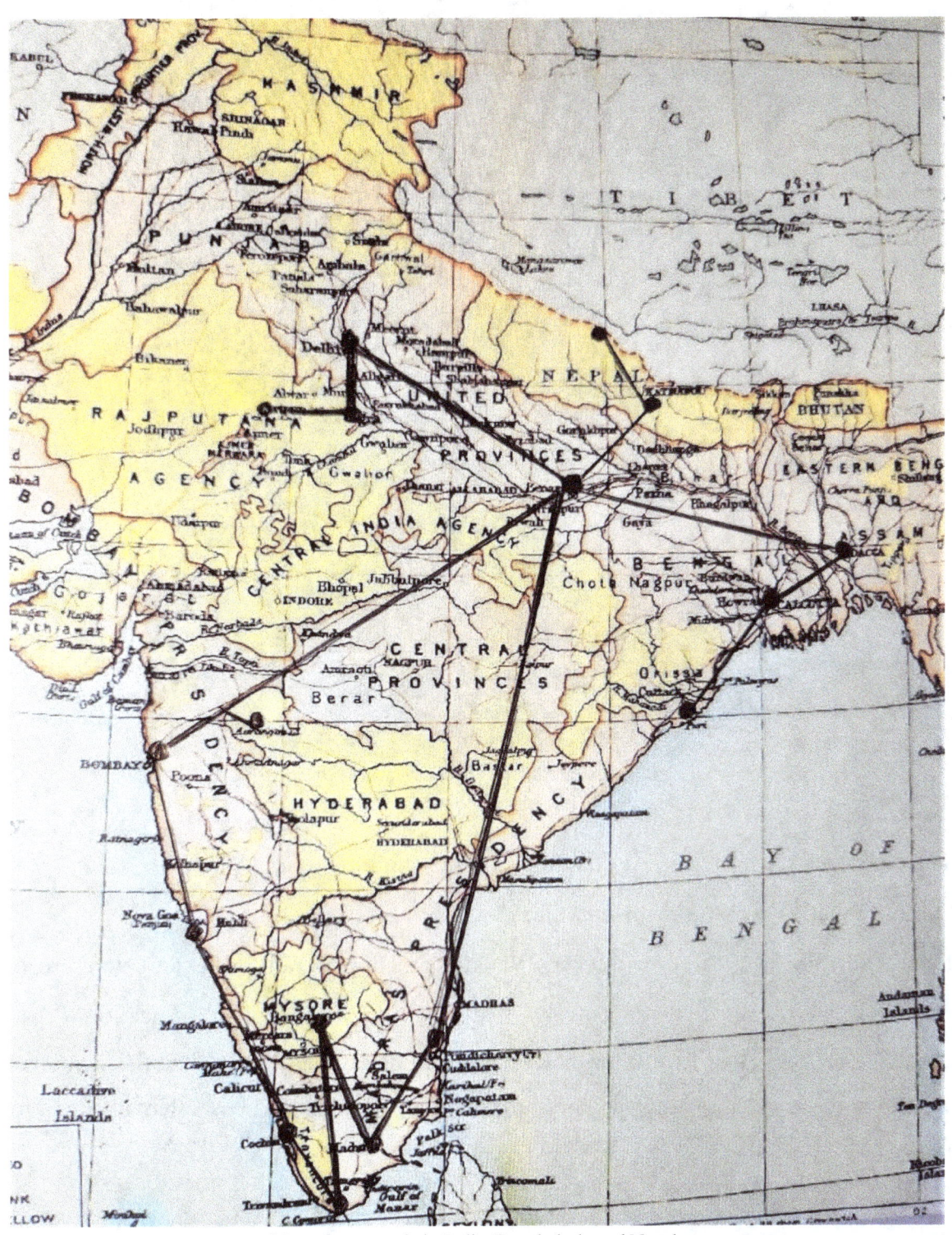
Map of my travels in India, Bangladesh, and Nepal.

"THE SCREAM" by Edvard Munch, 1910.

There are loud cries and shrieks coming from the adjoining room.

Soren: "What's the matter with you, Lars?"

Lars: "I just finished 'Stoner to Seeker: 1970s Asian Hippie Trail' and I can't stop screaming? Am I going insane?"

Soren: "You know that I work for the IRS and I'm here to help you. I had the same reaction when reading the book. Just watch an hour of golf on TV, it's the next best alternative to a frontal lobotomy."

Table of Contents

Introduction 1

India: First Impressions 3

Calcutta 5

    Chapter One: Calcutta - Dystopian City 6

    Chapter Two: On Poverty 12

    Chapter Three: Women in Indian Society - Past and Present 16

    Chapter Four: The Great Bangal Famine of 1943 18

    Chapter Five: The Black Hole of Calcutta 22

    Chapter Six: American Aid on a Personal Basis 25

    Chapter Seven: Rabindranath Tagore 28

    Chapter Eight: Dance, Dance, Dance 31

    Chapter Nine: The Freak Goes to the Movies 40

    Chapter Ten: Ravi Shankar 44

    Chapter Eleven: "You Can See the Forest for the Tree" 46

Bangladesh 49

    Chapter Twelve: Bangladesh 50

    Chapter Thirteen: Bangladesh II - the Islamification of Bangladesh 57

    Chapter Fourteen: Sufism and "The Perfect Man" 61

    Chapter Fifteen: A Simple Tale of Faith - A Bedtime Fairytale 63

    Chapter Sixteen: Nusrat Fateh Ali Khan 67

    Chapter Seventeen: Ibn Battuta 70

    Chapter Eighteen: Shipbreaking 101 73

    Chapter Nineteen: Furdos' Story 79

    Chapter Twenty: People of Bangladesh 88

The Heartland of India 103

    Chapter Twenty-One: Hinduism Demystified 104

    Chapter Twenty-Two: How the Caste System Began - A Fractured Fantasy 112

    Chapter Twenty-Three: The Academic Confronts Reality 116

    Chapter Twenty-Four: Khajuraho and the Kama Sutra 118

    Chapter Twenty-Five: Mahabharata - The Epic That Made India 122

    Chapter Twenty-Six: Ramayana 124

Chapter Twenty-Seven: Ramayana - The Hollywood Adaptation 128
Chapter Twenty-Eight: Kailasha Temple 135
Chapter Twenty-Nine: Waiting for Godot - The Indian Version 142
Chapter Thirty: Rachel 147

Bombay 152
Chapter Thirty-One: Bombay - Quiet Days and Wild Nights 153
Chapter Thirty-Two: Parsi - The Flame Is Flickering 162
Chapter Thirty-Three: How to Marry a Millionaire 167

Buddhism in India 170
Chapter Thirty-Four: West Meets East and the First Image of God 171
Chapter Thirty-Five: Sanchi - Beauty in Ruins 175
Chapter Thirty-Six: Buddha's First Sermon 179
Chapter Thirty-Seven: Ajanta - A Lost World Rediscovered 183
Chapter Thirty-Eight: Why Buddhism Died in India 187

Goa and Kovalam 194
Chapter Thirty-Nine: The "Magic Bus" 195
Chapter Forty: Goa - Freak Paradise 199
Chapter Forty-One: "Lover Shot Down" 212
Chapter Forty-Two: "Lusiades" (The Portuguese) - A National Epic Poem 216
Chapter Forty-Three: Gypsies of Goa 219
Chapter Forty-Four: Alfonso de Albuquerque 223
Chapter Forty-Five: Trish in Goa 227
Chapter Forty-Six: Cochin - Spices, Jews, and Christians 236
Chapter Forty-Seven: Kerala - Green Mansions 240
Chapter Forty-Eight: Dawn 245

The South of India 252
Chapter Forty-Nine: Life on Indian Roads 253
Chapter Fifty: Madurai 256
Chapter Fifty-One: The Hindu Concept of Time 261
Chapter Fifty-Two: The Curious Case of Wobble 263
Chapter Fifty-Three: Mahabalipuram 265
Chapter Fifty-Four: "Dawning of the New Age" 269

- *Chapter Fifty-Five: Srirangam Temple Complex* 272
- *Chapter Fifty-Six: Beedis* 276
- *Chapter Fifty-Seven: Jesus as the First Freak* 278
- *Chapter Fifty-Eight: From Idol to Figurehead* 284

Auroville **286**
- *Chapter Fifty-Nine: Pondicherry - France in India* 287
- *Chapter Sixty: Sri Aurobindo, the Mother, and Auroville* 292
- *Chapter Sixty-One: Ray - Build It and They Will Come* 296
- *Chapter Sixty-Two: A Man of Constant Sorrow* 299
- *Chapter Sixty-Three: A Walk of Song, Love, and Death* 306
- *Chapter Sixty-Four: Ray II - The Adventure of Consciousness* 309
- *Chapter Sixty-Five: Jacob's Ladder* 312
- *Chapter Sixty-Six: Gordon Bares All!* 316

Puri **325**
- *Chapter Sixty-Seven: June the Sixteenth* 326
- *Chapter Sixty-Eight: Puri - Welcome to Sesame Street* 331
- *Chapter Sixty-Nine: Magic and Mystery in Stone - The Sun Chariot Temple Konark* 334
- *Chapter Seventy: Reise Mit Kinder (Traveling With Children)* 339

Nepal **343**
- *Chapter Seventy-One: The Road to Kathmandu* 344
- *Chapter Seventy-Two: The Ideal of Kathmandu* 350
- *Chapter Seventy-Three: Kathmandu - The Promised Land* 353
- *Chapter Seventy-Four: "We Are More Than Cuckoo Clocks, Swiss Cheese, and Chocolate"* 367
- *Chapter Seventy-Five: Ingrid - The Heidi Redux* 372
- *Chapter Seventy-Six: Claire De Lune Part I* 377
- *Chapter Seventy-Seven: Cathy* 385
- *Chapter Seventy-Eight: Claire De Lune Part II* 391
- *Chapter Seventy-Nine: People of Nepal* 397

Benares **414**
- *Chapter Eighty: Benares - City of Joy* 415
- *Chapter Eighty-One: Hot-L Benares* 422
- *Chapter Eighty-Two: Charon* 425

Chapter Eighty-Three: Freaks, Houseboats, and Nietzsche 428

Chapter Eighty-Four: Alex's Tale (Room 1C) 435

Chapter Eighty-Five: Megan's Tale (Room 2D) 438

Chapter Eighty-Six: Remy's Tale of Woe - The French Connection (Room 2E) 440

Chapter Eighty-Seven: "We Hardly Knew Yah, Tommy Boy." 443

North India 445

Chapter Eighty-Eight: Delhi 446

Chapter Eighty-Nine: Partition 450

Chapter Ninety: Bangal Lancers, Adventurers and Novelists - The Creation of a Myth 455

Chapter Ninety-One: One Chooses to Forget, Another Clings To Remember 461

Chapter Ninety-Two: Frozen Infatuation - A Photograph 467

Chapter Ninety-Three: Agra Beyond the Taj Mahal 470

Chapter Ninety-Four: Fatehpur Sikri (City of Victory) 472

Chapter Ninety-Five: The Freak Buys a Sitar 477

Jaipur 480

Chapter Ninety-Six: Jaipur - "Pretty In Pink" 481

Chapter Ninety-Seven: Upward Mobility in the caste system - The Rajputs 484

Chapter Ninety-Eight: Mahavira and the Jains 488

Chapter Ninety-Nine: Hawa Mahal - Palace of the Winds 492

Chapter Hundred: Lakshmi's Prayer 496

Chapter A Hundred and One: People of India 499

The Parting Glass 519

Chapter A Hundred and Two: The Last Day in Asia 524

Chapter A Hundred and Three: Flash Gordon's Worst Fear 528

Bibliography 530

Illustration Credits 549

About the Author 571

About the Book: Stoner to Seeker - 1970s Asian Hippie Trail 572

Introduction

This is the final installment of my three-year-long Asian travels (Are we there yet?). I started off as a typical American: a soldier and Christian, complacent in my middle-class values. Then I discovered so many new and different philosophies, religions, and lifestyles that I began reevaluating my life's ambitions and goals ("And you don't know what's happening to you, do you, Mr. Jones." {Counting Crows}).

I overindulged in sex and drugs, but I always strived to understand the different cultures, worldviews and attitudes of the people in all the countries I visited. I did this by talking and listening to all manner of people in these countries, getting their views, doubts, hopes, and dreams. I call myself a freak ("Call Me Freak" - wait, that's stolen from "Moby Dick") and sought out other Westerners: freaks, tourists, ex-GIs, Peace Corps volunteers, academics, and religious seekers. From each of these individuals, I received bits of a huge puzzle that eventually formed into a whole.

Indian Snake Charmers 1900 Carpenter Collection,
Library of Congress (Public Domain).

When I started my journey, India was always my final goal, yet I did not know what to expect when I arrived there. Growing up, the first image I had of India was a man in a turban playing a flute and taming a king cobra in a basket. Now, I see this image as a metaphor for my time in India: I am the snake charmer, and India is the snake, dangerous, mysterious, yet ultimately understandable. What I have attempted in this book is to convey this understanding of India: the people, places, culture, religion, and poverty. I arrived with my own set of Western prejudices and slowly, by speaking with the people, changed my perspectives and viewpoints on ideologies, religion, and life itself. If nothing else, I want to share with the readers the sense of wonder and awe I experienced here. I was "A stranger in a strange land." The customs were bizarre, the people were otherworldly, and the daily frustrations would have tried the patience of a saint. However, I have never felt so free in my entire life. My life was a "tabula rasa," and I could literally write my own destiny.

I really enjoyed writing this book because I was able, through my written journal, recollections, and research, to reinvent myself into my younger self, experiencing my travels anew, or to paraphrase Proust, "In search of glorious time."

Everyone likes to think that their own experiences are unique. They are not! What is unique is the self- examination of these universal occurrences so they make sense and give meaning to you and to you alone. Descartes famously stated, "I think, therefore I am." I would tweak that to read, "I am, but I must think to know who I really AM!"

Well, I think the reader has enough of these word plays, dramatic symbols, worldly quotes, misty recollections ("It brings a tear to me' eye, laddie") and "mea culpa" ("Being in love means you never have to say you're sorry." Oh my God, I just threw up).

Drum Roll! Ed McMahon enthusiastically booms, "Here's India" studio audience goes wild: clapping, whistling, and stomping their feet.

India: First Impressions

What I found when I arrived at Calcutta's Dumdum Airport was that everything can be summed up in two words: too much. Too much heat; too much people; too much poverty; too much religion; too much hot food; too much cows; too much traffic; too much smog; and pervading everything, too much frustration. That said, India must be experienced by immersing oneself directly into this cacophony: absorbing the sights, smells, sounds, feels, and tastes of this impossible place. Only then, with your senses overwhelmed, can you finally begin to divine any sense of order in this place. The sheer beauty and ugliness are the yin and yang of your mind, slowly bringing the understanding out of chaos. Once your mind is in equilibrium, you find that this is the most fascinating place in the entire world.

This is not a postcard "Wish You Were Here!" vacation; it is life in all its rawness, a struggle of endurance and basic existence. India is a cruel mistress that seduces and challenges you. It can swallow you up and spit you out, lost and broken. And it can uplift you to heights you never dreamed you would attain.

India is multi-layered; you can choose your destiny. Many of my freak friends chose hedonism, always high, living on golden beaches and pristine mountains; others obsessively searched for meaning in life through meditation and ritual. I chose the "Middle Way," trying to understand the culture by speaking to Indians from all classes of society. Dope, sex, and even religions are the guideposts in my real-life bildungsroman to understand who I am and what I want out of life.

So, join me on my "Beagle" voyage of discovery (which at times feels like I am a clueless passenger on the Titanic, "Oh, look at all those lovely little icecaps bobbing in the ocean before us"). India is the "strange new world," more fantastic than any "Star Trek" adventure.

Calcutta

Calcutta street scene (Burra Bazar) 1945

Chapter One: Calcutta - Dystopian City

Calcutta is a festering sore: more poverty, more disease, more lepers, more homeless, more jobless immigrants from farming villages, more radicals, and more human distress than any other large city in India. Industry leaves because the workers are always striking. Everything is collapsing: buildings, from shoddy construction; the electrical grid, which fails daily; clean water supply (there is none); lack and enforcement of public education; overwhelmed mass transit; corpses lying in the street; beggars and thieves everywhere; and pollution so thick, you can cut it with a knife. To top this off, there is an "upper crust" that still goes to the old British Jockey Club for drinks and races.

Upper-class Indians pride themselves on aping the Brits, playing cricket, and sending their children to exclusive "public schools" dressed in copied St. Paul logoed uniforms; there are hundreds of intellectuals that discuss everything, from world politics to the latest fashionable book, but avoid the real issues of poverty, homelessness, and the breakdown of society. And yet, there are individuals who strive to make a difference. Mother Teresa, a frail little Albanian nun, started a hospice where the dying are taken in and given medical help. Most of these unfortunates were picked up from the streets, left there to die of disease or starvation, and now, they are given solace and love in their last few days.

There's also the Salvation Army. When I first heard of this organization in Calcutta, I thought of the well-meaning, overstuffed Santa Clauses outside of every department store, collecting money in their iron pots for the poor in America. I didn't know who the poor were that they helped. It was sort of like what your mother said to you, "Eat your food; people are starving in India." (Well, I silently thought to myself, let's send it there now, so I don't have to finish eating this meal). I pictured a stiff cleric dispensing food in a soup kitchen, saying to the drunks and homeless, you can stay the night if you attend the moralizing service after the meal. Thank God, this wasn't the case in India. The Salvation Army was in the front ranks of dispensing food, without the Christian morality, and keeping people alive, one day at a time. They were selfless, energetic people who genuinely believed in God's message: "He who does this for the poorest, does it for Me."

Mother Teresa 1995 Photo by Kingkong Photos, Laurel, MD: free to use with attribution of author (CC-Attribution-Share Alike 2.0 Generic License)

The Salvation Army was one of the first missionary organizations to recruit local Indians to further their evangelical mission in India. Colonel Weerasooriya was a native of Ceylon and joined the Salvation Army in the 1870s. He was a dynamic preacher and a great inspiration: over 100 idealistic Brits enlisted in the Salvation Army after one of his impassioned speeches on the overwhelming poverty of India. He was a tireless worker and rose quickly in the ranks. The director of the Indian mission entrusted him as second in command, overseeing all of the European missionaries in India and Ceylon. He was never mindful of his personal safety and personally treated cholera victims when no one else would go to help them. He contracted cholera and died in 1888 at the age of 34. His last words were singing the song "I will trust Thee, I will trust Thee, all my Life Thou shalt control."

THE LATE COLONEL WEERASOORIYA

When I first arrived at the airport, there was a group of people with a small stand draped with the banner "The Salvation Army," giving out leaflets and talking with the travelers. They approached me and gave me a leaflet, but I begged off, saying I had to go. I thought nothing of it;

the Seven Days' Adventists were always accosting you on the streets of New York and stuffing your mailbox with their pamphlets of God's redemption. I ignored the group just like I ignored the Adventists. However, after a few days of walking the streets and seeing the absolute misery and overwhelming poverty, I felt I wanted to help, even in a small way. So, I found the rumbled-up leaflet from the Salvation Army and decided to go there to volunteer my services.

At the Salvation Army headquarters, there were groups of us travelers, Bible students, and regular tourists, and we met with one of the "Army Officers." A middle-aged, frumpy "housewife" let us into her office. I expected a sermon, but instead, she detailed what the organization was doing to save lives here and now. We talked about the hopelessness of the situation, and she agreed, saying, "The Indian middle and upper classes don't care to help the poor; they're only concerned with themselves. What India needs is communism to save itself. Religion here makes and justifies the passive acceptance of poverty. If you are a good person, you will be born into a higher status in your next life. Communism worked for the majority of the people in the Soviet Union and China, here and now. It gives food, education, shelter, and, most importantly, self-respect; all of the life-giving essentials these people need to survive."

I was astonished to hear these fiery words from such a supposedly staunch pillar of Christianity. I was won over by her forthrightness and honesty; I volunteered on the spot. I was told to be here at six o'clock in the morning to assist in picking up food and distributing it in one of the poorest neighborhoods in Calcutta. I arrived shortly before six am and was greeted by an overweight, bear of a man, Major Gardner, who directed the idealistic volunteers showing up (five hardy souls). He was a no-nonsense, abrupt pragmatist, who quickly organized us into a ready working team. Our duties were to pick-up left-over food from luxury hotels and bulk supplies from wholesale food distributors and philanthropic organizations. We would then stack it in his huge Bedford truck. The truck was lined with shelves inside, and there were also huge stainless-steel pots that needed to be filled and then lifted on to the truck. These were filled with rice, lentils, chickpeas, and whatever surplus was available that day. We also had some packaged food that we shelved in the truck.

This took all the morning, and the hot, humid weather really got to us. Finally loaded, we fought traffic for another hour and reached our destination around one pm. We set up tables, neatly spacing the overloaded food pots and dry goods. We formed lines for the hungry and policed those lines, making sure the supplicants didn't loop around and return for second helpings. We also set out some disposable dishes and plastic spoons, but I found out that most Indians carry their own brass pots, which we filled and moved the line along. By two pm, we were ready and opened the line for service. On a good day, we could feed anywhere from 150 to 200 people, depending on the size of portions and the type of food we had to distribute.

As I was helping, ladling out food into pots that the Indians carried, Major Gardner came over to me and said, "See how selfish the Indians are; look at this mother with her two daughters, about nine years and eleven years old, respectively. She won't send her daughters to school because she wants them to help her around the house." We had just fed this mother a pot of rice with lentils and a pot of boiled ladyfingers (okra). First, she loaded the rice on her eldest daughter's head and then the lighter okra on the head of her youngest daughter. She walked off, with the children trailing behind her, carrying nothing.

We always had to turn back people when the food ran out. Now it was about three thirty pm, and we collected the pots, broke down the tables, and headed back to the Salvation Army headquarters. This took over an hour in traffic. Once we arrived, we had to unload and scrub the pots and wipe off the shelves of the truck; by then, it was five thirty pm. It was a long day, and we were exhausted; however, we felt good: we had made a difference.

Then that night, reality kicked in: *Oh my God! We're going to have to do this again tomorrow morning and the next morning and the next morning after that*. Major Gardner had been doing this job, day-in and day-out, for an unbelievable five years. That devotion and selfless love to keep carrying on really made me respect and care about this rough-talking crusader. The daily monotony, the infinite humility of accepting leftovers and table scraps, the same feeding exercise, the traffic jam, and the daily heartbreak of turning away starving people would have driven me insane after a week of this.

As it was, I lasted five exhausting days and then had to move on. I told him that I wouldn't be back and thanked him for allowing me to put a face on poverty, and praised the selfless work of the Salvation Army. He didn't show any visible disappointment and graciously thanked me for my (all too short) efforts. He had a mission, and like any good "soldier," he would find a way to accomplish it. Leaving, I asked myself, "Did I do any good this time?" Yes, but I was too selfish to do this for any extended period. Not only did I want to continue my carefree traveling, but I also wanted a big, immediate solution, like communism, to solve this problem. However, I was proud to have served with a man who achieved little victories daily in the fight against poverty. God bless you, Major Gardner.

Chapter Two: On Poverty

Begging Girl (author's photo).

"Another day in paradise,"

- Phil Collins.

Anyone arriving in Indian cities is struck by the huge amount of people who are homeless or in make-shift huts in shanty towns without electricity, potable water, and sanitation. What freaks out most people coming to India is the constant begging: women with ragged children, old men, cripples, blind individuals, lepers, and all manner of distressed people constantly besieging you for money. Something should be done, you say—but what? Most of these people arriving in the cities have no education, and manual labor jobs are very limited. There are soup kitchens to feed the very poor like I had worked in and there are always openings for rickshaw drivers, but this employment provides barely enough for food, let alone to save any money. Many of the extremely poor cannot even work due to infirmities and mental health issues. As a freak, I had very little spare money. After giving to the first three or four beggars, I just hardened my mental attitude, ignored and passed them by; only the most extreme cases, the lepers, the blind, and the cripples, sometimes received a few rupees.

City poverty is very visible, but it turns out to be the tip of the iceberg. In India, 70% of people live in villages, and most are subsistence farmers. Due to overpopulation and a disproportionate number of tenant workers as opposed to farm owners, poverty in the countryside is hidden away from the general public, and when there are famines, hundreds of thousands die of starvation or succumb to diseases due to malnutrition. Village landlords control most of the arable land and have tenants working the fields, giving produce in lieu of rent. If the crops fail, the tenants are thrown off the land; the ambitious ones migrate to the cities for work, leaving their families behind, and this is the poverty you find in the cities today.

What have other countries done to handle their poor? In Communist China, the landlord class was abolished: all land belonged to the State and collective farms were established. Society was controlled and you just couldn't leave for the city. In Taiwan, the landlord class was bought-out and tenants were given the land. People could move to the cities, and because of Chang-Kai-shek's economic policies, there was work in small factories, producing essential components for the American electronic industry. On a relatively small scale, this worked, and we have the Taiwanese "Economic Miracle," but India is so huge that buying-out the landlord class would be prohibitive. Even if this were to happen, you would just create a nation of poor subsistence farmers, who can barely raise enough for their families, let alone a surplus to sell to the cities.

Then there is the caste system with a particular group that just operates the irrigation system. A different caste just grinds the wheat, yet another caste solely makes bricks. The Brahmin class serve as priests and educate the various castes in the village (but not the Untouchables). How do you change this intricate structure, which somehow seems to work?

America has sent in thousands of agricultural experts. The Peace Corps alone has over a thousand agricultural experts advising the farmers how to improve yields, introducing fast-growing strains of rice and wheat and new vegetables as alternatives to stop the growing depletion of the soil. American Aid gave the villagers tractors to till the fields, but without mechanics. The tractors broke down and were left to rust. The oxen that were replaced weren't around to leave the manure that fertilized the fields and served as fuel in a treeless land. Furthermore, the improved hybrid rice produced didn't have the same taste as Indians were accustomed to eating. So, they stopped using the high-yield miracle seeds and went back to their old low-yield varieties. Everywhere the old system remained in place. Why get a machine to replace railroad tracks or move timber when you have thousands of laborers who live on subsistence wages; they can eke out a living doing this back-breaking work.

The World Bank set up a program where local villages or single individuals would come up with a project, apply for a loan, and then slowly pay back the loan with the profits from these ventures. Successful projects such as a dairy co-op, which supplied milk and yogurt to local villages, or a weaving co-op, which sold their weavings in the cities, helped thousands, but what of the millions left behind?

The only answer is communism, but India has whole state governments like Kerala, which are communist-controlled but support the status quo, and do not advocate a revolution against the ruling elite. For the most part, the communists are just a part of the Indian middle-class political system, a class that's as large as the whole population of Great Britain.

There was, however, a communist uprising in 1967; this was called the "Naxalbari Revolution," which took place in West Bangal. Peasants, under the direction of radical communists, advocated land seizures from landlords and formed communist cells throughout the countryside. The leader of this group was an Indian freedom fighter who followed the Chinese Communist Party as opposed to the Russian-influenced mainstream Communist Party. His name was Chara Majumdar. He preached a people's war, based on the Chinese Communist Maoist revolution, which conquered China in 1949. This initial revolt killed government officials, industrialists, and peasants, alienating most Indians, but was supported by the villagers in West Bangal and by the Darjeeling tea pickers. Government police forces quickly suppressed this initial revolt, imprisoning and killing the communist leaders. Majumdar went underground and hid from the forces while organizing other cells and further revolutionizing the peasants. He was finally captured in 1972 and mysteriously died while in police custody. However, the movement continued on a smaller scale and spread from Bangal to Bihar in the rural provinces. Finally, the Indian government sent in the army in 1971 and suppressed the main insurgency.

Communism: to Be or Not to Be, That Is the Question?

While riding on a bus in the Bihar countryside, I met two different educated Indians. The first was a "Petit Bourgeois," a telecommunications official with a son attending an engineering college nearby. We spoke of many things, including the Hindu religion and his respect for Sri Sathya Baba, the mystic holy man from Whitefield, India. The other Indian was an upper-caste Hindu who received his PhD in agricultural science from Kentucky University. He is a glowing example of a modern, forward-looking Indian who believes that only science and technology will save India.

Both men believe that India has greatly improved since independence, but the population increase wiped out a lot of these gains. The PhD man spoke realistically of corruption, inefficiencies in government, and the lack of general education. Both men firmly believed that India could survive without communism. Listening to these two educated Indians made me reflect on my own upbringing. I, too, was like the first Indian, a member of the "Petit Bourgeois." I was able to go to college because of the hard work of my parents, just as this Indian did for his son. This Indian viewed his struggle to educate his child as "dharma" (duty) to make the world a better place for his children, but I also saw the viewpoint of the second Indian.

The agricultural professor fervently believed that technological advancements and education were the only way that India could overcome its poverty. He had a son and a daughter; both were attending university and would be at the forefront of India's educated professionals: his son was studying structural engineering and his daughter was studying to be a physician. Both men firmly believed that you could work within the system to make changes. Both Indians were part of the rapidly growing middle class, which was already close to 75 million Indians.

Unlike the Salvation Army matron and I, who are "outsiders" demanding communism as the answer, these two Indians lived through partition, independence, and the growing pains of nationhood. They have an insider's view and see hope for the future. They know the Indian system, culture, and way of life and want to change India for the better from within the system. This should be possible in the world's largest democracy.

Chapter Three: Women in Indian Society - Past and Present

When I arrived in India, I imagined what women's lives were like for hundreds of years in the past. In Agra, while touring the fort, the seat of Mughal power, I visited the harem quarters. Their rooms overlooked the Yamana River, and their lives were confined to the fort only. Their existence was to serve the emperor, but they also learned valuable skills such as music playing, dancing, and social etiquette. Similarly, the young daughters of wealthy Hindus were also confined, having to sit behind lattice screens in buildings like the Hawa Mahal (Palace of the Winds) in Jaipur to view life from afar.

Marriages were (and still are) arranged by parents, and duty over freedom or happiness is always the rule. Muslim women were just as restricted from mingling with outside society, and when they go outside they are clothed from head to foot (purdah) so that no part of their body could be seen. Most Indians married very young since the social and moral requirement of virginity was paramount for a marriage.

In the villages of rural India, women aren't usually schooled since they should help their mothers with the farm chores. Also, daughters could be an unwelcome burden when it comes to marriage since they are required to have a dowry. The larger the dowry, the more marriageable the daughter is. In all of the village community governing councils, women aren't represented or allowed to speak. Once married, the wife moves in with the husband's family, and the patriarchal family makes all the important decisions, especially among the higher Hindu castes.

Once the husband dies, the widow is expected to sacrifice herself in a death ritual (suttee) where she throws herself on a sacrificial fire. This was outlawed by the British, but social and peer pressure still dictate that the widow never remarries once her husband dies.

Fast forward to the present, and we have an Indian woman as prime minister, Indira Gandhi. Indian women, especially the higher caste Hindus, are being educated and entering professions that were once the sole provenance of males. Education for women is now an advantage in advertisements for marriage in newspapers. Just like in the West, a two-income family is becoming a necessary norm, especially in large urban areas. However, in rural India, both Hindu and Muslim villages little has changed, and women are second-class citizens. The one bright spot is that Indian women can now vote, and I'm sure that helped elect Mrs. Gandhi. Also, there are opportunities for women in dance, film, and popular movies. International aid organizations are experimenting with low-interest mini-loans for village women who want to start small businesses in their local villages. As India gets more exposure to Western culture and lifestyles, more opportunities for middle-class women will develop in business, medicine, politics, tourism, sports, and fashion.

Woman sacrifices herself after her husband dies (suttee).

Chapter Four: The Great Bangal Famine of 1943

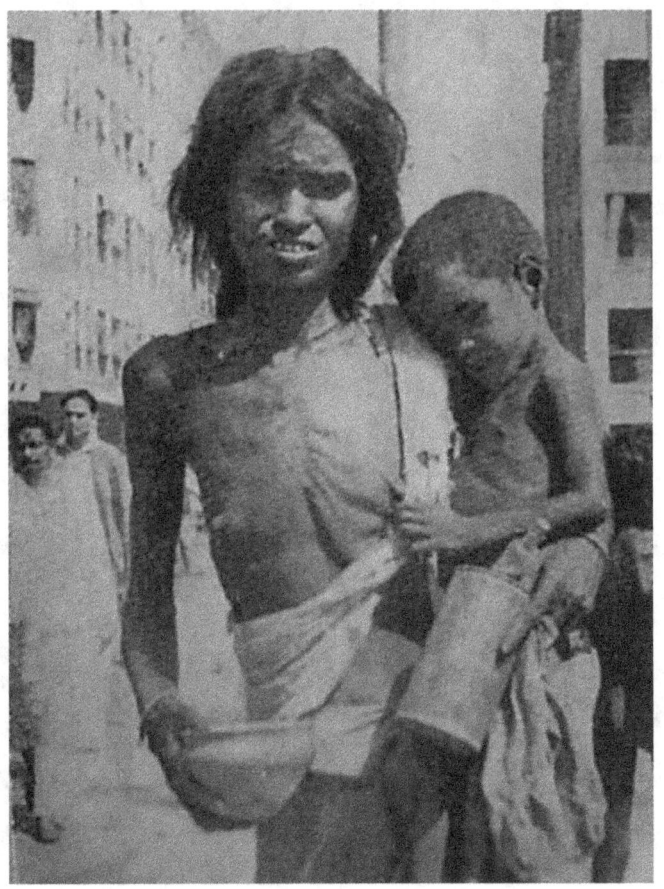
Starving mother and child, 1943, Calcutta.

My father had lived through the Great Depression. I only knew that he was the owner of a small restaurant in New York City that had to close because of the economic crash, but he never talked to me about the hardships he endured. Times were rough in America, but we did not have three million dead, as Ahmed (my hotel manager) told me. What caused this horror?

Bangal in 1940-1941 was 80% rural farmers, who eked out a poor subsistence living on small farms (Bangal included all of Bangladesh, the newly formed country and Indian Bangal, and was about 50% Hindu and 50% Muslim). Bangal farmers and their families suffered severely from malnutrition, and the Calcutta State Government had to import rice just to keep these farming families alive.

Then World War II started, and the situation got much worse. In 1941, the Japanese conquered Burma and shut off that rice supply to Bangal. The shortage of rice caused inflation; the Raj put in price controls that forced merchants to sell rice at artificially low prices. This, of course, led to hoarding, which further reduced the availability of rice.

The Raj, fearful of a Japanese invasion of India through Bangal, issued a disastrous "policy of denial." First, they burned rice fields in Eastern Bangal (now Bangladesh) and confiscated and destroyed 45,000 small boats: all to deny the Japanese foodstuffs and transportation. With this policy, the Raj ruined not only the Bangal fishing industry but also closed the network that supplied the Bangalis with a means to distribute food, medicine, and other essentials throughout the eastern province (during the monsoon and shortly afterwards, supplies and food moved by boat; there wasn't a good road infrastructure to fall back on).

The second disastrous Raj policy decision was to give priority to what rice was available to the people who worked in the "war industry." These were the munitions manufacturers, the army, the railroad workers, and the civil servants that were needed to help Britain win the war.

The third mistake was for the Raj to prohibit the movement of food from one Indian province to another, causing more shortages and black markets; the cost of rice doubled and then tripled in the countryside. Small farmers were desperate, selling heirlooms and, finally, their family farms. Over a million and a half small farms were sold to greedy landlords for cash, the profits of which were soon eaten up by inflation. The poor farmers were soon just as broke as before, but now they were tenants, dependent on the whim of their landlords.

Before the famine, the landlords often extended credit to poor farmers to be paid back when the new crops were harvested. Now, landlords abandoned their tenants. Credit was almost impossible to obtain, and less rice (about 25% less than the previous year) was produced. Then in the fall of 1942, Bangal was hit by the "Brown Spot" disease, which devastated the new rice crop for that year. This disease was like the Potato Blight of the 1840s in Ireland, which also caused mass starvation there. This disaster, coupled with the intra-provincial ban on rice imports, caused the first wave of starvation deaths in early 1943.

What was even worse was the breakdown of the family structure. Husbands abandoned wives and children to go to Calcutta in search of work and food. Homeless women and children wandered the countryside, dying of starvation by the hundreds of thousands. Young girls were sold to pimps for a kilo of rice; thousands were forced into prostitution. These women were never accepted back by their husbands or families after the famine was over. Many families abandoned small children, especially girl babies; elderly grandparents were left behind to die in deserted villages. The whole fabric of rural society, from families to religion to education to healthcare, was destroyed.

A further calamity occurred in the October - November 1942 timeframe when a cyclone struck the low sea-level coastal villages of East Bangal, killing hundreds of thousands. But worse than the actual cyclone was the aftermath: the drinking water for millions of Bangalis became polluted. This polluted water caused malaria and cholera on a huge scale. The sick and starving rural population migrated to Calcutta to die in the streets by the hundreds of thousands; so many died that they were left to rot in the open, spreading even more disease.

The Viceroy of India, Sir Lytton Linlithgow, desperately asked Britain for help, but Churchill refused, citing a lack of transport vessels. However, Churchill hated Indians because of the "Quit India" Independence Movement. Calcutta was especially a hotspot for independence agitation. Relief wheat shipments from Australia somehow got vessels to go to Ceylon and South Africa but not to go to Bangal. Churchill was overheard saying: "I want to feed only those (Indians) actually fighting or making munitions or working some particular railways."

When food and medicine were finally made available in mid-1943, a good portion of it rotted at the docks of Calcutta because there was no way to distribute it into East Bangal. This was because the Raj had destroyed the small boats that could have carried it via the interior waterways to the starving populace. About one and a half million Bangalis died from an outright lack of food from March to December 1943. But the other one and a half million of the total deaths were the result of severely malnourished people, who died of malaria and cholera because they had no immunity to it. This continued through May of 1944. Everywhere there were dead bodies, lying in ditches, eaten by vultures; the famine had destroyed millions of families, and no one helped the unfortunate people who were still alive.

When the famine finally ended, there were three million dead out of a Bangal population of sixty million. The blame is squarely on the Raj for this genocide. Nehru, at that time one of the chief independence fighters, spoke for all of India when he said, "The final judgment on British rule in India was the Great Famine of 1943-1944." This terrible event showed that the Raj was incapable of providing for their subjects and deserved to lose this "Jewel of the Crown" by the callous indifference they showed to the millions of lives lost.

A famine dead boy and his dog, 1943, Calcutta. (Public Domain).

Chapter Five: The Black Hole of Calcutta

While growing up, I heard the expression that this place or situation, where you had a lot of people in close, sweaty proximity, was as stifling as the "Black Hole of Calcutta." In college, I saw something like this when I witnessed a group of guys from a rival fraternity who tried to see how many people you could get into a Volkswagen Beetle.

Fort Williams in 1807- headquarters of the British East India Company: Calcutta.

The real "Black Hole" was actually a small prison room in Fort Williams, the headquarters of the British East India Company in Calcutta. At that time, in 1756, the company controlled a large portion of India. The British were always having conflicts with the local native authorities, in this instance, the ruler of Bangal was Nawab Siraj ud Daulah. The nawab attacked the fort and captured it on June 20, 1756. His commanding officer then gathered the surviving British company soldiers, civil servants, and civilians of the fort, including the wife of an administrator, and imprisoned these people, 146 in total, into a small holding room where they could barely get the door shut after forcing all the people inside. The room measured 14' long and 18' wide, with two small, heavily barred window openings high up near the ceiling. This was a small prison room meant to hold at most 20 people.

Prison Guards offered hundreds of Rupees for a bowl of water: Black Hole of Calcutta. Print from Hutchinson "History of Nations" 1910, copyright expired and now public domain.

They were locked in the room around seven pm on the night of the twentieth, and then the horror began. The sweating bodies, the lack of breathable air, and panic-stricken prisoners climbing over each other caused the first death by around nine pm. The desperate men climbed the wall, trying to bribe guards and shouting for water. The guards were too afraid of the nawab, who they didn't dare to awaken, to apprise him of the dire situation. Later the guards did pass some water through the bars, but most of this spilled. By midnight, asphyxiation and trampling upon each other killed dozens of prisoners. They stood on dead bodies to get to the windows. Many went raving mad, clawing the walls. The screams and cries sucked what little air was in the room, and more died. When the nawab was finally informed, he opened the door to the room at six am, and of the 146 prisoners that went in, only twenty-three came out alive, including Mrs. Carey, the only female prisoner. Many of the survivors were raving mad and others too weak to walk.

One survivor, John Holwell, wrote an account of that terrible night and sent it to the British press. The London press printed the story and added lurid illustrations of the carnage, with prominence given to Mrs. Carey, looking crazed, with a contorted expression, and men shown clawing at the walls and climbing over dead bodies to reach the windows. The British crown was outraged and sent reinforcements that defeated and killed the nawab, who publicly expressed no regret for this tragedy.

The fort, including this infamous room, became a company warehouse before it was torn down in the nineteenth century. There is a large monument in St. John's Anglican Church graveyard in Calcutta, commemorating this horrific night and the unfortunate who died.

Chapter Six: American Aid on a Personal Basis

U.S. Marine Corps delivering U.S. Aid.

"Oh! Shiva, help me! I need to get money for my family. Wait! Who is this getting on the tram? A tall, bearded foreigner, he looks just like one of those evil American hippies that I saw in the movie Hare Krishna, Hare Ram. He must have something worthwhile to steal. He is clutching his camera tightly, and I can see he carries his money in a pouch around his neck, tucked in his shirt. The bus is too crowded for me to get to that. There are only his pockets: maybe he has a few rupees there. I slowly made my way toward him, hoping he wouldn't get off before I could rifle his pockets. Then I saw my opportunity. Like a well-executed soccer move, I angled myself to his right side while a fat Indian (civil servant, I guessed) stood in front of him, and another two passengers had hemmed him in on the back and left side. I deftly groped his right pocket, grabbed a small pouch, and quickly zig-zagged through the crowded arms and bodies, heading for the exit. He felt my hands and started yelling, first shoving the fat man forward and then frantically moving around, still screaming that he had been pickpocketed.

The tram stopped at Chowringhee, and I got off with dozens of others. I wondered what I had stolen; it must be valuable! He stayed on the tram, frantically trying to find the culprit; I was safe. I walked into an alley and opened the pouch: Nothing! Then I felt a small wadded-up piece of paper. I unfolded the damp paper and found a strange-looking piece of money that I had never seen. It had the number 100 on top of each side and a picture of a fat, balding old man with square glasses. It had writing I couldn't read, but it looked like the store lettering in my neighborhood, so it must be English.

What do I do? If I take it to the local moneychanger, I will be cheated. Who can I trust? I was at Chowringhee Square and went to one of the large moneychangers who served the foreign tourists. They are always very busy, and I wouldn't be asked a lot of questions because it would hold up the line. I had my ID from the jute factory; it was still good, even though they had let me go a month ago, claiming the times were bad and they had to cut workers. I have been looking for work since then; pickpocketing hadn't been good, and I needed a steady income that would pay me every week to support my family.

I turned my judah (long draped skirt that covered my lower body) inside out so that it was relatively clean, brushed my hair back, and washed off the stains on my white desh (shirt). Afterwards, I looked in a store mirror and thought I looked presentable enough for a low-level civil servant. As I stood in the money-changing lane, I looked at the exchange board: 1 British pound = 950 rupees, 1 US dollar = 320 rupees, 1 French Franc = 78 rupees. Whatever I had, I had 100 of them, not just one. Finally, it was my turn. I handed the fat moneychanger my factory card and the unfolded bill. The moneychanger looked amazed.

'Where did you get this American 100-dollar bill?'

'I am cashing this for my boss; he deals with a lot of foreigners and told me to change it because he couldn't leave the office.'

'Hmm, the boss was too busy to change this?'

'Yes.'

'Normally, I take 5% of the total, but since this is such a large bill, I must charge you 10%. Take it or leave.'

I didn't know what to do; the people in line were shouting, 'Hurry up! Keep moving!'

'Yes, I will change it.'

The moneychanger laughed and counted out 28,800 rupees and handed it to me in a big wad of bills. I was dumbfounded! This was more than I made in a year at the factory. I walked around the square with this large wad of bills, thinking of how to spend it.

I would buy Lakshmi a new gold-threaded sari and my two boys new book bags and school uniforms so they wouldn't be the shame of their class in their old torn sets. I would get the greedy landlord off my back by paying past due rents and a few months in advance on our small apartment. But I thanked Shiva a thousand times because now I could buy a nice piece of gold jewelry for Shanti's dowry, so she could get married to a proper suitor when the right time comes. If there was anything left, Lakshmi would manage to spend it; I had no fears about that. Yes, it was wrong to steal. Forgive me, Shiva, but I thanked that hapless American for his 'donation' to save my family."

Chapter Seven: Rabindranath Tagore

Rabindranath Tagore is a literary giant and father of modern Indian literature. He was primarily a poet and won the Nobel Prize in Literature in 1913 (the first non-Westerner to win this prize) for his "Gitanjali - Song Offerings" poems. He was also the first modern Indian short storyteller, novelist, song writer, nationalist (for Indian independence) painter, filmmaker, and university teacher (Now, only if he had also been a famous chef, he would be a household name in the West!).

In India, his reputation is sacrosanct. However, today he is little known in the West, and that may be because his works are exceedingly difficult to translate. He composed the national anthem of India, and one of his songs has become the national anthem of the new state of Bangladesh. In his poems, he was greatly influenced by Bangali folktales, while his later poems extolled Hindu mysticism. I have included an excerpt from a poem from the Song Offerings, "Unending Love."

"I seem to have loved you in numberless forms, in numberless times In life after life; in age after age, forever

My spellbound heart has made and remade the necklace of songs

Take that as a gift; wear it round your neck in your many forms

In life after life, in age after age, forever.

You and I have floated here on this stream that brings from the font

At the heart of time, love of one for another

We have played alongside millions of lovers

Shared in the same shy sweetness of meeting, the distressful tears of farewell.

Old love but in shapes that renew and renew forever.

The memories of all loves merging with this love of ours and the songs of every poet past and forever

To me, this poem is beautiful and very romantic (written in 1912). I spoke to an educated Bangali, and he saw this poem as a heartfelt pean to the Hindu gods. This made me reevaluate the poem. Here romantic and spiritual love are fused together; the Indian mindset is very different from ours. I came to see how it was in the tradition of the singing chant of the Vedas I had listened to in the Indian temples. It would be great to hear this poem spoken in its original Bangali, to hear the musical rhythm and the cadence rhymes of that language to see how the tradition of the Vedas is brought into the 20th century.

I have felt the same way about Dante's "Inferno." The English language translation of Dante's poem left me cold. I asked myself, "Is this a great classic?" Then I got hold of a talking tape of the "Inferno" in Italian, and the musical beauty of the poetry overwhelmed me: so majestic and chromatic in the sonorous Italian language.

Rabindranath Tagore in 1941.

Lastly, Tagore looked the part of the father figure: long narrow face with flowing white hair and beard and piercing dark eyes. Like Tolstoy and Whitman, his dynamic appearance furthered the image of the poet sage, projecting an aura of assurance and authority.

Chapter Eight: Dance, Dance, Dance

Sri Chaitanya Mahaprabhu,(sage with the long white beard) who was born in 1486, is shown performing 'Nagar kirtan,' devotional chanting and dancing, in the streets of Nabadwip, Bangal.

Dance is one of the oldest cultural arts of India. There is an unbroken continuity from the Harrappan Indus Valley Civilization to the present-day dance spectacles of Bollywood. One of the first statues ever recovered from the Indus Valley Civilization was a tribal girl about 4 inches high, portraying her dancing.

The dancing girl of Mohenjo-dara; 2300-1750 BC; bronze; height: 10.8 cm (4 1/4 in.); National Museum (New Delhi, India).

The veneration of dance in Hinduism continued with the Cosmic Dancer, created in the 8th century in the south of India. Here Shiva is multi-armed, in a high-stepping dance movement, surrounded by a ring of fire with the headdress of a multi-headed cobra, trampling the demon of ignorance. His dancing symbolizes the dynamic nature of the cosmos, destruction followed by rebirth.

Indian dance was codified around 1500 BC in the ancient Sanskrit treatise "Natya Sastra," which gave instruction on hand and eye movement, phasing of steps, positions of standing and knee bends, acting, facial expressions, and other ritual movements. Following the rules of the "Natya Sastra" will give the viewer pleasure in watching the dance; however, the primary goal of dance is not enjoyment but to transport the viewer into a reality where they experience the essence

The Cosmic Dancer: 8th century South India.

of their own consciousness. Dance causes them to self-examine their consciousness and ultimately unite with God.

Perhaps the most fascinating Indian classical dance is Kathakali, which in the Dravidian language means "story play." This unique dance features elaborate costumes, hand-painted faces, using rice paste and vegetable dyes, and unlike other Indian classical dances, incorporates ancient forms of Indian martial arts and athletic traditions. Kathakali is unique in that it was first performed in the courts of the kings and not in the temples as most other classical Indian dances. Kathakali is also unique in that it separates the performers into two groups. One group of actors does the speaking parts, while the other elaborately made-up, face-painted actors do all the choreographic dancing.

Although Kathakali uses themes from the Ramayana and Mahabharata and is basically a drama of the eternal fight between good and evil. Kathakali dance is performed in a pompous, humoristic style similar to Mozart's "The Marriage of Figaro." In Kathakali, the dancers use hand signs and movements to symbolize words, and emotions are shown through facial and eye movements, as in most of the classical dances of Asia. The voice actors must make sure that their speaking parts are in sync with the dance gestures and movements so the audience does not become confused. Similarly, the orchestra must be on cue and adjust the music to fit the particular emotion or action being depicted. Kathakali performances usually start at dusk and go all night and sometimes for several nights at a time. Before electricity, the dancers performed around a bright coconut flame "lamp, "which illuminated their faces since the dramas were performed mostly at night. Similarly, the voice actors were situated in the front of the stage so that the people could hear what the dancers were performing in the age before microphones and speakers.

The dancers must not only master the hand movements and eye stylizations, but they also must be experts in the ancient martial arts, and they can be seen jumping around the stage in highly stylized martial art movements and positions. Modern kathakali dance plays have incorporated women actresses and have expanded their repertoire to include plays from Goethe and Shakespeare.

Elaborately costumed Kathakali dancer from Kerala (the green painted face with the ruby red lips signifies that this actor is portraying a God).

Kathakali has a great deal of similarity with Japanese Kabuki, with elaborately painted faces, stylized emotions, and eye movements. It is also akin to Peking Opera, where martial art-trained actors fly through the air in stylized positions, wear elaborate costumes, and hand paint their faces. I also noticed that the Kathakali dance is very similar to the Balinese Barong dance in the costumes, facial gestures, and stylized movements.

Tamil Nadu in Southern India developed a dance variation of the classical form called Bharatanatyam. This dance form was performed in theaters and villages and took its inspiration from classical sculpture. There is a 7th century A.D. stone Shiva at Kamalaka, which has 18 arms: each arm demonstrates a different dance position, and the classical dancer follows each stylized arm movement to mimic the Dancing Shiva.

From its earliest beginning, dance had a religious purpose. Every large temple had a troop of temple dancers who danced not for the public but for that particular God of the temple. Indian religious dance has become Indian classical dance, with each region having its own version of honoring their gods.

This is one of the classical dance positions copied directly from the 7th century Dancing Shiva statue shown above.

In the 17th and 18th centuries, many of the women temple dancers became courtesans called "nautch girls" in northern India and "devadasis" in southern India. There were dance rituals where the girls gave themselves to the priests in honor of the gods. This, however, was a corruption of the original religious meaning of dance in the "Natya Sastra." The British missionaries convinced the authorities to prohibit temple dancing because of the immoral character of the dancers. This prohibition, however, led to the religious dance moving to the countryside, as shown in the illustration above depicting Sri Chaitanya Mahaprabhu (16th century AD) chanting and dancing accompanied by a musician group called "Baul."

A typical Bollywood dance extravaganza (Photo by Tasneem Mandviwala from amalgame.co.uk).

Tamil Nadu in Southern India developed a dance variation of the classical form called Bharatanatyam. This dance form was performed in theaters and villages and took its inspiration from classical sculpture. There is a 7th-century stone Shiva at Kamalaka, which has 18 arms: each arm demonstrates a different dance position, and the classical dancer follows each stylized arm movement to mimic the dancing Shiva.

Mahua Mukherjee performing her modernized Guadiya Nritya.

While I was in Calcutta, I saw a classical Indian dance and was very impressed with the absolute control and confidence the dancers exhibited, following a tradition that went back over a millennium. In the 1970s and early 80s, Mahua Mukherjee, a classically trained Bangali dancer, revolutionized Indian classical dance by reconstructing an ancient dance called Guadiya Nritya, adding certain modern expressions, postures, and gestures to the classical framework. This caused a lot of controversy in India, from the purists who wanted to keep classical dance in its original form to the modernists who wanted to bring it into the 20th century and attract a widespread secular audience. Miss Mukherjee brought her revolutionary theories on classical dance to the world: teaching dance in America and performing throughout the world (see illustration above).

While classical dance is still popular in India, the average Indian satisfies his love of dance by watching a Bollywood dance spectacle. Most Indian movies are escapist fantasies, with extensive song and dance routines, sometimes involving dozens of dancers. This rivaled the Busby Berkley dance extravaganzas of 1930s Hollywood (although even Bollywood might find it hard to beat scores of high-kicking, scantily dressed chorus girls dancing on the windswept wings of a flying propellor airplane in "Flying Down to Rio").

Movie poster of "Flying Down to Rio" 1933.

Chapter Nine: The Freak Goes to the Movies

Between trains, I was stranded for the night in a small junction town. I had gotten a shoebox room, complete with huge horseflies and no ceiling fan. Added to this was the monsoon rain, which caused humidity so thick that I thought my clothes were part of my flesh. After dinner, I wandered around the town instead of retreating to my spartan bug-infested bunker. I passed a small Hindu temple, lit with candles and the smell of incense, with devotees going in and out. Then I looked down the main street and was awestruck. Here was a bright multi-lit marquee that shone like a huge incandescent Christmas tree banishing the night. As I got closer, I could see the posters of the leading actor and actress with Indian writing beneath the mammoth-size pictures (it's all Bangali to me).

I had not seen an Indian film since Bali, when I saw "Hara Krishna, Hara Ram," an immensely popular Indian film about evil hippies (westerners with long hair, playing guitars) kidnapping a pure Indian girl, who was eventually rescued, after song and dance routines, by her handsome brother. The evil hippies were banished, and all was well in the kingdom. However, in every place I traveled, little children ran up to me, yelled "Hippie" and then ran away, so I guess not all the evil hippies were banished.

I remember seeing a different kind of Indian film in New York in the 1960s: the social realism films of Satyajit Ray. Satyajit Ray's "Apu Trilogy" won international fame and offered a gritty real-life slice of Indian life. The film followed a poor Bangali boy from village life to success in Calcutta, after many personal heartbreaks and failed dreams. Ray went on to make several other acclaimed thought-provoking films. The Ray film that I loved best was called "Distant Thunder," and it showed how a Brahmin priest and his wife slowly changed from a pompous self-centered couple to a crusading self-aware couple that tried to selflessly help their fellow man during the Great Bangal Famine of 1943. Their story was a haunting microcosm of the larger tragedy that engulfed all of Bangal.

However, I had my own thunder to deal with. It was starting to rain, the heavy monsoon rain, so I paid my admission and joined the packed audience of Indian devotees staring enrapt at the big screen. I arrived after the start of the film (luckily or unluckily, depending on your point of view), missing the first couple of dance routines and solo songs, but I found I could easily follow the plot.

Boy falls for a girl, parents don't like the boy because he is poor, and they keep their lovestruck daughter from seeing him. Boy gets an inheritance and a respectable job from a distant relative, and that clears the way for boy to get girl with the blessing of the girl's parents after many song and dance interludes. Of course, there is no sex in the film, not even a kiss when the boy and girl are finally reunited for the happy ending. (And who says money doesn't buy you happiness?)

Satyajit Ray in New York 1981.

As I was leaving the theater, I observed the young people, who were excitedly talking about the movie and sounded like they really enjoyed the film. I smugly thought to myself: how could they like this hackneyed fantasy of an improbable and badly acted romance, where the plot is upstaged by the colorful dance and heartfelt love songs, mostly sung by the hero accompanied by his guitar? But then I remembered how another romantic song and dance extravaganza had deeply affected me as a young teenager: "West Side Story."

Columbia Album cover of the Broadway soundtrack recording of "West Side Story."

Shakespeare or not, the plot of "West Side Story" is just as sophomoric as the potboiler I just watched. The Hollywood acting might have been better, but the Indian film had the same lively dance numbers as I enjoyed in West Side Story, "When you're a jet, you're always a jet," and memorable love songs, "There'll be a time for us," which mesmerized me as an impressionable teenager. What made it stand out for me was that it was gritty "Lower Depths" New York, a time and a place where gangs were killing each other in real life. Just a few years before, an infamous Puerto Rican gang member, "The Cape Man," had stabbed to death two rival white gang members in a gang rumble. At his trial, he expressed no remorse and shouted, "Give me the (electric) chair! My mother can watch me burn!" I realized that "West Side Story" fantasized just as improbable a love story as I had just watched, and the experience I had at that time was that love would overcome hate and even death. I was not alone in these feelings: "West Side Story" was immensely popular with people of all ages, and I saw that both the young and older Indian moviegoers felt the same about this romance as I did about the doomed romance of Maria and Tony.

Chapter Ten: Ravi Shankar

Ravi Shankar performing at Woodstock, 1969.

Probably the most famous Indian known in the 1960s in the West, outside of politicians, was Ravi Shankar, a classical raga sitar player from Calcutta. Shankar was a master of Carnatic (South Indian) classical music, a collaborator with the great Israeli violinist Yehudi Menuhin and a pop star that played at Woodstock in 1969. He, above anyone else, was responsible for popularizing Indian musical instruments in Western pop music, influencing the Rolling Stones, Jeff Beck, and the Beatles. This music is called: "Raga Rock," and these pop groups emulated the tone and accompanying drone of the sitar in their own electric guitar playing.

The raga is the melodic formula, and the tala is the rhythmic beat cycle. The interplay of these two leads to endless improvisations that can change the mood, emotion, and tone of a musical composition. George Harrison of the Beatles became his pupil and friend. Harrison also played sitar in the Beatles hit "Norwegian Wood" and solo sitar in "My Sweet Lord".

He also was a composer, creating the musical score for Satyajit Ray's "Apu Trilogy" and wrote a classical symphony piece: "Sitar with the Violin" which featured Menuhin on the violin and himself on sitar.

At Woodstock, he disliked the drug scene that was associated with his music: "Music to us is religion; the quickest way to reach godliness is through music." He was particularly upset by Jimi Hendrix, who usually ended his set by destroying or setting fire to his guitar. Ravi believed your musical instrument is your access to the godhead, and it showed great disrespect toward God and yourself by this desecration. The most accessible (for a first-time Westerner listener of sitar music) introduction to his playing is his "Live at the Monterey Pop Festival," which I liked very much. His music was new and raw to his rock audience. At Woodstock, he played for about two minutes and then stopped, and the audience went wild with applause. Shankar looked at the crowd and said dryly, "If you liked my tuning that much, I hope you'll like my performance even better."

Chapter Eleven: "You Can See the Forest for the Tree"

First edition front cover of the novel "A Tree Grows In Brooklyn" by Betty Smith.

When I visited the Calcutta Botanical Gardens, I found one banyan tree that is four and a half acres in circumference! The tree spreads by its boughs, growing out of the main trunk, down into the ground, sprouting a new tree, creating a maze of trees of differing heights, each one budding a new tree. This banyan is at least 300 years old, and the amazing thing is that the central trunk of the original tree was fifty feet in circumference, but it died of disease in 1925.

The banyan tree (also called the pipal tree) was the tree that Buddha sat under for 49 days in a state of complete yogic meditation and achieved nirvana. For me, this magnificent Calcutta banyan is the perfect symbol of Buddhism dying out in the land of its birth. The original central trunk symbolizes Buddhism in India, but it died there, only to be reborn with new tree trunks, which symbolize the lands that adopted Buddhism as their religion: Thailand, Cambodia, Burma, Ceylon, Nepal, Bhutan, and Tibet.

This is all one tree: The Great Banyan Tree of Calcutta (This is only tree I know that you need a road map to find your way in and out of!).

The full expanse of the Great Banyan Tree, Calcutta.

It is ironic that in Betty Smith's novel "A Tree Grows In Brooklyn," the tree is called the "Tree of Heaven." It was brought to America by Chinese immigrants in the 18th century as an ornamental shade tree. Nowadays, we call this tree the Ailanthus, and it is known to grow where other trees cannot: out of concrete sidewalks, in sand, and in total shade. Betty Smith's family tried to kill this tree many times, but it always came back stronger than ever. For the heroine of the book, Francine, the tree symbolized the resilience and struggles of her family to overcome hardships and tragedies in Irish immigrant Williamsburg.

When I was growing up in New Jersey, we had two Ailanthus trees in the backyard, and my mother loved them. She would go out in the summer and pluck the lower branches off, leaving the top crown of leaves so they appeared as miniature palm trees and gave the yard a tropical feel.

Bangladesh

Bangali Woman reclining: Francesco Renaldi 1789 (Public Domain).

Chapter Twelve: Bangladesh

Ganges River scene in what now is Bangladesh 1824: watercolor by Lieutenant-Colonel Forrest (Public Domain).

Verse 1

Let's go children of the fatherland,

The day of glory has arrived!

Against us tyranny's

Bloody flag is raised! (repeat)

In the countryside, do you hear

The roaring of these fierce soldiers?

They come right to our arms

To slit the throats of our sons, our friends!

Refrain

Grab your weapons, citizens!

Form your battalions!

Let us march! Let us march!

May impure blood

Water our fields!

Verse 2

This horde of slaves, traitors, plotting kings,

What do they want?

For whom these vile shackles,

These long-prepared irons? (repeat)

Frenchmen, for us, oh! what an insult!

What emotions that must excite!

It is us that they dare to consider

Returning to ancient slavery!

Verse 3

What! These foreign troops

Would make laws in our home!

What! These mercenary phalanxes

Would bring down our proud warriors! (repeat)

Good Lord! By chained hands

Our brows would bend beneath the yoke!

Vile despots would become

The masters of our fate!

Verse 4

Tremble, tyrants! and you, traitors,

The disgrace of all groups,

Tremble! Your parricidal plans

Will finally pay the price! (repeat)

Everyone is a soldier to fight you,

If they fall, our young heros,

France will make more,

Ready to battle you!

Verse 5

Frenchmen, as magnanimous warriors,

Bear or hold back your blows!

Spare these sad victims,

Regretfully arming against us. (repeat)

But not these bloodthirsty despots,

But not these accomplices of Bouillé,

All of these animals who, without pity,

Tear their mother's breast to pieces!

Verse 6

Sacred love of France,

Lead, support our avenging arms!

Liberty, beloved Liberty,

Fight with your defenders! (repeat)

Under our flags, let victory

Hasten to your manly tones!

May your dying enemies

See your triumph and our glory!

Verse 7

We will enter the pit

When our elders are no longer there;

There, we will find their dust

And the traces of their virtues. (repeat)

> Much less eager to outlive them
>
> Than to share their casket,
>
> We will have the sublime pride
>
> Of avenging them or following them!

"La Marseillaise"

On April 24, 1792, Rouget de Lisle was a captain of engineers stationed in Strasbourg near the Rhine River. The mayor of the town called for an anthem just days after the French declared war on Austria. The amateur musician penned the song in a single night, giving it the title of "Chant de guerre de l'armée du Rhin" ("Battle hymn of the army of the Rhine").

Rouget de Lisle's new song was an instant hit with the French troops as they marched. It soon took on the name La Marseillaise because it was particularly popular with volunteer units from Marseille. On July 14, 1795, the French declared La Marseillaise the national song. This song exemplified in my imagination the struggles of the Bangali people against the savage rule of West Pakistan.

I had been in Calcutta for about three weeks, and I was awaiting my Bangladesh visa, so I could finally visit this newly independent country. The visa came through, and I bought a ticket on a small freighter that was carrying equipment and foreign aid from Calcutta to Dacca. The ocean journey from Calcutta to Dacca was not pleasant. There were still high winds and the last of the monsoon rains. I was traveling alone, the only foreigner in steerage. Needless to say, I was soaked the entire journey; only the ship overhang offered some relief from the rain, and that was jam-packed with the rest of the steerage passengers. I endured all these privations because I desperately wanted to see how the country was surviving after their bloody war for independence.

On the morning I arrived at Dacca harbor, the one thing that will be forever imprinted on my mind about Bangladesh was the greenness of the land. Everywhere there was new life sprouting up. The harbor was chock-block full of vessels: fishing trawlers, small ferries, foreign aid vessels, and hundreds of houseboats crowded with families. People were smiling and everyone seemed friendly, even after I told them I was an American. The country had been independent for five months now, and everyone was still in their honeymoon phase of "everything is possible." But there were also serpents in this green garden of Eden. As I started to walk off of the vessel, a group of Bangalis waved to me, shouting to come over. As the naïve traveler I was, I started for the group, but an older Bangali passenger, walking beside me, cautioned, "Don't go there; you'll be robbed or worse. There are many desperate people who would think nothing of killing you for your watch or camera." I thanked him and headed in the other direction, losing myself in the crowd.

Dacca by Frederick de Fabeek 1861.

I took a pedicycle to the city center, asking the driver to direct me to a cheap hotel. There were people everywhere, and the green garden soon gave way to the brown, ochre, crumbling buildings and streets deep in refuse-strewn mud. He took me to a small but clean hotel called the New Dacca Hotel, obviously getting a kick-back from the hotel owner. The room was small, but it had an overhead fan, a small table and chair, and a rope bed. The manager was exceedingly friendly and incredibly happy to see me since there were few tourists. The majority of the foreign aid workers stayed in fancy hotels at the center of the city.

My conversations with him soon turned to the liberation war and the hardships of that time. I had followed the independence fight closely while in Korea and during my travels. I had read about the atrocities committed by the Pakistani Army and was both indignant and ashamed of America's support for Pakistan in this conflict. We were supposedly the Land of the Free, but we actively supplied arms to a military dictatorship that was killing hundreds of thousands of innocent people. Like our American Revolution, these people just wanted their freedom from a cruel regime.

The hotel manager, Ahmed, was proud to say his nephew had been a freedom fighter, fighting with guerilla-style tactics to free his country. He told me that his nephew and other freedom fighters ambushed military convoys and blew up the Pakistani Army Headquarters here in Dacca. They also mined the harbor at Chittagong, destroying Pakistani vessels loaded with arms and troops. The Indian government helped by setting up training camps to teach young Bangalis military tactics and firearms training. They also supplied the freedom fighters with all types of weaponry. India finally stepped in to end the bloodbath when the atrocities became so horrific that not to have done something would have been a crime against humanity. Indian troops quickly defeated the Pakistan Army in Bangladesh, helped install the new government, and then selflessly returned to India.

Bangali Intellectuals and Teachers killed by the West Pakistan Army 1971.

The Pakistan Army butchered thousands of unarmed university students, especially seeking out and killing every teacher and intellectual they could find. Particularly horrific was the rape of 43,000 Bangali women. Many were kept captive in army compounds and raped daily for months. When the war was finally won by the Indians and the native freedom fighters, these freed women were disowned by their parents and husbands because they were defiled. The new Bangali government offered a stipend to husbands who took back their defiled wives and a bonus to anyone who would marry these martyred women. But since most were disavowed by their families and had no dowries, there were few takers. Here the relief aid organizations stepped in, housing and feeding these "orphans" and provided job training so that these women could support themselves. However, as one earnest Bangali university student told me, "Many of these women were committing suicide or turning to prostitution since no one would accept them."

Everywhere I went, I could see the destruction: bullet holes in buildings, limbless young men begging in streets, and people querying for food dispensed by international aid organizations. On every corner, there were idle groups of men; their jobs were lost since all the factories were looted or destroyed by the fleeing Pakistani soldiers.

My heart despaired for the Bangali people - where would they get the money to rebuild their country? India had their own poverty problems and America had supported West Pakistan. I had no answers, but I wanted to talk with the students and the freedom fighters to see if they had any solutions or ways forward to bring the country back on its feet.

Chapter Thirteen: Bangladesh II - the Islamification of Bangladesh

"Peace train,"

-Cat Stevens.

Cat Stevens converted to Islam in 1978 and became Yusuf Islam, performing Islam-influenced songs for the rest of his recording life.

The restored ruins of Vikramshila, the Buddhist monastery, school, and library.

Traveling around Bangladesh, I saw many ruined Hindu temples and the remains of destroyed Buddhist stupas. I wondered why Bangladesh is Muslim, while Burma is Buddhist, on the right, and Bangali Bihar on the left of the map is Hindu. In the case of Bihar, both peoples are of the same ethnic race, speak the same language, and were both conquered by the Delhi Sultanate around 1200 AD. The Delhi General Khaljil was particularly savage, killing thousands of Hindus and Buddhists and destroying universities, libraries, and temples.

Buddhism was very active in Bangladesh, and their university and library at Vikramshila trained thousands of priests. Most of these priests were slaughtered, and the university complex was razed to the ground. The surviving priests fled to the north, to Nepal and Tibet, where these countries offered them sanctuary. Now, it is a fascinating ruin to walk through and imagine the splendor of life there during its heyday. After the conquest, Khaljil left to conquer Tibet but was humiliated by the Assam King, who destroyed his entire army; Khaljil was later killed by his own son.

Unidentified Bangladesh Mosque 15th century. Watercolor by Indian painter Sita Ram 1817. Bangal mosques at that time featured multiple Roof domes, which became a unique characteristic of Moslem Bangal religious architecture.

This caused a power struggle within Bangladesh, splitting into many Muslim and Hindu kingdoms. The Hindu kingdom of Gour occupied the central part of Bangladesh and was the most powerful for two hundred years. Finally, the adjoining Muslim kings attacked Gour and conquered the land. Here's when the conversion to Islam really started. Along with the sultan's army came a group of Sufis. Sufis are the Islamic mystics. They are strict Muslims, but they strive to look inwards and have a loving, personal experience with Allah.

The Sufis are organized in orders (congregations under a master teacher), and their goal is "ihsan," to worship Allah as if "you can see Him, He surely sees you. If you can't see Him, He surely sees you." Because of this personal experience of "ihsan," the Sufis made great teachers and, above all, great missionaries to spread the word of Allah. The leader of the Bihar order of Sufis was a remarkable man named Shah Jalal.

Mughal Painting of Shah Jalal of Sylhet (18th century).

Shah Jalal

Shah Jalal was born in Konya, Turkey, in 1271 AD. He became a Muslim imam (teacher), traveling through Syria, Baghdad, and Punjab. Before he left on his journey, his uncle gave him a handful of soil and told him to propagate Islam, where the soil is like this handful. Dutifully, he kept this soil and, while in the Punjab, converted to Sufism. He became the master teacher of his order and accompanied Sultan Forez in his victorious campaign against the Hindu kingdom of Gour.

Immediately after the victory, he brought out his box of soil that he had been carrying since Turkey and found that it matched the soil here. Since this was the sign he was waiting for, he and his followers proceeded to go village by village, converting the inhabitants to Islam. They were remarkably successful, and central Bangladesh was converted to Islam, not by the sword, but through the loving message of the Sufis.

Shah Jalal became famous but always led a simple life: living in a cave with only one possession, a goat for milk, cheese, and yoghurt. Toward the end of his life, he was visited by the famous Muslim traveler Ibn Battuta. Battuta was very impressed with Jalal's learning and holiness, and they had many discussions on the nature of God. After Shah Jalal's death in 1346 AD, his shrine became the most venerated site in Bangladesh.

Chapter Fourteen: Sufism and "The Perfect Man"

(NO, THIS ISN'T MY AUTOBIOGRAPHY!)

Traveling around the Indian subcontinent, there are so many Hindu sadhus, saints, and mystics that we forget the Muslims also had saints, mystics, and holy men who perfected the Sufi doctrine of the "Perfect Man." There have been many "Perfect Men" in Islam: Adam of the Garden of Eden, Abraham, Jesus Christ, and the last and greatest, Mohammed. One of the greatest Sufi mystics, Ibn Arabi, who lived in the thirteenth century in Seville, Spain, first elaborated on the concept of the "Perfect Man." He used the concept of mirrors as a metaphor for God and humans. God is the object and humans are the mirrors. Humans are a reflection of God (i.e., there is no separation between God and man.). Humans are a part of the ultimate oneness with God. This oneness means that man's goal in "true reality" is to be reunited with the Divine. The "Perfect Man," through self-consciousness and self-realization, accesses the Divine in himself, so he is both God and man.

"Sufi in Ecstasy" Persian ink and watercolor
1650 A.D.

Ibn Arabi states that God is a "necessary" being (Pure Essence), and man is a necessary being by means of God (man cannot exist without God). Ibn Arabi asks the question: Why was man created? He answers with this saying, "I (God) was a hidden treasure and I wanted to give this knowledge to the world." God created man because only through man can God see the unity (the Divine Essence) with the temporal world (the physical world of plants, animals, and humans all imbued with God). This Ibn Arabi calls this the "isthmus" (bridge) between God and the living cosmos that man sees in the world around him. Man is both Divine and human; God is only Divine. The "Perfect Man" brings together and embraces all of the cosmos and shares God's essence with the corporal world. The Qu'ran states Allah is God (Pure Essence), and Mohammed (the Perfect Man) is His servant who spreads the voice of God throughout the world.

Christianity also has Christ as both God and human. This is the logos of St. John's Gospel: "the word made flesh." Jesus was Divine, but it was the human Jesus that spread God's message to the world. Jesus was the isthmus between God, the Father, and man.

All of the great religions teach the same message: that God (Divine Essence) is in every man. Once you access this state of pure consciousness (realization of the Divine), you can, as in Buddhism, merge with the universal soul: Nirvana, which is the cessation of individual existence, or as in Christianity and Islam, you can spread the word of God to your fellow man, sharing God's love for man since the Divine is part of you.

Since my aunt was a missionary in Africa and I listened to her stories of converting the local tribespeople, I imagined how the Sufis converted the Hindus by preaching love instead of the sword.

Chapter Fifteen: A Simple Tale of Faith - A Bedtime Fairytale

"To every thing there is a season, and a time to every purpose under the heaven:

A time to be born, and a time to die; a time to plant, a time to reap that which is planted;

A time to kill, and a time to heal; a time to break down, and a time to build up;

A time to weep, and a time to laugh; a time to mourn, and a time to dance;

A time to cast away stones, and a time to gather stones together;

A time to embrace, and a time to refrain from embracing;

A time to gain that which is to get, and a time to lose; a time to keep, and a time to cast away;

A time to rend, and a time to sew; a time to keep silence, and a time to speak;

A time of love, and a time of hate; a time of war, and a time of peace."

-Chapter Three, Ecclesiastes (King James Bible)

To everything (Turn, Turn, Turn)

There is a season (Turn, Turn, Turn)

And a time to every purpose, under Heaven

"Turn, Turn, Turn": The Byrds

The Byrds used the Bible song lyrics verbatim, adding "Turn, Turn, Turn" after each verse.

Once upon a time, there was a village in ancient India that faced an important decision. Now, we'll all have our hot chocolate; I'll tuck you under the covers and will read this little bedtime story to you (not recommended for children under 8).

"Everyone quiet down," the village elder Jama said in a forceful manner. "I have called you all together to discuss an important decision that we as a village must make. As you have heard, that cruel beast, Shah Forez, has burned Vikramshila to the ground, killing all of the Hindus and Buddhists there, more than 10,000 men, women, and children. He has destroyed our temples, butchered our priests, and killed all who do not accept Allah as the true God. His army is only 20 miles away and soon they will come to Jankar, our peaceful village. What should we do? Betray

Shiva and the traditions of our ancestors? Should we fight them with our farm sickles and risk the lives of our wives and children? Or should we submit to Allah, who is a fearsome brutal God that rewards its believers if they kill us Hindus just because we aren't followers of the Book?" (The book refers to the three faiths of Judaism, Christianity, and Islam. In the Qu'ran, both Abraham and Jesus are prophets, with Mohammed being the last and greatest of prophets; the Book is really the Old Testament, the New Testament and the Qu'ran collectively).

The village priest spoke up, "We must fight them. Shiva is mighty, and He will trample his foes."

Next spoke the village store owner, "We must accept Allah, or we will suffer the same fate as our brethren in Vikramshila. Think of your wives and children. Shiva has deserted us in our time of need."

Every villager had an opinion except the washerman and the handlers of the dead, the Untouchables, and the women of the village because they weren't part of the village council. The discussions were long and rancorous. Many of the villagers wanted to fight to the death, and just as many others desperately wanted to save their families and convert.

Jama finally spoke up, "As I feared, we can't come to an agreement. Each family must decide for themselves when the army comes."

The meeting was adjourned, and most of the villagers retreated despondently to the shrine of Shiva, pouring colored dye and draping the lingam with garlands of flowers, imploring Him to save them. The next day was bright and sunny, a perfect day to harvest the ripening rice, but the villagers were not harvesting today. Many gathered their farm tools and prepared to battle the army. Others prayed in their homes with their families, waiting for the inevitable.

By noon, the army had not come; there was no dust cloud from the horses of the fearsome enemy. Instead, a single turbaned figure, riding a donkey and dressed in ordinary robes, came into the village square. Jama and the council members hastily appeared to meet him. Surely, he was bringing them an ultimatum: "Convert or Die!"

This solitary figure introduced himself to the elders, speaking in a calm and reassuring manner. "I know you are frightened, but I come on a mission of truth and love. I come not as a messenger of Shah Forez but as a disciple of God. I do not bring fire and death but understanding and love. I want you to see that Allah is a merciful God. A God who treats all his subjects as equals before

His merciful Eye. I have studied your faith and see that you believe in one God, no matter how many visages of that God you worship. Allah accepts all equally in His Love. I am considered a holy man, a Sufi spreading the word of the true God, but I am not superior to the lowest of your village, the outcasts, the Untouchables."

The elders murmured loudly, "This is blasphemy; the Untouchables are unclean. We can't eat or drink with them, or they will defile us."

The Sufi spoke up in response, "I see you have two wells in your village, one for the Untouchables and one for the rest of the village. Yet you must know that the water is the same in both wells. The brass pots handled by you and the ones handled by the Untouchables all touch the same water source. The water is indifferent; it will fill any brass pot that is lowered into it. Allah is like your well water. He treats everyone equally. And you priest, you say if you adhere to the correct rituals and worship and are a good person, you will be reborn into a higher caste in your new life. Allah says, 'If you believe in Me, I will give you Paradise when you pass from this existence.' My god is a God of Love, who rewards all His followers with eternal life. Believe in Him, and you will become free, rich or poor; it is your faith and your equality before Him that will stop the endless cycle of rebirth. Love and equality to all is the message I bring."

The Elders and the village people were astonished. Here was a man who knew their religion and showed them that they were not as pure and undefiled as they thought they were. Jama asked the Sufi to stay in his house, and the Sufi stayed in the village for several weeks, describing what a proper Muslim must do, such as praying five times a day facing towards Mecca and not eating from dawn to dusk during the daytime for the entire holy month of Ramadan.

Slowly the villagers listened and talked about this new God. Here was a God who didn't have to be appeased by sacrifices. Faith alone and adherence to the simple regime of prayer and fasting is the path to salvation. After a few weeks, several individual villagers accepted Allah based on their own decisions, viewpoints, and advantage. The rich farmers wouldn't have to pay the onerous poll tax for non-believers if they converted. The Untouchables found a way to be equal with the villagers, ending their degrading status by converting. Even the high priest accepted Allah because he could retain his status as a spiritual teacher: now as imam of the village, reading and interpreting the Qu' ran, just as he had done with the sacred Hindu Vedas, to the newly converted.

Jama convened the village council again after a few weeks. This time it included the newly converted Untouchables. Jama's heart was full of joy. He and his family had converted and wanted the village to join him in praising Allah. The vote was taken, and the village became one before Allah. The Sufi prayed with them; then, he remounted his donkey and headed east toward the next Hindu village. And everyone lived happily ever after.

Now I'm turning out the light, and you get some sleep, give me a goodnight kiss, and in the morning, when you wake up, I'll make pancakes for you.

Sufi teaching, 1750, anonymous artist, National Museum, Delhi, India.

Chapter Sixteen: Nusrat Fateh Ali Khan

Nusrat live in an English concert in 1987.

Listen to any of his qawwali songs, and I'm sure you will enjoy this passionate singer. To understand Sufism, it is important to see and listen to how the faithful express their love of God. Just like in America in the tent revival and the black gospel churches of the south, music releases the passion and the love of Christ. The preacher and the congregation are swept away in song and movement, lifting their hearts and voices in ecstatic love. In Sufism, this singing and praising God is called qawwali. Qawwali originated in Persia in the 12th century. The lyrics are based on Sufi poems and often invoke images of romantic love or even drunkenness to show how the spirit of God envelops the believer. In Judaism, in the Old Testament, you have the "Song of Songs," heartfelt romantic love symbolizing the spiritual love of God. In medieval times you had the mystic saints like Hildegard of Bingen, who betroth herself to Christ as a bride in an ecstatic and mystical union with the godhead, celebrating this union in mesmerizing song.

Qawwali is traditionally performed at religious shrines, and the singer is usually accompanied by a tabla which is a pair of drums and a reed organ, sometimes with backing vocals. Here the faithful dance or sway to the music, sometimes joining in chorus to the lead qawwali singer. Up until the 20th century, this religious music was solely confined to the Sufi shrines and their followers. This all changed with one man who brought this obscure regional religious music into international prominence with millions of followers in the West. This man was Nusrat Fateh Ali Khan.

Nusrat was born into a musical family which had carried on the singing of qawwali for over 600 years. At an early age, he demonstrated a powerful vocal expression, and the music carried him away, sometimes performing for up to 10 hours at a time. His father originally wanted him to become an engineer or a doctor, but when he heard the magnificent voice of his son, he relented and taught him the basics of qawwali singing.

Nusrat started as a traditional singer, but as he got more experienced, he increased the tempo and added a melodic beat to achieve a more contemporary sound. Soon he was considered the leading singer of qawwali in Pakistan for his high-range vocalizations and dramatic phrasing. Then he took his show on the road, going to England and America to perform this hypnotic religious music. This bear of a man, weighing approximately 300 pounds, with a full round face and bubbling personality, captivated his audience everywhere. In England, he met Peter Gabriel and collaborated with him and Eddie Vedder, using Western instrumentation and melodic rhythms. He recorded soundtracks for Indian and Hollywood movies: the most famous being Mel Gibson's "The Last Temptation of Christ." He also collaborated with the Canadian artist Michael Brook, further expanding his audience by using synthesizers and other Western instruments to bring out the power of qawwali.

Here Nusrat was torn. He wanted to show the beauty and message of love that qawwali proclaims to a much wider audience and yet keep the traditional meaning. In a secular sense, this mirrored the development of Bob Dylan, who started as a wood guitar and harmonica folk player, but soon felt that he could reach a wider audience by becoming electric and entering the mainstream of rock and roll. However, Nusrat, throughout his career, always took the time to perform at local Sufi shrines, keeping the music traditional, singing it as it had been sung for hundreds of years. He recorded over 100 albums, and in his public concerts, he performed nonstop for three to four hours. This took a heavy toll on his health, along with his weight, and he developed kidney problems. He was treated for this in a hospital in England, and while at the hospital, he had a cardiac arrest and died of a heart attack at the age of 48. He was mourned all over the world, and in his native Pakistan, he was called the "King of Kings of Qawwali."

In my personal experience of listening to Nusrat, I have come full circle. I started listening to his traditional qawwali; it was interesting but not arresting. Then I heard his musical collaboration album with Michael Brooke, and I was blown away: the music was mesmerizing and haunting. I then went back and listened to the traditional music. Now that I can understand some of the musical expressions and techniques of qawwali singing, I find the traditional and the more Western-inflected singing of qawwali of equal power and beauty. I would recommend Western listeners follow the same path, seek out the more accessible collaboration albums with Western artists first, and then listen to the intonation and musical expression of the traditional qawwali.

Chapter Seventeen: Ibn Battuta

"I get by with a little help from my friends,"

-The Beatles.

Ibn Battuta in Egypt: An illustration from Jules Verne's book "Découverte de la terre" ("Discovery of the Earth") drawn by Léon Benett 1878. (Public Domain)

Ibn Battuta was the first real traveler in the modern sense. By this, I mean he traveled not as a merchant like Marco Polo nor as a warrior like Genghis Khan, nor as a religious monk like Faxien and Huang Tuang. He traveled solely out of curiosity.

He lived from 1304 to 1360 AD, starting from Tangiers, Morocco, and returning there twenty-four years later. His original purpose was to perform the sacred duty all Muslims are required to do: the Hajj to Mecca. This he performed three times during his travels. This was the golden age of Islam, and most of the countries (except for China and the Byzantine Empire) he visited were Muslim. In the thirteenth and fourteenth centuries, thanks to Pax Mongolia, you could safely travel with an ingot of gold in your pocket from China to Turkey on the main caravan roads and not be robbed or attacked. So too, Ibn Battuta depended on the hospitality of Muslims throughout his journeys. One of the central tenets of Islam is to offer food, help, and lodging for any stranger that knocks on your door. He also stopped traveling for many years, working as a judge in Muslim Delhi and the Maldives Islands.

Like the freaks of today, he traveled by horseback, camel, and boat over all types of terrain: mountains, jungles, deserts, and crowded cities. Ibn Battuta, however, was robbed and beaten by unbelievers and nearly died of privations in desolate deserts, but he persisted, always pushing forward to see new lands. His book gives valuable information on the customs and practices of these Muslim countries. Many of these countries were newly converted to Islam, and he recorded the old pre-Muslim traditions of these countries that were slowly disappearing. He was also a bit of a Muslim prude, describing women in Sumatra, Indonesia, who were scantily dressed as an affront to their newly adopted religion.

He had heard about the Great Wall of China when visiting that country and believed that the wall kept out Gog and Magog, legendary demons from the Qu'ran, and the Book of Revelations in the New Testament. (It is nice to know that the Great Wall kept someone out!). However, no one could tell him where the Great Wall was located, so he couldn't investigate this legend first-hand.

Ibn Battuta was not an abstinent holy ascetic. He had numerous wives and concubines and about half of a dozen children, all of whom were left behind (Unfortunately, he was never credited with being the first "modern" sailor with a girl in every port). His intense curiosity led him to speak with religious leaders, mystics, soldiers, merchants, kings, as well as the common Muslim man. He also passed by Bangladesh, at that time East Bangal, which had been newly converted by the conquering Muslim armies and Sufi missionaries and mystics. He was impressed with the Sufi mystic and teacher, Shah Jalal, in present-day Sylhet, Bangladesh. They discussed the divinity within each individual and how to access this, so one can feel the presence of Allah within you and see the wonders of His work all around you.

He went on to visit legendary Arabian Nights cities, like Baghdad and Damascus, fabled Samarkand on the Silk Road, rich Chinese and Indian cities, and even faraway, exotic Timbuktu in Africa. He started his journey as a young seeker and returned home as a middle-aged sage, wise in the ways and customs of the world (Been there, Done that!).

I identify with him because I, too, am innately curious about foreign religions, politics, economics, and different ways of life. And he did it on a shoestring budget like "Moi," the rucksack freak. The book he wrote after his return to Morocco is called "A Gift to Those Who Contemplate the Wonder of Cities and the Marvels of Traveling" (Great title: it sure beats Marco Polo's pedestrian title: "Travels"). All modern travelers walk in the shadow and awe of his prodigious achievement.

Chapter Eighteen: Shipbreaking 101

Jafrabad Chittagong Shipbreaking: A long line of workers pull the cutoff sheets from the beached vessel by hand with ropes.

There was not much to do in Dacca. A great deal of the infrastructure had been destroyed, including the buses, ferries, and bridges. During the day, I was able to rent a boat and see the countryside, but at night I spent it in the cafes, talking with the university students and in my hotel with the owner. There was a great disconnect that I saw: the university students were discontented about the future of Bangladesh and disheartened by the current regime of Mujib Rahman. They saw the government as corrupt and not listening to the will of the people. Mujib Rahman had taken the country in a socialist direction, confiscating and nationalizing what few industries were left in Bangladesh and giving ownership to his cronies. Production dropped precipitously, and where there were previous jobs, now there were none for the university students; unrest was spreading everywhere.

While traveling, I avidly followed the progression of the war for the independence of Bangladesh and thought perhaps here could be the birth of a new America. I really didn't know anything about Bangladesh other than it was a land of poor farmers, and because of the low-lying coastline, hundreds of thousands were killed when cyclones swept the region. There was a particularly bad cyclone in 1970 in which over 300,000 were killed, and many more died later of cholera from the polluted waters that the cyclone caused.

In reality, there was so much horror and suffering; besides the students, there were poor rural farmers who lived on small plots of land that eked out a minimum standard of living and only raised enough to barely feed their families. Adding to the misery were millions of rural landless peasants that worked for slave wages and had nothing to show for it. The state of education in the country was abysmal. In Bangladesh, the majority of farmers and rural poor were illiterate; they could not read or write and had no marketable skills. There were very few public schools outside of the main cities, and what instruction they got was from the imam at the local mosque, where they were taught the basics of the Qu'ran, and this was just for the male children. The girls and women were totally uneducated because they were seen strictly as wives and mothers with no need for education. Added to this was the destruction of the independence war, where schools and government buildings were destroyed by the Pakistani army.

I spoke with my hotel owner about the situation in the countryside: Bangladesh was over 90% rural subsistence farming. I tried to see the parallel between their freedom fight and the American Revolution, but in the 200 years since our independence, we have become the greatest industrialized and powerful nation in the world. At the beginning of the 19th century, almost everyone was a farmer. The more ambitious left the farm for the city and were able to find jobs because of the budding industrialism that was taking place in large cities like New York, Boston, and Philadelphia. Here in Bangladesh, hundreds of thousands converged on the city, but there was nothing for them to do. I saw Bangladesh as a larger Calcutta. I was horrified and guilt-stricken between the "have" nations of the West and the "have-nots" of Asia. In Bangladesh and India, millions were at risk of dying if there was just one lost harvest.

Then the owner told me about an industry that was unique to the Indian subcontinent: ship dismantling. This industry was started in Bangladesh by a certain industrialist Mizanur Rahman. The new Bangladesh government had nationalized his jute factory, and he was not compensated fairly. However, he was industrious and always looking for new ways to make money. The Bangladesh independence war had created a ready-made market for ship dismantling: Bangladesh's main port, Chittagong, was clogged with the half-sunken remains of Pakistani munitions and war equipment vessels, food carriers, and troop transports that had been destroyed in the war by the Indian army and Bangali freedom fighters. These destroyed hulks were left rusting and abandoned, clogging the harbor of Chittagong and impeding the use of the harbor for export and import and desperately needed aid and foodstuffs for a starving population.

What Rahman proposed to the newly-formed government was that he would buy these half-sunken and rusted freighters and have them towed to a beach nearby and dismantle them for the steel and the other products that are salvaged when a ship is dismantled. He paid the Bangladesh government $1 million rupees for a few of these derelict freighters and then had the ships towed to a beach which the government gave him for the dismantling process. He then proceeded to hire workers and came up with a plan on how to physically "cut up" a vessel on the beach. He contracted with the steel mills and promised to deliver standardized products they could use in their furnaces to create the rolling bars of steel required for the reconstruction of the bridges, tunnels, and buildings. This had never been done before, but Rahman was up to the task: hiring secondary managers to go out to the villages to get the unskilled workers, bringing them to the beach, and starting the vessel cutup. All these vessels were dismantled by hand with hammers and blowtorches, which was dangerous, and many of the workers were killed each year by residue oil explosions from the use of blowtorches in closed quarters.

All the steel was carried out by long crews of men dragging the huge cutup plates with ropes, manned by hundreds of workers, without any safety gear like steel-tipped boots and hardhats. Due to the mud and slippery footing, even carts couldn't be used to remove the heavy steel sheets from the beach. The first vessel took over six months, but Rahman still made a profit and was able to go out and bid on other vessels until all the wrecks were cleared from Chittagong harbor.

International cargo transport is a cutthroat business and works on very little profit margin: the ship owners were very pleased that they could sell their old and outdated vessels for hard cash and wouldn't have to pay to dispose of them. Other Bangladeshi industrialists jumped on the bandwagon, and soon there was a thriving industry employing hundreds of thousands of workers dismantling and transporting this cutup steel. The previously idle steelworks now had a product to work with. They melted down the sheets into rolling bars and distributed the finished product to a hungry building industry. Bangladesh could not afford to import steel, and now they had the raw materials needed for their construction industry. By the early 1980s, this shipbreaking furnished almost half of Bangladesh's steel requirements.

On paper, this sounds like a win-win situation for everyone: the poor were given jobs, the rich industrialists made money from the dismantling, and the country had the steel it needed to rebuild after the destructive independence war. However, looking a little closer, you could see the fallacy of this: the workers worked for a few dollars a day, doing backbreaking work, dragging the cut sheets and using dangerous blow torches in confined spaces, with no compensation if they were injured or killed, while the owners made millions with the finished product. This was a classic case of exploitation of the workers. However, digging deeper, it seemed like a self-supporting ecological system, however much we would condemn it in the West. The ships were completely recycled: everything could be used or sold for profit: the fire extinguishers, engine oil, expensive electronic circuitry, and even the furniture and furnishing of the ships. It benefited the poor laborers, who were paid three to four times what they would have made as subsistence farmers in the rural countryside. The millionaire owners, by keeping the workers' wages low, were able to buy more ships and therefore keep this industry growing and hire more poor, unemployed workers. Whole villages grew up around these vessels, and the workers supported restaurants, clothing stores, and basic necessities shops.

Chittagong Shipbreaking: Workers aboard ship using blowtorches to cut large sections of the vessel into manageable sheets.

There was also a huge downside in the environmental damage that ship dismantling was causing the country: the mercury, asbestos, oil residue, and other toxic materials polluted the beaches and affected the long-term health of the laborers. Yet it offered a livelihood for hundreds of thousands of people in a country that was one of the poorest in the world. We in the West look at the destruction of the rainforest and are furious with these governments for allowing this destruction to go on, but we have come up with no solution on what would be an alternative to these developing countries. In Borneo, a country I visited on my travels, they are now cutting down the rainforest and planting millions of acres of palms for palm oil. Here you are creating jobs, replacing wild trees with cultivated palm trees and earning valuable export dollars, so the Indonesians can be helped with much-needed health, water, and electrification programs.

Even more tragic are the policies of the current government, which has nationalized foreign industries and expropriated private Bangali-run businesses. America had supported Pakistan in the war and was not about to aid this budding socialist country. As I had described, there were dozens of demonstrations that were anti-American and alienated even the international aid workers. Since foreign capital was not coming in to pay for much-needed humanitarian projects, shipbreaking was a viable industry that provided valuable tax dollars to the struggling government.

Ship dismantling is now a huge business in Bangladesh, and the ships that are dismantled are getting bigger; there seems to be an endless supply. In the late 1990s, the European nations and North America established regulations to prohibit single-hull oil transporters. The normal life for an oil transporter ship is 25 years, but because of oil spills from the single-hull tankers, new vessels had to be constructed with double hulls to prevent the oil spills and the ecological damage. These perfectly good one-hull tankers are now obsolete and cost too much to insure in the event of a vessel being damaged and causing a huge oil spill. Added to the oil tankers were the cruise ships, which had to be up-to-date and offer well-heeled Western customers all the amenities for a memorable holiday vacation. These tankers and cruise ships were huge 40,000 tons vessels. These huge vessels were driven full speed onto the beach and finally stopped of their own accord out of the water so they could be dismantled on the shores of Chittagong. The dismantling has now become a set formula on "how to break up a ship." These large vessels are totally recycled in six to eight months, including delays due to the monsoon, which makes it impossible to work for weeks at times. To become even more profitable, the ship dismantlers are seeking billions to build steel furnaces next to the beach so they can save on the cutting and transportation process. The new mills would be able to take all forms of steel instead of the uniform sheets that were needed for rolling pipe production. With these new steel mills, different types of steel could be produced. They would employ even more workers in the mills and in the flourishing dismantling industry.

I remember crossing the George Washington Bridge and seeing the long lines of out-of-service merchant and naval vessels moored on the Hudson. They had served our country during World War II, bringing vital supplies to our troops fighting the Nazis and Japanese. Now they were anchored and rusting along Hudson river banks, all the way past West Point. Eventually they would be taken out and sunk, some to form man made barrier reefs needed to protect low-lying tidal-floods areas. I thought about all of those out-of-service ships and remembered how much I was moved by William Turner's painting, "The Fighting Temeraire," at the British Museum. Here was one of the major four-masted frigates that was at the forefront of the battle, along with Admiral Nelson's "Victory," which won the naval battle against Napoleon's navy at Trafalgar, Britain's most spectacular naval victory. Now the "Temeraire" was being towed out to sea for an ignoble sinking in a gold and crimson-infused skyscape. History was not lost in the heat of battle but in a whimper of senseless sinking. "God Save the Queen!"

"The Fighting Temeraire" William Turner 1838.

Chapter Nineteen: Furdos' Story

"The Night They Drove Old Dixie Down,"

-The Band.

This song represents my ambivalent feelings toward the Biharis. Yes, they supported a regime that did evil things; however, when you talk with these survivors, you find they're human beings struggling like the rest of us to make sense of the present reality. This was just like the rebel soldier in the song above that must come to terms with the South's defeat in the Civil War.

"Liberation War "by Zainul Abedin 1971 (Bangladesh National Museum).

There are large prison tent cities where the Baharis are kept captive. The Baharis are West Pakistanis living in East Pakistan; there are two classes of Biharis. The first is the powerful class of government officials, doctors, lawyers, and educators, who collaborated with their fellow countrymen, supplying information on the freedom fighters and, of course, siding with the Pakistani army. The second group are the Bahari farmers and landlords who lost all their farmlands due to their support of West Pakistan. Here you could see the racial divide between the two people: the tall, light-skinned, aquiline-nosed West Pakistanis, descendants of the original Aryan invaders, mixed with Mongol and Turkoman blood; the Bangalis, in contrast, were dark-skinned, small, and finely featured.

West Pakistan controlled the government, law courts, teaching positions, and industry. The Bangalis had no political power; whatever money was made in East Pakistan was used by West Pakistan and not shared with the local Bangali government. The Baharis, clinging to their leadership role, sided with the losing side, and now they were imprisoned. These camps are filthy, disease-ridden, lacking sanitation and food, causing hundreds of deaths. The Biharis are in political limbo: there are no jobs or even farmland to give these pariahs in West Pakistan. The West Pakistan government didn't want them back because they already had too many people for too few jobs, and the government was in chaos following their defeat in the war, and of course, they were hated by the native Bangalis. The new nation was slowly healing its wounds, and there was no room for these festering traitors.

The foreign aid groups were very efficient, setting up soup kitchens and orphanages, supplying clothing and job training. Factories were slowly hiring, opening under native Bangali management, and the jute exports (the largest agricultural industry) resumed production.

As I wandered the crowded streets, people came up to me, asking why did I come here and for what purpose. I replied that I was here as a representative of the American people, not its leaders, and supported their struggles. The students, civil servants, and ordinary pedestrians that I spoke with were all politically aware and articulate in their views. One young student talked of a further revolution because the people were getting nothing. "Mujeeb (Bangladesh's new leader) is a good, honest man, but his cabinet and party are all corrupt."

I sit in cafes, drinking tea and everyone comes up to me to talk about the future of Bangladesh, but sometimes about America. The questions they asked were very personal, for example: "Where do you get your money?" "Where do you live." "Why are you not married?" and the best one, "Don't you have a razor?" (And I thought I was growing a remarkably successful beard!). I heard from many students that over two million people were killed and from other students, who were freedom fighters, who claimed to have bayoneted many Punjabis during the war. Others asked me about studying in America. I was at a loss when one enterprising young student asked me, "Do you know of any jute technology schools in America?"

I stopped in a large restaurant, trying to decide what to eat. After looking at the bi-lingual menu, I was still no better off because they only had the names of the dishes listed and not what they were made of. I asked a young man at another table, telling him I didn't understand the menu. He looked at me incredulously, "It's very simple. The menu is in English, see?" Then I went through my explanation, and he laughed, realizing my dilemma. He helped me order a delicious Bangal rice and chicken dish. We discussed the future of Bangladesh and ate our food together.

The next day was Hunger Strike Day. Most of the shops were closed, and crowds thronged the streets, following one leader, chanting in rhythmic cadences. The crowd was chanting, "Death to America," so I thought that the best place to observe these endless throngs of protesters was from my hotel roof. I felt for the people, but I didn't see how these demonstrations would really help them get on their feet. Bangladesh needed millions of dollars in foreign aid to rebuild its infrastructure after the war's destruction and create millions of jobs so the people wouldn't starve.

Historically, Bangal was the richest province in the Mughal Empire, trading gems and timber, building ships, and raising and producing cotton clothing. When British rule replaced Mughal rule, Bangal became the intellectual and cultural center of India. Bangal was also the leader in the Indian independence movement, with many Bangalis jailed for their vocal and violent opposition to British rule. Then why is Bangal so poor now?

I attribute this to the policies of the British Empire, which used their colonies, and this includes the future United States of America only as a source of raw materials. They shipped Indian cotton, timber, and mining products to Great Britain, which produced a finished product and sold it back to the colonists. In the case of Bangal, there were no independent cities that fostered homegrown manufacturing like there were in America with New York and Boston. The British kept the Bangalis as subsistence farmers, producing cash crops such as opium which they sold to the Chinese to equal their balance of payments for the vast amounts of tea they were buying from China. The profits went to Great Britain, and the Bangalis received nothing. The West Pakistanis continued this exploitation, siphoning export dollars from Bangali raw materials directly to the West Pakistan government and leaving East Pakistan impoverished and powerless.

While sitting in a café, I met a young student, Furdos, tall with typical West Pakistani features. It turned out that his father was one of the biggest Pak Army supporters and is now in jail. He had to leave the university because of his West Pakistani nationality, so now he sits in cafes all day with nothing to do. He spoke excellent English and I was curious to meet a Bahari "collaborator," having listened to so many freedom fighters' stories and wanted to hear about the other side of the war. We agreed to meet the next day, which dawned cloudy and grey. I had been talking with yet another Dacca University student, who told me the best way to get a feel for Bangladesh was to get a boat and row through the waterways and canals. Here you can see the real village life, where the vast majority of the Bangladesh people live.

Chinese style fishing net vessel (author's photo).

I met with Furdos and told him of my plan, and he agreed to be my interpreter (he also spoke fluent Bangali, as well as Urdu, West Pakistan's national language) when we visited these villages. At the harbor, we found a wizened old man with a good-sized rowboat. I hired him and the boat, and we started exploring the countryside. We could have rowed from one end of Bangladesh to the other, and a year wouldn't have been enough time to see all of the countryside. I remembered Franz Kafka's short story "The Great Wall of China."

"The Emperor has sent a message directly from his deathbed to you alone, his pathetic subject. The messenger started off at once, a powerful, tireless man. But the crowd is so huge; its dwelling places are infinite… how futile are all his efforts. And if he finally did burst through the outermost door—but that can never, never happen—the royal capital city, the center of the world, lies before him. No one pushes his way through here, certainly not with a message from a dead man. But you sit at your window and dream of that message when evening comes."

We rowed slowly, away from the muddy, clay-colored city into the cool green countryside. We passed women washing, children cleaning themselves, relieving themselves, and swimming in the same muddy canal. We saw Chinese-style fishing boats carrying huge, elaborate fishing nets strung on huge wooden poles, which caught hundreds of fish when they lowered the net. After about two hours of rowing, we stopped at a village, with Furdos acting as my interpreter. My questions about the war were answered, "Yes, the Pak Army burned this village. Yes, they killed this man's mother by rocket-shelling the house." "They kidnapped two village girls and raped them," the horror stories just went on. However, the villagers moved on from the hate and were extremely friendly to us, even though Furdos was a West Pakistani, and I was an American. They even took one woman out of the courtyard and brought her into the open, so that I could take a photograph of her doing the typical woman's work of washing. We thanked them and got back in the boat and rowed for a few more hours, going deep into the countryside. We passed old abandoned Hindu temples and mausoleums, now housing small families that seven hundred years ago were vibrant shrines of worship.

All of the life of Bangladesh seems to be centered on the riverfront and the canals. The beautiful little girls with their eyelids all outlined in black, the banyan and pipal trees overhanging the canals, and the daily cycle of washing on the banks, cleaning, and bathing, all viewed from our roving vessel.

We returned to Dacca and proceeded to get dinner at one of the local cafes. While we were eating, a small child ran into the restaurant and quickly grabbed a big mutton bone from a fat customer's plate. The man was so astonished that he didn't even know what to say. We passed crippled, grotesque figures lying in the street crying, "Allah, Allah be merciful!" and shaking in a trance. This was contrasted with the oasis of air-conditioned splendor that was the Dacca International Hotel, with its high-priced rooms, food wastage, and pious relief workers, saving the starving and homeless for eight hours, then eating and sleeping in splendor, retreating to this paradise at night (now that's what I call relief!).

I had been spending the last week with Furdos: he translates my conversations with Bangalis, interprets menus, and guides me through the sights of the city. We visited ornately tiled mosques, the bustling port, and the old city of Dacca. We were waiting for a bus in one of the urban districts outside of the center of town when a surrealistic stagecoach pulled up. This coach looked exactly like all the stagecoaches I had seen in Western movies, and I half expected to see John Wayne riding shotgun on the buggy seat. The passengers got out and we got in, sitting on hardwood seats as the horse-drawn coach bumpily pulled away. I felt like I was in a movie, and the Indians (Southwest American Indians, of course) would be shooting arrows through the open windows. The Pakistani army had destroyed all the public transport buses, so this was the only public conveyance service still operating in many areas of Dacca.

After about a week of this, Furdos asked me to dinner at his house. I put on my best shirt and freshly cleaned pants and took a pedicab to his house. I arrived at this imposing, two-story British Colonial house with a fancy wrought-iron gate, surrounded by a brick wall, now very dilapidated with peeling paint and a few broken windows. I was ushered into a large family room, where I noticed the furniture and rugs were in a ruined state. However, the extended family, tens of uncles, brothers, cousins, and grandparents, were really lively and friendly. I realized that all the family, not just the father, were involved with the politics of the country and were very outspoken and intelligent. Before dinner, I talked with an uncle, who said that "our family opposed the cruelty of the Pakistan Army, but what could we do?"

We sat at a huge table and the meal was extremely tasty: roasted lamb over biryani rice with dal (lentils) and naan (bread). After dinner, the family entertained each other. One cousin, who was a natural singer, sang Bangali pop songs and accompanied himself on a vina (similar to a sitar). He was also the family comedian, putting on a show, imitating a hip disc jockey, making jokes, dancing, and generally entertaining his enrapt audience.

Finally, all of us stood while he sang the Bangladesh national anthem; all the family joined in the singing.

Where was John Wayne when the Bangalis really needed him? (author's photo)

"My Golden Bangal"

My Bangal of Gold I love you

Forever your skies your air sets my heart in tune as if I were a flute

In Spring O Mother Mine the fragrance from your mango-groves makes me wild with joy - Ah what a thrill!

In Autumn O Mother Mine in the full - blossoms paddy fields I have seen spread all over - sweet smiles!

Ah What a beauty what shades what an affection and what tenderness!

What a quilt have you spread at the feet of canyon trees and along the banks of rivers!

Oh Mother Mine words from your lips are like Nectar to my ears!

Ah What a thrill! If sadness O Mother Mine casts a gloom on your face my eyes are filled with tears!

(Taken from a poem by Rabindranath Tagore - Public Domain)

Five Hundred Taka Bank Currency (Public domain)

It was very moving, the love of a new country: golden Bangal, while a small child was suckling at his mother's breast nearby as we sang. The atmosphere was of peace and wonderment at this family gathering; I was so thankful that he had made me a part of this.

As I left Furdos, I wondered what would happen to his troubled family in the coming months. The father was still in jail and there were no jobs for any of the adult family members because of their "traitor" status. Yes, they had chosen the wrong side. I saw them not as faceless collaborators, but as individuals, with hopes and anxieties, struggling to survive in post-war Bangladesh. Returning to my hotel, the street was jammed with thousands of rickshaws, people everywhere and no end to the poverty on display.

The land of Bangladesh is just like the Five Hundred Taka bill (Bangali currency). Vast seas of muddy blue-brown water and simmering fields of tall-stalk golden jute. All of Bangal is very fertile, with dark, sweating men driving their oxen through fields. But it is not only the land that is fertile but also the people. I met a well-educated civil servant of about 40 years old who had six children and wanted four more. Overpopulation is already a huge problem, and the government doesn't help. For example, the director of Bangal Family Planning had three wives and twenty-three children! As I walk around the back alleys and the crowded streets, I have never seen so many vultures as I've seen in Dacca. They are like evil harbingers, remembering their last feast from the war and anticipating a new one from the looming famine to come.

On my last night in Dacca, I was saddened by the new country's prospects: so much poverty and corruption. I went up to the roof of my hotel one last time to view the sea of humanity below me. It was a beautiful night; the setting sun enveloped the landscape, and there was a cool breeze blowing. I looked over and saw a young boy playing on a nearby tenement roof, flying his kite in the setting sun, totally oblivious to the humanity below him. I felt here was the future of Bangladesh, and with young people like this, it would survive.

Boy with kite (author's photograph)

I got up early for the boat, stopping at my favorite café. The owner smiled at me and prepared my order of hot, spiced potatoes before I even asked. On the ship, we passed the small villages with their rusted iron sheeting, and soon the green fields were left behind, with the grey ocean and the leaden sky forming an ashen monochrome, enveloping the horizon.

Chapter Twenty: People of Bangladesh

Young girl on a dike: during and shortly after the monsoon all the road networks are flooded out and people had to walk on the dikes to get around.

Instead of the family car, you have the family boat. Here we have a family on a boat for an outing.

Bangalis gathering jute stalks in the low-level swamps and streams.

Jute is mashed and spun into fibers in a small village outside of Dhaka.

Along the waterways and shoreline of Dhaka you see hundreds of these small houseboats. This one is very bare: cooking and sanitation is done on the shore; the houseboat is only used for sleeping and privacy.

Loading the spun bales of jute for export. Jute is primarily used in our country for making burlap bags.

A typical fishing boat from the small villages outside of Dhaka.

Bangali fishermen pass by an ancient Hindu temple, reflecting Bangladesh's past history as a Hindu Kingdom. Many of these old Hindu temples were converted into mosques or abandoned and now are home to poor Muslim families.

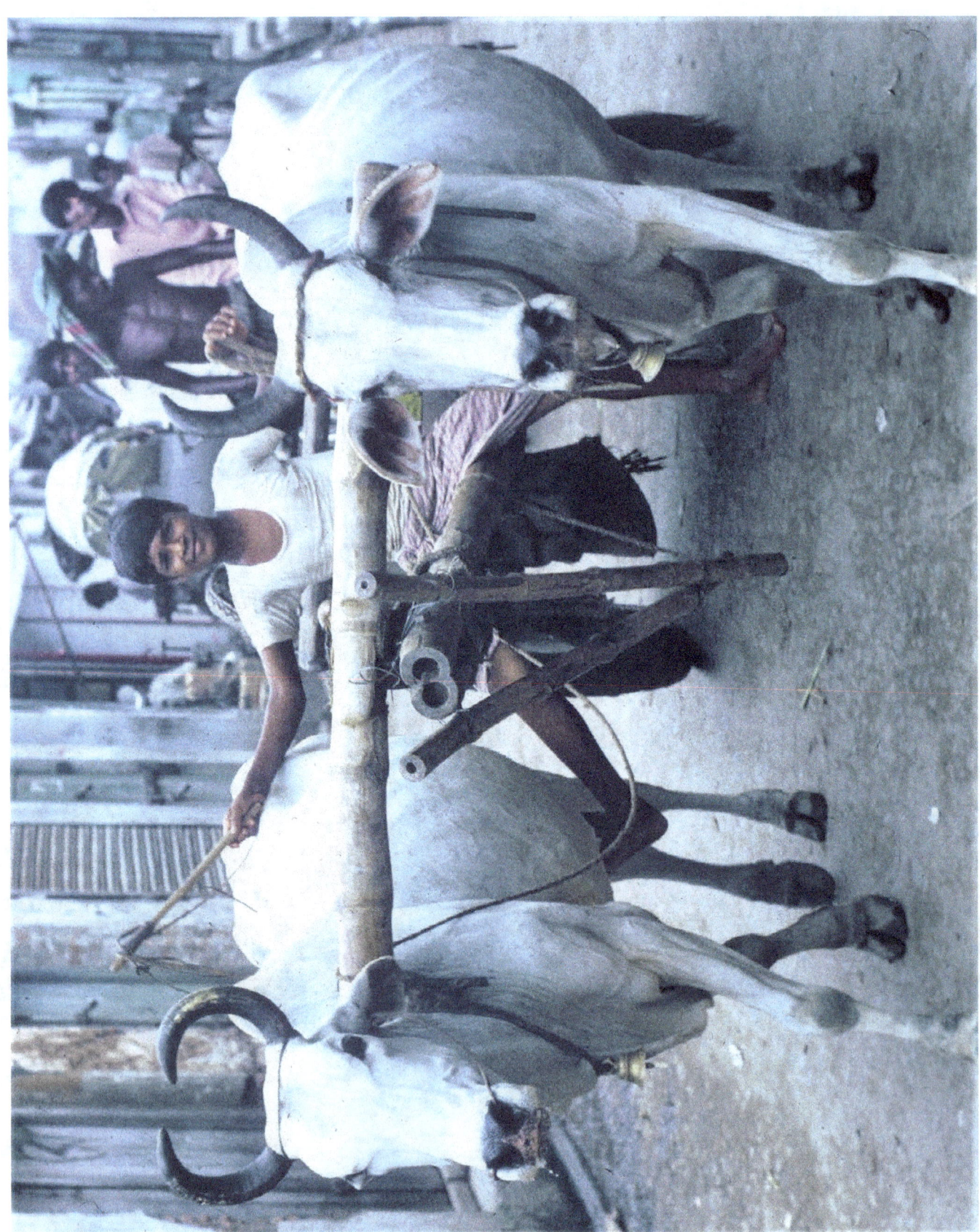
It is not surprising to see oxen pulling a cart on a busy street in Dhaka.

While I was in Bangladesh there were many demonstrations, mostly against America for supporting West Pakistan instead of Bangladesh during the independence war.

Young children in the countryside. The crippled girl may have been an independence casualty.

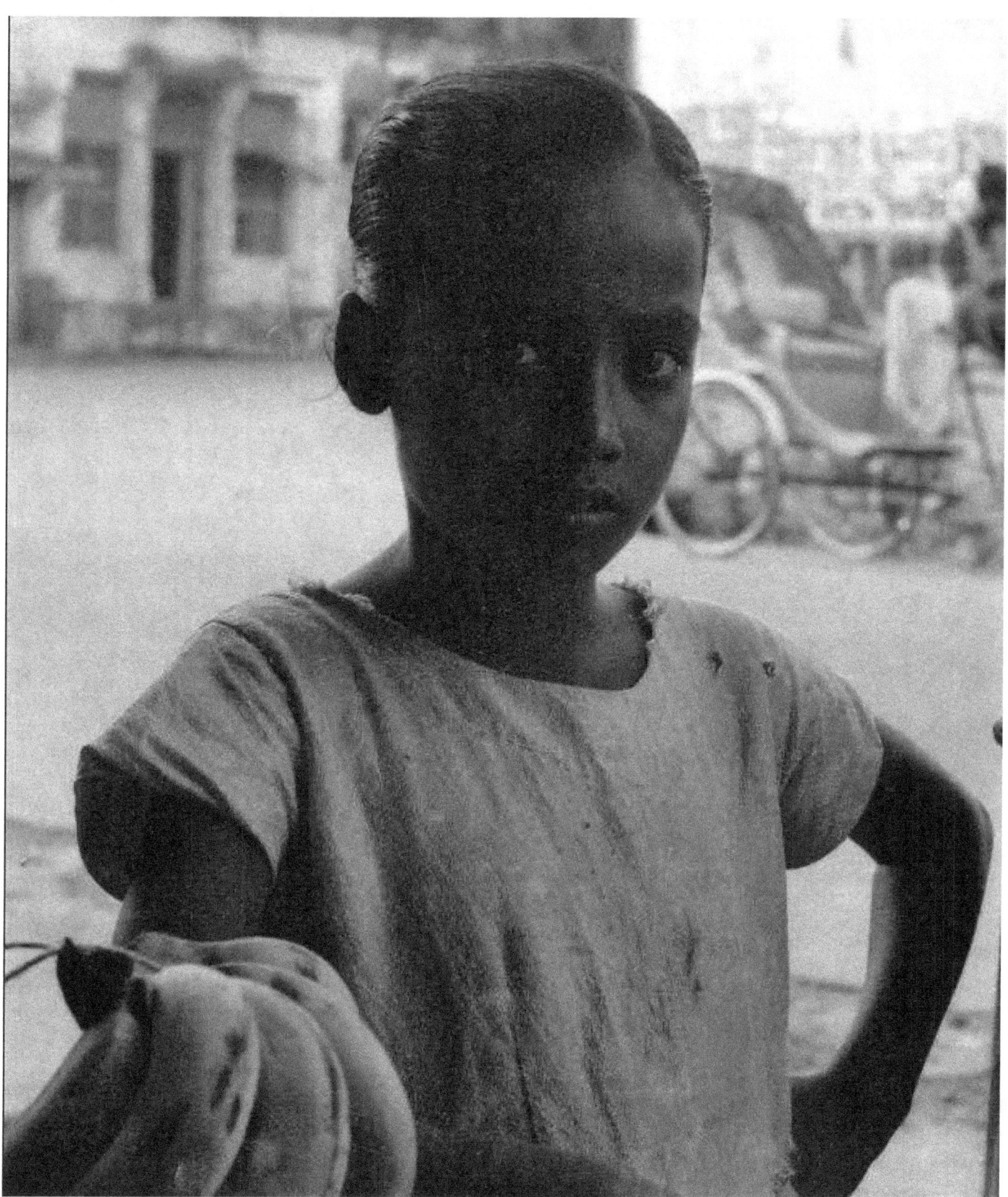
A beautiful young girl in the Dhaka market.

A scene at a village water well where the young teenager is washing his clothes, and the old grandmother is escorting her children to get water.

The man is smoking a chillum, similar to how I smoked, only my chillum had hashish and not tobacco.

Everyone in the village household has a task to do: here a young girl is cleaning the pots and pans for her family.

The Heartland of India

Ganges River in the Heartland of India: Lieutenant Colonel Forrest: color drawing 1824 (Public Domain CC-CCO-PD License)

Chapter Twenty-One: Hinduism Demystified

They swept down from the mountains in their horse-drawn chariots in endless waves through the Khyber Pass, moving their vast herds of sheep down into the great plains of the Ganges basin. They were fierce, fair-haired, light-complexioned warriors, speaking a strange language (Sanskrit) and worshipping the sky and fire gods in open-air altars. They had no temples but a priesthood that practiced the horse-sacrifice and the preparation of "Soma" (a hallucinogenic drink) to placate their God. These were the Aryans, and they vanquished the remains of the Indus Valley Civilization and the petty fiefdoms of the Indian plains.

Aryans Entering India 2000 BC.

To understand India and how Hinduism originated, we must study the Indus Valley Civilization and the legacy it left on Indian Civilization. For over 1500 years, the Indus Valley prospered: they built huge cities and traded ivory, gems, and spices with the Sumer cities in the Fertile Crescent (Iraq) and Egypt in 3500 BC. They developed a system of indoor plumbing that collected the waste from individual houses and funneled it into canals which dumped it away from the city. It is believed the people spoke a Dravidian language, but unfortunately, the written language has not been deciphered. Around 1900 BC, the civilization began to decline. What caused that decline has made the Indus Valley Civilization a poster child for climate change and the devastation that it wrought. In this part of India (now Pakistan), the monsoon came in two cycles: the stronger summer monsoon, which dumped most of the rainwater, and the lighter winter monsoon. Around 2000 BC, the summer monsoon started failing; this lasted for generations and affected the produce needed to feed the large cities of the Indus Valley. Previously the inhabitants were able to raise rice because of the abundant rainfall of the summer monsoon. They adapted by switching to millet and barley, which took less water to come to fruition. However, when the winter monsoon also failed, there was a general famine in the whole area. Coupled with this was the shifting of the major rivers in that area. The Indus and the Ghaggar-Hakra Rivers shifted, and a major river, the Sarasivati, disappeared.

Unlike their counterparts in Central Asia which also suffer from heat and drought conditions, there was no extensive irrigation system developed by the Indus Valley people. In Samarkand, due to the hot weather, the irrigation system was ingeniously constructed underground and could be tapped far from the Oasis city to provide produce for the huge populations of Samarkand. Unfortunately, this underground irrigation system which existed for hundreds of years, was destroyed by Genghis Khan when he sacked the city and killed all the inhabitants in the 13th century AD. The Indus Valley cities were now landlocked and did not have enough water to support their crops and large urban populations. This climatic catastrophe caused a decline in trade with their neighbors. Many of the major cities were abandoned, and the people moved into the Ganges Plain. The arrival of the Aryans dealt this decaying civilization its final blow.

Worship of the Lingam / Yoni

According to archaeological finds, the Indus Valley Civilization practiced a primitive fertility religion: the worship of the lingam (phallus)/ yoni (vulva). It's described in the sacred Vedas by the conquering Aryans as the religion of the "dark-skinned" people that they conquered.
One of the finest sculptures to come out of the Indus Valley Civilization is the Dancing Girl (see photo of Indus Valley Dancing Girl in my Chapter: Dance, Dance, Dance). Her features, however,

are negroid. Could the original Dravidian people have adopted the fertility religion of these Aboriginal Negroid people, or was this dancing girl a slave acquired in a trade with the Sumerians?

The Great Bath of Mohenjo-dara.

Excavations at the Indus Valley cities found no temples or palaces, but they did find a huge water tank which subsequently became a part of every Hindu temple complex in India up till this day. This is where the faithful cleanse themselves before doing their prayers to the gods.

There is also an interesting seal unearthed at Mohenjo-Dara, which shows a seated figure in the yoga position. This is the first representation of the ancient Indian meditation ritual. The figure is surrounded by animals, both real and imaginary, and the face could be an animal god or a three-faced God with horns (A forerunner of the Hindu Triumvirate of Brahma, Vishnu, and Shiva?). Below is the photo of the seal.

Pashupati seal: 2600- 1900 B.C. discovered at Mohenjo-dara.

The original Indian Civilization, the Indus Valley Civilization, had conquered or absorbed the native tribes and instead of imposing their form of religion, they took the tribal lingam (penis), which was originally a fertility God symbol, and made it a central tenet of the religion. There have been no statues of any of the present-day Triumvirate of Hindu gods: Brahma, Vishnu, and Shiva, in the Indus Valley ruins. However, Shiva, the creator and destroyer of worlds, is represented by the lingam, many times depicted emerging from the yoni (vulva).

Since Indian history is an "oral" history until about 500 years before the Christian era, the history of the lingam/ yoni was lost when the Aryans drove them into the Ganges Plain. The worship of the lingam continued, and when the nomadic warriors became sedentary farmers in the Ganges plains, this fertility lingam worship displaced the Vedic "Aryan" Gods. The Aryans believed in simple nature gods (Sky, Fire, Wind), and their rituals couldn't be sustained in the hot Ganges Plain. Their horses died of the heat, so the horse sacrifice was abandoned. The soma plant couldn't be grown in this hothouse environment so that ritual was also abandoned.

The second important concept that the Aryans adopted was reincarnation. Originally these warriors buried their dead under the "open" skies. They believed in the afterlife, giving their powerful chieftains slaves and horses that were sacrificed, as well as chariots and fine clothing in their burial sites. They practiced ancestor worship and, once settled, became influenced by the "rebirth" concept of their neighboring Indus Valley farmers. I believe the reincarnation concept for the Indus Valley people was originally derived from the farming of crops: they are planted, flourish, and die and then are reborn the next growing season. Similarly, people are born, flourish, and die only to be "reborn" with the next crop (new body) of a human. The philosophical constructs of Hinduism weren't developed until the Upanishad Era (1000 BC) that justified the "eternalization" of the soul, which is constantly renewed through reincarnation.

The simple fertility worship of lingam/yoni was transformed from the sexual symbol to the symbol of the cosmic energy of creation and destruction. The idea of stopping the endless reincarnation also developed during the Upanishad era when Hindu philosophers developed yoga to achieve oneness with the godhead within everyone.

Lingam, the symbol of Shiva, in a South Indian temple (author's photo).

While the Aryans couldn't stop the loss of their religion or rituals, they could try to stop the miscegenation of their people with the indigenous "dark-skinned" conquered people. They developed the caste system for their own people and encouraged the indigenous people to develop their own system. A "separate but equal" system that keeps racial lines pure between the two people. The Aryans used the Indian system of reincarnation to support the caste system: If you are a good person and practice good deeds, you will be born into a higher caste position in your next life. While the two separate caste systems and peoples intermingled and inter-married over time, the concept of power and authority of the caste remains intact to this day.

Like the American experience of settlers in Conestoga wagons pushing out the native Indians, the Aryans conquered an advanced, heavily populated civilization that had farmed the land and built great cities. This was the classic conflict between two ways of life: the herder vs. the sedentary farmer. Like the ancient Hebrews, the Aryans brought a vast body of oral history, the Vedas, which they chanted and sang for thousands of years from one generation to the next. On a larger scale, it was the fusion of these two world views, the Aryan and Indus Valley, that created the religion we call Hinduism today. After the initial shock of overwhelming poverty, the one thing that stands out in India is religion. Hinduism dominates every facet of Indian life; it is the glue that keeps India together.

In most of the major religions of the world, we have a single individual who, through his works, offers a path to achieve meaning in life and an everlasting life after death. We have sacred books: the Bible, Qu'ran, and Sacred Sutras, that expound the philosophy or essence of how we can achieve life everlasting or union with the godhead. Hinduism also has an ideology and pathway, but it is intrinsically bound up with the caste system and becomes a social and economic way of life. India's oldest sacred books, the Vedas (there are four Vedas), deal with how certain sacrifices are to be performed, hymns of praise to the Gods, and a manual of how to conduct your life. Ritualism, or the proper way to practice a ritual, is primary. It is not as important to worship your God as it is to follow the proper ritual in worshipping your God that is prescribed in the Vedas.

However, the conquered race took over the conqueror's religion, replacing Vedic gods with the elaborate ritualism of worshipping the trinity of Vishnu, Brahma, and Shiva, which is Hinduism today.

Bhagavad-Gita

The essence of Hinduism is in a compact three-page prose poem called the Bhagavad-Gita (The Song of God), and it was actually sung for over a thousand years before it was transcribed into Sanskrit.

Hinduism has the unique characteristic of accepting and incorporating all other religions into its pantheon of gods. The Vedas were dedicated to the Aryan sky and fire gods, but the Upanishads expound the concept of Brahman (the universal Soul): the infinite force and destiny of all existence, the formless infinite substratum, the transcendence of everything that is or was or ever shall be. Complementing this is the concept of the Atman: the immortal spirit of all living creatures, a pantheistic belief that the universal energy of existence is in everything. The Upanishads teach that most of these beliefs are one and the same. Every man can tap into his infinite spirit and merge with the oneness of the universal soul.

In Western philosophy, our approach to ultimate existence started with Descartes, who believed that the self is the most dynamic form of reality: "I think therefore I am." God created the self and is a perfect version of the self. Spinoza wrote that God is in every living thing: a pantheism that makes all living things sacred. The Hindu philosophers of the Upanishads take these concepts of self and sacred and synthesize them into the startling idea that God and the self are one and the same. How do you achieve this transformation, becoming one with God? The answer is in the Bhagavad-Gita ("The Song of God").

Arjuna and the avatar of God, Krishna converse in the poem Bhagavad-Gita (old lithograph print from 1932) (Public Domain).

The poem relates the conversations of feudal princes Arjuna and Krishna, an earthly avatar of the God Vishnu. Arjuna does not want to kill his cousins in a fight for the kingdom's throne, even though they stole the throne from him. Krishna expounds on the concept of dharma (duty): every man has a soul, and when a person dies and sheds his body, the soul (atman) is immortal. It is Arjuna's duty to fight because he is a warrior. He must fight, but he should not be eager for victory. His real goal is to achieve oneness with God by performing his duty. He must abandon his false ego, the material world, and enter the real world of Atman.

The Bhagavad-Gita explains the yogic understanding of action, service, and meditation. Karma yoga is selfless action, performing one's duty in life without wanting any reward. Bhakti yoga focuses on meditation of the godhead (the essence of the universe). Jana yoga stresses that all existence is ephemeral. Only meditation on the godhead is the way to bring understanding of the Atman.

All of these yogic teachings are just different ways to access the universal soul to achieve Moksha (enlightenment) and release the soul from the constant cycle of rebirth. There's only one true being, and the individual has a part of this being in his own self that seeks to unite with the universal being. By becoming part of all true existence, he achieves pure consciousness. "He who does work for Me; he who looks upon Me as his goal; he worships Me freely from worldly attachment; he who is free from enmity to all creatures; then he becomes part of Me" (Upanishads).

Chapter Twenty-Two: How the Caste System Began - A Fractured Fantasy

Once upon a time, there was a powerful but troubled king who called together his vizier, trusted administrators, priests, and astrologers to help him solve his problem. He spoke to the assembled group in a grave tone, "When we first came to this lowland from our mountain pastures, we had to completely change our lives. There were plenty of rich kingdoms to conquer and booty for our troops, but our way of life was changing irrevocably. We couldn't keep our horses alive in this infernal heat; there were no grasslands to support our enormous herds. We couldn't brew "soma" needed for our worship rituals because our elixir bush wouldn't grow in this climate. All of this we can live with; now we'll use water buffalo, become farmers instead of herders, and have sweet wine in place of soma. But the biggest threat to our being is that we're being absorbed into this inferior dark-skinned race that we conquered. Our soldiers are marrying these dark-skinned, pug-nosed slaves. They're deserting Surya and bowing to Shiva, a dark god, worshipping his phallus as their God. Everything we stood for is being debased and is being swallowed up by these slaves. What can we do to stop this?"

A trusted adviser spoke up, "You cannot legislate the passions of the heart. You'll alienate your subjects, who won't obey you, and there'll be much unrest and uprisings against your unjust rule."

The king's economist spoke up, "We could offer gold rewards if they would marry within their clans and more gold for each 'fair-skinned' child born."

The king's minister of civil affairs interrupted, saying, "Just look at our women; they've become fat and lazy. The slaves do everything for them. Who wouldn't want a comely, nicely figured slave as opposed to our fat, useless women who do not work."

Next, the king's chief priest spoke, "We could destroy images of Shiva, burn their temples, and force everyone to worship our sky god on penalty of death."

There were grumblings from all of the other counselors. "We can kill many of the false believers, but we can never kill the false religion. It was here 2000 years before we conquered them. And besides, we don't have the army to accomplish this. There'll be uprisings which will be the downfall of the kingdom."

Lastly, the astrologer spoke up, "The stars are not portentous to any of these so-called solutions. The stars are aligned to favor these slaves; there are too many of them. Our clansmen are favorably disposed to this new religion, and their women are strong, hard workers and capable of producing many strong babies who are needed in our largely agrarian society."

Everyone shook their heads and started arguing amongst themselves. Outside stood a shabbily dressed, matted, long-haired sadhu, a wandering holy man who had overheard the entire proceedings. He stepped forward and asked for an audience with the king, but the guards caused a commotion and pushed him away. Again, he tried to enter, and the royal guards were ready to spear him to death. Then he shouted, "I have a solution to the king's question." A minister near the window heard this and stopped the guards, escorting the sadhu into the king's presence. Ordinarily, the king wouldn't have permitted this intrusion, but he remembered that recently a soothsayer had foretold him of a man dressed in rags who would bring him the good news. The king admitted him into this regal chamber and bid him to speak.

Indian Sadhu with monkeys: Library of Congress Carpenter Collection (Public Domain).

The sadhu laughed, looking at all of these incredulous faces. "Your advisers really don't have a clue on how to solve your problem. Laws won't achieve this separation of the races. They are already a part of the fabric of our civilization. And destroying their temples will bring your downfall and still not solve the problem for your next generation. The solution can be answered in one simple but effective concept: the ritualization of purity.

Surya, the ancient Aryan God of the Sun.

"I see you have a statue of Surya, your God of the sun. Create a society based on the physical attributes of God. The head of the God, which possesses the mind and knowledge, would be the "brahmin" (priest) because only he can perform the proper ritual to achieve the salvation of the Soul. Now you have the arms and chest, the strongest part of the body, which would be the "kshatriyas," the king, nobles, and warriors to rule and defend the kingdom and enforce obedience to the Brahmin's role. Suryas' legs are the "Vaishya", the artisans, merchants, and farmers to create your art and wealth. Then we have Suryas' feet which are the "shudras," the manual laborers that build your palaces and roads. Lastly, there is a vast underclass that isn't a part of Surya: the slaves and untouchables who are necessary to society because they do the dirty work: tanners, latrine cleaners, and the buriers of the dead. You, as the king, must make it impure to move out of your present condition in life. If you try to marry outside of your group, you risk contamination and the ostracization of your group or caste, as I call it. The carrot at the end of this stick is that by properly observing these rituals and being a good person, you can move out of your caste when you die and be reborn into a higher one. If you're a bad person, you will be reborn into a lower caste. This keeps civil order in your society.

"To make this a viable solution, you must also include the conquered peoples into this hierarchical system of castes. You share the power but preserve your purity of bloodlines by not intermingling into the dark-skinned castes. Even the lowest members of your society, the Untouchables, can aspire to be reborn into the lowest shudra castes by adhering to the rituals."

The king and his advisers were astonished. "Yes, this would work." The king offered the sadhu anything he wanted, but he replied, "I have no need of riches. I renounced all of my wealth to find God through meditation and yoga, which is the physical and mental exercise to control your body through your mind. I will reach the state of non-being and leave this endless cycle of rebirth behind." He then walked out and was never seen again.

The king enthusiastically instituted the caste system. The old bloodlines remained intact within their castes. The people knew their place in society and there was prosperity and contentment in the land.

Chapter Twenty-Three: The Academic Confronts Reality

"Throw me a lifeline, save me,"

-Joan Armatrading, *Save Me.*

I met her at a small traveler's hotel outside of Allahabad. She was an intense young woman in her mid-twenties who was doing research for her PhD in Indian studies. She was living in a small Hindu farming village about 30 miles away and was in town getting supplies because there was no store in her village. Her name was Karen, and she was desperately lonely. She had lived among the villagers in a small room that belonged to the headman, yet she was isolated from the village's day-to-day life. She was still learning the local Hindi dialect and recording village life with her camera and her small battery-operated tape recorder. She was there to document how the Indians lived in this small village. If she could understand the dynamics of Indian life, then she could use this microcosm laboratory of the village to extrapolate solutions for poverty within the Indian tradition and not Western-style reforms that were alien to the culture she was trying to help.

Karen was from Ohio State University and had lived in the village of Udad for two months. Daily, she ate what the locals ate: chapatis and vegetables and roamed the fields with farmers, observed the local school taught by the village Brahmin and attended, as a guest, the local village council. She had no electricity, no running water and used the fields for her toilet. She wasn't accepted by the local village women, and her forays into the Untouchable part of the village didn't endear her to the ruling village council. This was her first trip out of the village, and she was splurging on the food and the company of fellow Westerners.

We talked about India, the incredible poverty, the seeming indifference of the Indian middle class, and how to change a way of life that had been the same for three thousand years. The American solution was education, but with the structured society where you did what your forefathers did, what were the opportunities?

Karen was a trained sociologist, not an agricultural expert. Her job was to observe, to see how all of the complex parts of the village melded together into a cohesive wholeness. She was there to record how the villagers endured famine, injustice, and the deadly tedium of everyday sameness. What she discovered so far was that everyone had their place; there was no loneliness (unlike her situation as an outsider) because of the daily tasks: a set time to get water, make dinner, sew clothes, till fields, answer grievances, wait for the life-giving rain and worship at the village shrine. The days melded into each other, everyone doing his or her part to ensure that the village functioned smoothly. She would finish up her field work in about six to eight months, go back to Ohio State, and publish a thesis on Indian village life, perhaps offering some minor solutions for improvements. However, the reality was painfully real: the only way out of this poverty was to migrate to the cities, where a different type of exploitation would take over; one without the safety net of shared village values and cooperation.

The enormity of this inescapable poverty overwhelmed me. I thought of Gandhi, Sister Teresa, Major Gardner, and countless other reformers that preached the non-violence, love, and equality of their fellow man. This wasn't working, and something more radical was needed: a Chinese type of revolution to sweep out the old and bring in a truly classless society. This was the only solution to this grinding poverty, but there wasn't a Mao-like savior.

As an American who wants to effect change immediately, I had no solution for India. We Americans couldn't end our Harlems or Watts; there was a persistent underclass in our great society. I hoped that I could be a part of changing that; I planned to teach in the inner city and do my part, like Hwa Ju, my former Korean teacher girlfriend. Maybe education is the best solution for India. I hoped that Gandhi was right: one person's effort can make a difference, whether in America or India.

Karen desperately wanted me to return with her to her village, basically offering sex as the carrot. She was an attractive woman, but what would I do there? She was there to document, not change, the traditional way of life. At least in the Salvation Army soup kitchen in Calcutta, I had distributed meals that kept people alive. Saving lives, not passively observing, made more sense to me. After buying Karen dinner, I wished her well and caught the night train to Ahmedabad.

Chapter Twenty-Four: Khajuraho and the Kama Sutra

"I will survive,"

-Gloria Gaynor.

I had just gotten off the train and grabbed a pedicab to the temple complex of Khajuraho. This was my first visit to a temple city as opposed to an individual monument like the Taj Mahal. Here spread out for over six miles, were various temples, either restored or in ruin. I walked around looking at the splendor that this city must have evoked in its heyday when it was completed in the 11th century AD. Khajuraho temples were built by the Chandela Hindu dynasty from 800 to 1000 AD and were sacked by the Muslim Delhi Sultanate under Sultan Quib-ud-din-Airbak in the 13th century AD, who destroyed many of the 85 temples that were originally there. Presently there are about 25 still standing, and the most magnificent is the Khajuraho temple.

The details of the "beehive" Spire of Kandariya Mahadeva: Khajuraho.

Khajuraho is built like many of the Hindu temples in north India, with a central beehive Sharia (Spire) (102' high) and many entrance porches and auxiliary buildings leading up to the Sharia. Khajuraho temple is a hexagon, which is called a cosmic yanta, representing the three faces or forms of Shiva. The entire temple is made of sandstone which allowed precise cuttings and has survived plundering, weathering, and general neglect for over 2000 years.

Khajuraho is famous for its erotic sculpture on the main shrine. There are many theories on what they symbolize. These explicit sculptures are stone illustrations of the Hindu Kama Sutra, which was originally part of the Upanishads, the early Vedic holy book. The Hindu religion has a text from the Upanishads which explains the four main goals of life. First is dharma, which means you must accept your moral duties and live a virtuous life. Second is artha, which means your career, wealth, and the means of living this good life. Third is kama, desire, emotions, the pleasurable things of life, and love with or without sex. Fourth is moksha, liberation, self-realization, and self-knowledge, which will enable you to escape the wheel of reincarnation and join with the godhead. So, love, including sexual love, is a proper goal of life. The following poem is from the Upanishads:

> A fire – that is what a woman is, Gautama.
> Her firewood is the vulva,
> her smoke is the pubic hair,
> her flame is the vagina,
> when one penetrates her, that is her embers,
> and her sparks are the climax.
> In that very fire the gods offer semen,
> and from that offering springs a man.
>
> -(Brihadaranyaka Upanishad 6.2.13, c. 700 BCE, Trans.: Patrick Olivelle)

So, the actual meaning of the erotic sculptures is that it is a normal function of everyday life (bathe yourself, cook dinner, enjoy kinky sex) practiced by gods, kings, and commoners alike.

I walked for hours in the ruins. This temple site was luckily built in the middle of nowhere, which saved it from complete destruction, and it was lost for hundreds of years in thick vegetation and forest until the British rediscovered it in 1830. There are also Jain temples; these were originally built together with the Hindu temples by King Vidyadhara, who showed extreme tolerance and acceptance of all creeds and religions.

An example of the erotic sculpture at Kandariya Mahadeva Temple: Khajuraho.

Ruin of an Entrance Porch to a destroyed Hindu Temple: Khajuraho.

Even stranger were the comments of the world-famous traveler Ibn Battuta, who visited the site in 1335 AD. He noted the destruction of many of the temples but also stated that Muslims flocked there to learn religious wisdom from the Hindu sadhus and ascetics. So even in that time of barbarism, there seemed to be a dialogue of religious thought between Hindus and Muslims. After seeing so much destruction, I was now glad to observe that Khajuraho is again a Hindu center for worship: priests and the faithful observing religious ceremonies, as well as the Jains returning to their worship centers. Religion is the binding glue that keeps India together, and this is a perfect example of it.

Chapter Twenty-Five: Mahabharata - The Epic That Made India

"All of our traditions, folklore, dance, and philosophy come out of the Mahabharata and Ramayana." An old, retired teacher told me while I was watching an Indian classical dance at a temple religious festival. I had heard of these two epics but did not know the details (where are my Cliff Notes, when you really need them?) and asked him to tell me the stories.

Manuscript illustration of the Mahabharta from the 18thcentury, author unknown, depicting the battle of Kurukshetra, fought between the Kauravas and the Pandavas , Public Domain, License: PD-Art.

The Mahabharata is a long epic poem concerning the battle between two clans of first cousins who are fighting for a kingdom in the Vedic Age (2000 BC). Unlike the Iliad, where the Gods orchestrate actions from above, the Supreme God Vishnu, in his human form, Krishna, is an active participant. Krishna is the chariot driver of Arjuna, the brother of the rightful king Yudhistira, who was cheated out of his throne in a game of loaded dice (welcome to Las Vegas: Indian style). They were tricked into exile for twelve years, and when they returned, their evil cousin Duryodhana and his ninety-nine brothers wouldn't relinquish the throne. There is a great battle to decide the kingship. Arjuna doesn't want to fight his cousins and older teachers, but Krishna counsels him on the duties of kingship. It is his dharma (duty) to fight evil. This conversation is part of the Bhagavad-Gita, which is really the essence of Hinduism (see my Chapter: Hinduism Demystified).

The Pandava clan is the victor after an eighteen-day battle where Duryodhana and his ninety-nine brothers are killed along with Arjuna's favorite teacher. Arjuna feels remorse at all of the bloodshed, momentarily forgetting what Krishna had told him that the laws of the universe transcend earthly notions of "good" and "evil." The Pandavas perform the Vedic horse sacrifice to pacify the great God, but still, they find no solace. They are then led by King Yudhistira to walk to Mount Meru to ask the Gods for forgiveness. One by one, all the Pandavas die along the way leaving only the old king and a faithful dog. When he arrives at the mountain, the gatekeeper would let him in but refuses the dog entrance. Yudhistira refuses to enter without the dog, who then reveals himself as the God Dharma. Again, he is shown heaven but only sees members of the Kura clan and is told that all the Pandavas are in hell. King Yudhistira then insists on joining his brothers there. The God Dharma then reveals that the Pandavas are really in Heaven, and he is permitted to join them.

What distinguishes the Mahabharata from the Homeric epics is the religious and moral lessons. Here the essence of existence is explained: how to reunite the individual soul with the universal; how man can truly achieve oneness with God because each man has the godhead within him; and through using the various yogas, he can self-realize this union. A closer comparison would be Dante's "Divine Comedy." Dante laid out the medieval worldview of existence: a guide to understanding Christianity that lasted theologically as "truth" until the Reformation and would last to our own age and beyond as "art," a poetic masterpiece.

Chapter Twenty-Six: Ramayana

The second grand epic of India is the Ramayana. Also set in 1500 -2000 BC Vedic India. Here the hero is Rama, the human avatar of Vishnu, the Creator/ Preserver God. Rama is the ideal conception of a Hindu prince: just, loyal, and faithful to his dharma (rightful duties and responsibilities as a king). He is married to Sita, the earthly incarnation of the Hindu goddess Lakshmi (the Goddess of purity and goodness). Throughout the Ramayana, there are the teachings of the Hindu sages: philosophical concepts are expressed in allegorical stories. Like the Odyssey, it was an oral epic, recited and sung at the Hindu courts for at least one thousand years before it was transcribed into written Sanskrit. The Ramayana differs from the Mahabharata; here, the Gods orchestrate most of the action, interceding in human affairs for their own benefit.

The villain in this poem is Ravenna, a demon king of Ceylon who's favored by the Hindu God Brahma, the creator of the world. Brahma grants Ravenna a form of immortality: he can't be killed by Gods or demons. Vishnu, as the Preserver God, hates disorder, as represented by the Demon Ravenna. He resolves to come to Earth as Rama, who can kill Ravenna because he is human and not a God or Demon. In this way, he can thwart Brahma's foolishness in granting Ravenna immortality.

Rama and Sita in the Forest during their 14-year exile (Rama takes out an arrow to kill a deer for supper. He cannot kill the deer in the picture because Disney has bought this deer to star in the movie "Bambi").

The old king favors his first-born Rama and intends to crown him king, but he's tricked by his second wife to place her son Bharata (Rama's stepbrother) on the throne. Bharata then forces Rama into exile for fourteen years. When it's revealed to Bharata what his mother did, he seeks out the exiled Rama and implores him to return as the true king. Bharata is the Hindu ideal of faithfulness, ceding to his brother, the rightful heir to the throne. Rama, however, following his dharma, refuses the kingship because that would be disobeying his father; he must serve out his exile. In a nice touch, Bharata takes the sandals of Rama and places them on the throne until Rama can wear them after the exile ("However," says Bharata, "I'm keeping his Nike Air Jordans, the girls all love me when I wear those blue suede sneakers").

Meanwhile, back in the forest Rama and his devoted wife Sita are wandering around, befriending various gods in human form. An important friend is Hanuman, the king of the monkeys, the embodiment of a true friend. Lakshmana, Rama's younger brother, is an Earthly representation of the snake god (Naga) that protects Rama and Sita with a crown of cobra heads to ward off any evil.

Ravenna kidnapping Sita: Cambodian Classical Dancers performing the "Ramayana" in 1922 Phnom Penh, Cambodia.

The main action in the epic is the kidnapping of Sita by the Demon King Ravenna. Assuming the guise of a wandering sadhu, he begs Sita to give him food. When she brings it, he grabs her and flies away with her, held captive on his winged chariot to Ceylon. Ravenna demands that Sita marry him; he threatens to kill her, but she still refuses.

Hanuman, the monkey king, finds her in Ceylon and offers to rescue her. She, however, refuses. Rama must kill Ravenna and "take me back with honor." A huge battle ensues between the forces of Rama and Ravenna. Rama finally kills Ravenna and rescues Sita. However, Rama doesn't want to have "used goods." He demands that Sita perform the fire ritual; if she is pure and undefiled the flames won't hurt her. (Oh God! The flames don't burn me, but the heat wreaks havoc on my makeup, running and streaky, I must look a fright!). Agni (the God of Fire) brings Sita through unscathed. Rama then embraces her, and they return to the kingdom of Ayodhya. Here Rama establishes the "ideal" state, where all castes can work together in harmony and unity, and the "ideal" king rules his subjects with benevolence and justice. After a long and prosperous reign, both Rama and Sita return to their heavenly abodes, again becoming Vishnu and Lakshmi.

The Ramayana differs from the Homeric epics in that the Gods take human form and actively participate in the action, not just squabbling on Mount Olympus. The "ideal" king is shown in Rama's brother, who was appointed king but rightly steps down and gives his brother, the true heir to the throne, the kingdom. Also, Rama, the human king, establishes a "just" kingdom treating all his subjects with happiness and prosperity. These homilies on kingship, dharma, and other Hindu philosophies give "moral" lessons to the listeners of the oral epic.

The Battle of Lanka where Rama's friend, the Monkey King Hanuman and his army defeat the forces of the evil demon King Ravenna: Painting by Sahibdin 1650 AD.

The Homeric and the Germanic Nibelungenlied epics deal with the "barbarian" concepts of honor and loyalty to their leader and clan. Loss of honor demands vengeance and the smallest "slight" demands a blood feud that ends up destroying the hero (to be fair, kidnapping the king's wife in "The Iliad" is not a petty slight; however, I don't believe Helen would have survived the "fire" test).

Coming from a Norwegian background on my mother's side, I read about the pagan Norsemen of the Icelandic sagas. Here the stories all deal with affronts to a particular character and how they all develop into blood feuds. The saga of "Burnt Njal" shows how trivial issues like who should sit where at the banquet table result in bloody killings because a person's honor was violated by his place-setting. Njal is taunted by being "less than a man" for not being able to grow a beard. For this, he seeks vengeance for the "disparagement" of his manhood.

In the "Vinland Saga," we see how the Norsemen came to North America five hundred years before Columbus. They faced savage Indians, but it was an "offended" wife that took a battle-axe and killed three Viking wives who "dishonored" her. The American colony disintegrated into a blood feud and the Vikings sailed back to Iceland and never returned to America to colonize as they did in Iceland and Greenland. It's intriguing to speculate that we Americans might all be speaking Norwegian if the first Norsemen had followed the "moral" precepts of the main characters in the Ramayana.

Chapter Twenty-Seven: Ramayana - The Hollywood Adaptation

Valmiki the Indian poet shown composing the
original Ramayana (unknown author and date)
Public Domain.

The Indian epic "Ramayana" was written by the poet Valmiki around 2000 BC. Like most of the classic epic poems, whether they be Indian, Homeric, or Norse, all were written by men and, of course, gave a man's point of view. I imagined if Hollywood decided to adapt the Ramayana and gave it to a woman director with a feminine viewpoint, you might have a whole different story. She would focus on developing the character of Sita: her reactions to living in the forest in exile, being kidnapped, and finally being rescued by the handsome Rama.

The Hollywood production would start with the lovers leaving the palace for their 14-year exile.

Sita: Rama, are you sure that I should accompany you on this 14-year exile? I could be a lot more help to you, taking care of your aging father, the king, here in the palace (aside: with all my privileges, servants, and grand lifestyle)

Rama: It is a wife's dharma to accompany his husband in good times and in bad, wherever he goes.

Rama and Sita leaving the Palace to begin their fourteen year exile (unknown date and author) British Library License: CC-CCO- PD (Public Domain)

Sita: Yes, dear (Aside: Oh well, I hope it's not as bad as that Girls' Summer Camp in the Poconos: the girls all hated me because the handsome camp director let me use his cottage bed (with him in it) while they had to sleep in tents on the bug infested forest ground. And when they found out that I had Chinese takeout every night while they had to eat that slop camp cooking, they were "fit to be tied," which I actually was, tied to the bedpost. This gave a whole new meaning to "roughing it" in the wilderness.)

The action now shifts to the forest, and we see Sita (the woman in grey) has just stepped on a thorn, and her loving husband, Rama, is now removing it. In the background, you can see Hanuman, the monkey king, and a slain deer which will be their supper.

Sita: Oh, Rama, this is just terrible! I've just stepped on a thorn, and it hurts so badly. I'm miserable! I haven't had my hair done in over a month, and my nails are broken and filthy. Be gentle when you remove that thorn! Why did you bring me to this hellhole? I had a beautiful life as the princess, with servants waiting on me, having anything I wanted to eat, not just this lousy deer meat that we have every night. There were so many things to do in the palace. Now all I do is walk around here, step on thorns, and get stung by bees. I must be allergic to bees; it seems I'm turning gray. I need a new life!

Rama and Sita wandering in the Forest during their fourteen-year exile: 18th century
Kanga Painting from the Metropolitan Museum, unknown artist, License: CC-CCO-PD
(Public Domain)

Rama: Be patient, dear; it's only another seven years until we get back to the palace and the good life.

Sita: (with a sigh) I'm going to the stream to bathe; there's nothing else to do in this dump!

Enter Ravenna, the king of Ceylon, who spies on the lovely Sita in the stream.

Ravenna: (Aside) Ah, look at this lovely naked maiden bathing. I'm going to take her back to my kingdom and make her my queen: Hello, darling, looking for a good time?

Sita: You're damn right, and who are you?

Ravenna: I'm Ravenna, king of Ceylon. I'm going to whisk you away to my kingdom, and you will be eternally happy.

Sita: Thank God someone's come to save me. Ravenna dear, I do hope you have in-flight movies and complimentary drinks for the long trip down South. (Aside) I hope he also has room service and NETFLIX down there in the sticks.

They fly away to Ceylon on his winged chariot. Ravenna installs her in the palace, demanding her hand in marriage.

Sita: Hold on there, big boy! What do you get to offer me?

Ravenna (the multi-headed demon) proposes marriage to Sita in his magnificent palace in Ceylon.

Ravenna: You shall be my queen and will have the whole kingdom to adore you, servants at your command, any foods you desire. I'll have lobsters and thick steaks flown in on my winged chariot and nightly entertainment direct from Broadway. You can wear a different sari every day, have a professional hairdresser at your command and have your own Starbucks espresso machine with a personal barista. We will go sailing on my yacht in the summer and skiing around my mountain chalet in the winter.

Sita: Now you're talking my language, big boy. I might just get to like you. Aside: You know a girl's gotta do what a girl's gotta do. I depend on the kindness of strangers.

Director: "Cut!" Sita honey, you can't use that line; it's stolen from Tennessee Williams."

Sita: "Damn! Oh, ok. How about "Why Little Ole' Me thrives on the goodness, grace and generosity of a gentleman such as yourself, sir."

Director: "That'll work."

Ravenna: Here, meet my son Prince Ashoka (in walks a handsome young prince).

Sita: Aside: (This is getting better all the time; now, if I could just lose the old fart, Ashoka and I could have some hot times in the kingdom tonight). Oh, dear Ravenna, can you have your charming prince show me around the kingdom? Don't wait up; I'll see you in the morning.

Ashoka: What would the queen-to-be like to see?

Sita: Well, let's start in your chambers. I always wanted to see how a prince lives. We could dine in: I haven't had champagne and lobster in seven years.

After a delicious meal with dozens of servants at her beck and call, she dismisses them all. She looks around the room and breaks into a wide smile, eyeing the big brass bed. Tonight, no more ants in the pants, no more spiders crawling up my legs (and then looks at the clueless Prince):

Sita: Well, I've heard so much about you southern lovers, let's see what you got, big boy!

She kisses him, throws him onto the bed, and ravishes him. Oh my God, I felt the earth move. (What made it so special was that I wasn't <u>on</u> the earth when it moved but in a nice comfy feathered bed!). They were right, Virginia is for Lovers. I'm beginning to like this arrangement; I hope I'm not rescued too soon. Now I better get back before Ravenna discovers what I've been doing.

As she enters her chambers, she's confronted by Hanuman, the monkey King.

Hanuman: I've come to rescue you, Sita, from that horrible Ravenna.

Sita: Oh, that's very sweet of you, dear, but I'm waiting for a better offer. Tell Rama to get off his ass and bring me some nice gifts when he comes to rescue me. (Aside): Until then, I'll just live the life of La Dolce Vita, pop another grape in my mouth, Ashoka.

After a month of heavenly bliss nights (I leave it up to the director to embellish in full Technicolor detail what happened during that period), Sita is awakened in the arms of her lover prince by the noise of a battle.

Sita: Oh my God, it must be Rama coming to rescue me. Quick, go out the window; he can't find me here with you! She pushes him out the window and throws his clothes behind him. He lands with a thud (it was three stories down) and starts moaning and crying loudly just as Rama enters the room.

Rama: I've just killed Ravenna and have come to rescue you.

Sita: My prince charming, by the way, what did you bring me for all my hardship and suffering that I had to endure?

Rama and Hanuman fighting Ravenna. In this illustration from the 16th century manuscript "Mewar Ramayana", now in the British library (unknown author), Rama is shown in a red chariot killing Ravenna with his bow and arrow.
License: CC-CCO- PD (Public Domain)

Rama: I brought diamonds, pearls, and a great book: "101 Recipes for Cooking Deer." Say, isn't this the prince's room? And what's that moaning and crying coming from the window?

Sita: Oh, that's only the palace cat; he must be in heat. Why yes, this is the prince's room; I was staying here because my room was being redecorated in a gorgeous pink, and the prince graciously gave up his room to me until my room was finished. Aside:(And if you believe that bullshit line, I've got a bridge to sell you in Brooklyn really cheap).

Rama: Oh, I see. (Aside: There's something rotten in the state of Ceylon). Sita, before I take you back, I want to make sure that you've been faithful to me. You will have to walk the ring of fire to prove your purity.

Sita: (Aside: Whatever happened to trust, anyway, you big boob?) Why of course, darling, I know dear old Agni, the God of Fire. Let me speak to him first before I walk the Ring of Fire.

God Agni: Ho, Ho, Ho! I am preparing the ring of fire, which separates the naughty from the nice girls.

Sita: Yeah, about that, do you still have that invisible cloak that protects you from the flames?

Agni: Yes, I do, but what's in it for me?

Sita: Well, I'm free next Thursday evening. My dance card isn't completely filled yet. I can squeeze you in between seven thirty and eight o'clock at your place.

Agni: You know what I like, "Fire in the Hole."

Sita: If you think it's hot now, wait till you see me in my Victoria's Secret negligee. I guarantee that I'll light your fire: I've been studying the Kama Sutra, and I know you'll like what I learned to do. I do hope you have been working out, practicing your leg and arm stretches and gymnastics. You're gonna need it! Now do we have a deal?

Agni smiles lasciviously and gives her the cloak.

Sita dresses in the invisible fireproof cloak and walks through the flames unscathed.

Rama: I knew you were pure, my darling. Come with me now; we will escape back to the forest. I'll kill a deer, and with your new cookbook, we can try one of those recipes. I can't wait for you to cook me "forest deer ala king."

Sita: (Aside) God, the things that a girl will do for love and the throne, of course.

The story ends here: an inspiring tale of a hardworking, struggling woman supporting her man in his time of duress.

Chapter Twenty-Eight: Kailasha Temple

Kailasha rock cut Sculpture Temple: Drawing by James Fergusson (1808-1886).

Asia has so many splendid temples that leave you awestruck, artistically and spiritually. Sometimes it is because of the massing of temples, palaces, gates, and waterways. Pagan in Burma is a good example of a huge temple complex that goes on for miles, and at every turn, you come across a huge sculpture or a stupa covered in vines: gods vying with nature for dominance. Other times it is just one huge building, for example, Borobudur in Java, which sits like a mountain on top of rice fields and is a didactic exposition of the Buddhist faith carved in stone.

There are also buildings that, because of their history, faith, and essence of the life of the community, <u>are</u> the city. For example, Koln (Cologne) Cathedral <u>is</u> Cologne. During World War II, Cologne was utterly destroyed; the only remaining structure was the huge cathedral (which incidentally took over 600 years to complete). In France, the Eiffel Tower <u>is</u> Paris, and before that was built, Notre Dame <u>was</u> Paris.

In India, the symbol that first comes to mind in representing or symbolizing India is the Taj Mahal; it is a beautiful building that is an everlasting testament of romantic love, but it is a mausoleum, a marble tombstone where a beloved wife sleeps for all eternity. This would be like making President Grant's Tomb Memorial the symbol of New York City. This confectionery wedding cake mausoleum was a very popular tourist attraction in the last quarter of the 19th century but now is forgotten, with the exception of the question asked laughingly by children trying to outsmart their peers, "Who's buried in Grant's tomb?"

President Grant's Tomb Mausoleum, New York City (photo by "King of Hearts", Wikimedia Common free usage).

The Taj is a conqueror's monument, not at all representative of the majority (80% of the population) of Hindu India. Hinduism doesn't bury its dead in mausoleums but burns its dead and scatters their ashes in sacred rivers. This corporal body is just a vessel of the everlasting spirit (soul) that will soon be reborn into another vessel. So why is the Taj Mahal the symbol of India? I believe it is because of the overwhelming power of absorption that is Hinduism. Hinduism swallowed up the Taj Mahal, just like it did communism and Buddhism. They were incorporated into a worldview where everything is accepted.

This introduction to Kailasha Temple is almost like Arlo Guthrie's "Alice's Restaurant." The first fifteen minutes of the song deal with an elaborately funny description of how an arrest for a petty littering misdemeanor affects your qualification for being accepted into the draft. The song is really about resistance to the draft on moral grounds. So too, Kailasha Temple; it is about a rock-cut structure, which symbolizes and glorifies the essence of Hinduism as a living religion and, in my mind, should be the symbol of India for Indians, as well as Westerners.

Kailasha is a temple structure carved out of a cliff of a single massive basalt rock. It's the largest rock-cut sculpture monument in the world, measuring 266 feet lengthwise, 154 feet in width, and 156 feet in depth: it represents Mount Kailasha, the sacred abode of the god Shiva. It was carved in the eighth century AD by order of the Hindu king Krishna I.

Overview of Kailasha Temple showing how it was carved out of a single basalt boulder.

What is truly mind-boggling about this temple is that it was carved from the top of the mountain down, which means the precise configuration of gods, gates, passages, and walkways was planned precisely; there could be no mistakes: you were creating a living temple out of solid rock. You can imagine the master planner directing armies of individual sculptors, each concentrating on his own portion of this huge architectural sculpture according to his detailed master plan. You can think of it as a gigantic 10,000-piece jigsaw puzzle, where you are crafting individual interlocking pieces with only the picture of the completed puzzle on the outside package! Amazingly this was completed in the short time frame of 20 years! This is truly one of the seven wonders of the ancient Asian world, and I believe that modern man, with all of his technological improvements and instruments, could not duplicate this with the exact precision and grandiose master planning these ancient sculpturers accomplished using only primitive hand chisels and hammers.

Ramayana carved panel at Kailasha Temple.

You enter this carved mountain through ornate gates into a spacious courtyard guarded by two life-size stone elephants. Walking further, you come across two tall 56-foot obelisks carved with lotus blossoms that flank each side of the Nandi Pavilion. Facing the entrance to the pavilion is an imaginative stone carving of Lakshmi (Goddess of Light and Krishna's Consort), being bathed by an elephant on each side of her, pouring water from their trunks for her bath. As you enter the pavilion, in the center, is the life-size sculpture of Nandi, the sacred bull of Shiva. You continue walking through the pavilion to the mandapo (assembly hall), which is part of the main temple structure. This hall is decorated with pillars and sculptures; on one side, scenes from the Hindu epic, the "Ramayana" and on the other side, scenes from the other Hindu epic, the "Mahabharata" and other legends of Krishna. This gigantic complex is supported by a frieze of stone elephants completely encircling the complex and supposedly holding up the structure.

Stone Elephants supposedly holding up the temple.

Off to one side of the mandapo is the Hindu demon Ravenna (from the "Ramayana"), shaking the mountain to awaken Shiva and Parvati, his consort. Opposite is the Hall of Sacrifices, with the feminine life-size images of Durga, Chamesnda, and Kali (destructive symbols of Shiva). The hall also contains other gods, goddesses, and avatars: Ganesha, Shiva's elephant-headed son, seven mother goddesses, and the ten avatars of Vishnu. On the outside of the temple are the early Aryan Vedic gods: The Sun God and the God of Fire. Also, on the outside are the representations of half Shiva, half Vishnu and another half Shiva, half Parvati.

Lions dancing on a lotus bloom roof.

The roof of the assembly hall is a huge concentric lotus flower, with four Lions surrounding the flowering bud. The roof is held up with sixteen stone-carved pillars. All along the sides of the temple structure are rock-hewn, pillared monk cells. You continue walking into the central tower, underneath which is the sacred shrine of Shiva, the lingam sculpture, which symbolizes the creative and sexual energy of Shiva. The lingam itself was a prehistoric adoption by Hinduism of an Indus Valley fertility cult. Above this is the shikhara, the Dravidian tall tower (156 feet in height). This huge tower was once covered in white plaster, depicting the snowy peak of Mt. Kailasha, mythically located deep in the Himalayas.

Not only is this an incredible sculptural work of art, but it displays the entire iconography of the Hindu faith in one place. Through the ages, Muslims have defaced the carvings, broken elephant tusks, and even closed the temple to Hindu worshippers, but they could not destroy this essential majestic symbol of Hinduism. This rock-hewn temple stands out as the summation of Hinduism, from its fertility cult beginnings to the conquering Aryan Vedic Age Gods, to the present dominant worship of Shiva, Vishnu, and Brahma and all their popular avatars. I stand so much in awe of what Kailasha temple represents in Hindu iconography that I can only say, to paraphrase the beginning of St. John's Gospel: "The LOGOS, the word is God and God becomes living stone."

Chapter Twenty-Nine: Waiting for Godot - The Indian Version

I had made a special trip to Whitefield (a suburb of Bangalore) to see Sathya Sai Baba. All over Hindu India, people were talking about this holy man as if he were a god. He performs great miracles, and his message of love and service to the poor made me curious; was he the person who would give me answers to my personal quest?

Author: Government of India Postal Service.

It was a bright Sunday morning when I boarded the bus from Bangalore to Whitefield. I look back now and say it was probably fate that made me take that bus. If I had come at any other time, I wouldn't have met Cathy and Wendall.

Whitefield is a small suburb of Bangalore: green fields, well-kept apartments, a small college, and some fledging industries. The countryside is slightly wooded but not that attractive, being flat and too dusty. I arrived in the morning and got to the ashram of Sathya Sai Baba to find out he wasn't there (Elvis had left the building!), and not only that, but most of his followers had also gone with him. I was very disappointed and was ready to turn back when I saw this white girl walking out of a cafe.

"Excuse me, are you a follower of Sathya Sai Baba?"

She said, "Yes," and I came over and started asking questions, wanting her to explain some of the things about him. She didn't seem to have it all together but said she would get her painter friend Wendall to tell me about him. They appeared to me to be an odd couple as I approached them. She was young, in her early twenties, cute tending to baby fat, and said she had been in India for six months. She had run out of money in Delhi, and Wendall had offered to take her here. She had heard of Sathya Sai Baba, so she agreed to accompany him here.

Wendall was tall and thin, about thirty-five years old, clean-shaven, with short hair, and said he had come to India because someone gave him a thousand dollars. Now he is a true believer in Sathya Sai Baba. "This holy man has great powers. He can materialize different things: necklaces, even a rainbow. He's even supposed to be present in several places at one time. Like Jesus, he raised a man to life who was certified dead." Then Wendall asked me, "Do you believe these stories?"

"Perhaps," I answered. "I've talked with many people, a Dutchman who had studied in a Hindu ashram and said that every living thing is energy, so if all human life is energy, then someone can master this energy. Controlling this energy makes it possible to raise someone from the dead or move mountains; anything is possible."

Listening to Wendall tell stories of the man was like listening to stories about Jesus. Most incredible was that you don't have to practice yoga or meditation to get peace. Just being near him gives you inner peace. Wendall, "He knows everything about you not because he can read your mind but because he is your mind."

Cathy asked me what I thought of Jesus Christ.

I said, "I think that all religions are direct experience. If you haven't had the experience, you can't really believe it. It's like trying to explain mushrooms or LSD to someone who has never taken it. You can describe the experience but never really touch the essence of it because it is an experience that must be achieved by yourself to realize this new level of consciousness." I really believe that Jesus did all of those miracles. Every man, according to the Bhagavad Gita, has a godhead within him; he just needs the middle (inward) eye to see.

I carried the conversation to a nearby restaurant and we talked all day about India: her poverty, her spirituality, art, and the Untouchables. Wendall didn't believe that one out of every five Indians was an Untouchable. I asked why Sathya Sai Baba does all of those materializations and miracles. They answered in chorus so that people would believe in him.

I asked again, "If he has the power of Jesus, why doesn't he do something really good for India?"

Wendall answered, "He is slowly doing really good things for India: building schools, colleges, and water projects. He is working for the spiritual revitalization of India."

After I had said this about Jesus, I thought of how the Jews had treated Jesus. "If you are the Messiah, rise up and deliver us from the Romans and show us the Heavenly New Jerusalem." I seemed to be one of those doubting Jews: Sathya Sai Baba must prove himself before I would believe. I began to see the similarity between Jesus and his performing miracles: walking on water, turning water into wine, and raising Lazarus with the miracles of Sathya. I also remembered that Wendall had said that just being near him brought inner peace. This was exactly the way the disciples described being around Jesus. I had to find out more about this holy man, so I went to the local bookstore in town and found a book about him and his teachings. Before I left the store, I talked with the bookshop owner, who said that Sathya Sai Baba had proclaimed himself as the reincarnation of Shirdi Sai Baba, a venerable nineteenth-century guru. This twist has now become a detective novel. I can't know about Sathya until I know about this earlier holy man.

Shirdi Sai Baba

Shirdi Sai Baba lived all of his life in the Indian village of Sharda from 1838 to 1918. His residence there was an abandoned mosque and his teachings were a synthesis of Islam and Hinduism. His belief was that all religions worship one true god, no matter how many visages God has. He believed there was unity in all religions, and like the Sufis, he believed that the light of God is in every human being. He also believed, as the Bhagavad Gita stated, "every man has the godhead within themselves." They just need to look inward to become one with Him.

He was against the caste system and preached that to access the godhead, you must pray, chant God's name and read the holy scriptures. You should also have faith and patience. Shridi used

Hindu yoga meditations and believed in the Indian dharma (you should perform your duties without attachment to earthly matters). He would also recite and read the Qu'ran and listen to qawwali (Sufi) singing. He did not identify himself as either Muslim or Hindu; to him, these names we're not important, only belief in the one true God.

Shirdi Sai Baba found his godhead, pure consciousness, and his message was love and patience to all human beings. This realization of the self, the all-pervading consciousness that knows no boundaries, allows the divinity in man to go forth and practice true righteousness, peace, and love. He didn't start a new religion but showed the way for every man to achieve self-divinity, oneness with God. Shirdi Sai Baba also performed miracles and materializations and attracted many followers. He is still revered in India and has several ashrams that continue to spread his loving message.

Shirdi Sai Baba in the early 1900s.

Sathya Sai Baba

If Sathya is a reincarnation of Shirdi Sai Baba, then he, too, must have achieved self-realization of oneness with God and nature (all other beings). This is similar to Taoism, which emphasizes the oneness with the natural order of life and the understanding that you can only find peace if you become a part of the all-pervading consciousness of the earth. However, Taoism is passive; you shouldn't damn a river because that isn't a "consciousness" of the river; the river must flow freely to achieve order in the universe. Similarly, Buddhism teaches the extinction of the individual soul when it merges with the universal soul. Love and help for your fellow man is seen as an unwanted desire, and real life is an illusion (maya). This, in my mind, is an escape from and not a fulfillment of the divinity within ourselves. Sathya coined the following epigram: "Love all, Serve all, Help Ever, Hurt Never." I had asked for the truth, not of his miracles but of what he was doing for India. He had built free hospitals that serve thousands yearly and founded a university and ashrams to spread his message. Most impressive are his water work projects: one project gave fresh drinking water to 729 villages throughout India, servicing 1.2 million Indians.

Here again, he isn't starting a new religion. "If you are a Christian, be a better Christian. Show compassion for your fellow man," similar to what Jesus preached. Jesus also was not trying to start a new religion but a fulfillment of Judaism: He was the Messiah, the long-awaited Hebrew God that would establish the Kingdom of God on Earth for His chosen people. Sathya's followers sing devotional songs to God, just like the ancient Vedas were sung two millennia ago. His advice is "meditate, practice constant repetition of the God name, visualize the image of the godhead, and practice silence."

You may ask, "Where does he get the money to do all of this?" Sathya Sai Baba has a huge following in the Hindu upper-middle class. Wealthy Hindus donate thousands of dollars just to see and speak with him. He also has many Western followers who donate money to his ashram. There are Sathya Sai Baba ashrams in the U K, the Americas, and other European countries. Famous individuals like John Lennon have a personal guru, and Sathya also has similar wealthy Western patrons and donors.

He is a Sat Guru (spiritual guide) that hasn't turned away from India's problems, using his self-realization to better the lives of the poor through meaningful, long-lasting improvements.

Chapter Thirty: Rachel

"What's so good about goodbye,"

-The Miracles.

Portrait of Wally: Egon Schiele 1912.

There were so many questions I had about Sathya Sai Baba, and Cathy and Wendell were gracious enough to invite me to their place for dinner. Cathy had also invited an ashram friend, Rachel, so we had a foursome.

Rachel was a tall thin girl with long brown hair, an aquiline nose, piercing hazel eyes underscored with deeply furrowed crow's feet, and a longish face with creases around her large mouth. She gave off an aura of seriousness and intelligence, a Simone de Beauvier (without the haughty accent and dangling cigarette).

Jean-Paul Sartre and Simone de Beauvoir 1939.

She had graduated from Earlham College, a small Quaker school in Indiana. She came to India as a tourist and stayed on to learn more about Sathya Sai Baba. I asked her what she thought about Baba's miracles, especially the one about raising a dead man to life. She wasn't sure if they were real or just stories, but she did feel a sense of peace when she was near him. Then what about Jesus's miracles? Being a Quaker, she also had some doubts about these.

We then spoke about India and my thoughts that only communism could save India. Wendell joined in and said India could be saved by a spiritual revitalization. I chimed in, "How would that work: you have 80 million Untouchables that no one cares about and 150 million Moslems that care nothing about a Hindu spiritual revival. India will not change unless the caste system is abolished. Gandhi tried and failed; he wanted to give equal rights to the Untouchables, but this was only given lip service by the national government. In the villages, which is 70% of India, they are still totally excluded from any decision-making in the village councils."

Rachel responded, "Change will come incrementally. The first step is what Sathya Sai Baba is doing: building water projects, free hospitals, and universities to implement this change."

We talked for hours, and it was getting late. I offered to escort Rachel to her apartment. I thanked our hosts, and we left. Rachel's apartment was in a three-story cinderblock building. When we arrived, she asked me if I wanted to come up. Her room was clean and bare, except for a two-section bookcase crammed full of books on spiritualism, politics, and classic novels. She was a seeker and told me passionately that she thought and read about India, poverty, and answers to her personal spiritual quest.

There was a lull in the conversation, and I took advantage of the moment by leaning over and kissing her. She returned the kiss, French kissing me. Soon we were embracing and kissing each other. I quickly undressed, and she loosened her blouse and dropped her skirt. She turned off the light and we fell in her bed. I kissed her small, firm breasts, and she stroked my penis to hardness. I sat up on the bed and gently nudged her face down. She kissed my crown and then enveloped it, moving slowly up and down, rasping my erection. I raised her head, laid her on her back, and started kissing, my tongue massaging her vagina. After a few moments, I stopped and mounted her, now kissing her lips, as we started to move together. She thrust her body upwards, wrapping her legs around my waist, and we moved in unison. After a few moments, I came but continued thrusting in her to give her the pleasure she had given me. Soon we were both spent. I came off and held her silently until we both fell asleep.

When I awoke, she was already up, making tea on her hot plate (there was no formal kitchen in the apartment). We drank tea, and she said she had to get to work at her ashram job as a teacher's aide. Soon she would have a class of her own, teaching English. I asked her if she wanted to get together again, and she said yes. I picked her up that evening for a vegetarian dinner served on palm leaves. She showed me around the ashram, and then we returned to her room for more hungry lovemaking.

I had hoped to see Sathya Baba, but he still had not returned. My days fell into a routine: I wandered around the ashram and talked to the people; most were very sincere, but all had that dazed glaze of "born again" Christians and were always willing to proselytize and sing the praises of Sathya Baba. Rachel had a set schedule also: after teacher assistance at the school, she would do her yoga exercises, and then we would get together in the evening for a meal and discussions. Here is a woman that is a seeker. She is working to achieve the bliss that Sathya Baba has promised. I looked at Rachel not as one would look at a groupie to a rock group, but like the followers of Jesus: Mary Magdalene and the other women that just wanted to be close to Christ because of the peace that He radiated. I remembered a passage in Moby Dick called "The Mat-Maker." Here Ishmael and Queequeg are weaving a straw mat: I use the mat as a metaphor to understand my situation here: the warp (vertical strings) of the mat is the ashram; the weft (horizontal strings) is free will that Rachel is choosing to accept Sathya's teaching. The last ingredient, chance, is the stick that tightens up the weave, and this is what I am missing. I look at myself as a "Doubting Thomas." I believe Sathya Baba is a very holy man, but is he the answer that I am looking for? The chance of meeting or even being near Sathya Baba was getting more and more impossible since he was not expected to return to the ashram for weeks, as I was told.

Rachel is a very caring, loving person, and yet I feel it is her vision that I am experiencing and not my own. We talked for hours about the peace that radiates from Sathya Baba and how everyone is in awe of this holy man. As I found out at the bookstore, Sathya came from a long line of Hindu holy men who tried to prove their divinity by performing miracles to convert the disbelievers. I think that was part of the allure that Jesus had among his ignorant followers, that he could change water to wine, walk on water and even raise the dead. I did not want to be converted by a miracle or a shaman trick. I believe true divinity is in mind, and I think this is what Sathya Baba has mastered, but the reality is that I have not seen nor felt his presence while I was here. I was determined to move on, to keep searching until I found spiritualism that I discovered on my own, not dependent on miracles or sleight of hand tricks. It also bothered me that Sathya Baba was the "guru" of the Western elite: the rock stars, filmmakers, and beautiful people that had the money for a "personal" guru.

I tried to convey my feelings to Rachel and wanted to take her away to see if we could discover a different spirituality in Auroville or in the Hindu "Bible Belt" of southern India. I asked her to come with me, and together we would discover a new path, but she countered that her life was here and that she had true satisfaction in working toward her salvation with the help of Sathya Baba. She wanted me to stay, and we could build our life together here. I could get a job in the ashram, and we would both discover our own truths together.

After three weeks and no Sathya Baba, I decided I would continue my pilgrimage. Like the biblical Rachel mourning for her lost children, I'm sure Rachel felt like a scorned lover. She was not "good enough" to convince me to stay for her, nor could she make me understand that the "saving grace" of Sai Baba was the "true way." Suddenly I was haunted by my memories of Christine from Chiang Mai. I had tried to make her stay with me, promising her we would find an answer together to what she was missing in life, but she left me for "the stability of the familiar." Now I was doing the same thing to this passionate pilgrim. Would I also miss out on the "IT" that would give my life meaning? Would I always regret not taking "this less traveled road on a snowy night?" She had made her commitment here and found an answer to her search for inner peace, whereas I was still on my "Long day's journey into the night."

Our last night was bittersweet, and our lovemaking had an urgency. We fell into each other, and our bodies moved slowly to delay the climax, the pulsating rhythm gluing us together. When we came, we wanted this feeling to last forever. There were no tears, just a sad resignation that we would never see each other again. This time I awoke first and kissed her goodbye. It was still early morning, right after dawn; I walked to my hotel to get my belongings and got the first bus out of Dodge.

Bombay

Two views of the English Fort at Bombay 1665 (copperplate print from the Netherlands National Archives (License: CC-CCO-PD) Public Domain.

Chapter Thirty-One: Bombay - Quiet Days and Wild Nights

"Running Wild In the Streets,"

-Garland Jeffreys.

Leo and I came into Bombay via 3rd-class rail, he slept on the floor between the berths, and I had a third of a seat. We arrived via the scenic route: straight through shantytown, people sleeping on the streets, little children shitting openly in the alleys, and young Indian males washing themselves at the communal water pump. It was early morning, and as I groggily looked out, I saw a fleeting image of a slim, fair-skinned Indian mother fixing food for her children outside a sheet metal shack. She was dressed in a faded red sari and possessed that luminescent, fragile beauty which sadly will fade and coarsen in a few short years, given the hard life of the lower-class slums.

We found a travelers' hotel and met some of the transient travelers there. I met an Australian tourist, Lara, and Leo found a fellow German, Trudi. Trudi had a very interesting experience: she spent the last year living with a Chinese family in Taiwan to learn Mandarin and now is returning home to utilize this new language for an international business career. These girls were not freaks but normal tourists living economically.

"Ich bin ich" (I Am Me) Self Portrait
by Paula Modersohn-Becker 1907.

Lara

Lara was wholesome looking, rosy-cheeked with long chestnut hair, green eyes and a fresh "girl next door" demeanor. She had just graduated from university, and this was her one-time fling before a steady job, her marriage to her childhood sweetheart and integration into the Australian middle-class society. "That's the way I've always heard it should be," Carly Simon. She reminded me of the teenage Amish, who are given a period of time for "rumspringa" (jumping around). Here the young person, male and female, gets to leave the close-knit community and experience the American society. They are free to do anything they want, to see firsthand how normal Americans live, work, and play. They then have the choice to stay in our society or return to be baptized into the Amish church and community with its strict codes (about 90% of these Amish teenagers voluntarily chose to return to the Amish community). She was lively, fun to be with, passionate in her beliefs, and possessing a quiet self-assurance. Here was a girl like Margaret from Borneo that knew exactly what she wanted out of life and had the confidence not to waver from her goals. She didn't believe in one-night stands nor having sex just because it was convenient or that she was lonely. She had that sweet innocence that I hope she can hold on to for the rest of her life.

We started hanging out together for dinner and seeing the sights. We were lucky that we had arrived in Bombay just when they were celebrating Ganesh's birthday. This is a big deal in Bombay and the whole city goes wild celebrating the elephant-headed son of Shiva. Every community in the city and the surrounding villages makes these gaudily painted plaster images of Ganesh, which they carry around the streets, singing, dancing, and getting drunk. The men carry these images to the beach in Chowpatty, followed by strumming musicians and women giving out sweets to passersby. The images are blessed by a priest at the shoreline and then the faithful carry the image far into the water and drop it, breaking it in the surf.

We took a taxi to the beach around 8 pm, and the best and largest processions had not even approached the beach. We jostled our way into the crowd to get a view of the ceremony. At first, everything was fine; we were given red dye markings on our foreheads and young girls gave us small, sweet pastries. As the backlog of processions slowed, we found ourselves surrounded by drunk, manic Indian males who felt up the girls, pushing them and fondling their behinds. No sooner did we yell at one, then another started the same behavior. We tried to shield the girls, but it was like rush hour on the IRT local, and we could barely move; there were hands groping everywhere. We finally got them to safety on the sidewalk, but they were pretty shaken and disgusted. To these Indians, every Western girl traveling alone or with "hippies" was a whore and deserved what she got. A lot of this behavior was the result of movies like "Hare Krishna, Hare Ram"- the Indian males actually believe these depictions of hippies and the life of "sin" they lead (Put me in coach, I can "sin" with the best of them.). Even little children ran up to us, yelled "Hippie," and ran away. We watched the young girls, who moved in a series of circles, singing, laughing, and spraying red powder over themselves as the circle closed.

Ganesh festival in India.

We left and took a cab to the famed red-light district of Bombay. Here were hundreds of whores sitting in barred windows and beaconing us to come in. The girls were all ages, from hardened middle-aged pros to innocent-looking teenagers no more than 18 years old. Many were bought from poor farming families that could not afford another mouth to feed. Because of the Indian way that young men cannot have sex until they are married, these women served as a needed requirement for young males to teach them how to be with a woman. And there were plenty of takers: fat civil service bureaucrats, rumpled office workers, and burley construction laborers all ogling and leering at the merchandise offered.

Lara was frightened at this whole scene and gripped my hand tightly. We walked out of the district and found a restaurant where we ordered chai to calm the girls. This was not the innocuous picture-taking photo op at the Taj Mahal; this was "raw" India, and Lara could not handle it. She expected to see the tourist sights and buy a few souvenirs for the family back home; the worst that could happen would be an upset stomach from the spicy Indian food.

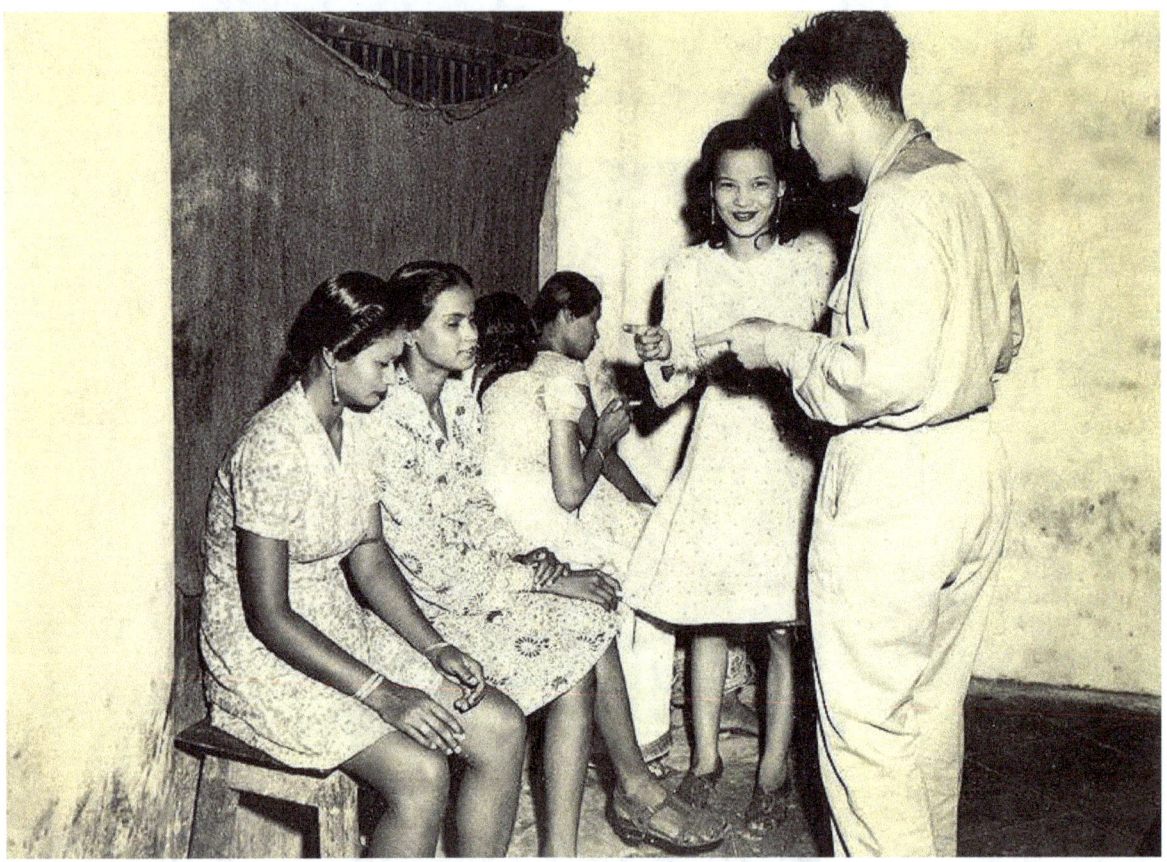

American GI negotiating for a prostitute in 1945 India.

"It takes a while to adjust to India," I said sympathetically. "So many people and they were all groping me. I felt violated, and then those poor girls and the disgusting men that take advantage of them." "India is a puritanical society. Most Indians do not have sex with an Indian woman until they are married. In the meantime, in the big cities, they have these legal red-light districts and look at all unattached Western women as "whores" and act the way they did with you." "Well, I feel like going home right now!" "Hey, what you experienced was the uneducated Indian; why don't we see what the middle-class Indians do for fun? I heard about an Indian discotheque called The Slip Disc. It will be a lot of fun and get you out of this foul mood." She reluctantly agreed; Leo and Trudi both wanted to go.

"Last Raga in Bombay"

We took a taxi to the discotheque: it was very modernistic on the exterior; the interior had a huge dance floor with strobe lights and a blue neon-lit long bar. The place was packed with young Indians and a few Westerners. The music was infectious: a combination of Indian drone raga music and a Western dance beat. They had a live band called The Elite Aces, whose music can best be described as Ravi Shankar meets Santana, very danceable. The dance floor pulsated with gyrating couples and young Indian girls dancing together. Everyone seemed to know all the dance steps and if I didn't know better, I would have thought it was a Brooklyn disco. The young people were all in Western dress, from jeans and colorful T-shirts to sleek dresses and leisure-suited dandies. I half expected to see a John Travolta Indian clone in a white leisure suit take center stage, strutting to the Bee Gees "Staying Alive."

I bought a round of drinks, grabbed Lara's hand, and we joined the fray. Lara was a natural dancer and quickly learned the dance steps. I followed her lead, and we were shaking with the best of them. Leo and Trudi were also swirling away, and we all had a rocking good time. These young people were the future of India, the middle class that was westernized with their own Indian twist. Lara was in her own private world; she and Trudi danced together when Leo and I had enough, soaked in perspiration. We stayed for over two hours, and when we got back to the hotel, Lara was still bubbly. I bought a bottle of rice wine, and we went back to the lounge lobby. We drank wine and laughed about our great adventures. "I'm glad you're not down anymore, you have a natural rhythm, and you were sensational on the dance floor." "The music was so danceable, and it was just what I needed." I said goodnight and promised I would pick her up in the morning, and we would tour the sights of Bombay.

She was up before me, knocking on my door while I hastily got dressed. She asked if she should get Leo and Trudi; I said we should leave them and see some of the sights by ourselves. We went to the King George Memorial Arch (Long Live Britannia), which has become the symbol of the city.

We passed a newsstand and saw a picture of the Duke of Windsor and his wife. I asked her if she thought he did the right thing - renounce his throne for love. She answered that it was very romantic and, yes, love should triumph. I then told her about the Bhagavad Gita, how Krishna the God convinced a vacillating Prince Arjuna to fight and kill his cousins who had unjustly usurped his throne. Krishna told Arjuna it was his duty to fight and kill but take no pleasure in the outcome.

I also related the stories of Chinese princesses who had to leave their whole lives behind and travel to faraway lands to marry barbarian kings and never return to China. It was their duty to do this, to preserve the Chinese Empire. Edward violated his sacred duty of upholding the British Empire by marrying for love. It seemed to me that they were a sad couple, never having children, pariahs wandering aimlessly without a true home. Love has its price to pay, and so does dharma. Lara reflected on this and was silent.

The Gateway to India, the Commemorative Arch built for King George V on his visit to India in 1901.

Elephanta Caves

ENTRANCE TO THE CAVE OF ELEPHANTA.

While in Bombay, Lara and I took a ferry to the Elephanta Sculpture Hall Cave. This magnificent shrine cave was carved out of solid rock, with huge Hindu stone gods guarding the inner sanctuary. The cave hall is immense; however, the carved figures are in a state of half ruin. In the sixteenth century, the Portuguese used the cave for target practice: shooting off the faces and bodies of the gods. Yet the whole cave is one majestic religious sculpture: even in its present state of ruin, the sense of awe isn't diminished.

You can smell the musty air, touch the sweating basalt rock, and recreate in your mind the ancient sculptors chopping away at the formless stone to make it alive with columns, statues, and altars in reverence to their God. I was especially impressed by the three faces of Shiva: an 18-foot-high statue in the middle of the Cave. Somehow it had managed to survive the Portuguese gunners, the Muslim iconoclasts, and the hordes of Indian tourists. Here more than anywhere else, you experience the majesty of the Hindu faith. Shining out of the cave darkness, Shiva is alive and speaking to you alone, no matter how many tourists are surrounding you and talking loudly.

Huge three face Shiva has survived almost intact and dominates the sculpture cave.

We went to the Tourist Bureau and found that there was a circus in a nearby suburb this evening. We all thought this would be a fun time; I had not been to a circus since I was a kid, going to a local circus with my 4th-grade elementary class. We took a taxi to the circus, which was in a large tent in an open field. It was very crowded, and the Indians were an enthusiastic crowd. From the opening procession of young girls carrying multi-colored banners to the dwarf comedy act to the gymnastics of an acrobatic group, the action never stopped, and the music was deafening. I especially enjoyed the young girl contortionists that twisted their bodies into incredible pretzel-like shapes. The "rope dancers" and juggler routines were all known to the audience, and grown adults to children cheered on their favorites. The twirlers could teach our high school cheerleaders some dynamite new moves. The show's high point was the flying trapeze troupe. They were flawless, with three sets of artists flying through the air in a syncopated ballet. They also performed trapeze acts with a very tame elephant. I was an awestruck nine-year-old again, and we all enjoyed "The Greatest Show In The World."

Performer with elephant in the Indian "Rambo Circus."

We came back, exhilarated by the fantastic performers and had a farewell rice wine party. Trudi was leaving in the morning for Frankfurt and Leo was going on to Delhi. Lara was leaving in two days for Adelaide, and I would be leaving for Goa in a few days. Lara and I spent the next two days together, getting to know each other and visiting sights. At the end of our time together, I felt a bond between us; we would finish each other's sentences, hold hands in crowded and dark places, and talk candidly about the life she was returning to after her "rumspringa," but we both respected that fine line between friends and lovers. We exchanged addresses, however, we both knew we would never see each other again.

Chapter Thirty-Two: Parsi - The Flame Is Flickering

"As I walk through the valley of the shadow of darkness, I shall fear no evil, for thou art with me" 23rd Psalm,

-Old Testament Bible.

As I walked in the Business District of Bombay, it seemed the name "Tata" was everywhere: construction companies, trucks, consumer goods, and even an airline. Who is "Tata," and how did this man come to dominate the Indian economy? Jamsetji Tata took over his father's small trading company in Bombay in the 1860s. He bought and sold textile companies and invested in the first native steel company. Profits from steel led to expansion in construction and hotel building. His Taj Mahal Hotel in Bombay was the first to have electricity throughout the building in all of India.

I went to the American Consulate library and looked up the Tata family and other Indian-owned businesses. The other large industries and shipbuilding were in the hands of the Godrey family, which controlled real estate assets, and manufactured household appliances and furniture. The Wadia family-controlled textile production, jewelry, and shipbreaking.

All of these family-owned Indian businesses had one thread in common: they were all Parsi-owned. The Parsi ("Parsi" is the Hindu word for "Persian") came to India in the eighth through tenth century AD, escaping Muslim persecution since they were Zoroastrian and considered infidels by the Muslim rulers of Persia.

Zoroastrianism: The Eternal Conflict of Good versus Evil

Zoroaster was born in the sixth century BC, a time of ferment, warfare, intellectual creativity, and the founding of new religions. Greek philosophy began with Thales of Miletus, who predicted the first solar eclipse. Anaximander postulated how the earth was formed, and Parmenides introduced logic as the mainstay of Greek philosophic discussion. Buddha and Mahavira both started new, reforming religions out of the caldron of Vedic Hinduism. In Israel, the Prophets Elijah, Jeremiah, and Amos were preaching against the sins of the Jewish rulers, and Babylon was the world conqueror, led by Nebuchadnezzar, who also created the Hanging Gardens of Babylon.

Parsi man and woman, 1870. Painting on Mica: Unknown Author, Walters Museum, Baltimore.

Zoroaster saw the world as a battleground between good and evil. Ahura Mazda was the prevailing God of Light and Good; he was opposed by Angra Mainja, who represented the destructive spirit and evil. Asha was the good cosmic order created by Ahura Mazda, who fought the chaos wrought by Angra Mainja. What Ahura Mazda asks of his followers is simply: "Good Thoughts, Good Words, Good Deeds (Good God, Let's Eat)."

Preceding Vedic Hinduism, Zoroaster states that you should be good without wanting rewards, as mentioned hundreds of years later in the Bhagavad-Gita. Zoroastrianism is the first religion to develop the concept of "last judgement," which determines whether an individual shall enter heaven or hell. In the final battle between good and evil, there is a Messiah-figure called "The Saoshyant" (one who brings benefits), who will ensure the triumph of good, and all mankind will be reunited with Ahura Mazda by passing through a cleansing ring of fire. This Messiah figure predates the Christian Messiah by six hundred years.

Zoroastrianism believes in two elements over all other matter: fire, through which spiritual insight and wisdom are revealed, and water which is the source of wisdom. They built "Fire" temples, airy, low-roofed buildings, open at all sides, within which is the eternal flame, which must never go out. The Zoroastrians also had a unique system of handling their dead: the body is cut into small pieces and placed on an open-air platform called the "Tower of Silence" for the vultures to feast on the remains.

A Parsi "Tower of Silence" in Bombay 1907.

The Parsi were always a small minority, and to avoid being swallowed-up by Hindu India, they set themselves apart. Their priests declared that to be a Zoroastrian, one must marry within the community of Persian believers. Religion, in this case, was cemented with race.

This was also how Christianity started: they were a small reformist Jewish sect that would have been absorbed by Orthodox Judaism and become, at best, a footnote as an obscure Jewish sect in the first century. However, Christianity was saved by St. Paul, a Roman citizen, who spread the creed to the Gentiles (foreigners). Christianity was foremost a proselytizing region, encompassing all races and people.

A similar transformation had happened with Judaism. When they were in Israel, race and religion were one. Once the Jews spread out to the Gentile world, they changed. Today you have black Ethiopian Jews, blond, blue-eyed American Jews, and Sephardic Spanish and Portuguese Jews that speak Ladino, a medieval Spanish dialect, in places like Istanbul, Damascus, and New

York City. A Jew is a Jew because he practices his religion wherever he is; even in the Jewish State of Israel, you are a Jew first and, secondly, a citizen of Israel.

The Parsi have kept their race and their religion pure, but their race numbers are declining, and therefore, their religion is declining. Today there are only about seventy-five thousand Parsi in all of India; more than half of that number live in Bombay. They are 100% literate, most with a college education or higher, and women are treated as equal to men. This emphasis on education and focusing on a business career has resulted in 20% of the males and 10% of the females never marrying (You can't keep a good, educated woman, barefoot and pregnant, down on the farm.) Many Parsi have immigrated to America and the UK, inter-marrying locally and falling out of the Zoroastrian faith. Only Parsi men can marry outside of the race, and their children must be initiated into the religion by a ritual called: "Novetias" by the age of seven. Even the Parsi that does marry has a very low birth rate as compared with the rest of India and Western economies. Unfortunately, this identification of race with religion will lead to the extinction of Parsi and Zoroastrianism, and one of the world's great religions will be no more.

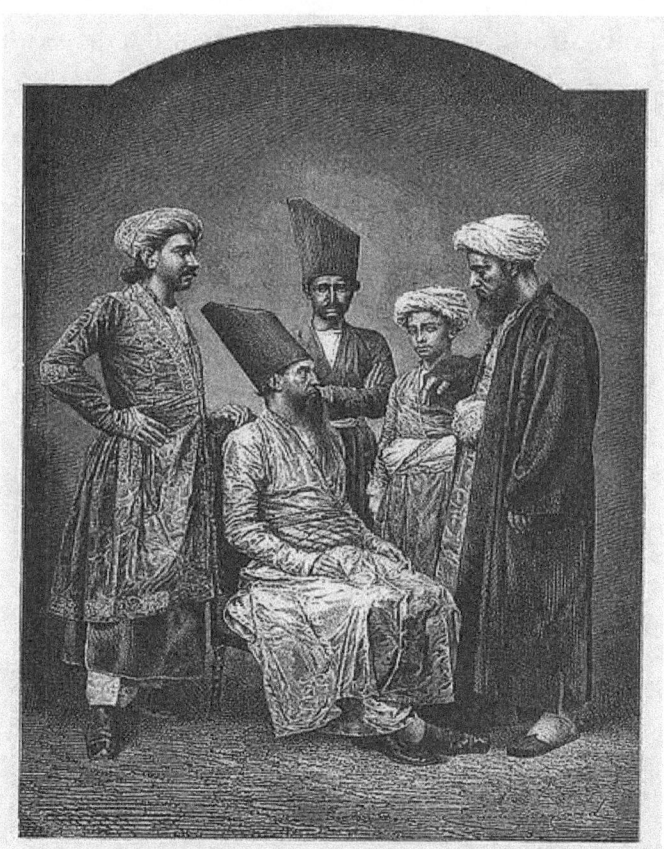

Parsees of Bombay 1878: Wood engraving by Emile Bayard from the book "World Tour: Journal of Geography, Travel and Costumes" by Alfred Grandidier. 1878. Public Domain.

The Parsi have their own housing complexes, hospitals, and schools in Bombay. They give huge sums to build hospitals and cultural venues for all Indians. One rich Parsi family started the Bombay Symphony Orchestra, and that founder's son, Zubin Mehta, became a world-famous orchestra conductor.

I look at the example of the Parsi and try to relate it to our own situation in America. We have a persistent underclass: the Blacks and I see the only solution to this is education.

The Jews came to America by the millions at the turn of the century, penniless and illiterate. They worked in New York City sweatshops, making garments and others hand-rolled cigars on tenement kitchen tables, while others pushed carts, selling everything on the streets. They sent their children to public schools and assured them that they would have the opportunity to escape a life of poverty. The second generation of Jews started the small tailor and food shops, working long hours to ensure that their children would have a college education. By the third generation, these Jews became doctors, lawyers, scientists, and politicians and now run New York City.

The Blacks and Puerto Ricans in New York need good teachers and good schools, but even more, they need their family structure to nurture and sustain the drive for education. This is the only way they will get out of poverty and secure their rightful place in American society.

Chapter Thirty-Three: How to Marry a Millionaire

"The best things in life are free but you can give them to the birds and bees. I need money."

-Barrett Strong, *Money*.

This is just one snapshot that goes on for pages and pages (Excerpt from the India Sunday Times, photographed and underlined in red by Shashwat Maheshwari September 26, 2010).

While in Bombay, I bought an English-language newspaper and threw everything away except the classifieds. The ads go on for pages and pages and are the most popular way to find a suitable woman or man for marriage. I spoke with many educated Indians, and they all agreed that it is the proper way to find a spouse.

Once a person answers this ad, then the fun begins. At that time, there was no internet, and people just asked for a photograph of the proposed spouse and the telephone number. Things have not really changed that much with the internet because once the matrimonial hunt begins, in seriousness, the parents get involved. Perspective couples meet under parental supervision and talk to each other very briefly to see if they are compatible and to find out what they really want in life, whether it be a career, children, or other goals, and how this would affect their marriage. Backgrounds of perspective partners are scrutinized: A suitable male should have a college education, a job, and be a morally upright citizen. There is also the important, maybe most important, question of the caste of the prospective marriage partner. In India, there are 25,000 sub-castes of the four main castes. You must find a suitable partner within the framework of your particular subcaste. Females are expected to be wholesome, fair, well-educated, and a virgin (although I have never heard of hanging the bloody sheet outside the bridal home after the first night of conjugal bliss). Lastly, there is the question of the dowry, which is very important for the parents of the groom. Parents can put the seal of approval or not, which saves the many disagreements many Western couples have over their in-laws. This is very important in India because, in traditional marriages, the woman leaves her parental household and moves in with the family of the groom. So, getting along with in-laws is taken to a whole new level if you must live day in and day out with them.

You may note that I didn't mention romantic love nor the attractiveness of partners for each other since the prospective partners do not know each other and probably will not see each other after the initial meeting until the wedding. Love is expected to grow once you are married, and only after marriage can you really find out about your bride or groom. The system apparently works since there are very few divorces in India.

We in the West laugh at this, but how do we find spouses? It's either the bar scene, work, college, or through friends and family. (Of course, there's always the public bathroom doors: "For a good time, call Judy 435-2810"). The bar scene gets stale quickly, and concerning the workplace, "You don't shit where you eat." You're usually too immature in college, and when you do grow up, you find you have nothing in common with your college fling and break up or get divorced. Friends are ok, but if you dislike your best friend's girl, good luck on the blind date she arranges for you (bring your own seeing-eye dog). Family is even worse: "You should meet my son, such a good boy and a doctor too."

Coming from New York City, we also use the classifieds of the "Village Voice" to meet prospective spouses or just to have a good time. "Single straight white woman, late 20s seeking man of any race for a non-commitment and fun relationship, most like outdoor activities, no S&M,

bi-sexual ok, send photo and brief description to PO Box...." (And this is one of the more conservative ads!).

A final note on classifieds to show that we Americans have just as many foibles as the Indians. In New York City, apartments in prime locations or rent-controlled units are as hard to get as panning for gold in your local creek. People buy the Sunday New York Times on Saturday night just to get a jump on the apartment listings. I would throw the rest of the paper away and sit for hours with the classified circling prospects. I would appear at eight o'clock on Sunday mornings just to be the first in line to see the new listings for apartments. Many unscrupulous New Yorkers even check obituaries to see where elderly widows have just died and contact building managers to get in first, even before the deceased's possessions are removed.

A note of caution: if you find a great apartment in a nice neighborhood at a cheap price, but there is a yellow chalk outline of a person on the living room floor, keep looking.

Buddhism in India

Buddha preaching the "Four Noble Truths" to his disciples: painting from Sanskrit Astasahasrika Prajnaparamita Sutra 700 BC (Public Domain).

Chapter Thirty-Four: West Meets East and the First Image of God

In all my travels, I have sought out what I call fusion art where two strong opposing cultures collide and create a hybrid art, combining the best of both cultures. In the Philippines, Spanish monks taught the local natives Christianity and art: how to depict Christ and various saints required by churches and private home shrines. Here the suffering Indians portrayed Christ as one of their own: sweaty, swarthy, and bloody, a Christ of flesh and bone who represented their struggles and not the sterile duplication of European Christian art.

After Alexander the Great died, his vast empire was divided into three parts: the European Macedonia, the Middle East and Egypt, and Persia, Afghanistan, and India. The Indian empire was under the Greek general, Seleucus. This Greek empire splintered into many smaller Indo-Grecian kingdoms, one of which was the Kingdom of Gandhara, which included Afghanistan and India (now Pakistan). The culture of these kingdoms was Hellenistic Greek and the ruler imported artists from Greece and Rome, who set up schools to teach the local natives Grecian-style art. At first, the art created was purely Grecian in content: Hercules, Adonis, Dionisius, and other Greek gods.

Fragment of a Hercules statue, Hadda, Afghanistan
(Free use through UNESCO,
http:www.unesco.org/bpi/eng/unesccopress/2001/Afghanistan.shtml)

But the people were Buddhist, and they had no connection with the Greek pantheon of gods. Buddhism was a major religion in India for over 400 years, but Buddha was never represented in human form. He was depicted with his footprint and an empty throne in the sculptures and temples of Buddhism. Gandharan art was the first art to depict Buddha as a young Greek God. Buddhist priests and monks saw the advantage of depicting Buddha as a human being, to give the people images of Buddha to counter the pictorial representation of the myriad gods of Hinduism.

Entire schools of Buddhist art were set up in Gandhara, providing sculptures and paintings for the millions of Buddhists in India. One of the most famous Buddhist sculptures was the huge Buddhas carved out of solid rock in Bamiyan (Gandhara). Here you see the Grecian face and the folds of his garment in the traditional Grecian style. The print below shows the Bamiyan Buddha with his face intact before it was destroyed by Muslim iconoclasts in the late 19th century.

Bamiyan Buddha, original drawing by Ivan Lawrowitsch Jaworski from his book "Journey Through Afghanistan and Bukhara 1878-1879" (Public Domain).

At the beginning of the Christian era, Gandhara was conquered by the Kushans, who came from Central Asia, but they also adopted Buddhism, and the hybrid art continued to flourish.

Head fragment of a Gandharan Buddha from the 2nd century AD Metropolitan Museum of Art, New York (Public Domain). Here you see the traditional Western nose and sensuous lips of Grecian art with the elongated ears, top knot and wavy stylized hair of Indian art.

However, the masterpiece of Gandharan and world art (and my personal favorite) was discovered by British archaeologist H.A. Dean at the end of the 19th century. He was digging in an ancient Buddhist ruin in Sikri, India, and unearthed a complete, almost perfectly preserved, life-sized Buddha.

"Fasting Buddha" second century AD (Public domain). The original life-sized sculpture (in the Lahore Museum, Pakistan) is a Buddha, who is starving himself, to focus solely on attaining Nirvana. The figure has almost no flesh; every bone in his neck and ribcage stands out, his face a hallow mask, only his eyes burn out of deep sockets. Flesh consumed by spirit.

Chapter Thirty-Five: Sanchi - Beauty in Ruins

Sanchi Stupa 225 BC

After the sensual Kama Sutra carved delights of Khajuraho, I boarded another over-crowded, stifling, and smelly bus and headed to Sanchi, the oldest Buddhist stupa in India. It was built by the famous Mauryan Emperor Ashoka in 255 BC. This stupa dates from the very beginnings of Buddhism in India and reflects the simplicity of the first Buddhist structures. Architecturally it's basically a burial mound and originally contained relics of the Buddha within. This is similar to the great cathedrals of Europe, which had pieces of the True Cross, the Shroud of Turin, and/ or various body parts of saintly martyrs.

What saved this one stupa while more elaborate Buddhist structures were razed by Muslim raiders was its out-of-the-way location and the overgrowth of nature. After a thousand years of Buddhism in India, Hinduism absorbed Buddhism and the site was abandoned. It was so overgrown with vegetation that it wasn't rediscovered until 1818 by a British officer while on a lion-hunting foray, which is rather ironic since carved winged lions were depicted on the gates protecting the Buddha.

What stands out isn't the plain masonry stupa but the four elaborately carved sandstone gates standing proud like the single Santori Gates of Japan. Here there are three cross bands on each gate. All are carved with scenes of the life of the Buddha. Unlike the many small towns of New Jersey that I visited where there is a plaque commemorating: "George Washington slept here." (I don't know how we won the American Revolution from the many plaques I've encountered - it seems that George slept through the war.) Buddha never set foot in Sanchi (unless you count his huge footprint near the stupa, which was a symbol of the Buddha just like the fish is a symbol of Jesus Christ).

The Buddha scenes are realistically carved tableaux, but what is amazing are the phantasmagorical animals: the winged lions, parrot-nosed griffins, stylized monkeys, and bejeweled elephants.

Mythological Griffin from Sanchi.

Here is the in-your-face aliveness of Medieval European Romanesque column capitals. Fantastic mythological creatures and bulging-eyed devils all bursting forth from the dark church interiors, frightening the illiterate peasants, graphically displaying the evils that await the sinners in the afterlife. At Sanchi, these creatures are more like the docile animals in Edward Hick's "Peaceable Kingdom." "The lamb shall lay down with the lion," as in the Book of Revelations. Here they meekly stand guard under the calming benediction of the Buddha.

Buddhism preaches that this life is "maya," but here you have the fecund sexuality of Yakshi, the female tree spirit which serves here as an architectural support. Here is life at its fullest: succulent mangos dripping from stylized tree branches and a full-breasted femme fatale beguilingly tempting the Buddha. This sculpture exudes sensuous desire even more than the Kama Sutra sculptures of Khajuraho.

Similarly, in medieval Europe, in the Romanesque church of Vezelay in France, you have this startling carved statue of Eve by a Medieval sculptor named Gilbertus. Eve is lying languidly naked, offering the apple of knowledge of good and evil to a now-destroyed naked Adam. She exudes an innocently bountiful sensuality that dangerously entices you. Here is the real world of carnal senses that overwhelms you, thrusting out from the cold stone more erotically than any Playboy pinup.

Eve by Gilbertus 1050 AD Vezelay, France (Public Domain).

Chapter Thirty-Six: Buddha's First Sermon

Seated Buddha preaching his first sermon after enlightenment: Hadda, Afghanistan 2nd century Christian era. (License: CC-CCO-PD, Public Domain).

I took a bus from Benares to Sarnath, the place where Buddha preached his first sermon after enlightenment. As I roamed the green park, photographing stupas and the ruined Buddhist university of Nalanda, I felt an air of calmness. I imagined the energy, passion, and sense of liberation on hearing the Buddha speak for the first time.

Buddha's First Sermon

"My fellow ascetics and seekers, I want to share with you how I achieved enlightenment. I am here in this lovely park with gentle deer surrounding us because this is the exact spot where the ashes of the ascetics fell.

For forty-nine days and nights, I sat under a huge pipal tree, determined not to rise until I achieved Nirvana. As I sat and meditated, I realized that striving for extreme pleasure and avoidance of suffering was not the way to achieve enlightenment. Nor was practicing extreme mortification of the flesh the way to achieve Nirvana. The only way to achieve true liberation is the middle way of the four noble truths. It was a great struggle to still my mind, being tempted by Mara, lord of earthly desires. He tempted me by sending me his beautiful, lasciviously naked daughters to seduce me. When I refused them, he unleashed ferocious monsters to break my concentration. But the four noble truths woke me up to see the world as it really is. These truths taught me to extinguish desire, hatred, and ignorance that cause suffering and the endless cycle of rebirth.

The four noble truths are:

First: All of life is suffering.

Second: Suffering is caused by desires and attachments.

Third: Let go of these desires and attachments.

Fourth: Follow the path of the eightfold truths.

Renounce desires and this will end the suffering and achieve true liberation. Like all of you, I was afraid of aging, disease, and dying. However, the eightfold truths showed me the knowledge of consciousness and how to extinguish desires and defeat fears.

The eightfold truths are as follows:

First is right view: All actions have consequences; death is not the end. Gain the right understanding of reality; clear your mind of delusion.

Second is right resolve: Resolve yourself to renounce desire and evils. Show no ill will to any being. Bring no harm to any being.

Third is right speech: Abstain from lying, abusive speech, spreading gossip, and speech that incites others to do violence.

Fourth is right action: Do not kill, steal, or engage in sexual misconduct.

Fifth is right livelihood: Living without attachments; take only what you need to live. Live in abstinence and show goodwill to all beings.

Sixth is right effort: Preventing the arising of unwholesome states, such as sensory desire, ill will, sloth, inability to calm your mind, and lack of trust. Practice wholesome states, which are awareness of true reality, and investigate the nature of reality. Use your energy for positive benefit. Practice relaxation and strive for joy (rapture), maintain clear awareness, and accept the world without desires or hatred.

Seventh is right mindfulness: Be conscious of what you are doing and be aware of the teachings that lead to the right path of enlightenment.

Eighth is right concentration: Letting go of desires and unwholesome states to feel the joy of detachment. Practice inner silence and unify your mind; let go of earthly joys and be aware of what true reality is; and practice complete mindfulness by controlling your mind while being indifferent to everything around you.

Now that I've shown you the way to liberation, I want you to meditate on this so that you, too, can achieve Nirvana."

"Buddha Giving His First Sermon after Enlightenment" from Gandhara 2nd century AD. Freer Gallery of Art Washington, DC (Public Domain).

There was no standing ovation, applause, or even "Tell it like it is, Reverend!" There were only five ascetics listening to the sermon. (However, one faithful ascetic came up to Buddha and said quietly, "That was a great sermon, Siddhartha, and you should have had a much bigger crowd.

Only next time, don't pick Super Bowl Sunday for such an important sermon, and I'm sure you'll get your message across to the people.").

Each of the five ascetics was greatly inspired by this sermon, and, one by one, they each achieved liberation. When the Buddha saw that they had achieved Nirvana, he directed them to form a sangha (community of monks).

"You must now go all over India and preach the way to enlightenment. You must spread this teaching not only to kings and nobles but also to the common man, the farmer, the soldier, and the merchant - every man must know how to achieve liberation from this life of constant suffering and rebirth."

The monks obeyed the Buddha's orders and went all over India, converting kings and common people: Buddhism as a religion was born here with this one sermon.

Chapter Thirty-Seven: Ajanta - A Lost World Rediscovered

Partial view of the 36 caves that form the Ajanta Cave site. (Photographer Soman released image to GNU Free Documentation License, Version 1.2)

Trying to get to Ajanta caves reminded me why they remained undiscovered for over a millennium. On one dusty overcrowded bus, filled with farmers carrying their produce in the aisles, I met another intrepid traveler, Leo, from West Germany. Together we felt like early 19th century explorers, only when we finally arrived at the Caves, it was take a number (or as they say in the Army: "Hurry Up and Wait!"). There was a long line of middle-class Indian tourists queued up at every cave, who had arrived in the comfort of dozens of air-conditioned buses.

What amazes you about the Ajanta caves is, first and foremost, that architecture is sculpture, and sculpture is architecture. By that, I mean all of the worship halls, monasteries, and stupas are building types which, in the pre-Christian era, were originally made of wood and, of course, subject to fire destruction and rot. Over a period of 700 years, these early Indian sculptors recreated wooden buildings in stone. The stupa in the cave you see below is not a masonry stupa but a stupa carved out of solid rock.

The Ajanta caves were carved during the heyday of Buddhism, and they served as monks' homes, way stations for weary travelers, and pilgrimage sites. Early Chinese Buddhists visited these sites and were very impressed with the level of artistic achievement and the hospitality they received there. I did not visit all of the caves, but I sampled enough to understand the majesty and the sheer human endeavor required to create this Buddhist world view.

I came for the beautiful ceilings and wall frescoes of dancing girls, court musicians, and a lifestyle that disappeared 1000 years ago. Here you see royalty, elite nobles, commoners, monks and merchants in their fancy and everyday clothes, depicting the worldly pleasurable life they lived: the festivals, the dances, and everyday business - a snapshot of medieval Indian life.

As a Westerner, it is very hard for me to understand why you would have scenes of lavish courtly life, banquets, exotic dancers, and myriad examples of a pleasurable existence, yet Buddhism teaches that all this is Maya (illusion). Why would monks want to view this daily when they are trying to achieve Nirvana by letting go of all these worldly pleasures?

After thinking long and hard on this issue, I concluded that this art was the earliest form of corporate advertising! (I imagined the Prince that donated the most money to carve the caves would have had a huge banner draped over the cliff, "Welcome to Prince Rama's 'Ramaland': see how royalty, the rich and famous live and play in colorful ceiling paintings, attend a candlelight service worshipping Buddha in the curved-stone stupa cave with real monks, and view our Buddhist gallery with over a hundred buddhas in various positions, all this for one low admission price (package tours and lodging available upon request). As a bonus, the first one thousand visitors will receive a free imported Tibetan prayer wheel (while supplies last). You can also eat at our tasty vegan cafeteria, and when you finish your tour, don't forget to stop at our moderately priced gift shop for that Buddhist statue, colorful thangka painting, or a framed sutra for your loved ones *back home*").

Buddhism survived on royal and elite patronage and what better way to reward the patron than to portray their lifestyle in the palaces, court performances, and everyday life of the people of the kingdom for the temples, prayer halls, and monasteries that they financed and built. I would not be surprised if the luminescent figures depicted in these paintings were actual portraits of nobility and elite noblemen and women. This would be similar to the religious paintings of northern Gothic

Europe: the 15th century Netherlander primitive paintings of Van Eyck and Hugo van der Goes, where the central religious painting is flanked on both sides by the male patron on the left and the female on the right.

The Portinari Triptych by Hugo van der Goes (1432) Portinari was a rich Florentine merchant in Bruges (Belgium) and he is depicted kneeling with his two sons on the left panel and his wife and daughter are kneeling on the right panel. (Public Domain)

Buddhist Prayer Hall: Cave 19 Ajanta by James Fergusson (1808-1886) (Public Domain)

The cave paintings were poorly lit, and the humidity, amplified by the thousands of tourists' carbon monoxide, caused the paint to flake off and the pigments to lose their vibrant colors. We, the well-meaning and curious tourists, are destroying these fragile works of art with our breathing in the close quarters of the cave. If this continues unabated, the frescoes will be lost forever.

The Bodhisattva Vajrapani Cave I Ajanta (photographer Sadai Thailand released photo to CC-Attr SA-2.0 Generic License)

The art would be better displayed in a "mock cave" with color photographs of the paintings and good illumination so that the artwork could be examined up-close: the delicate beauty and sweeping medieval culture seen as a whole, the way the Buddhists monks viewed the paintings over a millennium ago.

Chapter Thirty-Eight: Why Buddhism Died in India

What killed Buddhism in India? I love a good mystery story, so I put on my Sherlock Holmes thinking cap, lit my hash pipe and after a thorough investigation (I found that the Butler did not do it!), I told my assistant Watson (Leo, my German companion): "Elementary!" There were a number of factors in the decline of Buddhism in India that took place over several hundred years. Buddhism survived by royal patronage. The greatest patron of Buddhism and the one person credited with spreading Buddhism throughout the Asian world was Emperor Ashoka of the Mauryan dynasty, 3rd through 4th centuries BC. His domain spread almost the entire length of the subcontinent from Afghanistan to Bangladesh. He built numerous stupas, monasteries, libraries, and schools for the Buddhists. After the Maurya Empire fell, the next largest supporter of Buddhism was the Gupta Kingdom in the third to fourth centuries AD. They originated in Central Asia and supported Buddhism in Afghanistan and along the Silk Road in Central Asia, again building monasteries, universities, and libraries.

Emperor Ashoka from the Southern gate of Sanchi Stupa (Public domain).

A Chinese monk, Faxian, who traveled overland from China in 400 AD, found thriving monasteries all along the Silk Road and in present-day Afghanistan and Pakistan. Buddhism was at its height in India at that time. He stayed at Palatiputra, which was the former capital of the Mauryan Empire, now a prosperous commercial and religious city. There he copied Buddhist Sutras, brought them back to China and spent the rest of his life translating these for the fledgling Buddhist community in China. Another Chinese monk Xuan Zang visited India three centuries later and found deserted monasteries and destroyed Buddhist schools and libraries on the Silk Road and in Gandhara, Afghanistan.

Xuan Zang on his journey to India:
14th AD painting (unknown painter)
Tokyo National Museum (Public Domain).

In the 8th and 9th centuries AD, Muslim invaders from the mountains of Iran and Afghanistan swept through Central Asia, destroying thriving Buddhist kingdoms along the Silk Road, Afghanistan, and current-day Pakistan. The largest Buddhist stupa in the world, in Peshawar (Pakistan), was so utterly destroyed that not even the foundation is found today. All that remains of Buddhism in Afghanistan is two huge Buddhas in Bamyian with their faces shaved off by iconoclastic Muslims.

However, at that time, the Buddhists in India were thriving, still building libraries, universities, and religious ashrams. Xuan Zang studied at the Buddhist Nalanda University for two years and returned to China with 657 sutras. This fully explained the Buddhist philosophy to the Chinese Buddhist priests. Xuan Zang returned to China after 17 years to great acclaim and honors. However, he refused all official government posts and spent the rest of his life translating the sutras to revitalize the Buddhist way of life in China.

Journey to the West

Xuan Zang is, at best, an interesting footnote in the history of Buddhism in India. However, in China, he is the most famous Buddhist monk of all time. However, this is not for his life's work of traveling to India to learn how Buddhism is practiced there in its original form and bringing back the sutras and translating them to purify the Buddhist religion in China. It is because of his fictional depiction as Tang Sanzang, the Buddhist monk hero of Wu Chengen's "Journey to the West." This 16th-century Ming classic "novel" defies definition. It is a combination of folktale, spiritual homily, fantastic supernatural adventure, and a Buddhist allegory comparable to Bunyan's Christian allegory, "A Pilgrim's Progress."

The novel begins with Buddha directing the monk Sanzang to travel to India to procure the original Buddhist sutras and to bring them back to China so the Buddhists here can follow the true path of Buddhism. To safeguard him, he gives this pilgrim four unlikely heroes: the Monkey King who had mischievously divided Heaven in the first chapters of the book and was tricked by Buddha, captured and put under a mountain for 500 years. Buddha now releases him, and he agrees to accompany the pilgrim on his journey. The Monkey King is joined by the Pig, who is the comic relief with his gargantuan appetite and sensual desires. Then there is the monk Sandy who represents a loyal Buddhist priest who obediently follows the directions of Sanzang on the journey. Lastly, we have the magical White Horse Dragon, which is really a transformed prince (this horse, unlike Mr. Ed, has no speaking part but serves as the mount for the monk Sanzang).

This merry band has many adventures, both real and fantastic, battling bandits, demons, and giants in their journey toward India. One of the highlights of the book is the kidnapping of Sanzang and how our heroes use their wits and magical powers to overcome insurmountable odds to rescue him.

Painting depicting a scene from the Chinese classic Journey to the West. The painting shows the four heroes of the story, left to right: Sun Wukong (Monkey King), Xuanzang (the Pilgrim Monk), Zhu Wuneng (Pig), and Sha Wujing (Monk Sandy) and the White Dragon Horse. The painting is a decoration on the Long Corridor in the Summer Palace in Beijing, China.

This is unlike "A Pilgrim's Progress," where the pilgrim must defeat allegorical figures named Ignorance, Despair, and Obstinance while being helped by characters named Honest, Great Heart, and Hopeful. These depictions leave little to the imagination but were easily understood by the common man of the times. The everyman hero Christian finally completes his journey from the city of destruction (the earthly existence) to the celestial city (Heaven) (Don't you just love a happy ending!).

Pilgrim entering the wicket gate, opened by Good-Will. Engraving from "A PILGRIM'S PROGRESS"

In "Journey to the West," the allegorical characteristics of our heroes follow the Buddhist precepts of ordinary men transformed from sinners to achieve enlightenment. The Monkey King, with his magical wand, represents the impulsive nature of humans, doing anything they want to satisfy any desire. The Pig represents the base nature of humans: greed, lust, and gluttony. The monk Sandy represents goodness and obedience, subduing his wild nature to serve his master faithfully. The White Horse Dragon represents human will in all its irrationality and lack of discipline. Slowly we see these characters leaving their human desires behind for the greater goal of Nirvana.

The story ends happily with Sanzang and the Monkey King achieving Buddhahood, while monk Sandy becomes an arhat (one who achieves Nirvana and is on the enlightenment road for full Buddhahood, who says that nice guys finish last?) The White Horse Dragon becomes a NAGA, a supernatural snake being that lives in the underworld (He still has no speaking part.) and is worshipped by Hindus and Buddhists alike. Pig receives the title "Cleaner of Altars," whose job is to clean every Buddhist temple by eating the leftover food offerings. Due to his gluttonous nature, this is probably the best reward he could hope for ("You can call me anything you want except late for dinner.").

Journey to the East

I thought of my own journey in India and if I was to write an allegory like "Journey to the West," it would be something like this:

"I am a lonely Western pilgrim searching for enlightenment, but first I must fight the demons: Indian bureaucrats, who keep losing my India visa renewal forms. In my journey, the giant that I face is the 3rd-class Indian rail which packs me tightly as a sardine in a tin, gives me endless hours of sweaty agony, and threatens to never let me leave. As for the temptations on the road, there are the femme fatales that would delay my quest and even cause me to abandon it. Dawn, the beguiling Sheila that wanted to whisk me away from my pilgrimage to far away kangaroo land, where I would be bewitched into playing golf, having 2.5 kids, and driving a minivan. I am also seduced by the "Maya" of gorgeous beaches in Goa and Kovalam and breathtaking mountains in Nepal, places that I never want to leave. Lastly, there are the false prophets of hash, LSD, and opium which promise instant enlightenment but leave me disillusioned in the morning (and I didn't even mention the palm toddy morning hangovers)."

My steadfast companions on this journey are not fantastical creatures but my camera, which records faithfully the wonder and awe of life surrounding me and my written journal, which helps me make sense of all the good, bad, and ugly stimuli that daily assault my senses, which in a word is India. Will there be a happy ending to my story, like Xuan Zang found enlightenment at the end of his journey? Keep reading; you will have to make that judgement call for yourself ("Are we there yet?" or, in the words of one frustrated traveling companion, remarking on my navigational skills, "You couldn't find your ass from a hole in the ground!").

Meanwhile, back at the ranch and to answer the central question of why the decline and fall of Buddhism in India? In the 8th century AD, the Buddhist priests turned to esoteric (Tantric philosophy) Buddhism, which emphasized secret private rituals. The priests remained in their monasteries, not preaching the steps to achieve Nirvana to the ordinary people. When they preached this new esoteric religion, the people didn't understand these new teachings, nor could they practice the intricate (secret) rituals. These Buddhists then turned to Hinduism with its emphasis on shared religious ceremonies, involving the people and giving them colorful festivals to participate in. Intellectually, Hindu priests began borrowing Buddhist doctrines and incorporating these beliefs into their own philosophy and worship rituals.

Kingdoms that were formerly Buddhist became Hindu and were serviced by Brahmin Hindus. The Buddhist priests and monks remained in their monasteries, absorbed by their quest for Nirvana, while the Brahmins offered their services as teachers, public administrators, and advisers to the new Hindu rulers. The Buddhist heartland was now surrounded by strong Hindu kingdoms. Without strong backing from a large, centralized state to offer military protection and a lack of royal funding to build monasteries and schools as previous Buddhist rulers generously provided and the new Hindu Kingdoms did not, the religion started a precipitous decline.

Then the "Gotterdammerung" began. In 986 AD, Muslim Turkomans swept into India, conquering Delhi and converting hundreds of thousands of Buddhists by the sword. The Muslim ban on idols was savagely enforced by destroying hundreds of temples, stupas, and universities. The Persian word for idol was "Budd" (Buddhist). Sindh (the bottom part of Pakistan) and the Ganges plain was captured by General Khalji of the Delhi Sultanate. Bihar and all of Bangladesh were also conquered by the swift Muslim cavalry of the Delhi Sultanate in 1193 AD.

The end of Buddhist monks, AD 1193.

Khalji killed thousands of Buddhist priests in 1193 AD because they didn't offer any resistance due to the peaceful nature of their religion. I stood in the ruins of Nalanda University and Library, which was once the greatest Buddhist library and priest-training university in the world, but now nothing but a pile of broken bricks. This destruction mirrored a similar catastrophe in Egypt, where the great Greek library of Alexandria was also sacked by Muslim raiders and totally destroyed.

Once the Buddhist priests were killed, the populace was left without leaders and no places to train new Buddhist priests. The Hindus were also persecuted, but the Hindu kingdoms fought back. In Hinduism, any Brahmin (priestly caste) could become a teacher/priest, keeping the faith alive. Furthermore, Hinduism incorporated Buddha into its pantheon of gods. Many Buddhists were reconverted to Hinduism, while others, especially the former untouchables, who saw no advantage in returning to Hinduism, were peacefully converted to Islam by Sufis, as was the country of Bangladesh. The remaining Buddhist priests fled to Nepal, Tibet, and Burma, which are still the thriving centers of Buddhism.

Goa and Kovalam

Freaks tokin' and smokin': Anjuna Beach, Goa 1971 (Unidentified photographer from the FACEBOOK web site "I LOVE GOA" posted by Vikash Jain).

Chapter Thirty-Nine: The "Magic Bus"

"Come with me little girl on a magic carpet ride,"

-Canned Heat, *Magic Carpet*.

One of my favorite books of all time is Tom Wolfe's "The Kool-Aid Acid Test." Ken Kesey and the merry pranksters traveled all over the American West in a psychedelically painted school bus, constantly stoned on "acid."

The original Ken Kesey "Magic Bus" (1964) immortalized by Tom Wolfe's "The Electric Kool-Aid-Acid Test" (1968) (R. Carlberg released photo to CC-Attr-SA-4.0 International License with attribution of R. Carlberg).

They had no particular destination; the trip both metaphorically and physically was the road. Freedom, love, and Rock 'n Roll was the objective, and they accomplished these in grand style.

What I found most fascinating was the bus driver Neal Cassady. Neal is better known as the fictional Dean Moriarty, the manic driver hero of Kerouac's "On the Road." He endlessly zigzagged across America, never stopping, always in fast motion (freedom = motion squared, $F=M^2$). Now fifteen years later, he is the LSD-stoned magic bus driver. Neal Cassady successfully bridged the gap from "beatnik" to "hippie." While Kerouac drank himself to death, Neal thrived

Neal Cassady: GRAWLIN released photo to CC-attribution: share-alike 4.0 international license, free to use with attribution of author.

in this new psychedelic world. I believe the reason he could live simultaneously in two different worlds is because he had no real personality of his own. You never really knew what he thought about his experiences; he was the driver, only feeling alive when he was behind the wheel.

A "Magic Bus" (India Overland) on the London to Kathmandu Road 1972 (photographer unknown) (Pinterest).

The other magic bus in the popular imagination was the "Overland to India Magic Bus." Enterprising Brits started various long-distance bus trips: London to India or Kathmandu, in the 1960s and 1970s and carried thousands of travelers. These buses were cheap, and they took care of everything for you: visas, knowledgeable driver/ guide, lodgings, and most importantly, they didn't mind if the passengers used drugs. The passengers were a motley crew: druggies, spiritual-seekers, adventurers, and poor English immigrants bound for Australia. Here the bus was a means to get to India and Nepal, whereas in the "Electric Kool-Aid Acid Test," the bus was the means itself.

The bus also picked up travelers from continental Europe, mostly Amsterdam, but the trip really got interesting in Istanbul. Here was the first city in Asia and it was the point of "no return." Here the travelers gathered at the Pudding Shop to get advice/ information on foreign lands, where to score dope, and to buy last-minute necessities.

The scenery along this long route was at first interesting and later boring.

Many turned to dope to make the trip go by quickly. Many also got addicted on the bus and some got off of the bus in cheap drug centers. However boring the many endless miles of the desert were, the stopovers at various "Arabian Night" cities made the trip somewhat fun and lively. There was a strong camaraderie aboard the bus, and everyone got to know each other (some in the King James Biblical sense of "knowing," i.e., "Abraham knew Sara," if you know what I mean.)

There were also legendary pit stops like the restaurant Siggi's in Kabul, with Western food and desserts and up-to-date information on the road ahead. Many travelers got no further than Afghanistan because of the cheap dope (hash, opium, and heroin) and the no-hassle policy of the Afghan government. Those who got back on the bus traveled through places that they had read about, dreamed of, or seen in movies like the Khyber Pass and the Street of Storytellers in Peshawar, Pakistan.

Finally, you crossed over into India, and your true journey was only now about to begin.

Hippies smoking hash in a Peshawar Pakistan hotel 1972 (Eddie Woods) from the "Lollywood" web page. Note the rope bed, this was the type of bed I slept in throughout India, Bangladesh, and Nepal.

Chapter Forty: Goa - Freak Paradise

I was alone, traveling by boat from Bombay and arriving in Panjim, Goa Province. (Goa is now part of India since the Indians forcibly took it back from Portugal in 1961.) Panjim is a small city, best seen in the quiet back streets, with their small statues of the Virgin built into little alcoves on the sides of brightly painted buildings, innumerable churches, Christian children in their starched school uniforms, taverns and wine shops.

I found a colonial-style restaurant on the second floor of a hotel, overlooking other two-story buildings. The dining hall had sets of open French doors, which let in a cool ocean breeze. At one table were two pretty Indian girls and at the large end table was an Indian businessman and his family. This was gracious dining, under revolving fans with palms, bright-white washed walls, and dark-polished floors. It could have been a movie set from the 1940s, the center table reserved for Humphrey Bogart, in a white rumpled linen suit, cigarette dangling from his mouth, and Lauren Bacall, in a shimmering, black taffeta dress with her usual haughtily sardonic smile.

The first night I checked into the Panjim Tourist Hotel and went out to one of the local taverns for dinner. There I met a bunch of German tourists and proceeded to get drunk with them. We were drinking Kingfisher Goan beer and singing German folk and pop songs until the wee hours.

The next day I took a rickety bus to the beach at Anjuna Village. What I saw when I reached the beach could only be described as a living, updated reenactment of Hieronymus Bosch's "Garden of Earthly Delights."

There were naked freaks walking dazed in the surf, while one freak wore a bright red Beefeater Gin frock. Dozens of freaks with matted black hair and beards, dressed in Indian white cotton tunics and hand-knotted linen pants, were everywhere, looking like unpaid extras from a Charlton Heston biblical epic. There were blond-haired George Harrison doppelgangers playing portable organs and sitars on the sand and other freaks playing guitars and flutes, all surrounded by a loyal following.

Smiling Japanese tourists, clustered under colorful umbrellas, were constantly snapping photos of the freaks. Here long-haired, flower-garland girls in skimpy bikinis, arms covered in Sikh steel bangles, with Hindu symbols pasted on their foreheads, and the more adventuresome with a nose ring, were dancing in the surf, while stoned Brits in long flowing white robes with black bowler hats, played Monty Python crochet on the grassy portion of the beachfront.

Hieronymus Bosch's "Garden of Earthly Delights" (center panel of the triptych painting) Prado Museum, Madrid (Public Domain).

The Aussies were clean-cut but drunk, loudly smashing the ball at their opponents in a mortal kombat that was more dodgeball than volleyball, accompanied by bikinied sheilas, cheering them on or sunning in the sand. Hindu sadhus, with flowing black hair and beards, were sitting in the sand with their ointments, incense, and potions spread on towels before them: one-stop cure-all for arthritis, diarrhea, and sexual dysfunction. Overloaded Tamil vendors roamed the beach, selling everything from beer to ganja to Indian snack food. Strangest of all were these Indian "medicine fakirs." They were carrying these long thin steel needles, which they tried to sell the freaks on cleaning their ears by inserting this shaft-like needle fully into the eardrum (apparently ear wax prevented you from achieving full consciousness, "Can you hear me, Major Tom"). Everywhere the air was pungent with the smell of hashish and ganja. Countless Westerners smoking joints, passing chillums, or wandering around dazed on an LSD high. Welcome to the funhouse!!

A spontaneous beach jam at Anjuna Beach-1970s (photographer unknown) from the FACEBOOK web site "I Love Goa" posted by Vikram Jain.

I settled in, leaving dusty and congested Panjim and getting a room in the Anjuna Beach Hostel. However, this was cacophony personified: people coming in at all hours, thefts, fights over drugs or women, no hot water, and filthy rooms. I moved out after the first night to a bare, clean room in Anjuna Village (away from the beach) run by an Indian Christian family. The family was very kind to me and did not mind my hash smoking.

The beach and ocean are beautiful. The water, warm in the daytime and slightly cool at night, was ideal for moonlight swims. There are dozens of makeshift grass huts on the fringes of the beach inhabited by long-staying freaks and tourist bungalows further inland. Life in Goa is slow (sun, surf, smoke). The lack of refrigeration meant daily forays to the local markets to buy essentials or to eat at the small restaurants near the beach. However, there is the flea market, which harkens back to the old-time barter economy.

Dancing in the sands of Anjuna Beach in the 1970s (Photo by Sunny Schneider). From the FACEBOOK web site "I Love Goa" posted by Vikram Jain.

"Need a pair of jeans-here try this one on. Fits? It's the latest style, bellbottoms. How does three grams of hash sound? Do we have a deal?" Clothes, tools, jewelry, furniture, books, tapes, palm readings, and dope were up for barter or sale. This was also a great live "bulletin board" where you asked about freaks that you had traveled with, cheap or free lodging, the best hangouts, and when was the next "Happening."

"Happenings" are beach parties where hundreds of freaks gather on Anjuna Beach for music, dancing, and dope. The freak musicians either borrow or have their own gas generator and speakers, and Wallah! You have a "Happening'. There are a few freak bands that play everything from hit rock covers to raga-infused dance music. The dancing and tokin' go on for hours, and everyone is smiling, sharing chillums, and gyrating wildly to the hypnotic sounds. I missed Woodstock, but this is our own "love, peace, and rock and roll" festival (without the rain and mud).

Goa is the Holy Mecca for many freaks: they come by buses, trucks, and VW vans from London to Goa; they arrive by boat from Bombay and remain on the beach their entire time in

India. After a few days, you start to see who these people really are. The druggies here are hardcore; they lay on the beach stoned-faced. However, there were only a few of these, and they were easily avoided; more trouble came from the freaks on bad acid trips. Many became aggressive, threatening other freaks and the local Indians. Out-of-control freaks stole from the Indian stores, and one freak pissed in the communal water well at Anjuna, which had the local Indian community in an uproar against all freaks.

Hippie VW van on the overland trail from Europe to India.

Anjuna Beach Hippy Flea Market 1982 (photographer unknown) from FACEBOOK "I Love Goa" posted by Vikram Jain.

What made Goa so special is that for the first time, I saw hundreds of women freaks. These women were not tourists or religious seekers but bonafide freaks. Many arrived on the various "magic buses" from London to India, combat veterans of the drug trails. Others flew into Bombay from America or Europe, came to Goa on the ferry, experienced paradise, and decided to stay. There were even a few heroin addicted unwashed French women freaks (Channel does a wonderful job of masking body odor) who did everything from smuggling dope in artifacts back to France, fake losing American Express checks and the occasional "trick" with tourists to keep themselves supplied with dope.

A beach happening with a gas generator-fueled rock band performing on Anjuna beach in the 1970s." Photographer Unknown. From the Facebook page "I Love Goa"

The long-term freaks build themselves thatched teepee hovels, without even an outhouse, on the fringes of the beach, living in squalor with their druggie girlfriends. Goa was the first place in India where I encountered freak families. These freaks had similar attitudes to the hippies in the American communes in the 60s. They wanted to get away from middle-class values of conformity and commercialism and return to the land, raise their own food, and share their feelings of peace and love with others. They wanted their children to be raised in this Garden of Eden, free from racial prejudice, bullying, and in symbiosis with mother earth and the environment around them. They saw themselves as the "First Freak Nation," where people of all nationalities would come together and live in harmony.

Then there are the freak tourists, especially the Aussies. Three months in the sun and life is a party: Daytona Beach Spring Break: Kangaroo style. They found what they needed: Western food, a gorgeous beach, a ready supply of beer and hashish, and sanitary beach hotels and private homes.

Freaks building a thatched teepee-style home on the beach 1974 (unknown photographer) from the FACEBOOK web site "I Love Goa" posted by Vikram Jain.

Included in these tourists are native Indians, who come to gawk at the freaks. Sometimes you see a whole family of pious Hindus staring in amazement at the antics of the freaks: as if this was a trip to the zoo and these freaks were truly exotic animals.

There are also the "legendary freaks:" Ingrid, a beautiful German courtesan, has made her beach house into a Madame Pompidou 18th-century salon, complete with intellectual discussions, live music concerts, a drug market, and call girl-priced sex. She is the queen bee and her rich drones give her money, pay her rent, and fawn at every word she utters.

Dave from England.

Dave was one of the friendliest freaks I met in Goa.

Freak family shopping in Anjuna Beach (photographer unknown). From the FACEBOOK web site "I Love Goa" posted by Vikram Jain.

Eight-Finger Eddie

The most famous resident freak was an American named "Eight-finger Eddie" (he only has eight fingers; it was a birth defect). He was the first freak to arrive in Goa around 1965. An amateur musician and wannabe author, he was in his late 30s when he came here, running from a bad divorce and a sure prison term for dope possession and smuggling. He vowed he would never return to America again.

He rented a large bungalow near the beach in Anjuna and opened it to all the freaks: crash here, share my food and hash; the only thing I ask in return is that you must accept everyone in the house and be in harmony with them. Due to the generational difference in age, he was a father confessor to the younger freaks: talking down crazed freaks and acting as a go-between for freaks in trouble with the local Indian police. However, these incidents were rather rare. The freaks in Goa were generally peaceful, and as opposed to "Spring Break" revelers in America, there were very few fights, and everyone seemed to get along.

Eddie is a household name in Goa and very popular with the girl freaks. There were always a bunch of adoring groupies that vied for his nightly affections. He lived simply, smoked hash, and was a frequent singer at the Happenings. Eddie was one of the first freaks to perform the annual hejira from Goa (Medina) in the summer when it was too hot and humid to go to Kathmandu (Mecca), where he held court until it became too cold and reversed the hejira back to the beach in Goa. He was content in paradise, surrounded by lovers and friends, and that's how he chose to live his life: no commitments, no responsibilities, and no hassles.

8-finger Eddie with the band at a New Years Eve party in the late 70s (Photo by Sunny Schneider). From the FACEBOOK site "I Love Goa", posted by Vikram Jain.

There is also another longtime hash druggie that came in the late 1960s: an American named Goa Gil, who started a family here and then stayed on after his girlfriend and child moved back home. Gil found peace by discovering Hindu philosophy and religion, but he was an exception. The majority of freaks were here for the dope and free-love freak lifestyle, having little interaction with the local Indians or the Indian religion.

Goa Gil, long-term hippie resident in Goa from the 2001 documentary film "Last Hippie Standing." Author Marcusrobbin released photo to Public Domain world-wide, no license required.

Goa has become a way of life for the druggies. There is also another, albeit smaller, freak convention center in Manali, located in the Kulu Valley in northern India. Here the hashish has ideal growing conditions, and the so-called "Manali Shit" is the gold standard for hash in India. Manali has a temperate climate and colonial ambiance of the old RAG's hill stations like Darjeeling.

Old Manali house, typical of the houses where the freaks lived. (2004 Photograph by John Hill, who released photo to Public Domain).

However, Manali has one big disadvantage: if you overstay into December, you're stuck there for the entire winter. Due to landslides and dangerous icy conditions, the roads do not reopen until the spring. Whether it's Goa, Kathmandu, or Manali, the drugs, free love, and freak lifestyle do not change, only the food and local scenery.

Selling Hashish from Manali, LSD and jewelry in Anjuna flea market, Goa, 1976 (Photo by Michel Hilzinger). From the FACEBOOK web site "I Love Goa" posted by Vikram Jain.

The last group is the traveler freaks, and they are a mixed bag. For many of these, Goa is a way station, a last fling before it's either back to the UK or onward to Australia, depending upon their dreams and ambitions. For others, it is a last taste of pleasurable, worldly "maya" before they go off to ashrams and gurus to find Nirvana or to access their hidden consciousness. For myself, it was my first R&R (rest and relaxation) after months of traveling alone on hot, dusty trails, overcrowded third-class railcars, and squalid accommodations.

Goa makes you feel alive; there is a psychic energy that envelops you here. I was sitting on the beach, watching my French friends wading in the surf, when I was approached by a young blond Dutchman. Out of nowhere, he started talking to me about what I was looking for in life. We talked about energy over matter: how he is practicing yoga to attain Nirvana. He believes that everything is energy, "Einstein's E=MC squared." "If all human life is energy, then you can master this energy to achieve supra-consciousness. Everything runs like a straight line: no "ups" for happiness, no "downs" for sorrows. Everything is accepted in the same detached way. Once you have abandoned desires, you can look inward to achieve that higher consciousness." In his journey, this is a fusing with the universal soul and extinguishing the individual soul (for the Hindus and Buddhists, the end of the cycle of rebirth). As I was speaking with him, the red sun was falling into the ocean. The luminescence made the Dutchman glow bright bronze as if he were the "Burning Bush": "The Word of God Made Manifest."

"Burning Bush" Sebastien Bourdon 17th century, Hermitage Museum, St. Petersburg, Russia.

Chapter Forty-One: "Lover Shot Down"

"Bang, bang, my baby shot me down,"

-Cher.

"Portrait of Maude Abrantes": Amedeo Modigliani 1907.

I met Nathalie, a sorceress disguised as a languidly somnolent English girl, walking on the beach at Anjuna. I was already stoned on opium-laced hash but still cognizant (2 + 2 = 4; SMART: S-M-A-R-T). We started talking about traveling, spiritual states of mind, and the freak scene here in Goa. Nathalie had been in Goa for three months, enjoying the beach and drug scene; however, she never lost control like the unwashed, shabbily dressed French chicks who were always strung out and turning tricks for their next fix. As with most freaks, the conversation turned to the trip; each of us trying to outdo the other with details of the best trip ever. I won round 1 with my mushroom high, but she took round 2 with her LSD adventure. She then suggested we go back to her hotel room and trip out together.

Her hotel was a clean tourist bungalow, and she had a spacious, albeit austere room: small table and chair, rope bed, small stand-alone closet, and, of course, the mandatory single light bulb hanging from the ceiling. However, she had a battery cassette/radio player and a stack of tapes on her table.

Nathalie was about 5' 6", liquid mahogany eyes, black hair cut in a bun, a long well-featured face with a straight longish nose and a petite mouth that radiated a world-weary Simone Signoret wistfulness when smiling and transformed into a witch's cursing scowl when frowning ("Double Toil and Trouble, Fire Burn and Caldron bubble").

We sat on her bed, swigging fenny from the bottle that I had bought and listening to the Stones, "Play with Fire": "She gets her kicks in Stepney, not in Knightsbridge any more…" "very apropos," I said. She laughed and told me about the dinner-jacket nightclubs in Knightsbridge and the working-class pubs of Stepney. After we had downed about a third of a bottle of fenny, she confessed that she had never tried fenny; it was a little hard getting it down, but she was getting a good mellow buzz out of it. I said, "Well, you drink it in gulps, at room temperature, just like your bitter-tasting ales in the Stepney pubs." (A ha, I thought, I had just won round 3 of best highs, {hangover not included!}).

She got out her stash, a dot-filled paper blot, and we each ingested a dot of LSD and waited expectantly for the high (Are we there yet?). We kept drinking and talking about London when I felt a tingling sensation and, suddenly, a saturated kaleidoscope of intense color. Nathalie's face became luminescent: first, fire-engine red, then brocade gold in the afternoon glow. I reached over and kissed her, and soon we were shedding clothes, strewing them around the room, bright blobs of paint on the wooden canvas floor. We fused together in a ball of white light. Her breasts were golden hills, and her bright red nipples lighthouses that lit up when I kissed them. I moved down her body to kiss her vagina; her hair luxurious and high, my tongue an explorer, pushing through dense underbrush. Finally, I found the Holy Grail, caressing it as if I were lovingly polishing a prized diamond. I raised my head, sat up, and eased my hardened penis into her mouth as if I was the key and she the lock. She moved up and down on it as a slow-moving piston; I was holding her head, which was a silky bed of black coral seaweed, swaying gently in the current. After a few moments, I lifted her head and climbed on top of her, her face a day glow poster that kept changing as I kissed her. My tongue and penis worked in machine-like unison, slowly moving in her as I French kissed her serpentine darting tongue. This rhythmic motion stopped when I came in her, thousands of phosphorescent droplets, all cascading into her churning whirlpool. We lay motionless in each other's arms, two sponges absorbing our sperm, now gluing us together, cemented by our lovemaking.

I slowly disengaged and sat up, babbling about art and beauty, and continued drinking fenny, which helped me to crystalize my "four noble truths" (Eat your heart out, Buddha!).

Truth 1: You must be in awe of something to create. You must feel deeply, immersing yourself before you can make your art meaningful.

Truth 2: Poets should die young or go insane because you cannot see infinite beauty all the time without cracking up. You must shout the hosannas of beauty, even if you are incoherent or delirious. Beauty demands to be recognized; you either die or go insane, impossibly realizing this ideal.

Truth 3: Drugs help you to see beauty; they are the dogshit you step on. You try to scoff it off, but you never get it completely off; it sticks to you, reminding you of beauty's stark magnetism.

Truth 4: All organized religion is bullshit; all religions are based on one man with charisma. Jesus was the son of God, and he initiated his disciples into this experience. These men, because they had this "personal experience" with God, felt they must spread the "good news" to tell others of their joy. It was the bastards that came later, with their tedious creeds (an absurdity like the Trinity), their persecutions (the Inquisition), and their righteousness (My God is the only true God). You cannot proselytize this – you must experience it firsthand. This is the only way religion can be truly alive.

The sun was setting, and we decided the best way to end this trip was to go to the beach. We sat there watching the Goan fishermen pulling in their nets. Dark-skinned Tamil children were playing in the sand; they were so innocent and beautiful that I had to add a fifth truth.

Truth 5: How could anyone be racially prejudiced when they see children of any color? Everyone is the same under God, and only when we have the eyes of a child can we understand this.

The red sun was sizzling into the huge saucepan of water; mesmerized by the glory of it, we held each other without breaking the cocoon of silence enveloping us.

I went on a photography safari into the Goan countryside and was away for two days. When I came back, I searched for Nathalie on the beach. I asked some freaks who knew her if they had seen her. They said she was with a French freak that had just arrived in Goa. When I heard this, I was angry, puzzled and hurt. We had a mind-blowing experience together; I had unburdened my soul to her.

After I got over my anger, I realized that she was not an evil sorceress but an experienced chaperone to new perceptions. I was the naïve acolyte, a clueless Dante, and she was the worldly know-it-all Docent, guiding eager pilgrims on a perilous updated journey of the nine circles of the Goan freak scene.

Chapter Forty-Two: "Lusiades" (The Portuguese) - A National Epic Poem

Luis da Camoes by Francois Gerard (1770-1837) (Public Domain).

At the height of the Portuguese overseas empire, there emerged a poet called Luis da Camoes, who wrote the last epic poem in the classical tradition of Homer and Virgil. Like in Homer, the classical gods of antiquity take sides. Venus favors Vasco de Gama (the first European to voyage to India in 1497 AD), while Bacchus is against him. The nominal hero de Gama goes through many trials, finally lands in India, and then is rewarded with nymphs and goddesses on his return from India to the mythical island of love (the proverbial sailor tale of a girl in every port).

The major difference between the earlier epics of Homer and Virgil and the Camoes' epic is that the true hero of the Lusiades is not a man like Odysseus or Aeneas but the entire Portuguese race. The idea is that the ancient gods foretell great glory for the Portuguese people. The goddess

Tethys foretells the conquest of African and Asian territories of Mozambique, India, Malaya, and China. She predicts great wealth and heroism for the future Portuguese conquerors.

Venus gives fair winds to Vasco da Gama's' fleet on route to India by Ernesto Casanova 1880 (Public Domain).

Cameos lived in all these Portuguese territories, landing first in Golden Goa as a poor young man who traveled east to make his fortune and served in the army there. Then he embarked to Macau, where he wrote most of the "Lusiades" in a cave while serving as a minor Portuguese official administering the deeds of the dead in Macau. It seems our boy misappropriated some of the property of the dead and was sent to a prison in Malacca, Malaya. After serving his time, he returned to Goa as a soldier, continuing to write his epic, and then left for Portugal. On his return voyage, he was marooned in the Portuguese colony of Mozambique, where he finished his epic and, on his return to Portugal, presented the poem to the King, who received it with great praise and gave him a lifetime pension.

Vasco da Gama and the nymph Thetis on the Island of Love from the "Lusiades": Tile mural from the Palacio Hotel in Bussaco, Portugal. (How did I miss this island on my Asian travels?)

Unfortunately, Portugal's day in the sun lasted only a century (1500-1600) due to quixotic, disastrous wars against the Moors in Africa, extravagances in the royal court, and lack of manpower and ships to protect their empire from superior Dutch and English forces. They were banished from Japan because of their proselytizing of the Catholic faith, lost Malacca and Indonesia to the enterprising Dutch, and their spice-laden ships to English buccaneers.

I thought of America today; we are the richest, most powerful nation on earth, but who is there to sing of our greatness? We have one great national poet: Walt Whitman, who sang about himself as a democratic free American. In his beliefs, he created his own American epic, one in which he extolled the American people as creating their own destiny. This destiny emphasized the divinity of the common man, not beholden to classical Greek gods for favors or power as in the "Lusiades."

Americans are free in the democratic and religious sense to become godlike and share our democratic vision as a "beacon on the hill" for all the peoples of the world. Yet we are acting like Portugal: engaging in disastrously wasteful wars, losing our industries to the Japanese, and racially and economically divided.

Chapter Forty-Three: Gypsies of Goa

"Gypsy Woman" - The Impressions

Goa is such a lush and tropical paradise that I wanted to see the countryside and get away from the freak circus of the beaches. The Portuguese have been here for over 400 years and have intermarried with the local Hindu population. These Luso-Hindus inhabit small Christian villages throughout the province.

Goan Portuguese woman being carried on palanquin. Cordice Casanatense manuscript, 16th century (public domain CC-PD art).

I would love to live in Goa, but not on the beach, rather in one of the small Christian villages like Anjuna or Calangute, with their little taverns, fenny (palm liquor) shops, picturesque markets selling exotic fruit, fresh fish, and varieties of vegetables I've never seen before. I wanted to go out into the green countryside, dotted with white churches and tall green banyan trees. Here are the small shops, one offering decorated Marys, Christs, and Saints next to one selling Ganesh and

Krishna plaster statues. The green countryside has these beautiful, stately old colonial houses, many with a young boy figure on the tile roof saluting, a throwback to the heyday Portuguese colony. Also, in the countryside, you see the funny way the women wear their saris, tucked under their asses and bunched up, for mobility, but making it appear like they have incredibly fat asses.

I took a bus out of Panjim and went off to stay in one of the small villages in the interior. While riding in the bus, I saw whole gangs of brightly dressed what looked like tribal women working on the roads. I got off the bus at the next stop and went up to the camp where the women were preparing dinner after a long day of hauling stones and raking the gravel of the roads. What I noticed immediately was that the men were gone, probably still working different jobs away from the camp and it was only women and children there. I wandered around the camp, greeting the people and shooting their pictures. They seemed to enjoy my presence and went about their business of cooking chapatis and lentils for the evening meal and caring for their children. It seemed very strange that they wore their finest possessions: brightly colored saris, bangles, elaborate silver earrings, and ornate necklaces while working on the dusty and dirty roads.

Road working Gypsies making dinner at their temporary camp (author's photo).

When I got back to my bungalow in the countryside of Goa province, I asked the owner if he knew who these beautifully dressed, dark-complected road laborers were. He answered they were "Kalo," which in Hindi means "dark-skinned," and said they were Untouchables. They traveled all around the roads of India, doing non-skilled laboring jobs and never staying in one place for long. It was then I realized that they were gypsies and not tribal people. This piqued my curiosity, and later, in the American embassy library in Delhi, I researched gypsies in India and how they spread all over the world.

The gypsies were "Untouchables" in India, even before the Christian Era. They came from Rajasthan and Punjab, speaking an Indian-Aryan language related to Sanskrit and modern Hindi. From the earliest times, they were known as nomads, moving in bullock-pulled carts, doing whatever work they could find, and then always moving on after their jobs were finished. Many Indian gypsies were dissatisfied with their low status and their inability to make enough money to support their families. These independent wanderers left India in two major waves. The first wave, first and second century AD and the second wave in the eighth and ninth century AD. They left to escape the oppressive caste system and find work in the Byzantium empire for the first wave and to escape Muslim persecution in the second wave.

The first wave eventually settled in the Roman province of Egypt (hence their name "gypsies" from "Egyptians"). They were known as fortune-tellers, soothsayers, and even wizards. Their council was much sought after by local rulers, and they prospered. With the fall of Roman Egypt, they moved on to Europe via the Byzantine Empire and through North Africa to Spain. The Byzantine Greeks called them "Atsingani" (outcasts).

The second wave spread through the remnants of the Byzantine Empire and worked as soldiers and at other laboring jobs, but never settled down to farming. Many stayed in the Middle East until they were enslaved by the advancing Mongols of Genghis Khan's army and brought to Europe.

After the Mongols retreated from Europe, they were either slaves or wandered throughout Europe. However, their strange language, dress, appearance, and constant movement from place to place earned them the name "Children of Cain" (the Old Testament figure who slew his brother Abel and left home to wander endlessly under the curse of God).

They were banned on the threat of death from England in the sixteenth century AD and enslaved in Romania and Bulgaria, now part of the Ottoman Empire after the fall of Byzantium in

1453. In the seventeenth and eighteenth centuries, the Europeans became more tolerant of them, allowing them to roam freely, living by performing circus tricks with animals and telling fortunes.

They were swept up in the Holocaust and were sent to the same concentration camps as the Jews in WW II. Estimates of Romany (their name for themselves) deaths at the hands of the Nazis range from half to one and a half million. Many were killed in Eastern Europe with the help of local authorities and vengeful townspeople. After the war, the survivors resumed their wandering ways, telling fortunes, working menial jobs, and performing with bears, where you can still see them in modern Turkey. They were usually bilingual and adopted the religion of the particular country they wandered in. There is still a large population of gypsies in India, always keeping themselves apart from the mainstream Hindu population, doing only the most menial jobs, hence the road laborers that so fascinated me on the back roads of Goa.

Modern Indian gypsy woman" Sandy Saab (free to use with attribution CC – Attribution- SA- 3.0 license).

Chapter Forty-Four: Alfonso de Albuquerque

Alfonso de Albuquerque (Public Domain, C.C.-PD License).

The man responsible for laying the foundation of the first global maritime empire in history is Alfonso de Albuquerque, viceroy of Portuguese India. Albuquerque was a brilliant naval strategist, and through his naval victories in the Indian Ocean, the straits of Malacca, the Persian Gulf, the east coast of Africa, and even in the far away Moluccas, the Spice Islands, he was able to control the spice trade for Portugal for over 100 years. Spices originally arrived in Europe via the Silk Road. Spice laden camel caravans transported the spices to Near Eastern ports where Venetian and Genoan merchants bought the spices and loaded them on their vessels for redistribution throughout Europe. This long and expensive route was closed by the Seljuk Empire in 1090 AD. However, in the early 12th century AD, Arab traders pioneered a new sea route from India and Malaya through the Red Sea and overland to the Near Eastern ports where Venice and Genoa again took control.

Alfonso de Albuquerque conquered Goa in 1510, allying himself with the Vinayagar Hindu Empire in central India and making it the centerpiece of the Portuguese overseas empire. In 1511, he conquered the center of the spice trade for Southeast Asia, Malacca, and now made it a central hub and clearing house for the spices of the Moluccas Islands, sending them directly to Calicut and then on to Portugal. He was able to control access to the Red Sea and all of the shipping routes in the Indian Ocean. His victories ended the Arab domination through the Red Sea of the spice trade.

Albuquerque was also a brilliant administrator establishing diplomatic ties with regimes in Thailand, Burma, the Moluccas, and commercial trade relations with China through Macau and the Safavid dynasty in Persia through his conquest of Hormuz. With these treaties, agreements, and conquests, the Portuguese were able to control the spice, ivory, and silk trade without any competition and effectively drove the Arabs and the Venetians out of business.

Gold coin from Albuquerque's Royal Mint showing the Royal Crest of the Portuguese Kingdom and name of Portuguese King Manuel. (Author Hispalois released photo to CC-Attrib.-SA 4.0 International License free to use with attribution).

He built up the defenses in Goa and reduced the taxes that the Hindus had to pay, ensuring domestic peace. He built hospitals and started schools and was responsible for establishing the first royal mint in the Far East. In Goa, he encouraged the Portuguese to marry the natives and convert them to Christianity. This created a whole new race of mestizos. Luso-Indians and many of the Christian Indians in Goa can trace their ancestry from these early Portuguese-Indian marriages. However, he left the larger Hindu community alone, only forbidding the suttee, the self-immolation of widows after their husbands died.

Portuguese soldier in Goa: "Well who do I choose for my bride? Will it be white sugar or brown sugar, this is a really tough decision." Codice Casanatense Manuscript 16th century, Public Domain (CC-PD Art).

Powerful men have many jealous enemies, and they convinced the king to replace him as viceroy of Goa, claiming he was trying to usurp the overseas empire for his own gain. He died a heartbroken man, always loyal to the king and not understanding why the king would believe these lies. At his death, he was beloved by both the Portuguese and Indian inhabitants of Goa and buried in great pomp and circumstance in the cathedral in Goa that he founded.

It is ironic that Alfonso de Albuquerque's lasting legacy will not be his military victories nor his diplomatic treaties; it will be a mango! In the 16th century, Jesuits in Portuguese Goa grafted the Indian mango into a new variety with less fiber, thinner skin, juicy pulp, and a delicious taste that has now become the gold standard of mangoes worldwide. They named this mango Alfonso to honor the viceroy of India, Alfonso de Albuquerque.

Alfonso Mangoes (G. Patkar released photo to public domain with no restrictions).

Chapter Forty-Five: Trish in Goa

"She's one of those girls who seems to come in the spring,

One look in her eyes and you forget everything."

-The Lovin' Spoonful, Younger Girl.

Portrait of Angela McInnes: John Singer Sargent (charcoal drawing 1915) (Public Domain CC- PD Art).

Trish was an English university student on an extended sabbatical, traveling to all the old British Empire outposts: Hong Kong, Malaysia, Singapore, and India. In India, she had seen the teeming poor cities and the cultural sights, and now she was having fun in the sun before returning to the land of perpetual fog and rain.

I met her, sitting alone in a small taverna, eating spicy Goan shrimp. We started talking about Goa and the impact of Christianity on the Indians. I had been to the small Christian villages in the countryside and extolled the beauty of colorfully decorated houses and stately baroque chapels set among palm trees, overlooking verdant green rice fields.

I also told of my own church in the States, a small all-white wood frame building with a frontal steeple: a church that would have fit into a prosaic village square in New England. However, it was in suburban New Jersey, surrounded by tract houses and supermarkets. Inside, it was a luminous light box: unadorned white walls, high, light-infused plain-glass windows, rich mahogany-colored pews, a central nave leading to a simple altar table, overshadowed by a huge polished oak wood cross. Growing up, I always thought this was the perfect empty vessel to welcome Jesus, who would fill it with His ethereal encompassing presence.

Trish listened and then spoke of her home, coming from the limpid, rain-washed Lake country of middle England, with its moss-covered stone churches, quaint villages, and austere atmosphere. She had attended Anglican services when she was a child and sang in the children's choir, but she never really felt the presence of God. "I never felt God's presence in church, but found Him in nature, walking around the pastoral countryside, sitting by still ponds, reading Wordsworth's 'Prelude' - God was pantheistical alive, surrounding me, in the first bloomings of spring, in the golden phosphorescence of late summer dusks, the earthy smell of fresh cut fields of wheat and the majestic poetry of bare trees swaying in the winter wind."

We talked for hours, and I asked her if she had seen Old Goa, with its stately churches and ruined relics dating back 400 years. She said no, and I proposed a visit. We met at the same taverna the next morning and took a dusty, overcrowded bus to Old Goa, a scant 10 miles away.

"The Market in Goa 1580": Jan Huygen van Linschoten, Amsterdam 1596 (Public Domain, CC-CCO-PD).

While we were riding on the bus, I told her a little about my travel experiences in the other Asian Portuguese colonies. Macau, with its stately churches, impressive Fort, and Portuguese-style food, was a museum of "Remembrance of Things Past." Malacca had no impressive monuments of Portuguese rule but a vibrant Luso-Chinese/Malay presence. Here the people kept up the Portuguese language, religion, and way of life for over 400 years. Now we are going to Golden Goa, the Pearl of the Asian Portuguese Empire. For a century and a half, from 1500 to about 1650 AD, this was one of the richest cities in the world, with over 200,000 people.

Portugal used this spice trade wealth to build magnificent churches and to convert hundreds of thousands of Indians to the Catholic faith. The Jesuits under Saint Francis Xavier established seminaries to train missionaries that went forward to China, Japan, and one lone missionary, Antonio de Andrade (1580- 1634), made it all the way to Tibet, becoming the first European to visit that country and establish a church there. Francis Xavier traveled all the way to Japan to convert thousands of lower-class Japanese to the Catholic faith. He was about to enter China to continue his conversions when he died of fever off the China coast. This same Francis Xavier is now entombed in Bom Jesus cathedral in old Goa.

Saint Francis Xavier preaching to the Indians and inhabitants of Goa. 17th century painting by Andre Reinoso, Public Domain (CC-PD Art).

Yet this tropical paradise had a serpent in the garden and that was the Inquisition. Tens of thousands of newly converted Christians were imprisoned, and hundreds were killed for not following the true Catholic faith. Many Hindus and Muslims were accused of practicing in secret their old religious rituals, and the newly converted Sephardic Jews were persecuted for falling back on their old Jewish traditions. The Jews left en-mass for Cochin, then under the rule of the Dutch. There they were allowed to keep their Jewish faith and established a thriving community. It also seemed that old Goa incurred the wrath of an angry God, who sent epidemics of malaria and cholera, which decimated the populace. The Portuguese authorities finally abandoned the city in the middle of the 18th century and established a new capital in Panjim.

The Procession of the Inquisition in Goa 17th century, Public Domain (CC-PD) Jan Huygen van Linschoten, Amsterdam 1596 (Public Domain, CC-PD)

Old Goa at in the 16th century, Public Domain (CC-PD) Jan Huygen van Linschoten, Amsterdam 1596 (Public Domain, CC-PD).

Upon arrival, we rented bicycles and proceeded to explore the city. Our first stop was the cathedral of Bom Jesus. Here we saw the marble sepulcher of Saint Francis Xavier. The body of the saint is brought out every ten years for public viewing and is supposed to be in a state of corporal intactness, which would have been interesting to see. When this was mentioned, I thought immediately of Stalin in his climate-controlled coffin in the Kremlin, waiting to return to butcher more people, just like it is rumored that once the grave of Genghis Khan is discovered, he will rise up and begin his conquests anew. Bom Jesus' interior is beautiful, with an intricately carved pulpit and the main altar featuring a life-size wooden sculpture of Saint Francis of Loyola, the founder of the Jesuits. The church has been restored meticulously and attracts thousands of worshippers.

We pedaled past boarded churches, empty government buildings, and abandoned docks. It was hard to believe this was once the Pearl of the Orient, but the churches were magnificent. Many of the smaller chapels were still engulfed in jungle vegetation, sitting forlorn with their whitewash paint peeling off in the humid tropical sun.

We stopped for lunch near the ruins of Saint Augustine, an impressive church that had burned and was never rebuilt, now being slowly engulfed by the jungle vegetation. I told Trish of the many ruined cities I saw in my travels: the former Thai capital Ayutthaya and the thousand pagoda city of Bagan in Burma. When Trish first saw Saint Augustine, the first thing that came to her mind were the terrible photographs of the London blitz during World War Two: entire blocks were leveled by U2 bombs and hundreds of civilians were killed.

Interior of Bom Jesus Cathedral. The main altar features a life-size wooden statue of St. Francis Xavier, who is also buried in the Church's crypt. Old Goa. Errol Fernandez 2017 released image to CC-Attrib-SA 4.0 International License, free to use with attribution of author.

I told Trish, "I plan to live in New York City when I return from my travels, but it is very disheartening to read about and hear from friends how the city is collapsing. The entire Bronx is burning: whole blocks look just like Saint Augustine and the crime and junkies are driving everyone out of the city. It is even more heartbreaking to realize that this is not an external wartime bombing but a disease within: our own people are burning their city and committing these horrific crimes. Would there come a time when people totally abandoned New York? Will the last one out please turn off the torch on the Statue of Liberty?"

Ruins of St. Augustine Old Goa. Vyacheslav Argenburg released photo to CC-Attribution 4.0 International License, free to use with attribution of author.

We continued our exploration and saw one more church and an old, crumbling Portuguese fort overlooking the sea. We then headed back as the sun was setting. I was quiet on the bus trip back, seeing all this beauty that was just abandoned, and now it's become just a tropical Disneyland to gawk at, without Mickey or the rides.

We returned to Calangute in time for dinner: we went to another small taverna, where we feasted on garlic-infused sea bass, washed down by huge bottles of Kingfisher Goan beer. We also tried feni, a coconut-based toddy whiskey, which mellowed both of us quite nicely. Emboldened by the feni, I asked her if she would like to see my spartan room, which I had rented from a Christian Indian family. She agreed if we would get a feni bottle to go. When we arrived, I told her my accommodation was not like a room in the Raffles, where she had stayed while visiting Singapore. However, it had a special charm: the room, from the high shuttered window, overlooked palm trees and a little courtyard with a small stone, gurgling fountain. The bare room also caught the evening breeze, which compensated for the lack of a ceiling fan. The 25-cent-a-night charge also made up for the lack of Raffles' room service. Furthermore, our BYOBB feni toddy could give the fancy "Singapore Sling" a run for the money.

We toasted Goa, the Queen, Moms, and apple pie, managing to drink about half a bottle, laughing at everything we said. As we drank, I looked at her: she had long chestnut-brown hair, light brown eyes with a touch of green, high cheekbones, full thick lips, and a nose that tended to aquiline. This combined with her rosy coloring, gave her a fresh wholesomeness that was irresistible. I put the bottle down, pushed back her locks, and gave her a long French-tongue kiss. She responded by parting my long hair, holding my face with both hands, and staring intently into my face. We fell back on the bed, kissing and touching each other. She had a loose linen blouse, which I undid and massaged her small breasts until her dark red nipples became rigid. We undressed and lay there, kissing and stroking each other. I moved her head down and she started kissing my penis, her tongue darting at my crown while I held her hair back. Soon I was rock-hard and lifted her head, laying her on her back, so I could caress her vagina. Her pubic hair was luxuriant and soon wet with my insistent tongue. She moaned quietly and after a few moments, I came up and was on top of her, easing my penis into her moist opening. We thrust together slowly and then more frenzied, the rope bed creaking noisily. I came hard and continued moving in her until I felt a violent thrust-gasp, and I knew she also came. We kept moving, and I felt our bodies were one. Afterwards, we laid back and held each other until we fell asleep.

We woke up in the early morning and got breakfast with strong dark coffee, a welcome break from Indian milk chai. We met later at the beach, joining the freak scene, two pointillist figures in the background, sitting back enjoying the fun house in a freak update of Seurat's "La Grande Jatta."

We talked endlessly on every subject, but especially on literature: she talked about her love for D.H. Lawrence and his primordial instinct of lovemaking. Lawrence, she said, created so many strong women that take charge of their own destinies, whether it's the sacrificing mother in "Sons and Lovers" or Lady Chatterley affirming her own femininity, as an equal partner, in an extra-matrimonial relationship.

I told her of my admiration of F. Scott Fitzgerald. How all his main characters are idealistic outsiders, always looking from a distance at the monied brokers and the golden girls, a life that Nick will never have and ultimately rejects as corrupt in the "Great Gatsby." Our Dionysian idyll continued for 6 days: getting sunburnt on the beach, renting bicycles and touring the verdant countryside, trying every Goan dish that the small tavernas offered, getting drunk on feni and making passionate love on my well-worn rope bed, which definitely began to sag badly.

"La Grande Jatta" by Georges Seurat 1886 (Public Domain, CC-PD Art) . (The man in the foreground with the red short-sleeve shirt and black cap, smoking a hash pipe is me. The woman nearby with the brown and white hat is Trish, reading my copy of "Lady Chatterley's Lover". The unknown dog has just finished the remains of our picnic lunch).

Trish was leaving for a flight out of Bombay to London in two days. We had almost a week together and now reality was upon us. I felt so close to her, physically, intellectually, and emotionally, that I didn't want this relationship to end. I thought of Francois Hardy's chanson "All over the World:" "Just know that wherever you are, I will be thinking of you and missing you."

Chapter Forty-Six: Cochin - Spices, Jews, and Christians

I left Goa with a French freak, Anthony, and we arrived in Cochin via bus and train and found that what makes this place unique is the prosperity of the people; there are no beggars and no starving naked children. This has been a rich state for 500 years because of one thing: spices.

Vasco de Gamma landed here in 1497, and the Portuguese proceeded to build their churches and forts. For one hundred years, the Portuguese controlled the spice monopoly, ruining Venice and making Portugal very rich. What the Portuguese found here was a thriving cosmopolitan city filled with Jewish merchants and Nestorian Christians. The legend is that St. Thomas, one of the original twelve disciples of Jesus, came here in 52 AD and founded a Christian community.

Street scene in Cochin (authors photo).

This brings us to the Nestorian Christians. This heretical sect was created by Nestorius, the patriarch of Constantinople, in the Fifth Century AD. He believed that Christ had two natures: one human and one divine, whereas the Roman Catholic Church believes that Christ has only one nature: Divine. "Not identical but united with the Son of God who lives in Him and also is a human." He is fully man and God.

After the condemnation of Nestorius, his followers migrated to the Sassanid (Persian) Empire, merged with the existing Church of the East (a Byzantium church), and transformed this church into a Nestorian-belief church. From their base in Persia, they sent out missionaries to China, India, and all of Central Asia. At first, they were very successful, with churches all over these regions. However, the rise of Buddhism lost them China and Central Asia oasis cities. Then in the 8th century AD, the Muslim armies conquered Persia and wiped out most of the Nestorians. Only in Cochin, India, did they survive and even thrive.

Many of the Jews in Cochin see themselves as remnants of the Ten Lost Tribes of Israel, migrating here from the "Babylonian Captivity." Many Jewish merchants came to India to escape Muslim persecution and the political instability in Iraq and Iran. Others are Sephardic Jews that scattered over the Mediterranean and Near East when they were expelled from Spain in 1498. These Jews still speak "Ladino," a Spanish dialect spoken during the reign of Ferdinand and Isabella. Today there are only about 250 Jews left in Cochin and only a single beautiful synagogue, Paradesi, out of the original nine synagogues, is currently holding services. The vast majority of the Jews left Cochin in the 1950s and 1960s to go to the newly founded state of Israel.

Paradesi Synagogue showing the Ark of the Covenant, Cochin, India (Photo by jeem from St. Louis, CC-Attr-SA-2.0 Generic License)

The area around Paradesi Synagogue is called Mattancherry. It has hundreds of stores, restaurants, and toddy (coconut spirits liquor) shops. The restaurants use their trademark spices to create the most delicious dishes. My French friend Anthony and I must have gained five pounds each just sampling these delicacies. Being on the coast, the variety of fresh fish is the best in India. Shrimp cooked with ginger, chili peppers, cumin, and coconut is "to die for." The Keralans also make zesty cumin chicken and an endless variety of vegetarian dishes.

I knew that the Keralan government was communist, but I didn't see any demonstrations or street rallies. The students we met were more concerned with their examinations than politics. The people seemed content, as well they should be, living in such a paradise.

I stayed off the hash and drank the local toddy and gorged on the delicious food. We visited Fort Cochin, which is in the Christian district. One church, St. Francis, symbolized the ebb and flow of Cochin's conquerors. St. Francis was built by the Portuguese and, for one hundred years, was Roman Catholic. When the Dutch took over, they reconsecrated it as a Dutch Reformed Church. When the Dutch were driven out by the English, they converted it to an Anglican Church. Anthony and I stayed one week in Cochin and then another week traveling by boat in the green countryside. Kerala's true life is in the countryside: the beautiful mountains, the brightly painted buildings sticking out amongst the emerald foliage, café con leche, fine-featured people. We were riding in a crowded bus when I saw a surreal image: a beautiful dark-skinned young Keralan nun: her face shone luminously against her white smock and black habit, riding with an older bespectacled nun. The bus stopped at a small village, and the two nuns got out, carrying huge suitcases and golden-framed holy pictures of Christ and the Virgin. Standing forlornly in the middle of nowhere, with the villagers surrounding and gaping at them, our bus spurts away and they are gone forever.

Walking for hours in the red earth of the plains through rice fields and straight betel nut trees (Every Indian has a red mouth because they incessantly chew betel nuts, a mild narcotic), I came upon a small baby crying outside of a mud-walled, grass-covered hut. The mother was milling grain and I could see the father in the distance plowing a field with a huge water buffalo. The late afternoon sun shone through the tall green canopy, illuminating the dwelling with a bronzed glow: a bucolic image of pastoral life in India.

Typical rural thatched grass covered house in Kerala (authors photo).

Chapter Forty-Seven: Kerala - Green Mansions

Alas, my love, you do me wrong,

To cast me off discourteously.

For I have loved you well and long,

Delighting in your company.

Chorus

Greensleeves was all my joy

Greensleeves was my delight,

Greensleeves was my heart of gold,

And who but my lady greensleeves.

Thou couldst desire no earthly thing,

but still thou hadst it readily.

Thy music still to play and sing;

And yet thou wouldst not love me.

Ah, Greensleeves, now farewell, adieu,

To God I pray to prosper thee,

For I am still thy lover true,

Come once again and love me.

Greensleeves was all my joy

Greensleeves was my delight,

Greensleeves was my heart of gold,

And who but my lady greensleeves.

-Greensleeves Is My Hearts Delight (excerpts): old English folk song.

Kerala was created by Parasurank, an avatar of Vishnu, when he threw his battle-ax into the ocean. I convinced Anthony that we should spend some time in the backwaters, lagoons, and canals of Kerala (It really didn't take much cajoling after I mentioned that was where the best, strongest toddy was.). We left in the morning for our Sputzursergung im der Grunner Wald (A Walk in the Green Forest).

One of the many verdantly lush canals in Kerala (author's photo).

We boarded a crowded ferry that made all of the local village stops: Kerala's version of the Westside IRT #1 local. If we liked a place, we got off, and within an hour or so, there would be another ferry to continue our journey. We would stay on the ferry for a few hours, view the local villages, and sometimes catch a glimpse of wildlife, the creatures of the green lagoon, turtles, and cranes. We would get off the ferry, have a few toddies, eat lunch, and then catch the next ferry. By late afternoon we were both drunk; we got off the ferry at a large village to get lodging for the night and dinner.

If I had only one word to describe what we saw on this trip, that would be: coconut. Lining the shoreline for miles, we saw endless coconut palms. For drinks, we had coconut juice straight from the husk or fermented into toddies. For dinner, we had fresh fish cooked in coconut oil with coconut sauce, and for dessert: delicious coconut cake. We stayed in small guesthouses. Each room we stayed in always had a brightly designed coir (coconut fiber mat) and a coconut fiber rope bed.

We inquired the next morning if there was a large rowboat that could take us into the backwaters to see the whole coconut process. We found an old fisherman who spoke no English but knew how to bargain with finger signals for the day's outing. We finally agreed on a price for his services, which I'm sure was more than he would have made that day fishing, but at least now we had a boat, and we were off. We glided from village to village, stopping every so often when we found a toddy shack. Toddy is made from coconut palm sap that is fermented; the longer the fermentation, the stronger the toddy.

The waterways were clogged with all manner of boats; large dugouts that carried merchants, villagers carrying small animals to sell, and school children going back and forth from school. The larger boats that we saw carried produce: fruits and other agricultural products.

At our third toddy stop, we got the owner of the shop to explain to the fisherman that we wanted to see the toddy tappers and the villages where they process the coconut into fiber and finished products. Our fisherman now finally understood what we wanted and took us off the main canal to a small stream that took us away from the coastline. After about half an hour, we came to a grove of palms, where we saw nimble tappers climbing these palms. They carried a butcher's cleaver, a small bowl-like object and buckets to catch the palm sap. The tapper would climb the palm and find the coconut buds, which he would then cut the tip off and tie it tight with palm leaves. He would then hit the buds gently with the bowl to stimulate the flow of the sap. Then he would place the earthen jug over the top of the bud at an angle to collect the sap. He would later return to collect the day's sap accumulation and cut the bud again and place a new jug to collect more of the sap the next day. Once the buckets were filled, they collected the sap and poured it into large plastic containers for distribution to wholesalers or individual toddy shops. The shops would then process the sap into different strengths of toddy depending on the length of fermentation.

We paddled on further until we came to a village where there were huge, round fishing nets submerged in shallow lagoon waters. Each net holds hundreds of coconut husks, softening in the brackish water. The coconut flesh had already been removed for eating or to be pressed into coconut oil. We stopped in this village to see the village women pounding with wooden mallets these softened husks to make strings of fiber. In another part of the village, we saw the villagers spinning these strings to make mats or heavy ropes. In yet another part of the village, we saw large troughs of colored dye, where they would submerge the string fibers, dry them, and spin them for colored mats and ropes. It was amazing to watch these different processes that went from wet husk to finished products.

By the time we had finished watching this process, it was getting to sunset, and we paddled back, without our traditional toddy pick-me-uppers, to get back before nightfall.

The next morning, we boarded the ferry in the opposite direction, back to Cochin, albeit slowly, for generous toddy pit stops. Looking back at our drunken "Lost Weekend" spree (which lasted about a week) in the backwaters, I see it as a living reenactment of the film "Harvey," wherein I am the James Stewart hero, always desperate for my next drink. The one exception to that movie was that instead of a six-foot-high friendly white rabbit, I had a six-foot-high chestnut mongoose named Oscar that wanted to be my friend.

James Stewart and Harvey from the 1950 film "Harvey."
(promotional still for the film "Harvey" which was not copyright and therefore is Public Domain.)

My friendly chattering mongoose Oscar. (Photo by Shannon Wild) CC-Attr-SA-3.0 license, free to use with attribution of author Shannon Wild.)

Normally I don't mind animals talking to me (usually, they are better conversationalists than my pet rock), but this mongoose just kept on and on; it just wouldn't shut up! "You promised me a king cobra to play with! When are we taking another ferry trip? We never go anywhere except these toddy bars - I want to go dancing...." The only way you could escape this constant chatter was to get good and drunk. I did this quite well in the daytime, but it was the nights that were extremely bothersome. However, I stashed a toddy bottle under my bed (there was no overhead light fixture that would hide my emergency toddy bottle), easily accessible for a panicked midnight swig, to stop that damn annoying mongoose from talking to me and keeping me awake.

Chapter Forty-Eight: Dawn

"Judith II (Salome)": Gustav Klimt 1909
(Public Domain).

My French friend, Anthony, said that his friends had told him of an unspoiled beach just down the Keralan Coast. Good freaks, good dope, good beach; "Put me in coach; this one is for the Gipper. Where's my suntan lotion?" We took a series of dusty, overcrowded buses and trains, and finally arrived at Kovalam Beach. The scene here was very mellow: you didn't see the heavy, heroin-drooling dopers that are a fixture in Goa. The freaks here were very friendly, the accommodations cheap, and the seaside restaurants, with their variety of "day's catch," were even better than Goa. There were a lot of Aussie and English travelers. They were headed for more beach adventures in Ceylon and then on to Kangaroo Land. There were a series of beaches and some even had Indian families on vacation. We stayed at Lighthouse Beach (you never know when you're so stoned and need a guiding "beacon" to get you home). At night, the beach livened up with small parties, passing chillums of hash, and moonlight swims in this freak paradise.

Lighthouse Beach Kovalam (Photo by Hiker Wolf Tours India) (CC-Attr-SA-2.0 Generic License).

Anthony had found his French friends and he went off with them. The first night, I wandered around the beach, a short walk from my room, with my housewarming gift: a block of hash. I found a group of about ten freaks, guys and girls sitting around a kerosine hurricane lamp. I asked if I could join them, and one Aussie started up and shouted to the group, saying, "Hey, we got a Yankee here." In my best Southern drawl, I blurted out, "How did y'all know I'm American? I ain't wearing my Stetson or cowboy boots or my disco white leisure suit?" They made me feel right at home, especially when I broke out my hash house-warming gift and mixed some joints for the group. They were talking about where they'd been, where you find the best dope and the best restaurants to go to: standard cocktail party banter, freak-style.

Sharing a joint on a beach 1969. Author Wickiwatcher 1 released photo to CC-Attr-SA-3.0 License, free to use with attribution of author.

I surveyed the scene, trying to figure out which chicks were attached or by themselves. I spotted a brown-haired girl who was quietly listening to the boisterous crowd. I went over and sat down next to her. Her name was Dawn, and she was from Adelaide, on the west coast of Australia, so we played "twenty questions" in order to get to know each other. She had left a boring hotel job, where she arranged events, and now, for a few months, she was off schedule. "How did you discover Kovalam?" "A traveler in Bombay said it was a better beach than Goa." "Well, is it?" "The beach is great, but I'm trying not to stay stoned 24/7." "Well, I think you picked the wrong crowd. However, there is a Christian Revival tent, the next beach over." She laughed and I suggested we walk on the beach (just to clear our heads, of course.) She was about 5'6", a little chubby, and had a sweet, fresh look, especially when she smiled. We walked along the shore, and I told her about Sri Sathya Baba and about the people at the Baba Ashram. She seemed attentive and I asked her if she wanted a chai or something to eat. She said no, but since it was a hot night, I suggested we have a quick dip in the ocean. We found a shady spot, where we stripped and ran off naked into the surf. The water was chilling but refreshing as long as you kept in motion. We walked out, up to our head level, holding hands. I pulled her towards me and kissed her. She pulled her head back, "Whoa, cowboy, aren't we going a little too fast?" "I'm sorry, I had no idea we were waiting for your chaperone duenna." She laughed and gave me a peck kiss. We walked out of the surf, got dressed, and walked back to our group. When we got back, I said, "The offer of dinner still stands, you, me, and the duenna at 7 o'clock." She agreed, and I went back to my room.

The next day I spent with Anthony and his friends, drinking toddy and lying on the beach. I picked her up on the beach: she had on a colorful calico-printed summer dress that clung tightly in all the right places and makeup that emphasized her full, red, petulant lips and rosy cheeks. "Well, I couldn't get us into Maxims, but I still have tickets for the opera." "What's playing?" "Madam Butterfly, the sad story of an American sailor who takes advantage of a foreign beauty and then she kills herself, but her memorable death lasts about ten minutes after stabbing herself." "Well, we can't let that happen here." "That's true, I don't believe you have the vocal pipes to hit the high C's, especially after you've committed hari-kari."; to be safe, though, I should hide your kitchen knives."

We found a small restaurant that served fiery chili shrimps. "Well, if I can't get you hot, this certainly will." We joked and jabbed each other on Aussie and American foibles. "You don't mind if I call you, Hey Sheila." "Only if you don't mind me calling you Uncle Sam" (at that time, I had a good-sized and, I thought vainly, good-looking beard). After dinner, we walked along the beach until we found a secluded palm area, sitting down to enjoy the cool evening breeze. She was totally clear-headed, and my toddy high had totally disappeared at dinner. Taking my cue from last night's conversation, I abstained from breaking out a joint and enjoyed the beauties of nature, both the landscape and my fetching lady, au naturel.

We talked about freaks, what we want out of life, and how we would achieve this elusive goal. Since she didn't think drugs were the answer, I asked, "Have you tried yoga?" "No, I don't think I have the patience for it. I was in a rut back home: steady job, dependable boyfriend, comfortable apartment, yet something was missing in this kangaroo pie dream they're selling you." "So, you think the freak lifestyle is the answer?" "I thought so, but the drugs are just another rut (though it's a nice pothole to fall in, I thought silently to myself), a way to avoid the problem." "Weel," I said, in my best German accent, "Lay down on this beach couch here and let's begin with your vater." She laughed and we got up, walking toward the town; dusk was setting in and I asked her what she wanted to do. "I don't know, but I like being with you." "Ah, aber vas do we do about the docktor patient relationship?" "You know das is a nein, nein!" "Well, we haven't talked about my mutter yet." "Well then, this docktor will make a haus call; you do have a couch, don't you?" We stopped for a bottle of toddy and some fruit. She lived alone in a small room that was your basic traveler's hotel room, but she did have the luxury of a working ceiling fan.

We had some toddy and fruit, sitting on her bed, talking. Again, I kissed her and this time, she kissed me back. I felt her breast through the dress, and she asked me to unzip the back. She undressed and then started undressing me. She got everything off, my pants around my feet, dropped to her knees, pulling me over, kissing my penis and holding my behind, as I stood there. She moved slowly back and forth slowly caressing my crown, fully absorbing my erection. I was holding her head, then pulling her back, kissing her and then laying her on the rope bed. I stepped out of my pants and sandals, and we laid there kissing while my hand stroked her vagina. When I felt she was wet, I came on top of her, found the desired place, and we started to move together. She moaned quietly, as I thrusted back and forth. I came with an urgency, but she kept moving, until we were both exhausted and silent. I got up, cleaned myself in the hall toilet, sat on her sole chair, chugging toddy and smoking a cigarette. I looked at her outline in the darkness; her sleeping body seemed totally relaxed. I sat there thinking of what she had said this evening: how we are all lonely inside, masking it with drugs, alcohol, and sex. Could I feel a sense of belonging, like Rachel had at the ashram, or would I always be on the outside, looking in, always questioning, never answering?

In the morning, true to her name, she awoke me early with a kiss and then moved her lips down my body, kissing me until I was fully erect. Then she climbed over me, moved on top, and began thrusting her body against mine. I grabbed her breasts as we moved together. Her face shone glowingly in the morning sun, every muscle tensed as she came and shortly afterwards, I came with a full thrust that quivered over her whole body. She came off and we both lay sated in each other's arms. We finally got up, dressed, and went for breakfast. I told her I would see her later that day and returned to my hotel. I arrived at the hotel just to see Anthony leaving, saying he was going to move into a rented house with his French friends. I wished him well and later met Dawn on the beach.

We were now a "couple" and were always together. The scene was different here than in Goa. In Goa you had the flea market where you could score colorful clothes at bargain prices and meet other freaks. Nor was there a music scene where people had impromptu parties on the beach attended by crowds of gyrating and stoned-out freaks. The atmosphere here was more laid back with just a few freaks getting together at night, sometimes over a bonfire, smoking dope and chilling. We hung out with other Australian couples here on holiday and went out to dinner together and talked about life in Kangaroo Land. The Aussies were a great bunch: they were friendly, open, and out to enjoy themselves. Like Dawn, the people we were with were not freaks and kept their highs to beer and toddy. This was their month in the sun; a spring break from the boring nine-to-five routines back home. Here they cocooned themselves: enjoying the beach, great food, and cheap prices. I felt like I was back in 1950s America. This was a time when people felt confident and content with their lives. There was no questioning of the consumer culture and their complacent lifestyle. They have a good life: there was no war to protest, nor was there any racial divide, and the society was homogeneous middle class.

Here we became Mr. and Mrs. Jones of the suburban Joneses. In the morning, we bought fruit and toddy in the local stores, spent our afternoons at the beach, met our new Aussie friends for dinner, and then went back to her room where we made glorious love. In deference to her, I didn't smoke hash, being fully conscious when trying every Kama Sutra position that we knew about. This idyllic adventure in postcard paradise continued for two weeks, and then one morning, I lay in bed after a passionate lovemaking, realizing I hadn't taken a single photograph and my journal was blank since leaving Cochin. I felt like Kafka's beetle, not physically, but intellectually and emotionally. I had metamorphosed into a complacent middle-class bore; next, I'm sure I would have taken up golf and bought a minivan.

I tried talking about the different philosophies that I had learned about, the "other" real India beyond the beach, and my reasons for traveling. She was polite, but I could see she really wasn't interested and didn't offer any opinions on any of my pedantic babbling. She enjoyed the beach, the good food, and the lovemaking. I thought to myself, "I went all of the way to India, just to find a Valley Girl, with a lilting accent!"

I told her I was going to Pondicherry to find out about Sri Aurobindo and his teachings, that every human has the divine in him, and his teaching would show me how to access this.

She was taken aback, believing we would go onto Ceylon for more fun in the sun (same channel, same program, different set of palm trees and curry) and then return with her to Kangaroo Land. "Look, everyone, see what I brought back from my travels in India: a real live Yankee - isn't his accent just adorable" She felt betrayed that I had led her on, built up her hopes that we were a "permanent couple" and now I had trashed her dreams. "You fuckin' Americans. First you fuck up Vietnam and leave with your tail between your legs, and now you fucked this relationship up, you coward!"

She was inconsolable and screamed, "Get out, and don't come back!" I left, feeling terrible for her and seeing myself as the schmuck she said I was. I got the first bus outta Dodge; Eve had banned me forever from this fecund emerald Garden of Eden and from the manicured green lawn with a white picket fence Eden of her dreams.

Birmingham Museums Trust (U.K.) on UNSPLASH (A Pre-Raphaelite imagining of my relationship with Dawn).

The South of India

Group of Sadhus 1900 (Library of Congress Carpenter Collection: Public Domain (CC-CCO-PD License).

Chapter Forty-Nine: Life on Indian Roads

Photograph by Jakob Owens on UNSPLASH

In Tamil Nādu and the deep south of India, I traveled alone. This was far from the freak pilgrimage sites of Goa and Kovalam, where freaks cocoon themselves with fellow travelers, dope, and sex. Days are spent on hot, overcrowded buses and nights in hot, claustrophobic shoebox rooms. My only luxury was a ceiling fan to circulate the stifling air. The food at first seemed "exotic:" vegetable stews served on palm leaves, but the curry becomes over-powering, thankfully masking the tasteless gruel. The meal is saved by the varieties of sweet fruit: pomegranates, mangoes, and coconuts. Sweet milk tea becomes an addiction: stopping at least ten times a day to drink from these little clay cups, which are destroyed after each drink.

I'm on my own pilgrimage observing a living faith; the ritual bathing, the temple smells of burning incense and human sweat, the markets crowded with hagglers, a kaleidoscope of colorful dresses, flowing white robes and ornaments of every description on the faces of the people I encounter. Barefoot kids follow you around, shouting "Hello" and begging for rupees. Waiting in long lines in the baking afternoon sun as it snakes around temples, caves, or building entrances, I tried to isolate people, to catch them unaware with my camera. I am the fool Westerner: a symbol of change in a changeless land. Religion dominates every aspect of life here. I think back on my youth how accepting Jesus was so easy and natural, and now I'm an outsider to both Eastern and Western religions.

Charles Montagu Doughty 1908 Author of "Travels in Arabia Deserta"

I remembered the classic outsider traveler Charles Montagu Doughty whom I had avidly read in college. I had never been to a desert, but his descriptions brought Arabia alive in my mind, and his language is majestic: old school but similar to the poetic gravity of the King James Old Testament. His "Travels in Arabia Deserta" now took on a different and deeper dimension. Like

Doughty, I was traveling alone, trying to understand the people, customs, and beliefs of the deep South Hindu Indians. Doughty traveled for years in the 1880s among the Bedouin Arabs as an openly professed Christian in a fanatical Muslim world. He suffered numerous beatings, humiliations, and threats to his life because of his faith. However, what stands out is his steadfast belief in the Arab duty of extending hospitality to strangers. "Startling is the magnanimity of the Bedouin in the religious sacrifice of hospitality. Men who in their other dealings are commonly of so nearly vile, fraudulent, self-serving minds and endless misanthropy. The most honor of a man's life is the people's praise of his bounty" (Arabia Deserta). Doughty, like Ibn Battuta four hundred years before, was able to travel anywhere; he was sure that Muslims would welcome him and give him food and shelter. Similarly, everywhere I went in India, people would stop to talk to me and buy me chais and dinners. These Indians, like Doughty's Arabs, didn't have a lot of money, but they went out of their way to make me feel welcome. Whether it was out of curiosity or genuine kindness, I discovered the real India, engaging merchants, government officials, university students, pilgrims, and Hindu religious priests.

Doughty spent the rest of his life holed up in rain-soaked England, far away from the desert, and wrote of the soul of the Bedouin before dying in obscurity and being forgotten. The shame is that within fifty years of his traveling, the Arab way of life was utterly destroyed by the oil wealth of Arabia. India was becoming a world power in Asia. Would Hinduism succumb to Western Capitalism and wealth, or would it absorb this foreign influence the same as it had absorbed religions, philosophies, and ideals in the past? Would my observations and photographs chronicle a dying age as Doughty chronicled with his Bedouins?

Chapter Fifty: Madurai

Madurai is one of the greatest temple towns in South India. It's also one of the most fortunate cities. For over two thousand years, it was a leading center of Tamil culture, where large gatherings of poets, musicians, and writers would have annual sangmans (literary and musical contests) where they wrote the classics of Tamil literature and music. It served as the capital of the Pandyan dynasty from the seventh to the thirteenth century AD, becoming rich from trade with Rome and China. It was also an important trading city in the fifteenth century with the Vijayanagar Empire and once again served as a capital city for the Nayaka kingdom in the sixteenth and seventeenth centuries.

Today it's famous as the home of the "fish-eyed" goddess Meenakshi temple. What makes this temple complex so special are the twelve huge gopuras (gateways), each over one hundred fifty feet high, crowded with thousands of stucco gods, animals, demons, and mythical creatures in vivid colors. Approaching Madurai by bus is like approaching Chicago; for miles, you see only flat cornfields, and then, out of nowhere, sprouts a row of huge skyscrapers, a fairy Legoland of improbable jagged shapes that fill the flat horizon. Similarly, here you see nothing but rice fields, and out of nowhere are these skyscrapers: multi-colored gopuras which stand out like surreal mountains dwarfing everything below them.

An aerial view of Madurai city from atop of Meenakshi Amman temple.

The temple is unique in that it's one of the few temples dedicated to a goddess (although she does cohabit the shrine with her husband Sundareshvara, the "handsome god" and avatar of Shiva). What I found extremely touching is that every night the temple priests carry the Sundareshvara shrine (the lingam) to the Meenakshi (Parvati) shrine, where they spend the night together.

South India Gopura (author's photo).

(Novice priest to older temple priest, "What is all that rumbling, cries, and moans coming from the Goddesses' shrine? I better see what's happening." Old Priest, "Don't worry, it's only Shiva and Meenakshi enjoying their nightly nuptial bliss. And I wouldn't go in there and disturb them. The last time Shiva was disturbed, He was so angry that he chopped off the head of his son, and when Meenakshi insisted on finding a new head for their son, all they could find was an elephant's head, and Ganesh was the result. Now if Shiva chops your head off, you're out of luck since we don't have any elephants at the temple. However, we do have goats, and a goat's head might suit you since you are very stubborn.")

In the morning, the priests return the shrine to its usual position in the temple (I'm sure that most American women would love this arrangement: adored and worshipped by thousands, daily being dined and bathed, given flowers and sweet-smelling incense and beautiful dresses for special occasions during the daytime. Then in the nighttime, the goddess is serviced by her loving, handsome husband: a perfect recipe for a long-lasting, satisfying, successful marriage) (Eat your heart out, Suzy Cream Cheese!).

The temple has a magnificent thousand-pillar hall (Actually only 985 pillars, but who's counting?) with individually carved columns of lions. There is a huge water tank for the faithful to purify themselves. This is fascinating since the archeologists excavating the Indus Valley Civilization city of Mohenjo-Dara uncovered a huge brick water tank, which they believe was used for ritual bathing. If this is true, then you have an unbroken continuity of original Hinduism that has survived for three millennia. There are other halls, one dedicated to Nandi Shiva's bull and another to the marriage of Shiva and Parvati, where an annual "wedding" festival is held.

Indian bathers in temple water tank (author's photo).

The streets of Madurai are small and clogged with traffic. However, on the side roads, you have the farmers spreading their grain to be trampled by the cars and people who cross over it to loosen the chaff from the grain. This will separate the wheat husk from the chaff without the need of any modern machinery. Here is a true Southern Indian city; the dark-skinned Brahmin caste priests with the three-pronged trident mark of Shiva on their foreheads, the sidewalk shrines where passersby stop for a moment to pray and bring flowers and then go about their business. Madurai at night is totally alive with religious processions, temple music, priests' chanting, the cries of vendors and hawkers, children running naked or sleeping on crude mats right on the sidewalks, and the saintly-looking, stringy-haired holy men who live by an incanting blessing on the faithful for a small fee.

Hinduism won't die out with the machine age; it incorporates the machine. In the streets of Madurai, I came across a small religious procession: a huge statue of Shiva being carried on a cart-like chariot through the back streets of Madurai. This portable statue of Shiva was brighter than any neon sign, and the reason for that was that right behind it, being pulled by an equal number of devotees, was the gas-powered generator that kept the Shiva float ablaze. The town is dotted by small restaurants with their dirty, fly-infested kitchens, but the seating area of these restaurants is plastered with pictures of Christ, Krishna, Ganesh, the mosque in Mecca, Gandhi, JFK, Pope Paul, and a smiling, beautiful Indian model selling Brooke English tea. These restaurants are a trip: the waiter first picks his nose, then holds it and blows out the snot, wiping his nostrils with his stained judah (Judah is a skirt worn by Indian men.) and then giving you a vegetable cake with the same fingers (so much for your appetite).

The old and the new are always at odds with each other: I saw a political rally with a fiery orator haranguing the crowds. He stopped in the middle of his speech, so a religious procession, complete with musicians, chanters, and devotees carrying the god statue, walked right in front of him. He waited until the procession passed and then continued haranguing the crowd without a misstep.

Four little children, all lining up on a main street in Madurai, shitting on the pavement, and a young girl washing her ass at the community water pump. Other little children: two naked boys and one girl in rags, run by, and she says, "Hello." I catch up with them and give them each five pence. At first, they run away but then bravely return, sticking out their hands for the money.

Immediately, they ran off, screaming to their mother, telling her what had happened and how they had gotten money from this strange, bearded foreigner.

The beauty of the Tamil countryside at sunset: the toddy palm trees, the bullock carts, the small villages with their naked children running helter-skelter. Small Tamil girls in tattered clothing, holding restless naked infants, the pungent odor of human waste fertilized fields, and mothers ever-present combing out the lice in their children's hair. Then there is the well-to-do Sikh and his wife, a typical middle-class Indian family, taking their two daughters out, sitting in an American-style ice cream bar having (what else) banana splits.

Chapter Fifty-One: The Hindu Concept of Time

Time, time, time, see what's become of me

While I looked around for my possibilities.

-Simon and Garfunkel, *A Hazy Shade of Winter.*

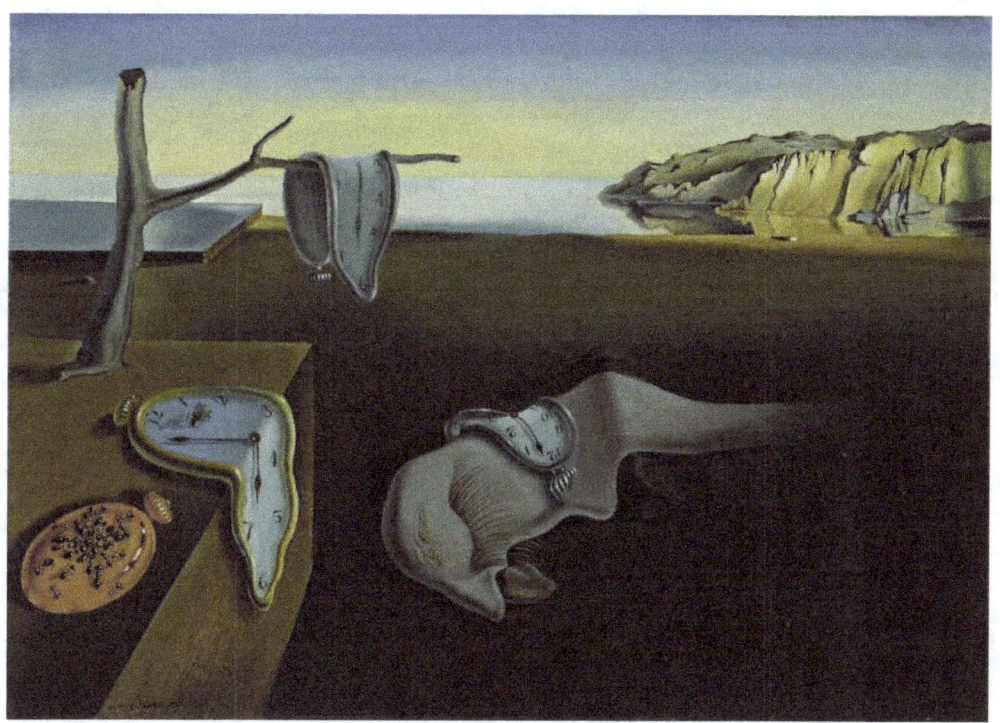

"The Persistence of Memory" by Salvador Dali 1931.

I always felt when I was in rural South India, that time stopped. Everything seemed to be in the present: the omnipresent temple rituals, the recurring daily rhythm of the farmers, and the ever-present enervating heat - nothing seemed to change or progress: everything is now.

Hindus believe that time is cyclical, not linear, as we believe in the West. We believe in progress; things will get better; we will correct the mistakes of the past and build our new utopia in the future. Similarly, Christianity offers eternal life at the Last Judgment, a progression point in linear time.

There are three components of Hindu time, represented by the trinity of Gods: Creation is Brahma; Continuous Existence is Vishnu; and Destruction is Shiva. The cosmos follows these three components, forever renewing itself from birth to destruction in an endless cycle. Hindus, like Buddhists, believe that the physical world is Maya (illusion). So, it is not important to record dates of kings or battles; if it relates to God, then it is important. Rita or Dharma is the cosmic rhythm: from man's heartbeat to the movement of planets to all creation. Dharma, the Eternal Law, protects this rhythm and gives man a way to access it through supra-consciousness.

Time is a mental construct of the senses and perception for man; for god, there is no time. There is only the present for all of eternity. Kalpa is the Hindu word for time, but it also means death (i.e., the world that man experiences). The Hindu gods have a different sense of time: Kalpa is one day in the life of the God Brahma. Interestingly, the Kalpa is divided into day and night; each last for 4.32 billion years, which amazingly is what modern scientists say is the actual age of the Earth. Each Kalpa is divided into one thousand Maha Juga (Large Cycles of Time), and each Maha Juga is subdivided into four Juga (mini cycles) like our year, divided into months and weeks. The first is Satya Juga, the Spiritual or Truthful Age, where man is spiritually close to God in an innocent, childlike manner (think of the Garden of Eden). Next comes Treta Juga, which is one-quarter less truthful (think of the hunter-gatherers, first farmers, and fertility gods). The third, Dvapara Juga is one half less truthful (think of national states, colonial exploitations, and endless wars). The last Kali Juga is only one-quarter truthful. We are presently in the Kali Juga, also called the Age of Materialism (think man exploits nature, mass genocide, and monetary greed). Man thinks only about enriching himself and neglects the spiritual life. Time is money. Man will self-destruct at the end of this age: Shiva will destroy the world and the cycle begins again, just like the Hindu concept of the endless cycle of rebirth.

The soul is immortal, and only if a man discovers the divinity or godhead within himself can he stop the endless reincarnation cycles, unite with God, and stop time. Pure consciousness, one with god, where everything is now and always will be and has always been now.

Chapter Fifty-Two: The Curious Case of Wobble

A Singing Bobble Head

The one thing you notice immediately when you're traveling around India, but especially in South India, is the Indian head wobble. This is basically a head shake from left to right and can signify many different things. A fast and continuous head wobble usually means "I understand." A quick one-time wobble usually means "yes/ ok." A slow, slight wobble with a smile is a sign of friendship or respect.

Why do the Indians use the head wobble? Scholars say the head wobble came from the ancient South Indian dance "Bharat Natyam," where one of the movements the dancer performs is shaking his head left to right, and this signifies "harmony." Another reason why the head wobble is so prevalent is that the Indians don't usually use the words "thank you" and substitute this nonverbal communication in its place. However, the typical Indian does not like to say no, so the nonverbal head wobble, if it's done slowly with a perplexed look, means "I don't know what the hell you're talking about." The interesting thing is that if you hang around Indians that constantly do the head wobble, you'll find yourself unconsciously doing the same when talking to fellow freaks, tourists, or other Indians.

The Indian wobble can be very useful: for example, if you are in a bar and this big, drunk bruiser "gets in your face" for some supposed slight (just because I am chatting up his woman, lighten up, Dude!), you can do a slight continuous wobble with a big grin. Once the bruiser sees this, he'll either think you're a complete idiot (What, Me Worry?) or a crazed psychopath high on PCP; either way, he will conclude it's not worth his effort to punch you out.

Chapter Fifty-Three: Mahabalipuram

I was traveling alone on my way to Pondicherry when I changed buses to see Mahabalipuram. This bus was jammed, but I was befriended by two engineers from Bangalore who were kind enough to share their two-passenger seat with me. One engineer spoke better English than the other, and he told me about the stories behind the grandiose temple and other sites in Mahabalipuram. The complex was spread out, so we decided to see the whole complex by bicycle, and they graciously agreed to pay for mine. They also treated me to my first betel nut experience. So, we all had orange-red teeth when we toured the temple complex. Betel nut is a mild narcotic that is similar to chewing tobacco and is highly addictive and chewed by all classes in India. First, we saw the Patch Rathas (five chariots). "These five sculpted chariots represent," Gorkum said, "the five Pandava brothers, the heroes of the Indian epic the 'Mahabharata'." Gorkum, the talkative engineer, explained that each of these temple chariots was carved out of a single huge boulder.

The smallest chariot is dedicated to Durga (one of Shiva's destructive avatars), and this shows him cutting his head off as a supreme show of sacrifice for mankind. This chariot is fashioned after a wooden tribal shrine like the tribal shrines in Orissa. The next chariot is Arjuna's chariot (Arjuna was the princely hero of the Mahabharata). Here Shiva is depicted with his bull in carving and there is a huge carved Nandi facing this chariot. Off to the right is the Nakal chariot, which Gorkum explained was sculpted to look like the back of an elephant and there was a life-sized stone elephant facing this chariot. The Bhima shrine is unfinished with a row of columns on the ground level but little interior carving. Lastly, the Dharmamaja shrine is the largest and most profusely decorated. Gorkum pointed out the set of two life-sized figures joined in stone depicting Harihara, a God that is half Vishnu with a conical crown and half Shiva with a head of matted hair. All of these five rock-cut chariots are set in a field of huge boulders and one huge, rounded boulder is perched precariously on a small incline. This Gorkum said was Krishna's butterball (I shudder to think what he spread that butter on!).

We then toured the Shore Temple, which is dedicated to Vishnu with two smaller Shiva temples adjoining it. All I can say, in the parlance of a real estate salesman: "location, location, location."

Author with Indian engineer friends, Gorkum (left) and Ashoka (right) at the Shore Temple, Mahabalipuram.

The temple is built on a promontory out into the ocean with waves splashing the sea boundary wall, which consists of a row of Nanda bulls. The interior features a huge reclining Vishnu, a polished and faceted lingam (Shiva), and a stone sculpture of another composite god Samoskanda (Shiva-Parvati and their two sons Shanda and Elephant-headed Genesha; four-in-one surely beats our Father, Son, and Holy Ghost Trinity God!).

We pedaled up a high hill to an ancient, ruined lighthouse, and the view was breathtaking. On one side, toddy palm trees, huge boulders, the Five Chariots and some distant temples, and on the other side, the blue sea lapping the front of the seventh-century Pahlavi dynasty Shore Temple.

We stopped for chai, and I asked about their personal lives. Gorkum and Ashoka were engineers in a small company. They were both unmarried and had gone to Bangalore Technical University. These are middle-class Indians who are not unlike their Western counterparts. Gorkum was a structural engineer, and Ashoka was an electrical engineer. They remained in Bangalore after their schooling because that's where the opportunities are. They were building small offices and hoped to get experience so that they could get jobs with a larger firm. They were articulate, bright, and knew and respected their Indian heritage. Their future was in India, not the UK or the States.

It was now about five in the afternoon, and I thought we were finished with our tour. Gorkum looked at Ashoka and grinned, "We are saving the best for last." We peddled into the town center and off on a small road, we came to a huge carved rock called "Descent of the Ganges."

"Descent of the Ganges" Mahabalipuram (Photo by Bernard Gagnon, released to GNU Free Documentation License, Version 1.2).

This monolithic basalt boulder was cleft in two with phantasmagorical carvings of gods, animals, and temples. On one side of the cleft are two life-sized elephants. The top was divided with ribbed stone resembling hair, and there were mythical beings below it on both sides of the cleft. "What is this?" I asked. Gorkum now told me the story of the birth of the Ganges, India's most sacred river. "There was a famous Hindu holy man Bhagiratha, who wanted to spread holy water on the ashes of his disgraced ancestors. These unfortunate souls had defied the god Vishnu and he struck them dead. Bhagiratha knew that this holy water would save their eternal souls from damnation, so he prayed to the gods to get this holy river to come to earth. His prayers were answered, but the mighty river fell from the Heavens with such force that it would destroy everything on earth. So, Shiva in Heaven took pity on man by letting his matted hair slow the single thrust into hundreds of streams and saved humankind. You can see one stream of the Ganges when it rains and the water channels into the cleft at the bottom." I don't think I'll ever look at these matted Hindu sadhus the same ever again. They are a living re-enactment of Shiva's stone-matted hair.

We returned to our bicycles, and they invited me to dinner. We had a highly spiced vegetarian meal of lentils, lady fingers (okra), and chickpeas in a Madras curry with rice served on a banana leaf. While we were eating, I started to talk about poverty and politics: "Do you think that India would be better off under communism?" Both looked at each other in amazement, and Gorkum said, "India does not need Communism; just look at what happened in Calcutta ten years ago: thousands killed, the economy at a standstill, and the majority of the people suffered terribly. Is that what you are proposing?"

"I see so much poverty; people dying of starvation, lying dead in the streets. Almost seventy percent of the country is illiterate, and just three years ago, twenty-five thousand people starved to death in Bihar." Gorkum replied, "India has a middle class in population, the size of all of the UK, and it's growing by leaps and bounds. Sure, there's poverty, but my parents weren't rich, and they saved so that I could get a good education. I am also helping my younger brother so he too can go to university. Soon I'll marry and I'll be looking not only for a beautiful girl, but a smart one, who has a university degree. We will then have two salaries, so that we can buy a car and be able to provide for our mothers and fathers in their old age." This sounded like my own background, and I could not argue against this. We in America have our own underclass: urban poor blacks, illiterate hillbillies, and isolated American Indians. It was almost like "the kettle calling the pot black." America should solve its own problems before we put our prejudices on other people.

I thanked them both for their generosity and knew in my heart that they would succeed and maybe their story will be India's story in the future.

Chapter Fifty-Four: "Dawning of the New Age"

"This is the dawning of the age of Aquarius."

-"Aquarius" from the soundtrack of Broadway Musical "*Hair.*"

Helene Blavatsky, the founder of Theosophy.

Growing up in the 1960s and 1970s, I felt like many of my generation: we could do anything. We are living in the greatest country in the world. The American Empire is at its zenith. We can remake society so that there is no poverty, racial injustice, and opportunities for everyone. Many of us were rejecting the comfortable way of life, choosing to "get back to nature," living in communes, and raising our own food; we saw a new age dawning where the human potential possibilities were limitless. Others believed that you could unlock the mysteries of perception and knowledge through yoga or mind-enhancing drugs. The wisdom of eastern religions and the Hindu concept of self-mastery of the mind attracted scholars, poets, and rock stars. Allen Ginsburg and the Beatles went to India and found gurus to realize the hidden potential of the divinity in each of us.

In India, I met dozens of seekers who were dissatisfied with their lives back home and wanted to discover a new path. Their philosophy of life was a pastiche: a jumble of living the "country life," the brotherhood of man, belief in a pantheistic spirituality that encompassed all living things, use of tarot cards or astrology to divine the future, or to practice a secret occult ritual to get spiritual enlightenment. Freaks carried with them "The Tibetan Book of the Dead," attached themselves to an ashram, and consulted Hindu soothsayers and fortune-tellers. They saw themselves as trailblazers, but in reality, they were in a long line of Western predecessors who had espoused identical views.

In eighteenth-century Europe, the Swedenborgians believed that you could communicate with angels through occult practices, and these angels would show them a new age of brotherhood. However, the most interesting "sect" was the Theosophists. This was founded by a Russian immigrant, Helene Blavatsky, in New York City in 1875. Blavatsky was an occultist and medium who communicated with an ancient and secret brotherhood called "the Masters." The Masters possessed age-old wisdom and supernatural powers. They telepathically told the divine Ms. B that they were reviving an ancient universal religion that would replace all present-day religions. This new religion would bring spiritual emancipation, universal brotherhood, and social improvement to peoples' lives. She wrote two books: "Isis Unveiled" and "The Secret Doctrine." These books revealed the Masters' plan for mankind. The books borrow bits and pieces of Hinduism, such as reincarnation and the spiritual mastery of the mind; all based, however, on the Masters' revealed instructions and not on vigorous Hindu yogic disciplines. Her teachings of the brotherhood of man and revitalization of religious, ethical, and moral ideals attracted thousands, especially members of the upper class, who generously funded her society.

Through Helen Blavatsky's charismatic leadership, the Theosophy Movement was one hundred thousand strong at the time of her death in 1891. Her influence was profound in numerous fields. She single-handedly transformed Theosophy from a "spiritual religion" to an all-encompassing cosmology of human evolution. Man can now master the innate divinity within all of us by following her guidelines of Theosophy. She took outdated crystal ball occultism and transformed it with tenets of Hinduism and Buddhism. Women were given equal status with men in this movement, and many women became inspiring spiritual leaders.

Her race and language ideals, extolling the accomplishments of the Indo-European ancestors, influenced Gandhi and Nehru since the Aryan conquerors established the great Indian civilization and subsequently spread to Europe and the Americas. India was the crucible for all later Indo-European achievements; this new-found pride of being an Indian greatly influenced the independence movement for a free India.

Spiritual prophet, flower child, or fraud- any of these descriptions would be true for Madame Blavatsky at different times in her life. As far as being a fraud with her Secret Masters, one critic stated that Madame Blavatsky invented the Ancient Masters, who explained the mysteries of the universe, because she felt that as a woman no one would listen to her. They would listen to great male authorities like the "Hidden Masters."

As I mentioned above, the "New Age" believers took her ideas of the self-mastery of the Mind deeper, studying Hindi Yogic techniques, spawning the Hare Krishna Movement and imitating Blavatsky's occult practices to divine the future. The West learned about the mysteries and theology of Indian Hinduism from her books and teachings. Her revival of Buddhist philosophy gave emphasis to studying Zen Buddhism and the founding of Transcendental Meditation. Blavatsky herself became a Buddhist while staying in Ceylon.

After she became a Buddhist, she preached love and brotherhood of man and would fit right in at Woodstock. With the decline of the Theosophical Society, she is fading into obscurity, but all of the new age people with their tarot cards, crystal balls, and vague ideas of the brotherhood of all people should rightly credit her as the Mother of their movement.

For our generation, what started as a Golden Age of Optimism under the "Camelot" years of JFK to the "Great Society" of LBJ, with achievements such as starting the Peace Corps, rebuilding our inner cities, ending rural Appalachian poverty and landing a man on the Moon. However, suddenly the promise of the American Dream turned into the American Nightmare: a charnel house of war, horrific assassinations of the Kennedys and Martin Luther King and the destructive and divisive race riots.

The "Age of Aquarius" is dawning, foretelling startling technological advancements and promising a renewed spiritual regeneration, similar to Blavatsky's vision in the late nineteenth century. Will Americans embrace this "New Age," truly becoming John Winthrop's "Shining City on the Hill" or will we implode from social injustice, class wars and failure of will like the Roman Empire did before us?

Chapter Fifty-Five: Srirangam Temple Complex

Srirangam Temple Complex 1870 (unknown photographer).

I had been following my guidebook, traveling on over-crowded dusty buses from one obscure temple town to the next. Everything seems so changeless; these temples seem to have been here for eons. Then I arrived on Srirangam Island. Here was a huge complex spread out over 148 acres with 21 huge gateways (gopuras), all profusely decorated with garish colors and innumerable gods. Srirangam shows how important the religious complex is and the extraordinary efforts to constantly renew it. The main temple: Raagantha is dedicated to Vishnu (not Shiva as is usual), and his central shrine is Vishnu as Raagantha, reclining on a golden cosmic cobra.

The original temple was destroyed by the Delhi Sultanate in the tenth century AD. It was restored slowly, finally completed in the fourteenth century, with further additions made in the seventeenth century; gateways' construction finished in the twentieth century. Just like in medieval

Germany, the present Cologne Cathedral was built on the ruins of a burned-down Romanesque church. The Gothic church that survives today was started in the fourteenth century. Every print you see of medieval Cologne shows a primitive crane atop one of the bases of the yet-to-be-built spires. Wars, lack of funding, and plague slowed the work, but the people persisted. It was their duty to God to give him a magnificent church. Cologne Cathedral was finally finished in 1846 (after 500 years) and was the only large building to survive the Allied bombings that flattened the rest of the city.

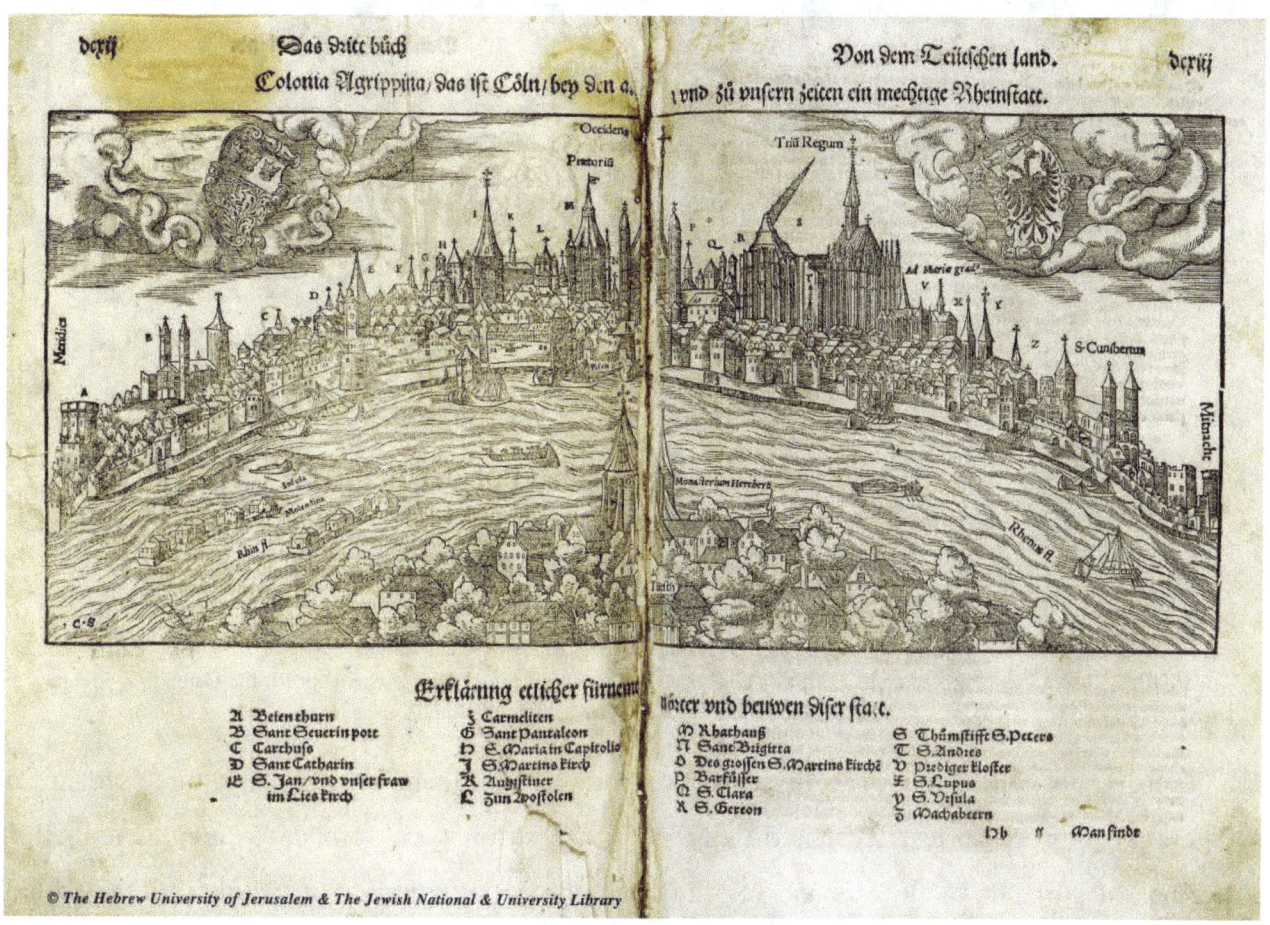

Cologne in the 16th century: the Cathedral is shown on the top right page with a huge medieval crane atop one of bases of the unfinished façade.

Srirangam Island is formed by the confluence of the Kaveri and Kolidam rivers. The Kaveri is one of the sacred rivers of India, named after Brahma's daughter. The Cholas, who ruled from the ninth to the thirteenth century AD, built great temples all along the Kaveri banks and developed irrigation projects that made the region around Srirangam the rice bowl of Southern India. Srirangam attracted many sages, gurus, and philosophers. In the eleventh century AD, the Indian philosopher Ramanujan lived there and developed "Bhakti" yoga, a form of yoga which emphasizes personal devotion and is widely practiced all over the world today.

Here in this US Army photo taken in April 1945, you can see the utter ruin of Cologne, except for the Cathedral, which stands proud and undamaged. (Public Domain)

There are seven boundary walls surrounding the temple complex: the first three are full of white-clad pilgrims, priests with red-painted pitchforks on their foreheads, merchants selling offerings of garlands of flowers and religious pictures, and hundreds of wandering matted-hair sadhus. (The other four boundary walls are for Hindus only.) This is what medieval Cologne must have been like, and I felt as though I was stepping out of a time machine into the sights, sounds, smells, and religious atmosphere of fourteenth-century Cologne. Especially impressive is the magnificent Seshagerirayer Hall with its larger-than-life rearing stone horses, trampling evil spirits beneath their hoofs.

Seshagerirayer Horses of Srirangam Temple.

I spent two days here, wandering the streets, imbuing the religious fervor: faith dominated every aspect of the devotees' life and, for a brief time, saw how my ancestors had lived and ruminated on what we had lost in our modern materialistic Western Civilization.

Chapter Fifty-Six: Beedis

"If you got 'um, smoke 'um." John Wayne talking to his battle-weary soldiers, telling them it's OK to smoke in a WWII combat action film.

When I was in college, the "powers-to-be" developed a vegetable cigarette, purportedly to be a safer alternative to tobacco cigarettes. This product never lasted very long because when smoking, it smelled like a cross between rotten eggs and overcooked cabbage. Furthermore, it had an unpleasant taste and, of course, no pleasing nicotine high. It reminded me of New York City tenement walkup apartment buildings. You no sooner start to go up the stairs, than the smell of cooked cabbage comes wafting down the hallways. It doesn't really matter what ethnic group lives in the tenement; they always have the same over-powering cooked cabbage odor.

In India, the most popular "cigarette" is the tobacco leaf beedi. You take the "tendu" tobacco leaf, dry it for a week and fill it with tobacco flakes and powder. Then you tie it at one end with a string to keep it together. It, too, has a strong odor, but it isn't unpleasant to smoke. Beedis are dirt cheap, and each beedi is hand-rolled; most companies farm out the ingredients to enterprising individuals for a small-time home cottage industry. When I was in India, everyone, Indians and freaks alike, smoked beedis. Beedis is the most popular cigarette and employs three million workers making these little cigarettes.

The workers, mostly women, hand cut the leaves using scissors and a metal stencil guide. After cutting a sufficient number of wrappers, they will move on to roll approximately 1,000 beedis each per day.

In India, the average wage for a worker doing unskilled manual labor or farm labor is about fifty cents per 8-hour day. Beedis cost about one cent for a ten beedis pack, which is the usual way they are sold. They satisfy a need at a price the average Indian laborer can afford.

Beedis in their distinctive packaging. In the 1970s they were about one US cent per pack (Ten beedis in a pack).

Beedis, unlike normal tobacco cigarettes, go out if not puffed regularly and must be relit frequently. The lesson you learn from this is: if you constantly need to relight your beedi, it means you are talking too much and not listening enough.

Chapter Fifty-Seven: Jesus as the First Freak

In 1887, a Russian explorer named Nicholas Notovitch visited Hemis Monastery in the Indian province of Ladakh. Ladakh is known as "Little Tibet" because this isolated northern region professes Tibetan Buddhism and follows the Tibetan way of life (pre-communist Tibet). There, a monk showed Notovitch two hand-written sutras over two-thousand years old that purportedly tell of Jesus Christ's visit to India.

Hemis Monastery in Ladakh, India.

Jerusalem, in the first century AD, was a thriving commercial and religious center. Many Romans imported their religion from the Near East. For example, Mithraism is the worship of the "sacred bull" and was very popular with the Roman soldiers. The cult of Isis from Egypt was a popular mystery religion with the men and especially the women of the Roman ruling classes. It wouldn't be unheard of if an Indian fakir traveled to Jerusalem, crossing the Arabian Sea with the monsoon winds to the Horn of Africa and then by camel caravan to Egypt and onto Jerusalem because it was a melting pot of religious fervor. Here, the fakir could spread his religion and teach the yoga discipline to attain an Everlasting Life.

There is nothing in the Bible concerning the sojourn Jesus had for 40 days and nights in the desert. Buddha discovered Nirvana after sitting under a banyan tree for 49 days. Could Jesus have mediated and accessed a prototype yoga similar to what Sri Aurobindo developed two millennia later, which doesn't involve physical exercises as does most yoga but rather an inner examination of the mind achieved by looking inward to the divine? I will explain integral yoga in detail in my chapters on Sri Aurobindo and Auroville. Looking at Jesus' life and teachings through this lens adds an extra dimension to our understanding of Him.

I thought of Sri Sathya Baba, who believed himself divine, performed miracles, did "good works," and said he would be reborn (come again) as an avatar of God. This could also describe Jesus' life. Jesus went into the desert and came back with a mission from God. Could Jesus have met a holy Indian fakir (spiritual guide) in the desert or followed an Indian fakir into the desert and discovered the divine in Himself? If every man is divine, every man has the potential to be one with God; hence, the Son of God could, via yoga, access the pure conscious state. He has attained pure consciousness; He is one with the divine, but He is also a man. "My God, why hast thou forsaken me?" he cries out on the cross. Is this a moment of doubt or a moment of sorrowful resignation that he didn't convey his notion of accessing the inner divine and now must be reborn (Second Coming) where the Kingdom of God will reign on Earth? The Second Coming will show how every man can have an everlasting life through discovering the divine in himself.

If the above sounds like an episode from the "Twilight Zone," it gets even stranger. As I was doing my research, I came across the "Gospel of Mary;" this is an apocryphal gospel that was discovered in 1895 in Egypt. The gospel is incomplete; what remains is half of the gospel on a torn papyrus written in Sahidic Coptic, the Egyptian language at that time. Two other fragments of the Mary gospel were also discovered in the early 20th century; however, these were written in Greek, but they all date to the same time, which is sometime in the 2nd century AD.

The Gospel of Mary is written in a question-and-answer format, where Jesus speaks with Mary Magdalene and Mary speaks with the original 12 disciples. The first and middle parts of the gospel are missing in all three versions that were found. It starts with Christ appearing to Mary in a vision after his crucifixion. Mary asks Jesus was it the soul or the spirit that allowed her to see him. Jesus answered it was the mind that allowed it. By looking inwards into your mind, you can access the divine. Here, the message of Buddhism and Hinduism comes forth: it is through self-examination of the mind that permits union with the divine. Jesus says, "The Son of Man and the Child of True Humanity lives within each of you." This is a clear reference to the divine, which can be accessed through introspection to achieve Nirvana or cessation of the reincarnation cycle.

Part of the Gospel of Mary on this torn fragment of papyrus, 2nd century AD
(Ashmolean Museum Oxford, Public Domain)

Mary then asks about sin and Jesus replies there is no sin. Sin is when the body is out of balance and attached to worldly things: greed, desires, and material goods cause sin. Again, the parallel to Buddhism, where suffering is caused by desires and attachment to the world. Jesus goes on to say that all these corporal things will pass because they are not real. Buddhism preaches that all life is maya (illusion).

The gospel goes into great detail on the struggles of the soul to overcome these worldly temptations to unite with the supreme consciousness (the divine). Once the soul has achieved this unity with the divine, which Jesus calls "silent restfulness," the mind and the soul are at peace.

"Silent restfulness" can be interpreted as the extinguishment of the individual personality, absorbed by the supreme consciousness, the Nirvana of Buddhism.

The very end of the Mary gospel shows the patriarchy revolting against Mary. Peter says how could God trust this to a woman when he did not tell the secret wisdom to his loyal male disciples. Mary was pushed aside and the whole direction of Christianity focused on salvation through Christ's sacrifice instead of becoming one with the divine by looking inward to your own mind.

The New Testament is also completely blank about Jesus' life from the ages of 13 to 26. These Buddhist sutras fill in this timeframe, describing in detail where Jesus visited in India and how he took lessons from Hindu and Buddhist sages during his time away from home. Jesus spent his early years in India in Puri, learning Hindu religious yoga techniques and the Hindu religion. He then went on to Ladakh and Tibet, where He studied the Buddhist Eightfold Path to enlightenment. According to Notovitch, what Jesus learned was accessing the divine in Himself. Like the Hindu sages, Jesus learned how to levitate (walking on water as mentioned in the Bible), perform miracles (raising Lazarus from the dead and changing water into wine), and master his mind "melding with the godhead" ("I am the Son of God.").

Notovitch had a monk translate these sutras from the Tibetan into French. Then he wrote a book about these truths called "The Unknown Life of Jesus Christ" and published it in 1894 in Paris. He portrayed Jesus as a wandering, penniless Sadhu absorbing the mysteries of Hinduism and Buddhism. Jesus then returned to Israel, proclaiming himself to be the Son of God, based on the self-mastery of his mind, where he accessed the divine. "Believe in Me and I will show you the way to the Way to Salvation." (i.e., to be one with the Divine). Jesus was the first freak!

Notovitch gained immediate notoriety (as well as a whole lot of money). He was eventually proved a fake (not a fakir) and a liar. British officials, religious leaders, famous anthropologists, and renowned Buddhist scholars all visited Hemis to examine these sutras. There were, of course, no Buddhist sutras on Jesus Christ and the Tibetan abbot of the monastery had never spoken to or heard of Notovitch. However, Notovitch did manage to convince some Indian scholars and the American mystic, painter, and set designer Nicholas Roerich that this was the "gospel" truth.

Various ethnic depictions of Jesus Christ. Any of these depictions of Jesus could be of a Hindu Sadhu (if you lose the halo).

Author's photograph of Indian Sadhu.

In 1922, Swami Abhedananda, a renowned yogi master and teacher, visited Hemis monastery and talked with monks there who showed him a copy of the Jesus sutras. The Swami had this translated and published his findings in Bangali. The monks also told him that the original manuscript is in a Tibetan monastery. Nicholas Roerich corroborated the Swami's story; again, talking with monks in Hemes monastery and they told him that Jesus spent six years in Nepal and Tibet studying Buddhism. I find it hard to believe that this charlatan can continue to deceive otherwise scholarly and learned academics.

His book is still in print and selling copies; all I can think of is P.T. Barnum's sign in the middle of his circus: "This way to the Egress." The gullible blindly followed the sign, hoping to see an exotic animal. Instead, they found themselves outside of the circus and having to pay a second admission fee to re-enter the circus.

Chapter Fifty-Eight: From Idol to Figurehead

Doc: Tell me, Future Boy, who's President of the United States in 1985?

Marty: Ronald Reagan.

Doc: Ronald Reagan? The actor? [rolls his eyes] Ha!

-"Back to the Future," 1985

While I traveled around South India, I always tried to talk to students: "What they wanted, what they were concerned with, and what they thought of India?" What I found was a little disconcerting; the majority of these students were not focusing on their studies but were very concerned about a popular Indian actor turned politician. This actor, Maruthur Gopalan Ramachandra (known as MGR), has been a heartthrob for over twenty years. His movies are highly profitable, and he parlayed this fame by getting into politics. Once there, he accused the other members of his party, the ruling DNK, of corruption. Because of this, he was expelled from the Party. Now the students were rioting and demonstrating for him, even stopping buses to get the riders to sign petitions for his reinstatement. They did this not for his anti-corruption stand but because he was a glamorous movie star, a hero of the people.

MGR as seen on an Indian Postage stamp.

Movies are the most popular entertainment in India. Students even burnt down a theater that wouldn't give them discounts on admission fees. Every little town in India has one or two temples and at least one movie theater.

Getting back to MGR, he did simply fine. He went on to make his highest-grossing movie in 1973, "Ulgan Sutrum Vaalibban," which was filmed at exotic locations all over Southeast Asia. This movie portrayed him as a virtuous man that stood up for the people. He was also one of the few actors that was extremely popular with both the young and old Indians. As for his political career, he founded a rival party, ADMK, that soon achieved power, and MGR became prime minister of Tamil Nadu.

"Tell me, Ashoka, my student friend, who is the prime minister of Tamil Nadu?" Ashoka answers, "MGR, of course." "MGR, the popular actor? "Yes." (Rolling my eyes) "Ha!"

Auroville

The Mother 1950

Nationalist Freedom Fighter Aurobindo "mug shot" in British India jail 1908.

Chapter Fifty-Nine: Pondicherry - France in India

Pondicherry Waterfront 1900 (Public Domain)

I arrived on a dusty, overcrowded bus that had followed the seacoast to Pondicherry, which was bordered by a cement promenade. Old town Pondicherry is filled with French-style villas with high walls, dripping bougainvillea enclosing heavily shaded gardens and houses with intricate wrought-iron balconies. The streets are narrow and lined with two-story light grey and red painted buildings set off by palms and frangipane trees. It is very quiet, like an early Sunday morning in a Cote d'Azur French village. The buildings still have their French surnames, but the French-named schools are now filled with dark-skinned Dravidians, but here and there, you see the occasional blonde Gaelic child. There are bicycles everywhere, even some of the expensive French racer styles. When you see Europeans, they are almost always French, speaking their flowery "Je ne sais quoi." In a large square, there is a beautiful Colonial-style building shaded by huge frangipane trees, which houses the "Allegiance Francoise." Walking around the town, you see beautiful, manicured squares with bubbling fountains and shaded trees. A small park has a statue of St. Louis. In the park, Indians play European-style bowling, similar to bocci as well as tennis. The huge, white-washed church named after St. Louis is typically French: fleur-de-lis bedecked and the large cast Virgin with the peculiarly French halo of gold stars surrounding her head. The church still holds service in French and many of the clergy are old French nationals who chose to remain in India after Pondicherry was returned to India in 1951. The French have laid out the old town like many French village towns, converging on a roundabout with a gaily painted L'Arc de Triumph in the middle, surrounded by French-cut shrubbery and benches for contemplation.

I walked around for about an hour and a half, letting the quiet French atmosphere sink in. Pondicherry was a former French colony for two hundred years before they gave it back to India. I was struck by the quality of the light shining pristinely on the two-story buildings, the deserted streets, and the blue ocean as a backdrop. This created a surrealistic feeling, the same as one gets from looking at a de Chirico painting. On the concrete promenade, I saw one Frenchman with red hair, the red changing to purple in the waning afternoon, and this further heightened the surrealistic feeling. The Indians I encountered were all dressed in white with long black hair, quietly discussing among themselves: an atmosphere not unlike what Plato's academy in Athens would have been like. There were also freaks wandering the streets in rainbow colors, heading toward the beach.

It was a bright sunny afternoon when I finally got an aged rickshaw driver to take me to the ashram at Auroville. He brought me to the main office, which was closed, so we went to the guesthouse, which was part of a larger hall. When I entered the guesthouse, an Indian asked for my card, which I didn't have ("Badges, we don't need no stinking badges" {"Treasure of Sierra Madre"}) and then sent me back to another office, where I could procure the card, to gain admittance to the ashram. I finally paid for the card, but when I returned to the guesthouse to get it stamped, there was no one there. So, I walked around until I could find someone to authenticate the card - no luck (All dressed up and nowhere to go!).

When I got back to the guesthouse, it was like an old-time comedy of errors, viewed from the top. I knew no one and was desperate to find a friend, but I went in and out for over an hour without meeting anyone. The guesthouse was a concrete box partitioned with flimsy walls that didn't even reach the ceiling. Over the top of the room dividing wall, I heard a familiar voice: it was my French friend Anthony, with whom I had spent weeks in Cochin and Kovalam Beach, speaking with another traveler. I went next door, reunited with Anthony and another Frenchman, Ricardo, who had shoulder-length blonde hair. We celebrated our reunion with a large blunt of Manali grass. Ricardo told us he had been there two weeks and hadn't met a soul either. Anthony then asked him in French what he had done for those two weeks. He replied, "I sleep a lot."

The next day Anthony and I rented bicycles and were off to visit Auroville. But first, we had to find our way to this mystical Oz. We stopped in a small boutique called "Auro Creations," which was managed by three women: a young Burmese girl, an older English woman, and a "Mama Cass," a heavily-set American. They told us they made all of the dresses and clothes by hand that they sold there and were plowing the money back into the shop for more materials to expand their operations. As with all enterprises in Auroville, it was community-owned: a percent of their profits went to the ashram to fund Auroville's building and educational programs. They gave us directions and off we went down the yellow brick road. We stopped at a coffee shop; only in the south of India do people drink coffee in great quantities, perhaps reflecting the French influence in that area. Our waiter was a little Tamil guy who was the best showman that I had ever seen, serving coffee. He poured the milk with one extended hand all of the way down to his other extended hand, which was down by his knees holding the coffee. His extended arm had the milk arcing down into the coffee. It was pure poetry-in-motion. I snapped a photograph and promised to send it to him, which made him very happy.

Starbuck Barista, eat your heart out! You ain't got nothing on this Tamil coffee pourer.
(Author's photograph)

After many misadventures, bicycling in and out of many small Tamil villages for two hours, we finally found Aspiration, one of the small villages of Auroville. Aspiration is set near the beach and consists of a few brick and cinderblock modern buildings and dozens of thatched huts. This is a "town" with many civic buildings: a modernistic school, which we visited and talked with many of the school children as best we could. They had a modern cafeteria complete with lounges for sitting where we met some of the inhabitants. Afterwards we walked around the village, which consisted of thatched walls and roofed residences, butted up to a large Tamil village.

Here everything was very barren, just the red earth and a few large trees which shaded our path. We bicycled through the Tamil village down to the sea. There we found a beautiful beach: children playing with their mothers, women collecting cow dung which they kneaded into paddies for cooking, men drying fish and repairing nets in the midday sun. We went into the water, which was very gentle, clear, and perfect for swimming. We left the beach as the sun was setting, pedaling through the little Tamil villages and trying to find our way home before darkness set in. I reflected as we peddled back on the pervading energy and a sense of purpose that I found in Auroville.

Auro Beach: Creative Commons: Attribution-Share-Alike 3.0 free to use with attribution of author Sanyam Bahga.

I thought back that I had tried five times to see Sri Sathya Baba and he was unavailable. Yet I decided to wait five minutes before leaving and found that couple that explained everything about their visionary community.

Anthony and I moved out of the Ashram into a beautiful colonial hotel in the old French district of Pondicherry, overlooking the ocean. We had a little alcove with a balcony accessed by huge French doors. At night we could see through the French doors the full moon bathing its fluorescence on everything in the room. There we had a comic misadventure: dragging our mattresses out onto the roof to capture the cooling ocean breezes only to drag them back an hour later when the heavy rains started.

Chapter Sixty: Sri Aurobindo, the Mother, and Auroville

Sri Aurobindo 1900

Sri Aurobindo was a larger-than-life personality: A nationalist freedom fighter, a polemist against the British, and most importantly, a philosophical holy spiritual leader. What I found out is that Aurobindo is in a long line of Indian holy men who tapped into their subconsciousness to achieve a state of pure consciousness.

Shirdi Sai Baba, in the 19th century, emphasized love and patience as a means of accessing the divine, which is in all of us. He followed in the tradition of the Sufis, whose mystical doctrine states the light of God is in everyone. Furthermore, the essence of Hinduism, the Bhagavad Gita states that everyone has the godhead within; you need the third eye (introspection) to look inward to achieve self-realization. Sri Sathya Baba, in our time, achieved this pure consciousness through love and compassion for his fellow man. Being selfless leads to self-realization, which is the control of consciousness. (See my chapter "Waiting For Godot" for more detailed portraits of these two holy men.)

Sri Aurobindo takes it further by developing a yoga, "integral," that allows you to achieve the highest experience of reality: the pure consciousness that goes beyond the ordinary mind to the "Overmind," which is the divine. Aurobindo utilizes Western philosophy and ancient Vedic and Upanishad scripture to buttress his integral yoga. Moreover, Aurobindo carries it to a new level, stating that the man of pure consciousness will evolve into a new being: a God. His philosophy posits three states of being: the outer being, man in his current physical existence; the inner being, integral yoga opens the mind, and he looks inward to discover his divinity; the psychic being, divine essence crosses over to the Overmind, which is God.

Integral yoga is not physical exercise but an introspection of your life. It emphasizes work (serving God through devoted service); analysis, observation, and knowledge (using intuition to look inward) and divine love (chanting the praises of God). A central doctrine is "The Triple Way," peace, calmness, and control of the body. To achieve the above, you must practice the seven quadrants: calmness, primordial energy, inward knowledge, control of the body, work as a devotion to God, understanding of Brahman (ultimate reality), and self-realization (attainment of the godhead).

All of these holy men were able to attain a level of pure consciousness. Some developed spiritual guides, and others turned to the world, helping people through good works, building hospitals, and water projects. Still others broke through dogma, ritual, and creed to show there is only one God and how you can be at one with Him. This striving for self-realization and work as a devotion to God is what I saw in Auroville. The name means "City of the Dawn," a new beginning, a place you can live in peace and harmony with all races.

The Mother (on Indian Postal stamp).

Auroville was conceived by Aurobindo's fellow guru, a French woman named Mirra Alfassa, who everyone calls the Mother. She founded the Sri Aurobindo Ashram, started the first school to teach integral yoga, and founded this new city. In a way, she is like St. Paul, spreading the message of Jesus Christ to all the people of the world, not just the Jews, in this case, Indians. The Mother created this "New Jerusalem" for all the races to live in harmony and achieve their individual self-realization.

St. John of Patmos watches God descending the New Jerusalem in a 14th century French tapestry

Auroville is an amorphous complex of small villages: Far Out Beach, Aspiration, and Forecomers are the ones I visited. It was envisioned as a spiritual community for up to fifty thousand people; there are about five hundred people now: half were French, German, and American, and the rest were middle-class Hindus. The important message was that they might be small in numbers, but they were dedicated to building this community and finding themselves, all striving for Sri Aurobindo's religious vision. Most have a beautiful seaside location with a view of gentle surf, surrounded by small Tamil fishing and farming communities. The closest ideal to Auroville would be a medieval monastery: a self-sufficient community where everyone has a duty to perform and yet you still have time to pursue your individual spiritual quest. Unlike the monastery, there is no central authority; this is much more decentralized. If you have an idea that would benefit the community: go for it. There is also an all-hands-on, can-do attitude that permeates this society. One individual thought they were paying too much for cooking gas, so he is now building a solar cooker as a solution. Another saw the wastefulness of the forestry program (a good source of income for the community) and started techniques implemented in West Germany to improve yields, clear-cutting, and an aggressive new-growth initiative.

This is a working community, people who performed their 9 to 5 jobs and then chipped in to build schools, meeting houses, and residential homes. No one owns anything, there is no money; when you work, you are given a ticket which is debited for food and other necessities. You can stay as long as you want, but you must contribute through building, teaching, or volunteering.

Would Auroville have the sustaining commitment to keep the original vision alive? Or would it be like a rehab center - you fly in for two weeks, take a yoga course, feel renewed, and leave? Or could it become a beacon for lost souls from all over the world to put in the hard work and achieve individual inner peace? In my next few chapters, I will share the experiences, hopes, dreams, and disillusionments of some of the pioneers in Auroville.

Chapter Sixty-One: Ray - Build It and They Will Come

When the wagons leave the city

For the forest and further on

Painted wagons of the morning

Dusty roads where they have gone

                       -"Theme for an Imaginary Western": Mountain

Self Portrait: Thomas Eakins (Public Domain).

I had gotten my ticket for entrance to Auroville (now I can finally see Mickey, Donald, and the Fairy Tale Princess), but it wasn't stamped. So, I still couldn't enter the Ashram buildings. I felt like a guy at a Chinese Laundry who had lost his dry-cleaning stub, and the owner was adamant, "no tickee, no shirtee." I walked around the old town and saw this long black-haired freak sitting on the steps of an Indian house, playing a sitar. I hadn't met anyone from the Ashram, and I had so many questions that I wanted to discuss with a member. I approached him and asked him if he was an ashram member, and he said yes.

This is his story in his own words: "I'm Ray Walker and I come from a small town outside of Boulder, Colorado. I came to India because I couldn't take the government establishment. Nixon and his cronies have screwed everybody. All I wanted to do was make my pottery, live like a hermit in the mountains, and to Hell with everyone else! I had heard that India was cheap, but what really convinced me was this chick back home, Diane. I had met her when I was taking yoga classes; she raved about Sri Aurobindo and his integral yoga. She split for India, but before she left, she laid this book on me, 'The Adventure of Consciousness.' After reading it, I wanted to see this place for myself.

"I got here about a year and a half ago; there were only about 250 people living here and about half were Indian. Meanwhile, Diane had long since split for other parts of India. The lodging and food are cheap here, but to stay, you must do work for the community and be committed to the principles of Sri Aurobindo's teachings. Right away, I liked the spirit of the place. The idea of each person pursuing his own destiny and yet united in trying to live on a 'new consciousness level.'

I really had no skills other than making pottery. Then it hit me: I would build a pottery kiln to be used by the community. I worked steadily for about two months, building the kiln, finding the whetstone and clays. Then I realized we really needed a building to create, house, and store all these things. I worked like a madman, digging earth, moving it, bringing bricks, and laying out a cement foundation, all in the hundred-plus Fahrenheit sun. I was sick the whole of the next week and laid up in bed with heatstroke. Finally, an American girl, Megan, offered to help and slowly the building went up. I lived on site for eight months, but now I live with an Indian family, who are also Ashram members.

"I gave up my physical yoga because it was just too strenuous with my work. However, as you can see, I took up the sitar. I bought a good used sitar, and although I'm not very proficient, it's a hell of a difference from a guitar, which I can play. It does give me a very relaxed feeling when I pick away at it.

"Yeh, it's been a strange journey here! When I first arrived, I thought this wasn't for me, but watching others in the community do their 9 to 5 jobs and then selflessly working on community projects; this made me look at my own life, and I'd say I was predestined to be here. What I found was a purpose to my life. I never feel bored or discontented. I have a real sense of fulfillment. But not to stand still; I constantly need to push myself, keep improving myself. For the first time in my life, I fit in somewhere and I believe in this community. Once this pottery project is done, I plan to get deeper into the consciousness-raising ideas of Sri Aurobindo. There are so many people in the community here that I can work with to realize my full potential as a human being. I want to be in harmony and understanding with all the people that are represented here. You know, we have over a dozen nationalities from all over the world as well as India. For me, there's nothing back in the States. Here, I can discover a new world and grow with the community that has a shared vision of life."

Chapter Sixty-Two: A Man of Constant Sorrow

> I am a man of constant sorrow
> I've seen trouble all my day
> I bid farewell to old Kentucky
> The place where I was born and raised
>
> For six long years I've been in trouble
> No pleasures here on earth I found
> For in this world I'm bound to ramble
> I have no friends to help me now
>
> It's fare thee well my old lover
> I never expect to see you again
> For I'm bound to ride that northern railroad
> Perhaps I'll die upon this train
>
> For many years where I may lay
> Then you may learn to love another
> While I am sleeping in my grave
>
> Maybe your friends think I'm just a stranger
> My face, you'll never see no more
> But there is one promise that is given
> I'll meet you on God's golden shore
>
> -Nineteenth-century Appalachian Spiritual (Public Domain)

"Man is not yet a finished creation but rather a challenge of the spirit, a distant possibility dreaded as much as it is desired,"

-Hermann Hesse, *Steppenwolf*

While sitting in the cafeteria at Aspiration Village in Auroville, I spoke to a young German, Joacheim, who told me about his experiences here. He was going to another ashram for further study. He had come to Auroville because he saw it as a new commitment - a group of people striving and working to create a new utopia. He met many dedicated individuals who believed they would find their spiritual needs fulfilled by working together to build something entirely new. This would be a society that shared equally, accepted everyone, and gave each member a chance to reach self-realization. I immediately thought of Ray and how this community had given him a purpose in life. I asked Joacheim what he had learned here. Joacheim replied, "I believe that life is basically tragic: you live and then you die. You seek the comfort of a religion that promises you everything in the afterlife: if you only believe in this particular God or system. I don't buy this. Every man is alone and must struggle to find his own salvation. The communal life here is exciting, with so many new ideas and new solutions. But I didn't find answers to my spiritual quest here."

Self-Portrait: George Tooker

"But didn't Sri Aurobindo believe that by dedicating yourself to work and helping others and looking inward, you could control your mind to reach a level of pure consciousness?"

"Yes, I believed that and tried to achieve that; I worked at self-analysis myself, but it became an intellectual exercise: good and evil, abstracted in a Socratic dialogue that led nowhere. I see the pioneers in Auroville and admire their hard work in trying to create a utopia on earth, but it is a worldly dream they are building: a classless, moneyless society that offers a distinct worldview as opposed to communism and capitalism. For most of the people that I talked to, Auroville is an attempt to achieve freedom, not bound by the constrictions and morality of the Western cultures they came from, but it is a societal freedom, not a religious one."

I saw Joacheim as a Romantic Siddhartha, following in the footsteps of the 19th-century Germanic literary and philosophical tradition. Listening to Joacheim, I thought of Goethe's "Meister Wilhelm's Lehrjahre," the original Bildungsroman, a young man exploring the world to find answers to life's eternal questions.

Johann Wolfgang Goethe 1775, Engraving after painting by Georg M. Kraus (Public Domain).

Goethe's novel deals with a young man who leaves his meaningless bourgeois life and joins a theater group. There he has many affairs set against the backdrop of the conflict between the new ideas of the French Revolution and the old bourgeois values, as well as the literary excitement of discovering Shakespeare and performing his plays on the German stage. Throughout the book, the hero, Wilhelm, is immersed in life and learning and is growing in maturity, despite his hardships and sufferings. Although the book now seems a little dated, the idea of a young man discovering himself by going out into the world and experiencing life to its fullest had immense influence and formed the basis and framework of all "coming of age" novels.

Joacheim had studied philosophy at a German university, and I'm sure he was familiar with the German philosopher that is very close to the Hindu and Buddhist religious traditions: Arthur Schopenhauer. Schopenhauer sees the physical world as a "representation, not the real thing in itself." What is real is the will and this will is a "wild, striving force existing outside of space or time." It is this will that causes suffering and the only way to end that suffering is to negate the "will to life." In other words, control your mind to accept the godhead. This is what Hinduism and Buddhism have taught for millennia, the union with the godhead is only achieved by annihilating your own consciousness and being absorbed by the supreme consciousness.

Arthur Schopenhauer in 1815 Painting by Ludwig Sigismund Ruhl (Public Domain).

"I'm going to a Buddhist ashram at Dharamsala in northern India. Now I see that for me, the self-negation of my individual soul or personality, if you will, is the path that will lead me to a uniting with the supreme consciousness. And I hope to meet the "Living Buddha," the Dalai Lama, who is in exile there."

"I tried to empty my mind, staring for hours at the Zen Garden Ryoan-ji in Kyoto, but there were always some distractions. I couldn't focus. The real world kept intruding, preventing me from clearing my mind."

"That's because you need discipline and a good teacher to show you how to apply that discipline to control your mind. Once you have mastered the yoga techniques, you can work on self-negation."

"And then there is the concept of Maya, that all of life is an illusion. There is so much to discover, learn and experience. My senses are overwhelmed with the sights, smells, sounds, tastes, and feel of the real world. How can all this be an illusion?"

"Yes, I believe that the world is Maya, an illusion. Let me give you an easy example: you're American, you must have seen the movie 'Groundhog Day' starring Bill Murray. The basic premise of the movie is the hero relives the same day, over and over, for an entire year. Everything he does that day: discover a cure for cancer, write a symphony, make love to a girl, get hit by a bus, is wiped clean. He wakes up the next day and starts all over again. The movie is very funny, but if you take the metaphor of the movie and apply it to life, you can look at each day as a new life, and you are reincarnated into a different life when you wake up in the morning. The concept that we call reality has no meaning, what was so important and so tangible is gone at the end of the day, an illusion and you will keep repeating variations of that illusion until you learn how to master your mind to end this cycle of rebirth or a new day."

"Wow! Say it ain't true, Susie Cream Cheese!"

I admired Joacheim, for his religious or philosophical ideas but even more for the passion that he imbued these ideals with.

I remembered the struggles of one of my favorite authors: Nikos Kazantzakis. Late in his life, he wrote a spiritual autobiography, "Report to Greco." The book describes his "odyssey" from Christ, whom he depicted as a flesh and blood individual: Jesus coming to terms with his divinity and the worldly desires that tempted him. In his book "The Last Temptation of Christ," Christ's last temptation is to live an ordinary, normal life: he marries Mary Magdalene, has children, and becomes a loving, respected patriarch. While he is leading this dream life, he tries to come to understand his destiny: that he was not meant for everyday existence but that he is the Son of God and must sacrifice himself for the good of mankind. He rejects this final temptation and returns to his real fate, dies on the cross, and is resurrected.

Nikos Kazantzakis 1904 (Public Domain)

Kazantzakis came from war-torn Crete and experienced the human misery, starvation, and senseless warfare of Christian Greeks versus Muslim Turks. There had to be a way to end all this savagery in the here-and-now physical world, so he turned to Russia and communism. Here were idealistic, passionate people trying to create a new spiritual utopia on Earth, where man is the new God. The purges, concentration camps, and repression destroyed this utopia. Disheartened, he delved into Buddhism; here, he saw the striving and the ultimate achievement of Nirvana as a negation of life. However, Kazantzakis abandoned Buddhism because he believed fervently in life. His fictional character, Zorba, imbues his ideals. Zorba has a zest for living, sensual pleasure, food, and the physical earthiness and sensuality of daily existence, good or bad. In Kazantzakis's mind, Zorba is Nietzsche's Superman (Übermensch). The individual who sees life's suffering and meaninglessness, accepts these flaws, continues to struggle to find answers, and lives his life to the fullest.

Kazantzakis is constantly moving forward, passionately embracing new ideologies, religions and philosophies, never satisfied. He created his own meaning of life by embracing it; the quest became even greater than the goal. He returns to his Cretan roots, becoming a real-life Odysseus, not the complacent nobleman sitting before the fire with his wife and son at the end of the Odyssey. But the endless wanderer, struggling to find meaning out of the chaos of the world.

Chapter Sixty-Three: A Walk of Song, Love, and Death

What wondrous love is this, O my soul, O my soul,

what wondrous love is this, O my soul!

What wondrous love is this that caused the Lord of bliss

to bear the dreadful curse for my soul, for my soul,

to bear the dreadful curse for my soul!

When I was sinking down, sinking down, sinking down,

when I was sinking down, sinking down;

when I was sinking down beneath God's righteous frown,

Christ laid aside his crown for my soul, for my soul,

Christ laid aside his crown for my soul!

To God and to the Lamb, I will sing, I will sing,

to God and to the Lamb, I will sing;

to God and to the Lamb, who is the great I AM,

while millions join the theme, I will sing, I will sing,

while millions join the theme, I will sing!

And when from death I'm free, I'll sing on, I'll sing on,

and when from death I'm free, I'll sing on;

and when from death I'm free, I'll sing and joyful be,

and through eternity I'll sing on, I'll sing on,

and through eternity I'll sing on!

"What Wondrous Love Is This?"

-19th century Appalachian Spiritual Hymn.

While walking back from Pondicherry Beach in the late afternoon, I experienced something I can only describe as a hallucinogenic religious vision. The sky was dark steel gray, as if it were ready to downpour. Suddenly, a shaft of sunlight pierced this foreboding curtain, bathing everything in a luminescent effervescence. At the very same time, I heard a subdued chant-like song in the distance. I turned toward that hauntingly beautiful music and saw an indistinct column of people coming toward me. Slowly they came into focus: a procession of nuns singing a medieval hymn in French. The lead nun was an older white woman, dressed in an all-white habit, carrying upright a large gold cross, leading a group of about 20 younger nuns and novices. The nuns walked two abreast: dark, fine-featured Tamil faces, dressed in crisp gray habits, with white breastplate blouses. They continued singing as they walked past me, a vision of spiritual loveliness, heading for the large St. Louis French Cathedral at the end of the square.

Suddenly in my mind, I was mystically transported back to 4th-century Cologne. Here was St. Ursula, leading the Eleven Thousand Virgins, singing praises to God, and marching through the muddy lanes of medieval Cologne. They were marching, oblivious to the horrific death awaiting them at the hands of the savage Huns. I was witnessing a living tableau of a painting by the French artist Jean Bourdichon (circa 1503-1508). Their beautiful voices and virginal innocence could not save them from being beheaded en-mass because they would not yield and sacrifice their virginity to the brutal barbarians. However, amid this carnage, the glowing shaft of sunlight was God's beacon of saving grace: their steadfast faith would grant them a place in Heaven to sing forever at the right hand of the enthroned God.

Saint Ursula and the 11,000 Virgins, painted by Jean Bourdichon (circa 1503-1508) (Public Domain)

Chapter Sixty-Four: Ray II - The Adventure of Consciousness

Later that week, I bumped into Ray again. He wasn't working that day and offered to show me the pottery kiln. He told me that he generally doesn't talk to many people, but he thought I needed help or maybe encouragement to understand what Auroville is really all about. The pottery building was sturdy and spartan. White-washed walls, two small glass windows, a cement floor, and a single electric bulb hanging from the ceiling. Inside, there was a huge grinding stone, a wet wheel, two tables, some chairs, and assorted earthen jars holding clay and dyes. The building also had a single copper-tubing tap, which was the water supply and shelves that were in-the-making, with cut wood piled up at one side of the building.

We talked about his life in Auroville; how he thought he was predestined to come here. I asked, "What happens next? You've built this pottery kiln that will serve the community, but what about your personal goals?" He told me that he must continue serving within the community. He will find himself by helping others in the community. I asked him, "Don't you feel this place is like a medieval monastery, set apart from the world? You are concerned and committed to your fellow brethren, but your real goal is to find your personal salvation, to truly discover God." "Only by being a part of the whole can you transcend yourself," he countered.

"Yes, I believe that; we are all striving for oneness with nature in the Taoist sense of understanding the cosmos. There is only one God, whether we find him through our Dharma (duty), through our uniting with the supreme consciousness (Nirvana), or through love for our fellow man as Jesus preached and died for us."

"The way I see it, God works through us to achieve his plan for man. This kiln was built to give great devotion to Him and to satisfy a basic need in our community. Only by giving of yourself, can you find yourself." I thought of Jesus when he preached, "It is more blessed to give than to receive," and Ray was living that life.

While we were talking, I remembered Thomas Merton, the American Trappist monk, who wrote of his struggles to find God in his highly popular "Seven Story Mountain." Later Merton studied Eastern religions, especially Zen Buddhism. God is transcendent, unknowable: like Zen philosophy, the concept of God cannot be put into language. He must be approached intuitively or through yogic exercises to discover His real nature. The elaborate doctrine of Christianity gets in the way of truly understanding God. Merton, as a Trappist monk, believed in solitude and silence, like Jesus, Mohammad, and Moses; they all retreated to the desert, where the silence and solitude freed or, better yet, emptied their minds to accept God as their personal Savior.

Merton moved to a small hut in the monastery complex, away from his brothers, so that he could meditate in silence; this fervent meditation brought his thoughts to see beyond his Ivory Tower, to the problems of the real world. He believed you must be concerned about the well-being of your fellow man to find God. Merton wrote polemics on social issues such as pacifism, the waste of war, and racial injustice in America. To truly understand God, in the Christian sense, you must love and help your fellow man. He emphasized, like Jesus, that love must be selfless and performed without ego, "Do unto others as if you were doing it for yourself." This could just as well describe the Hindu concept of Dharma (duty) or the Sufi mysticism of accessing the God within each of us. This brought me back to Sri Aurobindo and his own revolutionary concept: Every man is divine on the same level as Jesus, Mohammad, or Sri Sathya Baba.

I shared these "revelations" with Ray; he listened and then hesitated before concluding that "Every man must approach God in a way that fulfills his own set of values and beliefs; to work steadfastly and selflessly for the common good of our community is the way I'm seeking God, and this gives me the inner peace that I've never had before."

As I left Ray to cycle back to my hotel, I reflected on our discussion. What came to mind was a book that greatly influenced me when I was growing up: "Childhood's End" by Arthur Clarke. I now see it in a totally different interpretation. Like all great literature, each generation finds new meaning, new ideas, and a deeper understanding of what a piece of literature represents. Before, I looked at it as a foreboding science fiction tale of humanity's end. A race, the Overlords, takes over the Earth and gives us everything we want: prosperity, peace, and an end of hunger and racial strife, but the price is human creativity. The Overlords foster the development of special children, those who exhibit clairvoyance and telekinesis. This new generation, the last human generation, connects with the Over Mind, a distant cosmic intelligence force or "Mind." These children work in concert as one mind, becoming a part of this supra-consciousness of the universe. They leave their humanity behind and migrate to the Over Mind. Earth is destroyed and humanity ceases to exist.

Now I see it as a philosophically "religious" novel. Clarke has taken over verbatim Sri Aurobindo's concept of the "Overmind" (without acknowledgement!). Aurobindo believed that the Over Mind was the last step of man's control of his consciousness - the discovery of his individual divinity. He saw this as the next huge evolutionary advancement. Before, it was Ape becomes Man; now it is Man becomes God. Clarke accepts this radical concept and then carries it one step further: what happens to this God-like creature? He is absorbed into this "Over Mind;" he has no need for his Earthly body or a firmament like the Earth. Or, looking at it another way, if every man achieved Nirvana, the supreme consciousness, then there would be an end to humanity. In Buddhism, this is the extinction of the individual soul to become part of the universal consciousness or, as in Taoism, a complete union with the way of the cosmos.

"Childhood's End" by Arthur Clarke (front cover of paperback version).

Chapter Sixty-Five: Jacob's Ladder

Print from the original Luther Bible of 1534 (Public Domain).

"And Jacob went out from Beer-sheba and went toward Haran. And he lighted upon the place, and tarried there all night, because the sun was set; and he took one of the stones of the place, and put it under his head, and lay down in that place to sleep. And he dreamed, and behold a ladder set up on the earth, and the top of it reached to heaven; and behold the angels of God ascending and descending on it. And behold, the LORD stood beside him, and said: 'I am the LORD, the God of Abraham thy father, and the God of Isaac. The land whereon thou liest, to thee will I give it, and to thy seed" Genesis 28:10-14.

Jacob was a pale, fine-featured young man with a sallow complexion and piercing brown eyes. He was also the son of a Holocaust survivor. His mother was rescued from Auschwitz, and she married another Holocaust survivor. Jacob was born in 1948 in Krakow, Poland. His parents resettled in Israel in the early 1950s; he was partly raised there and worked at a kibbutz. The interesting thing about Jacob was his passport: his mother had been living in a camp for the Holocaust survivors and the UN gave his family UN passports which stated they were "Stateless." His mother and father chose Israeli citizenship, but he kept his UN passport because he was not at home in Cold War Poland and hated the siege mentality of Israel, with the sword hanging over his head, reminding him that the Jews could again be subject to elimination, this time by hostile Arab nations. He started traveling in the late 1960s all over Europe, never finding a place where he could settle down or feel at home.

Portrait of Robert Minton: Lucian Freud

He was good with his hands and knew about farming from his kibbutz days. Like almost all of the residents in Auroville that I met, he was not into drugs. He came here to see if this would be the home he never had. While he was in Amsterdam in the early 1970s, he boarded a "Hippie Bus" to India and wound up in the village of "Forecomers" in Auroville. I spent an afternoon talking with him. He shared with me his hopes and dreams, searching to find a community here in Auroville where he could build his future. He had spent over a month visiting the different communities to see if he would fit in and if this was what he really wanted.

The different villages had their own personalities. "Aspiration" was dominated by the French; "Forecomers" was more laid back and predominantly American and British. "Far Out Beach" was a polyglot of nationalities: Germans, Brits, and ashram Indians.

Jacob was a loner and dissatisfied with the European and Israeli way of life, yet like Ray, he felt he could probably fit in here at "Forecomers." He was also looking for a niche that he could dedicate himself to for his work requirement. Now Jacob had a decision to make; would Auroville be his new home? If so, he contemplated changing his passport from Stateless to Indian citizenship. In Genesis, the Biblical Jacob wrestles with an "angel" all night. Jacob held his own in this struggle and, at daybreak, demanded a blessing from the angel, who blessed him with the name of Israel, which means "one that struggled with an angel." The Biblical Jacob stated: "I have seen God face to face and lived."

The present-day Jacob is also struggling with an angel, the angel of doubt and uncertainty, to determine his future life. I thought of the quote from Genesis, where God told Jacob, "The land we're on thou liest to thee will I give it and to thy seed." I hoped that this would be the "Promised Land" where Jacob could find the home he was always missing. Unfortunately, I never saw him again after that day, and I don't know what decision he made.

Jacob Wrestling with the Angel: Eugene Delacroix (Public Domain).

Chapter Sixty-Six: Gordon Bares All!

The Lord will be our God, and delight to dwell among us, as His own people, and will command a blessing upon us in all our ways, so that we shall see much more of His wisdom, power, goodness and truth, than formerly we have been acquainted with. We shall find that the God of Israel is among us, when ten of us shall be able to resist a thousand of our enemies; when He shall make us a praise and glory that men shall say of succeeding plantations, "may the Lord make it like that of New England." For we must consider that we shall be as a city upon a hill. The eyes of all people are upon us.

-John Winthrop: "Dreams of a City on a Hill Sermon,"

-Massachusetts Bay Colony, 1630.

GORDON BARES ALL!

I had spent about three weeks in Auroville: meeting settlers, eating at the cafeteria, sleeping in the ashram guest house, and observing the creativity and hard work that was all around me. I had come to India as a seeker to find answers to who I am and what I wanted out of life. Here was a community that gave me an opportunity to answer these questions. What I found was energy, but it was civic and not spiritual energy. This was a community, and everyone worked together. You saw a need that would help your fellow settlers, and you would do it for them, not for the glory of God. This was like the GIs in World War Two, who would risk their lives not for the ideal of defending democracy, but they would put themselves in harm's way for their buddies; they wouldn't let them down, and they had their backs. Auroville is a living organism that grows with the people helping each other to create a Garden of Eden out of this barren red earth.

However, what I saw was not a classless heaven but a decentralized monastery. Here the inhabitants were not assigned duties; they assumed them depending on their skills, desires, and what would help their fellow settlers. Like the medieval monastery, there was no real need for money because it became a functioning, self-supporting village. Monks farmed, raised livestock, created goods, and shared their spiritual vows in communal dinners and private meditation. The central authority was not Abbott, but the Mother who decided what was best for the community. In this light, I thought of all the previous utopias and how they had failed.

Brook Farm in New England was an American utopia in the early 19th century, modeled on the writings of a French socialist named Fournier. He advocated a society where all men are equal, there is no money, and everyone works and lives together in equality whether they be common laborers or university professors, in a communal farm self-supported by selling farm produce and livestock and other handicrafts created by the community. Many of these communities sprang up in Europe, but they soon failed. This, unfortunately, was the problem at Brook Farm. Many of the prominent settlers felt they should be given more power or authority because of their special skills, such as medicine, engineering, architecture, and other vital professions that were needed to build this utopia and to keep it running ("I should get an extra slice of bacon because I built this building and am more important than the common laborer!"). It attracted many intellectuals and prominent businessmen, among them the young idealistic author Nathaniel Hawthorne.

George Ripley, Literary Editor of New York Tribune and founder of Brooke Farm in Massachusetts in 1847.

From the beginning, Brook Farm was in debt: the land was too poor to sustain cash crops and too small for large-scale farming, and there were not enough laborers nor skilled farmers to turn a profit on the land. The women in Brook Farm created handicrafts that were sold in Boston but did not generate enough income. More importantly, there was no skilled businessman to balance the books and keep the society self-sustaining. However, disagreements over leadership and direction caused the failure of this experiment within one generation. The ideals of Fournier were very influential in France and must have attracted the attention of an idealistic young woman who later became the Mother of Auroville. Then there were the Shakers with Mother Lee, who was the binding force that kept this puritanical society together. The Shakers believed in the absolute separation of the sexes and forbade any intercourse with either men or women. What sustained the

Engraving of Shakers dancing 1840, unknown author (Public Domain).

society from the 1850s to the end of the century were orphans that were raised by the Shakers and adopted the Shaker lifestyle. The community was self-sufficient because of the beautiful furniture and planting seeds that they produced and sold to the outside world. After Mother Lee died, the Shakers continued, but the changing mores of American life resulted in fewer orphans left to fill the ranks of the older ascetic Shakers. This grand experiment finally ended with the death of the last two Shakers in the early 1920s.

18th century Jesuit Priest in Brazil. Unknown artist
(Public Domain)

The most fascinating experiment in attempting to achieve an earthly utopia was in the Jesuit Rio de La Plata missions in Paraguay and Brazil in South America in the 18th century. The Jesuits founded these "reductions" (settlements of Indians) specifically to protect the Indians from the slave owners that were constantly raiding the villages and kidnapping the young men for work in the mines and the sugar cane plantations. There was also a system in the Spanish settlement of Paraguay where Indians were forced to do labor called "encomienda," which meant they had to devote a portion of the year to working for the Spanish landowners, where they worked in the fields, tended to cattle, and serviced the family of the landowner as domestic servants.

These "reductions" were a theocratic state run by the Jesuits and controlled by the native chiefs. The Jesuits taught Christianity and gave the Indian skills such as raising cattle, cultivating gardens, and growing a lucrative product called yerba mate tea. The cattle were used for food and the hides were sold along with the yerba tea for a profit so that the settlement could become self-sufficient, and they were able to buy tools and learn other skills to bring in more revenue to keep the settlements flourishing.

The settlements indeed flourished: there were over 140,000 Indians at their height in the middle of the 18th century, living in 30 "reductions" missions in Brazil, Paraguay, and Bolivia. However, this attracted the slavers called "banderitas," who attacked the missions and enslaved many of the natives. These banderitas were particularly active in Portuguese Brazil, so the Jesuits moved the missions to the Spanish territories. But they still had to fight off the slavers, which they did quite successfully by buying arms and forming militias. The missions taught the Indians practical skills, Christianity, and, most importantly, how to defend their communities. The "reductions" valued women in Indian society and provided a dowry for each of the women in those missions through the bounty of commercial profits.

Here was a classless society, where Indians worked together under the leadership of their own people and yet looked to the Jesuits for their spiritual enlightenment. The settlements were not only self-sufficient but gave the Indians pride, saying that they were equal to the Spanish and Portuguese overlords. This golden heyday of independent Indians in their own country estates ended with the expulsion of the Jesuits from South America in 1767. Afterwards, the Indians melted back into the jungles. They once again became myriad separate tribes, which were finally enslaved or overwhelmed by the superior arms of the Spanish ranchers.

Each of these experiments had a charismatic leader that supplied the driving force, the vision that would sustain the faithful. Auroville had the Mother, who also headed the Sri Aurobindo Ashram and envisioned a theocratic classless city-state where every nationality would come together to build this utopia. The charter of Auroville, which was drafted by the Mother, emphasized the teaching of Sri Aurobindo, the glue that kept this society together. The first settlers were a couple: an artist from New York and a dancer from California, the Lawlers, and they settled appropriately in Forecomers Village. They built a straw thatch house and paid for a well to be dug. Soon others came, planted trees and orchards, making the barren red earth into a virtual jungle of tropical growth. The Lawlers had their own garden, which supplied the food for them, and later, the produce from these mini gardens would feed the community through the cafeteria. What you had here was first-generation idealism: the hippies reclaimed the land and shared everything in common similar to an American commune of the 1960s. Then conflicts arose when this idealism was pitted against the governing body, the ashram officials, businessmen, and religious leaders responsible for getting donations and hiring the workers to keep Auroville viable and growing. I talked with an Indian who told me that the settlers, with their innovative projects: tree reforestation, incense and candle making, and community gardens paid for about 1/3 of the operating budget of Auroville. The other 2/3 was the responsibility of the ashram central governing committee (CIY) in getting donations and grants to keep the community alive. Every large project, whether it was a reforestation project, building a pottery kiln, or setting up a shop to sell candles, was funded by the CIY, who supplied the raw materials, the machinery to do the work, and, in some cases, paid the local Indians to make the dream a reality. The CIY also ensured that everyone received a small monthly salary, whether they were a doctor or just a food worker: everyone was equal. However, there were constant conflicts on how the money should be spent and who actually controlled the community: would it be the people that did the sweat equity, or would it be the people that brought money in to sustain this vision? The Mother kept these two opposing forces in equilibrium through her charismatic leadership. The governing committee wanted a planned sterile city, similar to the lifeless Chandigarh in north India, which was designed by the modernist French architect Le Corbusier.

However, what evolved in Auroville was the collection of villages, each self-sustaining and building what the settlers thought would be their home for life. It was almost like Professor Malcolm said in "Jurassic Park:" "Life finds a way" to evolve and not follow a strict sterile rule.

Many of the settlers that I talked with viewed the Mother with the same adoration as that of the Virgin Mary. She knew all the answers and her presence was that of a living saint. Being raised a Protestant, I did not have the love or reverence of the Virgin that many of my Catholic friends did. I saw it almost as cult worship, which bothered me greatly. I looked at the building of the Matrimandir, which, when I was there, was just a large hole in the ground, as the Biblical "golden calf" for the worship of the Mother.

The completed Matrimandir in Auroville (When I was there in the early 1970s, there was only a huge hole in the ground.)

Then there was the ideal of a classless society, which was also a myth. Many of the foreigners had money or were wired money to construct their MacMansions in the jungle. They hired local Indian laborers to dig wells and set up generators for electricity, and although they didn't own these houses, they could live there for all of their lives, and their children would be able to live there, also. This contrasted with the poor foreigners and ashram Indians who had just enough money to purchase materials for a small, thatched house and perhaps a dug well; otherwise, they would have to carry water by hand or bullock cart from miles away.

There was also one burning issue that I found fault with in Auroville and that was the education of the children. In the school I visited in "Aspiration" village, the children were running wild. Learning was confined to helping their families build their houses or tending to their gardens. "Readin', ritin', and 'rithmetic" were solely missing. Auroville was the selfish dream of the parents and the children they had (there were 66 when I visited in 1972) were wholly unprepared to carry on this vision. The philosophy of the settlers was that children are naturally curious, and they will learn what is important to them.

I've always believed that success in life is dependent on education, especially in this fast-changing world. If the Auroville experiment failed, or if the children were not satisfied with a farmer's existence or running a shop, what would happen to this new generation of illiterates? I had personally seen how our schools could not teach basic learning to our underclass to get out of poverty. The children of Auroville are not given a structured learning environment that would prepare them to deal with modern life outside of society or even to offer skills within the community because of their lack of education and training.

I looked inwardly at my own life, realizing that I did not have the commitment nor the manual skills to go off into the wilderness, build my own house, become a farmer, or even want to make incense candles. I had worked hard as a busboy in restaurants and in a factory, assembling hundreds of eyeglass frames daily. I had my clothes eaten with chemicals while making mothballs and worked every summer for four years as an underground zinc miner just to fund my college expenses and education. I joined the Reserve Officers Training Corps to fund the last two years of tuition at my college in return for service in the army. My parents had struggled and worked hard to send me to college, and I was proud to be the first in my family to attend and graduate. I felt I owed them and myself a responsibility to be the "best of the best, sir" and strive to do something meaningful with my life.

Life on the road is usually a solitary journey: you put up with the overcrowded third-class trains, the fleabag hotel rooms, the filthy stall food, and the frustrating nightmare of Indian bureaucracy because the excitement of discovery and the opportunity of learning keep you motivated and eager for the next adventure. The idea of settling down and committing to a community alone frightened the hell out of me! I thought of Rachel; I had begged her to come with me: we would discover our path together. However, she had her own vision and dreams and had found a peace there that eluded me here.

The last reason why I chose not to stay in Auroville may sound overly patriotic (would someone please turn down the volume of "America the Beautiful"!). I am an American, and I believe in the ideals of our country. I wanted to give something back to my country. I wanted to teach children, whether it was a ghetto school or a college campus, to impart to them the skills that they would need to succeed in our ever-evolving society. As Malcolm X said, "Education is the passport to the future, for tomorrow belongs to those who prepare for it today." I thought America needed me more than I needed this well-meaning, idealistic society here in India.

However, I will never forget the idealism, perseverance, and spiritualism of people like Ray, Rachel, and Jacob. They have found their own "shelter from the storms" of life, and I was happy for them. However, this was not my goal: I am the "wayfaring stranger just going over Jordan," trying to make my way home.

Puri

Puri Temple drawing from the book 'LINDE DES RAJAHS Voyage Dans L' Inde Centrale', 1877 Louis Rousselet (Public Domain).

Chapter Sixty-Seven: June the Sixteenth

Unbearably hot, the smell of body sweat, clothes grafted to my body, 27 hours-Madras to Calcutta, 3rd class, 3rd circle of "Inferno," barely hanging on to a seat, halfway in the aisle, clogged with burlap bags of produce, children screaming, running, shitting - dehydrated and delusional. An Indian reading a paper opposite me - the date June 16th. "Ulysses," the entire world in a day, a young student trying to find the parallels with the Odyssey: Stephen Dedalus as the surrogate son, Molly as the earth-mother goddess fucking everything in sight, Leopold the cuckold "Wandering Jew." What the fuck is he talking about? A clever parody or just an elaborate leprechaun tall tale? I, too, was going home - what is home? Parents fighting; my cat Rin Tin Tin waits for me every day on the front steps when I come home from school; late lunches; Mom busy watching soaps "Search For Tomorrow;" and no I can't go out, Chris I have to do my homework. In my sandbox, my first love at five, Mary McCormack teaches me English; I only speak Norwegian.

Going home - to teach? High school, Dr. Funaro, old Sephardic Jew - love of books - joy of sonorous "Inferno" in Italian, Sons and Lovers, my story, not in black coal country Britain, but blue-collar Jersey.

"Chai, please," sweet nectar of the gods, need to keep drinking, or I'll get really dehydrated and sick.

Neighborhood kids, bullies yet wanted to be there, be a part of the group, walking on railroad tracks, Butterfingers and Twinkies and genuine US Army canteen - off to discover the world or at least Jersey City; my church - our father figure minister, teaching Sunday school young children the gospel not believing half what I taught them. Going home.

"When Johnny comes marching home again, hurrah!"

Too much hate, antiwar assholes picking on returning soldiers, not fat cat politicians, perform my Dharma - US Army, Salvation Army: "We all have to serve someone." Going home. I love my parents, but I am Oedipus: kill the father, marry the mother. I can love and talk to each other separately, but not together. Must go home, the prodigal son returneth. To what? Nothing there: no lover waiting, friends gone following their dreams.

The rest were "raised to do what your daddy did" ("For my 19th birthday I got a union card and a wedding coat:" Bruce Springsteen) work in a factory, construction, plumbing, or electrician. Only the dead know Brooklyn.

Number 10 school, smartest kid in class ODed first year in college; another friend spent three tours in Nam just so he could bring back the Vietnamese girl of his dreams. Thought everyone in the whole world was Italian, I had nothing in common: cars and the latest fashion, greased hair, and teased hair: "When you're a Jet, you're always a Jet." Our leader of the pack killed himself in a hot rod collision.

I must get up, or I'll pee in my pants, toilet a smelly hole in the floor, sweat pouring down, wiping face, holding glasses, train jolts, glasses fall in hole covered with shit, it doesn't get any better! Yes, it does! I didn't have a seat anymore, standing with the sweat pouring down. My steadfast companion was a live goat brought by the villagers to sell in the market. Goat kept nibbling at my rucksack, braying at me while I shooed him away from chewing my belongings. Goat took its cue from children, shitting whenever it wanted.

Home, my spiritual home, New York City, the magic Disneyland across the river, peddling my bike to the hill where I gape at the magnificent skyline. Loetz from Berlin, the Berliner Luft, freedom in the air - that is New York, you can be anything you want. Now, my home is the road. Not the endless highway of Dean Moriarty, Dean as Charon driving a "cigarette speedboat" across the Styx filled with the damned. Streets lined with gold, life's answers at end of the hippie rainbow, new experiences around every bend. I feel alive! I don't want to go home, fuck Odysseus and Bloom, responsibilities. You must listen to your Dharma Arjuna, be "the best of the best, Sir," get a meaningless job, "Plastics, that's the wave of the future, son." 8 Finger Eddy: no cares, no responsibilities; is this what I want? My alter ego, Flash Gordon, defeats Ming, saves the world and then returns home to a boring 9 to 5 with the insipid blond Dale.

"When Johnny comes marching home again, hurrah!"

Home - physical space not as important as relationships: the feel of the girl in your arms in the dark night of the soul, discovering ancient, ruined cities, dirt-caked, sweat pouring, bad breath, yet you are as one making your destiny together, bodies glued in sweat and semen as you lie exhausted from lovemaking. Love on a two-week soldier pass, army brat, why bother when she'll be gone, and I'll never see her again. Rachel lost in religious reverie and Christine always missing the one "It" that makes life worthwhile. "I've been waiting for a girl like you all my life."

Home. Odysseus, bored out of his mind, leaves wife and kids, and hits the road again. Ambrose Bierce, an old fart recapturing Civil War glory, goes to fight new war in Mexico and disappears. Muslims and Vikings: die in battle, and you enter Paradise. Hindu time always the present: no past, no future - make the best of it; this is your life, Susie Cream Cheese. Spin the wheel of fortune: success, money, happiness. Don't want to be Dorothy, an old spinster; nothing at home compares to that past magical fairyland, now foolhardily facing every twister, hoping for the special one to return to Oz. I am in Oz; why leave? Floating in a Taoist Chinese painting, at one with the universe. "When I was small and Christmas trees were tall," the Bee Gees reminisce. I have lost my childish beliefs- a snake that sheds its skin. I am American, but what is America? An ideal to die for or just a place to make a buck? Pilgrims, smugglers, dopers, vacant-eyed GIs, naïve farm boys - all come to look for America, for our mythical home, that "green spit of land, Manhattoes," after months of gray sea-sky monochrome, a new world.

"When Johnny comes marching home again, hurrah!"

Thank God! Puri, this is my stop. Now I can get off this "Streetcar Named Hell."

Chapter Sixty-Eight: Puri - Welcome to Sesame Street

I hailed a pedicycle to take me into Puri town. The pedicycle driver took me on the scenic tour, passing Puri beach, dotted with fishermen with their boats and small little villages. We passed dilapidated peeling Victorian mansions; this was the summer residence of the British Raj when the seat of government was still in Calcutta. These crumbling white elephants, many of them now Somerset Maughan colonial-style hotels, stood out in the harsh Indian sun like the washed-out houses of an Edward Hopper painting.

Indians have replaced the Raj, but they come here from Calcutta for the cooling ocean breezes, the temple, and the excellent seafood; no one goes to the beach for swimming. The beach was eerily quiet except for fishermen pulling in their nets.

Old Puri is a maze of small, narrow streets, cluttered with roaming cows, long matted hair sadhus, white-clad Hindu pilgrims, beggars, merchants, and most interesting of all, exotic tribal people with steel bangles, nose rings, colorful dresses, others with tattoos all over their arms and faces. These tribal people come from the nearby hills for day labor or to sell some of the handicrafts that they create in their mountain villages.

Bonda girl from the forest tribes of Orissa

The Bonda tribes number about 12,000, and they are unique in that they are an Austro-Asiatic people and were the first settlers of India, coming out of Africa 60,000 years ago. They settled in the forests and mountains of Orissa and were able to keep their unique ethnicity, culture, and language intact, even though they are surrounded by millions of Indo-European language Hindus.

The houses are thatched two-story buildings with whitewashed exterior walls that are covered with painted images of peacocks, the God Krishna, and strange primitive childlike paintings of Lord Jagannath. The rickshaw driver brought me to a large, crumbling Victorian mansion hotel (a euphemism). The only good thing was it was a traveler's hotel, so there would be a bunch of interesting freaks to talk and toke with.

Lord Jagannath at 2011 Festival

I came to Puri for the beach and the Jagannath temple. The next day I visited the temple, and I couldn't believe my eyes: here was a deity that was a cross between a Sesame Street Muppet and the Pillsbury Dough Boy. I wondered how such an outlandish caricature could be worshipped by millions of devout followers. Coming from a background in Christianity where God is depicted as majestic and a fatherly figure (with blue eyes, of course), and then to see this Muppet, who is an avatar of the God Vishnu, Preserver of the Universe, referred to as Lord Jagannath, the Supreme Being, was, to my Western eyes, preposterous.

I did some research and found that the Hindus had incorporated this tribal god, which was originally a long pole of wood, into the Parthenon of Hindu deities. Lord Jagannath is usually depicted with stumps for hands and sometimes no feet at all, harkening back to the tribal totemic god. Once again, Hinduism, the dominant religion, allowed the tribal god's primacy over Shiva, Brahma, and Vishnu. As I mentioned in my chapter on Hinduism, this also occurred in the Indus Valley civilization, where the fertility tribal god symbol, the lingam, became the central worship object of Shiva. Hinduism has always been an encompassing religion, absorbing different religions, philosophies, and moral systems into its belief systems. However, if the lower pre-civilization tribal fertility and animistic gods take center stage of worship, it speaks of a lack of confidence by the believers in the central deities and world view of mainstream Hinduism.

In Puri, the main festival is transporting Lord Jagannath and his sister Subhadra and brother Balabhadra in three huge chariots, which are paraded around the town, pushed and pulled by the faithful, and attended by millions of devout followers. The English word juggernaut comes from this festival, meaning unstoppable, and when you see these huge chariots, you'll know why.

The Temple Festival where Lord Jagannath and his sister Subhadra and brother Balabhadra parade around Puri.

Chapter Sixty-Nine: Magic and Mystery in Stone - The Sun Chariot Temple Konark

The ruined Sun Chariot Temple in 1847: James Fergusson (Public Domain)

I had been taking a little R&R on the beaches in Puri and now decided it was time to leave the sun and surf for some cultural enlightenment: close to Puri is the Sun Chariot temple at Konark. While I was in Puri, I saw the huge wooden temple chariots that were pushed and pulled by the faithful carrying the statue of Lord Jagannath. This theme is echoed in the sun temple only the chariot is the temple, and the stone wheels of the chariot also serve as sundials, and the huge horses that pull it are carved schist stone. The Sun Chariot temple was in a state of ruin in the 19th century when the British partially restored it. The print below shows how the monument looked in 1847. You can see the remains of the central tower to the left of the drawing called the Vimana, which collapsed in 1837.

The Sun Chariot temple had been abandoned for hundreds of years after the devasting attack of the Muslim sultan Sulaiman Garrani in 1508.

The temple is dedicated to the sun god Surya, who is not part of the popular triumvirate of gods, Brahma, Vishnu, and Shiva, but is an earlier Vedic god sung about in the "Rig Veda," the earliest Hindu holy book. Here, you see the fiery sun god worshiped by the Indo-European Aryan horsemen who conquered Mohenjo-Dara and the entire Ganges plain. The statue of Surya seen below shows us the God-wearing boots, revealing his Central Asian origins. From the pen and ink drawing below, you can see the stone horses pulling the stone chariot, a legacy from the time when the Aryan tribes rode horses and chariots to go into battle. As befitting the sun god, the entire temple is set up as a huge sundial. Each of the twelve wheels and their spokes still gives an accurate measure of time today. The temple is positioned so that in the first morning light, the sun illuminates the huge statue of Surya shown below.

The largest building standing is the audience hall called Mandapa. This is intricately carved with scenes of ordinary life at the time. It was created in 1244 by King Narasimhadeva. Here, you see royalty and commoners alike going about their normal business, and you also have the erotic sculpture that you saw at Khajuraho.

One of the Stone Chariot wheels: the spokes of the wheel are a huge sundial- still accurate today.

The magic and mystery of the Sun Chariot temple are further enhanced by a little-known fact. When the temple was built, the king installed a huge magnet on top of the mandapa audience hall and inserted magnets throughout the sanctuary so the large metal statue of Surya (now gone), probably similar to the one shown below, was magically suspended in the air, showing the great power of the God who can self-levitate. The watercolor below shows two British officers exploring the ruins of the mandapa. I look up at the ceiling, which was where the huge magnet had been placed, and the sidewalls where smaller magnets were positioned to keep the god in equilibrium, now all ruined, as well as the floor filled with crumbling stone blocks. These magnets were so powerful that they affected the instrumentation of the sea-going vessels, causing many of them to crash into the rocks by the shore. The magnets and the huge statue of Surya have disappeared through Muslim raiding and European desecration, but it was a magical wonder for hundreds of years and has never been duplicated in any other Indian temple.

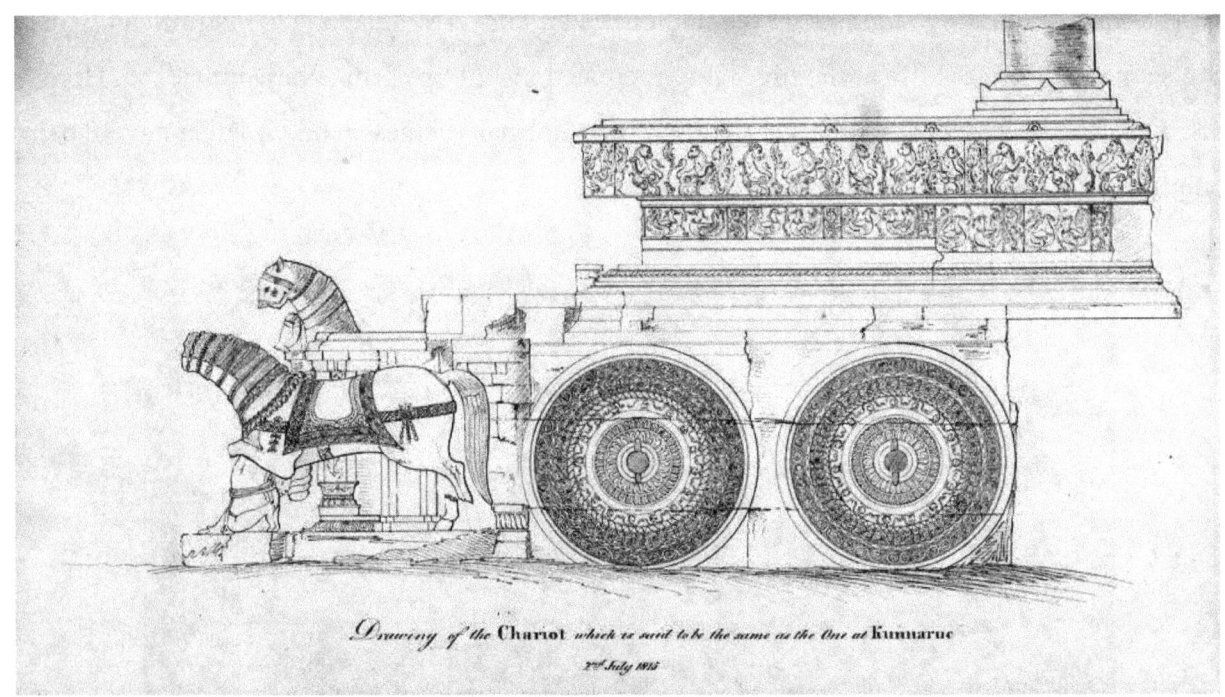

Stone horses pulling the Sun Chariot: anonymous pen and ink drawing circa 1815 (Public Domain)

I spent my last day here traveling to a small village outside Puri to see Orissa's art. I took a dusty bus to mile marker 10 from the city and then walked a mile to the village of Chaurapur. This is a one-horse town and that horse left years ago, which spreads out into fertile rice fields, green lagoons, and forests of coconut and palm trees. Halfway through the village, I saw a small house with paintings hung on the exterior walls and painters working at their art in the courtyard. They were very friendly and brought out all their paintings for me to see. I picked out a long horizontal painting of a Hindu god festival, complete with gods in a horse-drawn chariot, cows, and lovely flower-strewing maidens, for a very low price. They rolled it up for me, and I headed back to Puri.

Sun God Surya : Sun Chariot Temple: Konark

British officers explore the ruins of the Sun Chariot temple in 1847: Watercolor by William George Stephen (Public Domain)

My painting from Puri, framed and cherished.

On the way out of the village, I spoke with a friendly local policeman, who went out of his way to flag down a government highway truck and told them to take me to Puri. So, there I was, sitting on top of a huge pile of red earth, watching the green Orissa countryside go by and freaking out the local villagers with children running after the truck and yelling either "hello" or "hippie," the only two English words they knew.

Chapter Seventy: Reise Mit Kinder (Traveling With Children)

Traveling with children: Freaks with their children in Goa in the early 1970s (Photo from I LOVE GOA: FACEBOOK post by Vikash Jain) (Photographer: Jacques Lasray, who later became a famous music composer and started a successful band in France.)

In my stay in India, I met single moms and dads and couples traveling with their pre-teen children. Many of these travelers were on a spiritual quest, others were druggies, and some were just extended-vacation tourists. Each parent saw this as a great learning experience for their offspring. In Auroville, I saw many Westerners: single parents and couples with children born there, living in houses they built themselves. At that time in the early 1970s, there were 66 children born in Auroville, happily adjusted and playing with kids of all colors and nationalities. Goa had many hippie couples with children (as seen above), and the ones that I met were great parents and kept their kids protected from the wilder elements of the large freak colony.

My aunt was a missionary with her husband and two small girls in Swaziland, South Africa. The children, Lois and Juliane, were born and lived there until they were 16 and 14, respectively. Their playmates were all Africans. They grew up without racial prejudice, were receptive to different customs and languages, and were resilient to any changes thrown at them. Lois, Juliane, and the children of Auroville had a stable environment and were gradually exposed to new ideas and lifestyles with nurturing parents to guide them.

From my experience in the army, I met many "Army brats" of all ages, colors, and sexes. These kids were also exposed to different cultures, circumstances, and lifestyles. Some adapted very well, but many felt a rootlessness, a sense of not belonging anywhere. The cycle of making friends in a strange environment and then losing them forever after 2-3 years gave them a deep sense of insecurity. As they grew older, they had a reluctance to start meaningful relationships. What's the use if you have to move on and never see these companions again?

I dated an Army brat in college. Corrine was a loving, beautiful person, but she saw me as a fly-by-night passerby. In one or two years, I would graduate, be gone, and she'd have to start all over again. She dropped me and married the first person who offered her stability and a chance to spread roots in one place.

The druggies were different. Some went wherever the drugs were cheap; others stayed at freak beaches like Goa, living with various partners and only out for themselves. Their kids were either shunted aside or treated like a smaller brother or sister to be initiated into their "glamorous big sister or big brother lifestyle." This meant introducing them into the world of "mother's little helper." I am not a Puritan (don't let the buckle shoes, gray frock, and black stovepipe hat fool you), but giving kids drugs at an early age sets a bad precedent on how these children view life. Either they use it as an escape from their current situation or see it as a pleasurable lifestyle, free from responsibilities and a moral compass. (Well, so much for the "moral" admonishment - I know a lot of freaks that don't "Cotton" to being lectured to, not that it "Mathers").

REISE MIT KINDER (TRAVELING WITH CHILDREN)

INTRODUCTION

The following is a true incident that could have been a scene from an unwritten Eugene Ionesco play.

SCENE 1

Setting: A lounge in a small traveler's hotel in Puri, India. Marie, a young Italian woman about 25, comes in smoking a marijuana cigarette. She addresses a group of travelers as follows. "Hey, it's our last night here. Let me make everyone a real home-cooked Indian and Italian meal."

She turns to Pur Mamoo, the owner of the hotel, who is also smoking a joint, and asks: "Can we use the kitchen to cook, and do you have lady fingers (okra), Japan wheat noodles, tomatoes, and ghee?"

Mamoo: "Yes, and I also have cumin, garlic, and chickpeas."

He then sits back in his armchair and resumes smoking a thick joint.

Marie starts the cooking, stopping every few minutes to have a toke off of her joint.

Gordon, an American freak with long hair, beard, and aviator glasses, is sitting at the table smoking one joint and making more Manali grade #1 joints. Two children, Franco, age 9 (son of Maria) and a blond Dutch girl, Veska, age 10 (daughter of Jan, another blond Dutch character), were playing on the lounge floor.

Franco stealthily reaches up and takes a joint from the lineup of joints that Gordon has just made. Gordon is already stoned and doesn't even realize that a joint is missing from his lineup. Franco takes the joint, and he and Veska go to the corner of the lounge.

Franco lights up the joint and takes a long hit. Veska looks on in envy and says in perfect American English: "Hey, give me a toke on that joint, please."

Franco, deeply inhaling, has the joint removed from his mouth by Veska, who then proceeds to inhale a long drag. The two children start to fight, each grabbing for the joint.

Mamoo wakes up startled, "What's happening?"

Jan, the blond Dutchman, comes into the room, walks up to his daughter, and says, "You know you're going to get sick. Give the joint to me. I wouldn't mind you smoking it if I thought you'd get something out of it."

Maria, again stopping her cooking, comes over and says to the two children, "Hey, don't be greedy. Let the other people in the room have some."

The kids reluctantly give up the joint, which is then immediately shared by Maria and Jan. Maria says, "Oh, those silly kids," laughing.

The smell of marijuana, mixed with the spicy smells of cumin, curry, and garlic, creates a heady food high. The dinner is finally ready, and everyone eats ravenously, a result of the "marijuana munchies."

After dinner, the kitchen boy, Farook, comes over to clean the table. Gordon gives him a joint, saying, "Hey Farook, try this: it will blow your mind."

Farook takes the joint and inhales in long, deep snorts. Farook gets stoned very quickly and sits down, gazing into space. The dinner dishes need to be picked up and cleaned, but Farook doesn't respond. Mamoo stops smoking, stands up, towering over him, and shouts, "Get up and clean this mess." Still no response.

Everyone at the table begs Mamoo to stop shouting at Farook. Maria runs to get the radio and puts on some fast-beat Hindu raga music to distract Mamoo. However, Jan saves the day when he brings out his chillum filled with a special blend of Afghani hashish. Everyone stops talking as the God of Intoxication is passed around. Even Franco and Veska are allowed to have a hit. Farook, however, is still sitting sphinxlike without moving.

Jan starts dancing to the music, and he is soon joined by Maria, gyrating together to the rhythmic beat. Then the kids get up and start hopping up and down and laughing. Gordon finally staggers to his feet, attempting his best Motown routine, complete with half splits, until he falls down in the middle of a song, too stoned to get up ("The Gipper is off the field and outta' the game"). Mamoo claps and starts singing, and Farook just sits there staring into space.

Scene ends.

Nepal

A rani or Nepalese lady of rank 19th century (Public Domain).

Chapter Seventy-One: The Road to Kathmandu

That's why I'm going to Katmandu

Up to the mountains where I'm going to

Hey, if I ever get out of here

That's what I'm gonna do

Oh, K-k-k-k-k-k-Katmandu.

-"Katmandu:" Bob Seger

I arrived exhausted in Calcutta and checked into a traveler's hotel, looking for a partner in crime to accompany me to Nepal. There were the usual stoned freaks, doing their best Sphinx imitation of staring into space or walking aimlessly about, then I noticed an incongruous traveler: short cropped blond hair, clean shaven, dressed in clean khaki pants and a white linen shirt. He had that rugged Hemingway handsomeness and a good-natured smile that put you immediately at ease.

Self-Portrait: Phillip Otto Runge 1801 (Public Domain)

At first, I thought that Freak Central Casting had sent him to the wrong film stage: this is a zombie movie set, not the Rock Hudson/ Doris Day romantic comedy stage. I went over and started talking with him (I restrained myself from pleading for his autograph!). His name was Tom Gates, and he was from Iowa. He had just graduated from Grinnell College, majoring in philosophy, and was taking a year off to see how Eastern philosophy answered the basic questions of life. He had been to Japan and studied Zen Buddhism. Now, he was in India to find out about the Hindu sages.

We spoke for hours about the significance of the Ryoan-ji temple garden, the ways to clear your mind, to accept the nothingness of Nirvana and then the pantheism of Spinoza, of how God is in every living being and then the teachings of Sri Aurobindo, where through inward self-examination you can access the divinity in each of us. Then, like all good freaks, I gave him my well-rehearsed "Amway" spiel on the benefits of drugs (it's very simple to operate: you take the clay chillum, stuff it with hash, light the chillum, inhale deeply, wait about five minutes and Wallah, you're high, no cares, no mess, no cleanup), how they relaxed your mind, opening your senses to accept new ideas. He had done a little marijuana smoking in college but never enjoyed the drug scene. Aha, I thought, a virgin to seduce and deflower, figuratively speaking, of course! We went out for dinner and afterwards, I mixed a strong blunt of Afghan hash. We both got very high and laughed at everything we said. I felt like Samuel Morse, sending the first telegraph to Tom in India with his famous words, "What hath God wrought?" Tom and I smoked regularly for the next few days, "And another one bites the dust." The pod aliens had taken over another body, and I convinced him to accompany me to Nepal.

The trip from Calcutta to Nepal was a horror show. Of course, we didn't get a sleeper rail car, so we stood for twelve hours. The train was packed with Bihari Muslims celebrating the end of Ramadan. When they finally got off the train, in came an onslaught of hundreds of Hindus, all eager to get back to their little farming villages to celebrate Diwali, the festival of lights. This time, we shared a crowded seat with the celebrants and got a chance to see the countryside. Bihar is very flat, filled with yellow paddy, green sugarcane, and high-stalked jute. We rode on all night through the darkness, surrealistically lit by hurricane lamps and occasional bonfires of the villages we passed. In the early morning, we awoke, the first rays of the sun striking the dark green banana leaves, the golden crown of corn, and fields of turmeric-colored paddy. There were huge luminescent green pipal trees, with new shoots sprouting from the gnarled central trunk and phosphorescent glowing water buffaloes grazing lazily in its shade. I made myself mushroom-trip through this technicolor brightness, reveling in this veritable Garden of Eden. That night, we crossed over the border into Birguni, Nepal. We exited our overstuffed hell on wheels and found a small dormitory hotel. My first impression of the town was a disappointment. It looked and smelled like a dusty, rat-infested Mexican border town: garbage strewn, mud lanes, worn cinderblock houses, and runny-nosed children, all clamoring for baksheesh. Moreover, it was very disappointing that there wasn't a lively red-light bar district (Hey soldier, looking for a good time?), not to mention a Mariachi band to welcome us.

The dormitory was a concrete shoebox with rope beds and nets; unfortunately, it came complete with mosquitoes inside the nets! The next morning, we hitched a ride and were picked up by a Nepali businessman, who drove us halfway to Kathmandu in style in his late model Land Rover. He let us off at a Nepali truck stop, and there we found a good-natured Sikh who offered to take us all the way to Kathmandu (about a 6-hour trip).

A typical colorfully painted Indian truck, similar to the truck we rode on top of the cab all the way to Kathmandu
(PUVVUKONVICT Photography: UNSPLASH)

His gaily painted truck was filled to the brim with sacks of rice and lentils, but he told us we could ride on top of the driving cab. So, we climbed aboard, grabbed the back rail, and the adventure began. We dipped into rice-terraced valleys, the sides of the road lush with banana and papaya trees; the sky above was the darkest Dresden blue, and there was not a cloud to be seen. We looked back and in the hazy distance, were the flat, dusty plains of India; we were leaving the hot, sun-scorched purgatory for the Heaven of the Vale of the Gods. We climbed steadily, passing rushing waterfalls and small red-painted earthen houses; from the ridge tops, the houses looked like little red dots in seas of green and yellow fields. We saw honeysuckle vines blooming pink against the ochre and burnished gold millet vistas; here, the red adobe houses were hung gaily with multi-colored field corn. The sun warmed us and toward dusk, it radiated day-glow pink on the snow-capped mountains far ahead of us. With the refreshing breeze in our faces and the technicolor landscapes surrounding us, I felt an epiphany of anticipated excitement: I would finally realize my childhood dream of visiting a real-life Shangri La.

Indian Painted Truck driving through the Himalayas: Anirudh Thakur
(UNSPLASH)

We drove past Nepalese women beating clothes in the meandering streams, washing their hair or quietly sitting, picking fleas out of their children's jet-black hair.

Nepal is a riot of colors - from the embroidered red velvet blouses to the pink coral and lapis-lazuli stone necklaces, to the silver and gold nose rings and earrings that Nepalese women wear, to the old men in tight-fitting black pants, that baggy out on the bottom, black vests over white homespun linen shirts and Moslem style fez caps. Mothers carrying their children on their backs while they go about their chores or spreading black grease on crying children's faces, to protect them from the harsh ultraviolent sun. The fading sun sent shafts of light through huge pipal trees, bathing the women, carrying huge baskets of millet, transforming them into shimmering copper silhouettes.

Girl swinging, Kathmandu. (author's photo)

We rounded a bend in the road, and I glanced down and saw a stony outcrop overlooking the verdant valley below. Here was a large tree hung with a swing. The view was breathtaking: a young Nepali girl swinging, with the whole valley spread below her. The image was gone in a second, but it was déjà vu, a flashback to a small, rundown farm in Appalachian East Tennessee. There was a small swing in the backyard, near a "hollow" brook and a ragged-dressed, hauntingly beautiful mountain girl swinging blithely, her swinging motions stopping time: the girl, swing and brook suspended in calmness, like being in the eye of a hurricane, where the savage storms of life cannot penetrate this quietude.

Kathmandu in 1811: Engraving by English artist William Kirkpatrick (Public Domain).

Chapter Seventy-Two: The Ideal of Kathmandu

For the world is wondrous large,

Seven seas from marge to marge,

And it holds a vast of various kinds of man.

And the wildest dreams of Kew

Are the facts of Khatmandu,

-Rudyard Kipling

Kathmandu I'll soon be touching you

And your strange bewildering time.

-"Kathmandu": Cat Stevens

Kathmandu's Durbar Square 1852: Watercolor by British artist Henry Ambrose Oldfield (Public Domain)

Kathmandu is one of those magical exotic places whose name conjures mystery, remoteness, and a sense of liberation: a mountain retreat where one can be truly free. My fascination with Kathmandu was not really about Kathmandu at all but about my imagined Tibet. As a young boy of about 10 or 11, I read one of the seminal books that has influenced me for all my life: "Seven Years in Tibet" by Heinrich Harrer.

Original Tibetan Buddhist Altar, 1900. Photo courtesy of Newark Museum, Newark,

"Seven Years in Tibet" tells the story of Heinrich Harrer and Peter Aufschnaiter, two mountain climbing Austrians captured by the British in India and imprisoned because of World War Two. They escaped from a British internment camp in India in 1944, made their way across the mountains, and finally received refuge in Lhasa, Tibet. There, Harrer became friend and tutor to the 14th Dalai Lama, Tenzin Gyatso (The present Dalai Lama, currently living in exile in India). Harrer writes of the everyday life and culture of the theocratic feudal state before the Chinese communists invaded in 1950. What I remember from the book are the Tibetan people themselves: warm, friendly, religious people who would stop digging a building foundation if they found worms, which they carefully removed so they would not have to kill them. This realistic portrait of Tibet carried over and was transformed by James Hilton's "Lost Horizon." Here was a mystical place, a Shangri-La deep in the Himalayas, where people never aged and lived in harmony with God.

This fairy-tale Tibet was furthered by my visits to the Newark (New Jersey) Museum. This museum has one of the most extensive and comprehensive Tibetan art, artifacts, and culture collections in the United States. Early in the 20th century, the museum bought hundreds of household objects, artworks, and a complete Tibetan altar from Christian missionaries who had returned from that country. Here, you could see how the Tibetans worshipped and lived in a medieval society similar to 15th-century Europe.

Both Harrer and Hilton painted this magical picture of a paradise in the Himalayas, reality and fiction intertwined in my thoughts of life in Tibet. However, when I grew up, Tibet had already been conquered, and while I was in Asia, the Tibetan religion was being destroyed by the Cultural Revolution of the Chinese Red Guards.

While I was traveling in India, I imagined Nepal to be another Tibet - not the present-day Tibet but the mystical Shangri-La, an exotic Buddhist culture untouched by Western capitalism and materialism. The reality was even stranger than my wildest fantasies.

Tibetan Lamas from "India Illustrated" 1905 (Public Domain).

Chapter Seventy-Three: Kathmandu - The Promised Land

Mister, I ain't a boy, I'm a man

And I believe in the Promised Land.

-"Promised Land": Bruce Springsteen

We came to Kathmandu in the early evening. The entire city was aglow with electric lights; there were people and cows everywhere. The crisp mountain air gave me the feeling that I was experiencing Christmas in September. However, as we continued into the city, I felt that I stepped back in time to medieval Nuremberg: the crumbling brick houses, with their wood-carved overhangs, the open-air markets, the smells of spices, rotted fruits, and animal and human waste filled the crooked lanes. Small, stocky Tibetan and white-clad Hindu shoppers, people smoking bubbling hokums in front of imposing, carved-wood doorways, and children running helter-skelter, laughing, crying, or begging. This was a living tableau of Bruegel's "Flemish Peasant Dance" painting.

"Flemish Peasant Dance": Pieter Bruegel the Elder 1568, (Public Domain).

There were oil lamps burning everywhere we turned in honor of Laxmi, the goddess of light and wealth. We checked into a freak hotel and headed to Freak Street (no kidding, that's the name of the street!) to get dinner.

The business-savvy Tibetans run most of the small hole-in-the-wall restaurants. These restaurants consist of two long wooden tables and benches, where you are all huddled together, and invariably, a freak stranger starts passing a chillum of hash along to you, so you are quite stoned before you even order your food. The menu is quite extensive and aims to please every nationality: there are fish and chips, bully beef and porridge for the Brits, pasta and pizza for the Italians, schnitzel for the Germans, tripe for the French, and hamburgers, pancakes, and mom's home-baked apple pie for the Americans; the only food not represented was Nepali, but they made up for that by serving chang (Tibetan barley beer).

Photo shows the "Annaporee (Kathmandu) Loaf Store" delivery pedicycle on the streets of Kathmandu 1970 (Photo by "rustyproof" on Flickr)

The enterprising Nepalis made Western-style bread for the freaks and tourists. My father's heimat, Switzerland, as part of their aid to Nepal, set up a cheese-making factory in Kathmandu to make genuine Swiss cheese (holes included). Bread, cheese, and chang beer: what more could a starving freak ask for?

"THE WILDEST DREAMS OF KEW"

How do you define the essence of such a magical city: write volumes about the history, culture, and soul of the place like Lawrence Durrell did in his "Alexandria Quartet," or do you sing praises in songs like Billy Joel's "New York State of Mind"? At best, I can only capture it from an outsider's point of view. I walk the streets in awe and amazement, taking photos of people and places. You would like to stop time and keep this place a fairy tale come true. What made it even more pleasurable was that there were very few cars, mostly the big black Indian Ambassador taxi, which stood out like the yellow Checker taxi in New York City.

I have said that Kathmandu is like a medieval European city. I have visited many preserved medieval cities in Germany, especially Rotenberg an der Tauber, which has its medieval walls intact, and you can walk around the whole town. It is a jewel of frack-work houses, majestic stone churches, and colorful open-air markets. Cars are banished from this museum piece, and unfortunately, that's what it is. What are missing are all of the five senses. In Rothenburg, you have the physical appearance of a medieval town, but you don't have the sound, feel, smell, or taste that can truly transport you back to medieval Germany. In Kathmandu, all your senses are assaulted and alive: the city is a jewel (dirt-covered diamond in the rough, to be more precise) to walk around, a visual feast; you can also touch and feel the statues covered in flowers and incense, run your fingers over the intricately carved wood doorways, eat fruit and vegetables that you have just bought from open-air market stalls. But then the other senses kick in: the smell of human and animal excrement, strong rotting meat hanging by hooks and covered with flies, the sickly-sweet burning incense, the savory aroma of hundreds of cooked meals, many prepared on the sidewalk as you walk by. You stop in the early morning for a samosa and a hot chai: the taste awakens you and stimulates all of your senses. Then there are the sounds of merchants hawking their goods, the shrill boisterousness of little children running everywhere, the sounds of bells welcoming you to the temples, and the cacophony of different languages spoken on the street. The sounds of work: the ditch diggers shoveling, the jewelers hammering gold, and the potter at the humming wheel. The city is alive, but what makes it truly medieval is the religion. We in the West are used to going to church once a week and then we go about our ordinary business. Here, religion is a daily part of everyone's life.

Scientists have said that there is a sixth sense: one of equilibrium, where your body adjusts to outward stimuli and keeps you upright. In Kathmandu, your equilibrium is out of balance: you are reeling with sensory overload. Everywhere you turn, people are coming and going out of temples; children are playing in the temple courtyards; women are decorating statues with pungent incense and garlands of flowers; and men are cleaning themselves in the public baths before they enter the temple. Religion is the glue that transports you back in time.

In Kathmandu, I caught a glimpse of a living goddess, the "Kumari Deva." This is a young girl who is chosen, like the Dalai Lama in Tibet, to be the "living goddess" who protects Kathmandu. She is chosen from a caste of Newari gold and silversmiths, usually between the ages of four and puberty. Like the Dalai Lama, she must pass many tests to prove to the priests that she is the chosen one. Once she is picked, she rarely leaves the palace, where she has a balcony and appears before the faithful once a day. This little elf of a girl, dressed in a colorful sari and jeweled headdress, waves at the crowd and then disappears. However, the crowds of Nepalis return to their daily business satisfied, knowing that the goddess is protecting them and Kathmandu is safe from evil. The only time she leaves is for a religious festival and again she cannot touch the ground and is carried everywhere in a palanquin or chariot for the festival. Once she has her first menstruation, she is relieved of her duties, given a large dowry and a new living goddess is chosen.

There are religious festivals where hundreds of bulls, goats, and roosters are slaughtered, sacrificed to the gods of Hindu temples. Just as important as the visual splendor of the temples, monasteries, and stupas is the tactile feel of the city: the muddy earth of the roads, the weather-darkened wood of the temples, and the worn stone and wood of the temple carvings. You walk around the Buddhist eye stupa at Swayambhunath three times, touching the rough white stucco, feeling the same religious awe that the monks do walking alongside you.

Your hearing is assaulted by the temple drums and bells. Every night, I walk by the main temples in Durbar Square and hear the priests chant the Holy Scriptures (Vedas) and temple musicians play the monotonous dirges using cymbals, drums, and the vina (sitar-like instrument).

There are temples, pagodas, and stupas everywhere you turn. From the Swayambhunath Stupa, which the Indian Emperor Ashoka was supposed to have built 2500 years ago, to the smallest Ganesh roadside altar, worn smooth, through generations of touching, yet still gaily decorated daily with fresh flowers and smeared with ochre and reddish incense. The all-seeing "Double-Eye" temple is always following you (Thank God, I'm glad I'm not paranoid!).

Buddha and Shiva statues are at every square and corner of the street. The carvings are as detailed in the roof rafters, high above eye level, as in main altars. (It pays to look up because on many Hindu temples, the roof struts visible from the street are decorated with explicit Kama Sutra carvings). This, again, is like medieval churches in Nuremberg, where even the gargoyles are carved with as full a detail as the Virgin on the main altar: these were made by anonymous artisans to show reverence to God alone.

Swayambhunath Stupa, a Buddhist sanctuary in Kathmandu (author's photo).

There is an old man who runs a small cigarette shop near our hotel. He sits in the evenings, playing his vina and chants the old hymns in a voice full of anguish and monotone beauty - a voice similar to the throaty, impassioned John Jacob Niles in 1920's Appalachia, singing "Black is the

Color of My True Love's Hair." This old Nepali has no audience to perform for; it is only sung for the God he reveres.

You walk down a side street, and you see the people spreading wheat on the roads for bicycles, children, and passersby to separate the chaff from wheat. You bend down and take a wheat morsel in your mouth; it is dusty and chalky. You spit it out, but the taste lingers. You thirstily drink a chai to get rid of the taste and after you've finished, the earthen cup is thrown on the ground and destroyed, never to be used again for the sake of purity.

Life here is elemental, following the seasons: the planting and, when I arrived, the harvesting of the grain. Everyone is working feverishly to get in the new crop before the rains and cold of winter.

Business selling "hippie gear" on Freak Street in Kathmandu (photographer: HOLLYNOW) License: GNU Free Documentation, Ver 1.2 free to use with attribution of author HOLLYNOW.

Then you walk back to Freak Street, and it is as if Scotty had beamed you up back to the 1970s. Here, your senses are again put in overload: the smell of hash chillums, the taste of homemade apple pie, and the sight of freaks everywhere. The rough splintered touch of the hardwood benches as you eat your meal and the incessant blare of Janis Joplin and Led Zeppelin.

Although we are just a thin veneer in Nepali society, we are the freaks, hundreds of us, the guys in torn jeans, baggy Chinese fisherman pants, multi-striped jester costumes, complete with bells on their pointed caps and shoes. Freaks in Afghan shirts with Muslim skull caps, flowing white Indian robes, leather sandals, and sturdy Alpine hiking boots. The gals range from 1960s Summer of Love, flower power embroidered Guatemalan blouses and faded, multicolored bell bottoms to completely native: brightly colored wedding saris, complete with steel bangles, beaded sandalwood necklaces, heavy gold earrings, and delicate filigree nose rings. We are friendly, always offering a chillum smoke in the small Tibetan-run restaurants, outside of the surreal hashish government-regulated shops, and on temple stairs. We have our own drone orchestra: Western rock and roll blaring out of every shop and restaurant. The Nepali authorities didn't hassle you; it is a joy to be young, alive, and in Kathmandu!

After a few weeks here I realized that Kathmandu was more than the exotic Buddhist kingdom that I had longingly fantasized about; more than a living medieval museum of faith and filth; more than the home of the fabled Nepali hashish, the gold standard to judge the "quick and the dead" of all other hashes (Gordon Schwerzmann, famed international Freak and "bon vivant gourmet" gives it "Two thumbs up" and five stars); and even more than the end of the Hippie Rainbow Trail that stretches from London to Kathmandu. It is all the psychic energy of an entirely new "Lost Generation" directed toward this mystical place at this special time ("Maybe it's the time of year or maybe it's the time of man" {Joni Mitchell "Woodstock"}). This is the new Paris, and we are the "stoned" updates of Ernest Hemingway, F. Scott Fitzgerald, and Henry Miller, fervently believing that the "Summer of Love" will go on forever.

"Tokin' outside of a government-controlled hashish shop 1970 (photographer unknown) Pinterest and The Italian Touring Club's review of Emanuele Giordana's book: "Viaggio Ail' Eden" 2017

Some unknown force ("The Force" be with you, Gordon Solo) has sent all the myriad freak tribes in America and Europe a subliminal message: "You must go and be part of this once-in-a-lifetime defining moment of peace and love. This is the biblical "Promised Land," the land of "milk and honey" that Yahweh gave his chosen people, a Paradise where the "Freak Nation" makes its stand; everything was possible, we could change ourselves and society. This turns Woodstock on its head: here, you are the rock stars, not the adoring mud-splattered audience. You are making your own destiny, creating your own anthems of love, universal brotherhood, and acceptance and understanding, a "Brave New World," here and now and forever. Here you are in a country where you can be totally free, where what you stand for is respected by the locals. You are a seeker, a sadhu in their eyes, and you are looking for life's answers. The mountains are calling you for a new spiritual rejuvenation. Here, the "luft" of high altitudes and Dresden blue skies seem to bring you closer to God. Here, we have a community of freaks and the power to transform ourselves. To build a community where "bombers riding shotgun in the sky, turn into butterflies above our nation," as Joni Mitchell poignantly sang of "Woodstock." We are young and idealistic; we have come to a land of belief in strange gods and yet we feel as one with the place and people. We are the new romantics. We feel like the father of English romantic poetry, William Wordsworth. We experience a visionary view of life.

"With an eye made quiet by the power of harmony, and the deep power of joy, we see into the life of things" (William Wordsworth: "Tintern Abbey").

The next morning, the whole city was enveloped in fog; the sun an ivory disc, visible through the still silvery leaves of a majestic weeping willow outside our hotel. We walk to Durbar Square (where the most famous temples are located) just in time to catch the now reddish-yellow sun baptize the old temples with a cleansing purity to show the elaborately carved detail in almost blinding white light.

Kathmandu was originally a destination stop on a branch offshoot of the fabled "Silk Road." This trade route was still an operation until the Chinese closed it down in the early 1950s. The Gurkhas, known for their fierce fighting in World War Two, conquered Nepal in the 19th century and established a secluded Hindu kingdom, shut off from the rest of the world.

A Freak wedding in Kathmandu 1973 (Photo by 365 security solution@securitycamy on Pinterest.

Nepal only opened to foreigners in 1953. At that time, there was one dirt road going into Kathmandu; the first tourist bus consisted of nine Americans and nine Brazilians. The new king of Nepal opened the country to all tourists and the freaks first discovered it in the late 1960s. What appealed to the freaks was the image of Kathmandu as a Shangri-La, a mystical land of peace and love, and the hash, which was legally sold in government shops when I was there. What appealed to me about Kathmandu was that the people were generally glad to see you and they went out of their way to create a friendly atmosphere: shops and restaurants that catered exclusively to the freaks. Later, I found out why, and it was because of the caste system: the first restaurants, bakeries, and chai shops were founded by Untouchables and later by the Buddhist Tibetans who treated everyone equally. The higher caste Hindu Nepalese wanted nothing to do with the foreigners because they were impure. So, the Untouchables created restaurants in their district and the freaks knew nothing about this. They just went to this district because the food was good and cheap. In the early 1970s, freaks were the majority of tourists and there was a whole section of town, Freak Street, that catered exclusively to this clientele.

Nepalis living in the back streets still gawk at you, like they do in the remote farming villages of India. However, here, the attitude is different: they smile at you. Even the old beggars joke with you, whether you give them backsheesh or not. The shopkeepers, monks, businessmen, and government officials all smile and are very helpful. Perhaps it is the tolerance of Hinduism, which can absorb everything from freaks to tourists to communists.

Everyone is up by 7 AM, setting up the vegetable stands (cauliflowers, radishes, and tomatoes predominate at this time of year) and displaying their fruits (I'm eating juicy persimmons - the first time since Korea). The shops are displaying their spices and brass pots, even the government-regulated hash shops are open for business (unfortunately, there are no free samples; where is COSCO when you really need them?).

Kathmandu government regulated hash shop 1970s with two freaks deciding to purchase the "catch of the day" (photographer unknown)
Credit: "r/Old School Cool" posted on "Reddit" by u/mOmOtamatar

Tom and I decided to visit the Chinese border and get a close-up of the Himalayan Mountains. We got a room in the Nepali town of Duelikel. At sunrise, the sight of the snow-covered peaks rearing up directly in front of us was awe-inspiring, but the light show got even better when the early morning sun rose red, striking the mountains and turning them chameleon-style into deep crimson. We trekked around the majestic landscape, exploring a picturesque gorge with a swift-running river that divided Nepal and China.

At night in the lodge, we met an English-fluent middle-aged Nepali, Ashoka, who was headed off to the mountains to an obscure village to live for a year, "to clear his head," in his words. Embracing the mountain air and solitude to examine his life without the daily cares of life to distract him. He was not particularly religious but felt a need to get a new direction, to develop a purposeful plan to find meaning, living his life to the fullest. In America, we would call this a "mid-life crisis;" our solution is to shed one wife for a younger woman, to recapture our youth, to find some illusive fulfillment in someone else's arms. We don't look within ourselves to find solutions for our emptiness like Ashoka is doing; we believe someone new will solve this for us.

It was raining heavily when he set off with two porters, each overloaded, stacked with his worldly possessions, yet still, one of the porters had one hand free to hold an umbrella over Ashoka's head. It was a comic Mutt and Jeff scene, he two feet taller, carrying nothing, while the porter balanced his precarious load and still kept him dry.

Back in Kathmandu, we spent evenings in a small Tibetan beer hall. The hall fronted a temple courtyard, with a looming all-seeing-eye temple watching us as we drank chang beer.

Two women Freaks on a Kathmandu street 1970 (from the web site "India mike", photographer "Wanderer 22") .

Kathmandu has dozens of freak chicks, women tourists, women mountain climbers, Buddhist neophytes, and idealistic, wholesome Peace Corps volunteers. During the summer months, the "magic buses," London To Kathmandu, arrived weekly, disgorging a new crop of wide-eyed, adventuresome women. Surveying the scene, I thought I was in heaven, not the Christian do-gooder Heaven nor the ascetic Buddhist Nirvana, but the Islamic Garden of Eden paradise: I had put my time in Hell, sweating on the dusty roads, eating the roadside slop meals, and enduring the horrors of the third-class Indian rail. Allah now took mercy on me and transported me to this magical garden filled with lovely maidens to woo and win.

Here, we met two young Peace Corps volunteers. Ida from Michigan was headed for a small village, half a day's journey from Kathmandu. She will be teaching English in a place that has no electricity, no indoor plumbing, and only well water. She has a guitar and books but is splurging on food and a bicycle before she starts her assignment. Phillip from Wisconsin is headed into the mountains to a remote village to teach English and science, only taking books and his favorite fishing rod. He also will have no electricity and no indoor water or plumbing. He will probably not see another Westerner until his teaching is completed. The idealism and dedication to service that these young people exemplify make me proud to be an American. I only hope that more Americans will have this same dedication in teaching at inner-city schools, serving as doctors and nurses in underserved urban and rural areas, or as contractors, building low-cost housing to replace slums in our country.

I have been exploring the countryside by bicycle, visiting many of the small medieval towns close by in the valley. Incidentally, I ate at "The Camp" restaurant shown above the cyclist, and the food was excellent. Also, note the Volkswagen bus on the right of the photo that carried freak travelers to Kathmandu from Europe.

This is harvesting time in Nepal, and everywhere you see farmers cutting down, threshing, and sifting the chaff from the rice. Kirtipur is a typical medieval village filled with temples and no cars. Here, the main square is completely filled with communal fresh wheat; the people walk over it to loosen and separate the chaff.

Renting Bicycles was the easiest way to see the Kathmandu Valley 1970 (photographer unknown) Pinterest and The Italian Touring Club's review of Emanuele Giordana's book: "Viaggio Ail' Eden" 2017.

The days are autumn mellow. I wander around and sit in dusty Nepali tea shops, drinking hot chai. The people here are strong and hard-working; the women carry baskets full of paddy, strapping the basket to their back, with the main strap on their forehead that carries the load. The village has cobblestone walks and the houses are two or three-story, reddish-brown brick with all the windows, balconies, and doorways covered with exquisitely detailed wood carving.

It was on this bicycle trip that I met Claire, whose story follows.

Kirtipur's Main Square at harvest time (author's photo).

Chapter Seventy-Four: "We Are More Than Cuckoo Clocks, Swiss Cheese, and Chocolate"

Nepal, even more than Tibet, was a closed country to Western foreigners. One man who came to Nepal as part of a diplomatic aid mission changed all this. That man was Toni Hagan and he spent 12 years in Nepal, crisscrossing the entire country on a geographical and geological exploration. He trekked over 14,000 miles, studying the people, their culture, and their living conditions. Hagan explored the best sources for hydroelectric projects and spent years cataloging and mapping the country's heretofore unknown mountains. An expert botanist, he collected and recorded the extraordinary fauna of this varied land, which has the highest mountains and densest tropical jungles in the world.

Toni Hagan holding his book "Nepal" (unknown date) (Photographer Bhuwan Maharyan released photo to CC-Attr-SA-4.0 International License with attribution of author).

Hagan wrote a book about his experiences and even made a short documentary movie about the country. I saw this video and found that in the 20 years' interval from his visit to my own, most aspects of life in Nepal remain the same. My photographs of village life outside of Kathmandu were the same as his film: the way the porters carried goods with a band supporting the basket on their foreheads, the hand-knotted rope bridges, and the mud and brick houses of remote villages, which are still lacking electricity and functional sanitation. Hagan, however, was more than just a scientist; he was also a humanitarian. When the Tibetans revolted against Communist China's rule in 1959 and caused the Dalai Lama to flee to India, Hagen, through his diplomatic connections, was able to secure sanctuary in Switzerland for over 1500 Tibetan exiles in Nepal. He personally met and became friends with the exiled Dalai Lama and worked for the betterment and welfare of the Tibetan exiles who remained in Nepal.

Hagen's book "Nepal" is still a standard for its scientific and geological research, but when he was interviewed, he said, "I found the people of Nepal much more interesting than the rocks."

Toni Hagan was from my father's heimat (country), a Swiss, and was just one of the great explorers to come from that small mountainous country. The first and most famous was Johann Ludwig Burckhardt from Basel, Switzerland.

Johann Ludwig Burckhardt, Swiss traveler and orientalist (unknown painter and date) (Public Domain).

He was intensely interested in the Middle East and went to Oxford to learn Arabic. From England, he went to Egypt and then all around the Middle East, Syria, Lebanon, and (now present day) Jordan. He wanted to blend in with the camel herders and merchants so he disguised himself as a fellow merchant and joined caravans where he could do his exploring without being exposed as an infidel and probably killed.

His greatest discovery was the ancient trading and oasis city of Petra. He was with a camel caravan when he heard about this foreign ruin, which was located near the tomb of Aaron, Moses's brother in the Bible. Aaron is a revered figure in the Qu'ran, and he convinced his companions that he was going to sacrifice a goat to honor him at his tomb. He went off to the tomb and explored the countryside around there and discovered the lost city, making notes and sketches so he could research it later. However, he was sure that it was the Roman-ruined Petra and was the first Westerner to rediscover it in a millennium.

El Deir Petra, 8 March 1839, David Roberts. Library of Congress (Public Domain).

He returned to Egypt and went down the Nile River as far as it was navigable and discovered Abu Simbel, the great temple of Ramses II. This temple was in the news because it had to be cut out of the rock and moved in a massive engineering feat to the hills above where it was originally carved. Otherwise, the temple would have been flooded out by the massive Russian-built Aswan dam and lost forever.

His next great adventure was to disguise himself as a Muslim merchant and make the pilgrimage to Mecca, one of the first Westerners to enter the holy city of Mecca. His Muslim disguise and thorough knowledge of the Arabic language allowed him to enter the city and leave without being discovered as a Westerner, which surely would have brought his death. This remarkable journey was accomplished decades before Richard Burton, who also wore a Muslim disguise and traveled to Mecca and wrote his famous book about the journey.

Burckhardt returned to Cairo and was about to embark on an exploration to discover the source of the Nile. Unfortunately, he contracted dysentery and died in 1817 at the age of 32.

To this great list of explorers, I must add my father, who, in his early 20s, bravely decided to leave the comforts of Switzerland and immigrate to America in the 1920s. Here, he had no family and very little money, but he was able to get into the restaurant business because he had been trained in Switzerland as a saucier. He saved and started his own restaurant in New York City, which was doing good business until the Great Depression. He had to close his own restaurant, but he still worked in other restaurants and was drafted at the start of WW II into the US Army as a cook at the age of 43.

I, in my travels through Asia, carry on the legacy of my father's Swiss ancestors. I, too, am a keen explorer and especially interested in the flora of the country. I have sought out and tried many variations of the genus "cannabis sativa" plant to determine which is genetically the best adaptation and most potent (for medicinal purposes). I am experimenting with new varieties daily for scientific research, of course.

However, if I had followed in the footsteps of my mother's Norwegian ancestors, the Vikings, I would have to loot and burn the Buddhist monasteries, kill the monks, rape the Nepali women, and enslave the young boys for servants. Then I would hastily exit for the safety of India, steal a Dhow sailboat, and travel down the Ganges to the open sea and home.

Typical Dhow sailboat (Photo by Muhammad Mahdi Karim) (CC-Attr-SA-3.0 License, free to use with attribution of photographer).

Chapter Seventy-Five: Ingrid - The Heidi Redux

Little Miss Bopeep, Where Are Your Sheep?"

"Little Bo-Peep has lost her sheep,

And can't tell where to find them;

Leave them alone, and they'll come home,

Bringing their tails behind them.

-"Little Bo-Peep": Mother Goose

Shirley Temple 1937, the movie "Heidi".

I was walking around the Hindu temple with the Kama Sutra carvings and spotted this blond girl staring intently at the carvings. I approached her, saying, "Getting any ideas for something different for your boyfriend back home?" She turned around, "Some of these positions look like fun, but for others, you need to be a contortionist to accomplish." "Tibetan tantric Buddhism believes you can access the godhead through sexual union." "Any luck at that?" "Well, I'm just a novice monk and need a lot more practice to get there." She laughed, and I introduced myself. She said her name was Ingrid. She was very Germanic-looking with rounded, rosy cheeks, a straight nose, and full red lips. She exuded wholesomeness rather than beauty. She could have been a poster child for a skiing resort or a Heidi movie.

"Winter in Germany" (author's Poster) Image is Public Domain since original copyright was not renewed. It is not copyright in Germany or the United States (CC-CCO-PD license)..

She had gone native with a clunky sandalwood necklace, huge round metal earrings and multiple bangles on both arms, and rings on every finger. She looked a little incongruous with her goldilocks braided hair, dressed in a fancy red Indian sari embroidered with gold thread, and Arabian Nights pointed felt shoes. I thought to myself, Freak Central Casting really got it all wrong: this is supposed to be a Heidi Redux movie set in the Himalayas, not a "Hara Krishna, Hara Ram" sequel. She should have been dressed in a dirndl with a lacy white apron and a bow in her hair and staff in hand.

"Kathmandu is a fantastic timepiece. I imagine 15th century Nuremberg must have been like this." She looked at me amazed, "I thought the same thing, the crooked streets with overhung wooden balconies, the dusty, cramped stores, even the dirty, garbage-strewn muddy lanes: this is medieval Germany." "Have you been to Rothenberg an der Tauber and walked along the old walls and seen the medieval burger frachtwerk houses and the gorgeous carved church altarpieces?" "Yes, you have traveled all over Germany!" "I was in the army stationed in Pirmasens an der Plafz. Where are you from?" "I'm from Mainz an der Rhine." "One of my favorite memories of Germany was sitting in a cozy beer garden overlooking the Rhine on a beautiful summer Sunday afternoon, being serenaded by a German Um Papa band, and drinking Weissbier." "What's an Um Papa band?" "That's what we Americans call a traditional German dance band because of the sound the tuba makes: um papa, um papa." "Oh, I see," she said laughingly. "So, are you traveling with friends?" "Yes, I'm with German friends who took off yesterday for the mountains; I wanted to stay in town to see more of the sights." "Well then, let me show you my Kathmandu. There is a small Tibetan restaurant that serves real European food. I'll pick you up at your hotel, and I'll treat you to dinner."

The restaurant was a hole in the wall with long tables where you sat next to other freaks. Invariably, someone would light a chillum and pass it around. Ingrid was still in her sari, and I had bought a woolen Nepali side-tie shirt since it could get chilly at night. I told her about Auroville and the divine in everyone. She had been raised a Catholic but stopped going to church. She saw that in Nepal religion is all pervasive and dominates everything you do. She found this a little uncomfortable. She had given up on one faith and was not up for "Nirvana;" she just loved the "strangeness" of the place. "But to carry the Nuremberg analogy further, the Nepalese are like the medieval German peasant. For medieval man, there was Heaven and Hell, and he felt the weight of God in everything he did. Many of the Nepalese are illiterate. They follow the rituals of their priests to appease their gods; they strive to do good so they will be reborn into a better life, just like the German peasants strived to avoid the horrors of hell as depicted in Roger van der Weyden's graphic Last Judgement."

The Nepalese know their place in society and have a steadfast goal, unlike us in the West who are floundering for answers as who we are and what do we want out of life. "Do you feel your life is fulfilled?" She looked at me incredulously, as if I were trying to sell her a Hoover vacuum cleaner after a 20-minute rehearsed spiel. "I don't think much about it. I like my life in Germany and came to Nepal to experience exotic people and places. I could have stayed on a beach in Greece, but here, everything is so different: the wood-carved temples, the festive atmosphere, and the friendly people. This is a fantastic vacation."

Detail of Rogier van der Weyden's "Last Judgement" (Public Domain).

She was not a stoner, refusing the chillum, so we drank Tibetan chang (barley) beer, and at dinner's end, we were both a little tipsy. We walked around, going into the clothes and jewelry stores, where she tried on a variety of items, which all looked good on her. After about an hour and a half, I asked her if she wanted to see how a novice monk lives. We went to my room and started to play "Show and Tell:" I showed her my Tibetan "thangka" (wall-hanging silk painting) of Buddha in a mandala surrounded by his disciples; she told me all about her jewelry and described the intricate way of wrapping of a sari.

I approached her, fondled her necklace, and kissed her. We held each other, kissing, and the ritual undressing followed. First the necklace, then the bangles, and finally the unwinding of her sari. She was quite chubby naked; the sari disguised her figure well, but she was very buxom, and my hands were quite full, not to mention my mouth as I kissed her breasts in bed. We were stroking each other, and I moved her down to my erect penis. She kissed it and slowly enveloped it, a perfect re-enactment of the temple carving. I moved her head up and went down on her vagina, spreading her legs apart, kissing her soft spot. After a few moments, I raised my head and climbed on top of her, easing my penis into her wet spot. We were kissing and moving slowly together. I increased my thrusts, she grabbing my behind and lifting upward. As we were absorbed in our lovemaking, thoughts of our earlier conversation flashed through my mind: I may not achieve Nirvana, but I was surely "Knocking on Heaven's Door." I came and continued moving in her, and she moaning quietly. I came off and we held each other in exhaustion.

That was the only time I saw Ingrid; she must have joined her friends, looking for her lost flock of sheep in the alpine-like mountains of Nepal.

Chapter Seventy-Six: Claire De Lune Part I

(TOM AND GORDON: THE NEW HARDY BOYS TAKE ON FRANCOIS TRUFFAUT'S JULES AND JIM IN KATHMANDU: A FREAK FILM UPDATE)

Tom and Gordon (The new Hardy Boys): Marc Rafanell Lopez (UNSPLASH)

Claire de Lune: Gabriel Silverio (UNSPLASH)

Characters:

Gordon (Jim)

Tom (Jules)

Claire de Lune (Catherine)

(Camera/ Action/ Roll)

Music Background: The First Time by Ewan McCool.

"The first time ever I saw your face

I thought the sun rose in your eyes."

Gordon, on a bicycle, is visiting a small medieval town in the Kathmandu valley. He sees a girl on a bicycle ahead, struggling to pedal up a hill, and he pulls alongside.

Two Cyclists: Ivan Rohovchenko
(UNSPLASH)

Gordon: You can make it. Just put your head down and grind away.

Claire de Lune: I was doing just fine until this mishap. I just need a Prince Charming to rescue me. I think my chain is slipping.

Gordon: Fear not, sweet lady. I am at your service. And whom is this damsel in distress?

Claire de Lune: I am Lady Claire of the Wiltshire Claires.

Gordon: Well, let's see… your sprocket is sticking; however, I just happen to have some snake oil from a wandering sadhu, and I'm sure it'll do the trick.

Gordon takes out some Indian generic WD-40 and greases up the gears. He slowly turns it, and the sticking sprocket loosens.

Gordon: Well, my Lady, your stead is ready. Twas only a thorn in its hoof. However, this will cost you a pretty penny.

Claire de Lune: Oh! And what will that be, kind Sir? The Wiltshire Claires have been disinherited by a cruel queen and left me nothing but my title.

Gordon: Tis' not lucre I desire, sweet lady, only your delightful company for dinner. I shall pick you up at seven if my lady shall deign to accept my heartfelt offer.

Claire de Lune: Well, I usually don't associate with commoners, especially Americans, but it might be fun to see how the lower classes amuse themselves.

Gordon: Your humble servant accepts your gracious noblese oblige. It is not everyday that we have royalty at our humble dining establishment. Oh, dress will be informal. We wouldn't want to embarrass my sans culottes companion.

The scene switches to Kathmandu in the early evening. Gordon picks Claire up and they go to a local Tibetan restaurant with long tables for dining where Gordon meets his friend Tom, another American.

Music score: "Take My Breath Away" by Berlin.

Gordon: Tom, this is Lady Claire of the "Wiltshire Claires."

Tom grabs her hand and kisses it.

Claire de Lune: Well, you two are a jolly pair!

Gordon: Yes, my lady, I must confess that you now have met Prince Hal, and I am his humble servant and companion, Falstaff.

Tom: Come now, Falstaff. Do not keep the lady waiting; break out your good cheer!

Gordon: Your Highness has spoken. Does the lady care for a special hors d'oeuvres: Afghani hash served in a simple earthen chillum?

Claire de Lune: Please let us not stand on formality here. Pass the chillum!

Tom: And what brings so fair a damsel to this mystical Shangri la?

Claire de Lune: I have been sojourning from my castle as a vacation from my studies at Miss Parson's Academy of Etiquette. One must know the proper placement of dinner service and how to seat and address nobility at formal tea parties.

Tom: But of course, my lady. Maybe you can teach my boorish servant here about the proper way to pass a chillum.

Claire de Lune: Aye, that's the rub. It's all in the cupping the hand…Watch!

Claire grabs the chillum, cups her hand around it, and takes a deep hit, slowly releasing her breath after she has held it for a long time.

Tom and Gordon (they look at each other in amazement and speak in unison): My Lord, a stoner wench!

Photo by Heleno Kaizer (UNSPLASH)

Claire de Lune takes another deep hit from the chillum.

Gordon: My lady, thou hast a goodly set of pipes on Thee.

Claire de Lune: Yes. It comes from wearing those tight-fitting corsets under our regal gowns. Breathe in and keep it in.

Tom: Ah, I know it well: the trials and tribulations of royalty.

Claire de Lune: And how long have Rosenstein and Guildenstern been together? You two are such an odd couple.

Gordon: I have humbly tried to keep my master straight as an arrow. But the lure of wine, women, and song has possessed him, as if under a magic potion spell.

Tom: Tis' true. I have been a dissolute rake, but my eyes now behold a vision of loveliness. A fairy princess, who will make me abjure all others for thy sweet grace.

Claire de Lune: Doth that line really work with the local damsels?

Gordon: What my master really means is that he is in awe of your delicate beauty and comely manner and hopes that you'll bestow on him a tiny morsel of your bewitching charm.

Claire de Lune: With such flowery entreaty from a love swoon prince and his buffoon mouthpiece, how can I deign to "Love's Labor Lost?"

Tom: Well-spoken, my lady. Now, shall we have our repast?

Music Score: "And I Love Her" by The Beatles.

After dinner and a few more tokes off the chillum, the threesome wander around Jhochen Tole (Freak Street), stopping in small shops. They try on Nepali clothing and jewelry, browse used bookstores, and marvel at the Buddhist thangkas at the handicraft shop.

Tom (takes Gordon aside and says): I really like this chick. Do you mind if I go for her?

Gordon: Hey, give it the old college try (even though Gordon is also smitten with Claire). Aside: Well, all is not lost. I still have my dog-eared photograph of Dana Wynter in my rucksack.

Dana Wynter 1962 (Heroine of "The Invasion of the Body Snatchers" 1956)

The scene changes: a collage of restaurants and shops on Freak Street as the three walk around the town.

Music score: "Do You Believe in Magic" by The Lovin' Spoonful.

They hang out together for days: role-playing royalty, red-neck crackers, and sometimes just three young people enjoying each other's company and getting high together.

One day, they bicycle to the outer villages of the Kathmandu Valley (the scene switches to the countryside where Gordon, Tom, and Claire are all riding bicycles).

Gordon: Hey, Queen Bee, slow down; your work-a-bee drones can't keep up.

Claire de Lune: The cool wind and the mountain air in my face make me feel I could go on forever. The world is out there, just around the corner for us to discover.

Tom: Yes, it's great to be free from responsibility, material possessions, and your life back home. You are totally free here.

Gordon: Are we truly free? I gave up my personal freedom to serve in the army to preserve my personal freedom back home. But if freedom is a concept that the mind can control, then you are only free if you put aside all of your worldly pleasures and suffering and look inward to access your consciousness. If you master this consciousness, then you have released the divinity within yourself, that which truly makes you free because you are one with God.

Claire de Lune: And are you at that level of freedom yet?

Gordon: No. I put that on hold. I'm having too much fun being with you and Tom.

Claire de Lune: Well then. Let's crank up the fun meter (and she sped up, leaving Tom and Gordon in the dust.)

The scene changes: night in Durbar Square.

View of the temples of Swayambhu Hill, Kathmandu ,1920. National Geographic Magazine Photo now Public Domain.

Music score: "Nights in White Satin" by The Moody Blues.

Claire is a wild thing, totally uninhibited. She loves roaming the back alleys for fortune tellers and sadhus on the streets and even playing soccer with the local Nepali youths. The night air is crisp, but the full moon gives the shops and houses an ethereal glow.

Tom: God, this is like fairies sprinkled silver dust over everything.

Claire de Lune: Yes! It feels magical tonight. I remember being a little child going out late at night, romping in my yard during the first snowfall of the year, which coated everything a powdery white. It gave off a luminescence that just made you want to dance, kicking moonbeams off your shoes.

They walked past a small Tibetan restaurant that was blaring a rock and roll tune.

Music score: "Foxy Lady" by Jimi Hendrix.

Claire de Lune: Oh, this is one of my favorite songs!

She starts swaying to the music, then kicking up her heels, totally immersed in the rhythm of the song. Her body throwing off phantasmagorical shadows as she glides through the pixie wonderland.

Gordon: My lady, I now pronounce you Claire de Lune, a name that suits you much better than Claire of Wiltshire.

Claire de Lune: I accept my new nom de plume. Now, both of you give your ladyship a christening kiss.

Gordon comes over and gives her a peck of a kiss. Tom, however, gives her a long probing French kiss. At first, she is thrown a little off balance but then returns it with a long kiss, as though she is inhaling a full chillum bowl of hash.

Gordon: Don't mind me, but I think you two should get a hotel room: kissing in Kathmandu in public is a "no-no."

Claire de Lune: You are so right! "Let's give 'em something to talk about" (Bonnie Raitt plays in the background).

She comes over to Gordon and gives him a sloppy French kiss. All laugh together, lighting another joint, and walk slowly back to her hotel.

Tom (after she had gone to her hotel): I really want her. What am I going to do?

Gordon: I'll give you some time alone with her. I'm going to the mountains, to Pokhara, for about two weeks. If it goes OK, I'll see you in two weeks. If it doesn't work out, come up and join me.

Music score: "500 Miles" by Peter, Paul and Mary.

The scene shifts to the bus station, where Gordon gets on the bus for Pokhara, gives Claire a wet, sloppy kiss, and then does the same to Tom (this is a remake of a French flick, so anything goes!). The scene ends with the bus taking off.

End of Part I

Chapter Seventy-Seven: Cathy

"Mazella" by Ernest Ludwig Kirchner 1909.

Relax, don't do it

When you want to go to it

Relax, don't do it

When you want to come

-"Relax:" Frankie Goes To Hollywood

After arriving in Pokhara late, I found a travelers' hotel. I rose early at dawn to see the sunrise - the incredible panorama: the deep blue lake hung over with mist, the rice fields burnished gold, and the steel gray basalt boulders twisted and sculptured into weird formations surrounding the lake shores. These rocks were like gigantic cousins of the small, naturally sculpted scholar rocks that Chinese officials kept on their desks. Slowly, in slow motion, a fisherman's boat emerges out of the mist. It has the appearance of flying slowly out of a surreal cloud. It reminded me of those grade B horror movies where Dracula's horse and carriage glide in slow-motion through the Transylvanian Mountain mist without touching the ground.

I was sitting in a small Tibetan chai house in the warm autumn sun, watching fishermen pulling up their catch. The village men were cutting bamboo and the freaks started to cluster at the lakeshore like zombies, wandering around with no purpose. All these "outcasts of the islands" had their sad stories: the Canadian woman who lost her child in "an accident" and was heavily into heroin to forget. A quiet, balding New Yorker told me he always regretted not marrying his Korean girlfriend while stationed in the army there. Now, he was in his late 30s, facing a dead-end opium habit. Especially heartbreaking was this pencil-thin wisp of a young girl, nodding off by herself, totally strung out on smack.

Lost girl on pier: Ben Waardenburg (benwubbleyou.com) UNSPLASH

I wondered if I could help this lost soul. All the people I had met in Auroville believed in the divine in each of us. My Christian upbringing taught me we should help people in need, "Do this for the poorest and you do it for Me."

She was obviously high on opium or heroin and "cold turkey" demanded around-the-clock supervision. I thought of a middle way: bring her down with hash so she could still feel high but get back her life. I was fumbling in the dark here, but wanted to give her hope and understanding, not as a preacher or medical clinician, but as a fellow freak who knows what she is going through.

She looked wane, with sunken eyes, matted black hair and a gray pallor. I approached her and asked how she was doing? She looked up, trying to focus, and then gave up, returning to her private reverie. I persisted, introduced myself and sat next to her. "I noticed you don't talk to many people, so as president of the Freak Welcoming Committee, I'm here to greet you." This got a slight rise out of her; she said her name was Cathy. "Well, Cathy, as part of my duties, I'm inviting you to dinner. No formal dress required." She seemed more alert, focusing on me, and replied lightly. "Well, thank you. Will there be a carriage to pick me up?" "Unfortunately, this is my valet's day off, but I will serve as your faithful escort, door-to-door service." I bowed and she gave her hand, which I kissed, and we walked off together to the local Tibetan restaurant. I gave her the menu and said, "I hear the mutton stew is based on an old French monk's recipe that is all the rage in Paris. Unfortunately, I don't see Chateau de Blanc 1934 on the menu." "Well, we'll have to drink what the ordinary people do." "My sentiments exactly, two chang beers, s'il vous plait."

She told me her family was originally from Rhodesia; they left when independence came. They were now in London. On a whim, she quit her job and booked an overland bus to India. She tried drugs on the bus trip and has been hooked on all different types of dope ever since. I asked what she was on now and told me she was snorting heroin. She seemed anxious, fidgeting in her chair. "Are you coming down hard now?" "It's not too bad yet." "I have some strong hash in my hutch: we can smoke it after dinner." After dinner, we went to my room and smoked a blunt of hash. She mellowed out in a few moments, talking and laughing about her travels. "Does this shit satisfy you or do you still need the hard stuff?" She looked straight into my face and said honestly, "This is like a pain killer, heroin is like entering another dimension. You are spacewalking, feeling totally free and floating above your problems. Nothing compares with this feeling." "I know the feeling from having tried opium, but when I saw those old thin Chinese blowing on the pipe, I knew that

I did want to be like them. Their reality was the dream world of opium, ordinary day-to-day life an illusion. Have you ever gone cold turkey or only used hash or ganja?" "Yes, I was fine on hash and keeping it together. Then I met this French freak who was heavily into heroin, and we snorted all the time. He split for Goa and left me here with this habit. I thought getting out of Kathmandu and breathing fresh mountain air would help me break the habit, but no luck." "Well, aspirin or not, we will walk in the Black Forest like Hansel and Gretel and banish the wicked witch with our blunt of Sumatra hash. Hey why don't you stay here tonight, and we'll leave in the morning for our adventure?" She agreed. We finished the joint, undressed, and lay like brother and sister until I fell asleep. I was awoken in the middle of the night by a strange sensation: I looked down my body, and her mouth was on my penis, kissing it to get it erect. Her magic worked and I brought her head up. She sat on top of me, and I found her opening. We started moving, my hands massaging her hard breasts as she pushed up and down with her body. After a few moments of this thrusting, I came with a forceful burst. She came off and we lay in each other's arms until we fell asleep again.

In the morning, we got up and had our "Breakfast of Champions:" a fat blunt that gave us a nice buzz. By the time we set off with mosquito repellant, beer, packaged mutton and rice, and a beach towel, it was late morning. I carried everything in my rucksack and started uphill on the earthen trail. We walked for about half an hour, sweating and out of breath in the hot noonday sun. Glancing down the side of the mountain, we saw terraced paddies, colorful red stucco houses, many with Pennsylvania Dutch-style hex signs on the sides (here they had Buddhist and Hindu symbolic meanings). The trial broadened and we encountered a caravan of asses and ponies, loaded with products for isolated villages, driven by fur-clothed stocky Tibetans. On the winding trail, we were passed by a group of four American girls, two with baskets hung on their forehead-Nepali style. Along the trail, we passed Tibetan prayer flags, stately banyan trees, and forests of rhododendrons.

We came across a small brook and she suggested we stop for a dip. We walked off the trail into a thicket of rhododendrons until we found a clearing near the brook. We stripped and waded into the water. It was freezing cold, but we immersed ourselves to get cool and then ran for the beach towel. We lay there naked, just absorbing the nature around us. Her body frail thin, but her face was red, flushed from the alpine waters. "Why is an American at a brook like this just like our flag?" She shook her head no. "Because he is white when he comes here, red after an hour in the sun, and blue when he jumps in the brook." We laid back until the mosquitoes got too bad. We doused ourselves with repellent but to no avail. We hurriedly dressed and pushed on up the mountain trail.

As we were walking along the trail, I noticed a strange wooden litter down in a valley below us. At first I didn't know what this was, but then I remembered from my "Seven Years in Tibet" book that this was a Tibetan burial litter, where the dead body is cut into small pieces and left out in the open air for the vultures to eat.

We walked about an hour more and we both had enough of trekking. We got off the trail again and found a rocky perch, where we spread our towel for our picnic. We broke out the food and ate and drank, saving the hash blunt for dessert. It was still hot, so we undressed and lay like naked salamanders in the sun. I moved my body so I was lying opposite her vagina. I pulled her body over me, kissing her dark, moist hair, and she sucking my penis. I found her moist vagina and sucked it until she started moaning quietly and I was ready to explode. I came with a thrust, but she kept sucking until I went soft. I nudged her off, turned around, and we lay exhausted, staring at the sky.

Tibetan Burial Litter (author's photo)

We got dressed as the sun was low in the heavens, bathing us in a golden glow. We arrived at the lake at dusk, watching the fishermen coming in with their catch. After dinner, we went back to my room, had a blunt, and I asked, "Do you miss the heroin?" "No, as long as I can keep making love to you."

The next five days went by in a blur of hash smoking and making love. I told her about Tantric Buddhism, achieving Nirvana through sex. This piqued her interest and she wanted to find out more about this practice.

I told her that I had briefly studied Tantric Buddhism and there is the "Sarma" (New Translation School), which has four types of yoga based on the level of the practitioner and how he uses and controls desire.

The first is "Kriya," for the beginner and the desire is like a couple laughing together.

The second is "Charya," for mid-level practitioners; the desire is gazing into a lover's eyes.

The third is "Yoga Tantra," for practitioners of high ability and the desire level is a couple embracing.

The fourth is "Anuttara," and this is the highest ability, and the desire level and practice of this yoga is fierce sexual union with an actual partner.

The goal is union with God, not sensual desire or pleasure.

Cathy seemed very interested in Anuttara and suggested we keep practicing our lovemaking until we achieve this level - I love an apt pupil!

After another week went by in a sexual and hash blur (Spoiler: we never reached Nirvana, but the fun meter was off the charts!), I told her that I had to return to Kathmandu in two days to see my friends, Tom and Claire. I asked her to come with me, but she said she was waiting for money from her family, which was coming in a few days. Once she got the wire transfer, she would join me. I gave her my hotel address in Kathmandu and would be waiting for her. On the morning that I was going, I gave her half of my hash stash and some money, telling her to spend it on food, not dope. She agreed and gave me a farewell kiss, promising we would meet soon.

I reunited with Tom and Claire, and we hung out together, having fun, but no Cathy. I waited over two weeks for her, but she never showed up. I hoped she stayed on the "soft" hash high, but heroin addiction is hard to fight on your own. I wish I could have done more for her.

Chapter Seventy-Eight: Claire De Lune Part II

(TOM AND GORDON: THE NEW HARDY BOYS TAKE ON FRANCOIS TRUFFAUT'S JULES AND JIM IN KATHMANDU: A FREAK FILM UPDATE)

Part II

Gordon comes back from Pokhara two weeks later to the same hotel where Tom is staying.

Music score: "Slave to Love" by Bryan Ferry.

Gordon: Tom, my compadre, how are you and Claire de Lune? Are we reserving the Elvis Chapel for a quickie Las Vegas marriage?

Tom: For the first few days, it was heaven on earth. We got high on hash cakes and made love. Got high on hash, made more love; I fell head-over-heels. But then, on the fourth day, she wanted to get out of the room. So, we hung out with other freaks in the Tibetan restaurant. I got really stoned, and she just disappeared. She came back in the early afternoon the next day, saying she'd met a friend from Bombay, and they'd partied all night. At first, I was angry, but I couldn't stay angry for long, and I forgave her. Then we made sweet love, but she was off again the next day. It's been a whole day and night and I haven't seen her; I'm sick with worry.

Gordon: Hey, Tom, get a hold of yourself! This isn't New York City; we'll find her.

The scene shifts to Durbar Square. Gordon and Tom wander around Durbar Square and Freak Street looking for Claire de Lune. After about a half hour, they find Claire spaced out and alone in a small restaurant off the square.

Music score: "Drive" by The Cars.

Who's gonna tell you when it's too late?

Who's gonna tell you things aren't so great?

You can't go on, thinking nothing's wrong, but now

Who's gonna drive you home tonight?

Gordon: Hey, Claire de Lune. Remember me? Why don't you come back home with us?

Claire de Lune: Gordon! My Prince Charming! Have you come to rescue me again?

Gordon: Sgt. Pepper is here to sweep you off your feet and take you away in his "Yellow Submarine."

She laughed, staggered up and they all went back to Tom's hotel room. Gordon leaves her with Tom; she falls asleep on the bed almost immediately.

The next afternoon, Gordon is smoking a joint and writing in his journal in his room when there is a knock on the door. There was Claire alone.

Music score: "For Your Precious Love" by Jerry Butler.

"Your precious love

Means more to me

Than any love could ever be

For when I wanted you

I was so lonely and so blue

For that's what love will do."

Claire de Lune: I missed you so much, my prince charming!

Gordon: I thought you and Tom were happy together?

Claire de Lune: I miss the Three Musketeers, swashbuckling around town.

She came up and kissed Gordon, massaging his pants below the belt.

Gordon: What about Tom?

Claire de Lune: I told Tom I was going out to see you. He just sat there and watched me go. I want you, my loving prince.

Gordon: Holds her, kissing her as they fumble to get out of their clothes. Finally, they are both naked, and he walks her to the bed, still kissing her. ("I can't deny that I have Designs on You:" Old 49's plays in the background). An amalgam of guilt and lust caroused through his brain. He fell on top of her, kissing her breasts and finding her soft, sweet spot. They made love in a frenzy of thrusts. When it was over, they held each other silently. After about half an hour, Gordon gets up.

Gordon: Well, Claire de Lune, where do we go from here?

Claire de Lune: We go back to our beginning. The circle is closed again, and we all have each other.

Gordon: (aside) I thought to myself, as Thomas Wolfe said in Look Homeward Angel, "You can never go back home again." We had lost our innocence and replaced it with jealousness, possessiveness, and random sex.

The scene changes. All are back in Tom's place.

Music score: "Take Another Little Piece of My Heart" by Janis Joplin.

Tom (looking despondent): So, you're back.

Gordon (with false bravado): Yes! We're all together again. Let's get stoned and I'll tell you about my climbing Mt. Everest and other "tall" tales over dinner.

Scene switches to a Tibetan restaurant. All are heavily stoned. Claire de Lune was her usual bubbly self. Tom was just happy to be with her and Gordon felt deep affection for both of them.

Music score: "Only Love Can Break Your Heart" by Neil Young.

Claire de Lune: I'm so happy we all have each other. I missed this more than anything.

Gordon: Claire, Tom and I just don't understand you.

Claire de Lune: I don't want to be understood. I want to live life spontaneously. Each day is a new adventure and I need both of you, just as the moon, my namesake, needs both of you. You're my sun for its light in the day.

We continued seeing each other every day and at night, Claire came to me for one night and spent the next with Tom. I was still waiting in vain for Cathy to come down from the mountains. My nights with Claire were different now. She was still exciting, passionate, and caring, but I felt like I was an "X" marked on her calendar. If it's Tuesday, it must be Gordon.

Music score: "It's Too Late" by Carole King.

"Somethin' inside has died, and I can't hide

And I just can't fake it, oh, no, no, no, no, no

it's too late now, darling."

The scene switches to Gordon's room. (After making love, they are both sitting, smoking a blunt of hash.)

Gordon: Is this working for you, tic-tac-toe lovers?

Claire: I love you both and this is the only way I can have you both and still satisfy my freedom. You said how important freedom is and you're right; it is at my core. My parents endured a loveless marriage and that's not going to happen to me.

Gordon: So, you're running from a commitment because you feel you'll be stuck like your parents?

Claire de Lune: It's more than that. This is a man's world and I'm not satisfied with this way of thinking. I want to be in charge of my own life. You said you don't understand me. Well understand that I'm not going to fit into a role that society gives me. I don't need a man, career, or a comfortable life to fulfill me. I need to fulfill myself by myself! Making mistakes, taking risks, being alone if I must. This is who I am!

She left and later Gordon takes Tom aside.

Gordon: This "menage a trois" isn't working for me. I'm leaving Kathmandu in two days. Will you come with me?

Tom: (Looking despondent) I don't know. "La Belle Dame Sans Merci" still has me under her spell.

Two Lovers: Kenny Eliason (UNSPLASH)

Music Score: "Love Portion #9": The Clovers

(Scene switches to Freak Street) The day before we were scheduled to leave, we walked around Freak Street. We were laughing and had gotten high at lunch (so what else is new?).

Claire de Lune: I want my fortune told.

Walking around until they found a sign that read, "You're Destiny Is Known by the Stars, Now Find the Answers to Your Questions." We walked up some dimly lit stairs and entered a room where an old man was sitting at a table. There were charts posted on the wall, but no crystal ball. We asked how much the reading would cost and after some haggling, we agreed on thirty rupees. He had Claire write down the exact time, date, and location where she was born. He told us to come back in three hours and asked for half of the fee.

The scene switches to Durbar Square.

Durbar Square 19th century (Artist Unknown, Public Domain)

We visited some Buddhist temples, drank chai, and returned to the fortuneteller, where Claire went alone to get her fortune.

Gordon: (To Claire, who has just returned from the fortuneteller) Did he tell you that you would meet a tall, dark stranger, get married, have a house in the suburbs, and 2.5 kids? I always wondered how you can have half a kid, but what do I know?

Claire de Lune: I'm not going to tell you everything he told me, but he did say I would have many adventures, live in a foreign land, and eventually find a partner, but it got vague after that. However, I do believe it was well worth the money.

Tom: Well then, Falstaff, "show us the way to the next whiskey bar, oh don't ask why." (The Doors)

The scene switches to a Tibetan restaurant. The meal has just been eaten and the threesome are talking.

Music score: "Hey That's No Way To Say Goodbye" by Leonard Cohen.

I'm not looking for another as I wander in my time

Walk me to the corner, our steps will always rhyme

You know my love goes with you as your love stays with me

It's just the way it changes, like the shoreline and the sea

But let's not talk of love or chains and things we can't untie

Your eyes are soft with sorrow, hey, that's no way to say goodbye.

Gordon: (Stares intently at Tom, who finally nods agreement and then faces Claire.) Tom and I are leaving Kathmandu for India tomorrow. We both still care for you, but it's time that we moved on.

Claire is taken aback, looking intently at both of us, but says nothing.

The scene switches back to Durbar Square.

Music score: "When You're Only Lonely" by J. D. Souther.

They walk silently around Durbar Square, letting the medieval atmosphere sink in. Tomorrow, they would be leaving this fairyland for the heat and dust of India. The "Silence of the Lambs" weighs heavily on the trio as they arrive at Claire's hotel. Gordon and Tom kiss her goodbye and promise to have a farewell breakfast before leaving.

Tom: Do you think we're doing the right thing? I miss her already!

Gordon: I don't know. Maybe we'll always regret it, like the song: "Me and My Bobby Magee." (Kris Kristofferson) "Somewhere near Salinas I let her slip away. Now I'd give all of my tomorrows for just one more time to have her here." She's a totally free spirit, a wild animal that we'd only try to cage. To tame her to our own romantic vision would destroy all of us.

Outside of Claire's hotel in the early morning. Music score: "Light Years": The National

Oh, the glory of it all was lost on me

'Til I saw how hard it'd be to reach you

And I would always be light years, light years away from you

Light years, light years away from you.

Tom: I tried her room, but she checked out early this morning. (despondently) Now she's gone for good!

Gordon: I know I'll miss her too, but what I really miss is that carefree time we had together. We were all so naïve. We believed that this magical time would go on forever and that anything was possible. But the reality is that we were not good enough for her. We could not satisfy that passionate longing nor keep up with her manic wildness: she is the "Chestnut Mare" that The Byrds sing about; she must always run free!

FIN

That's a wrap. Roll the credits.

Lili Fokken (UNSPLASH)

Chapter Seventy-Nine: People of Nepal

A young girl filling a water jug in a village outside of Kathmandu.

On a mountain trail I passed a girl on a typical Nepalese rope bridge and she decided to pose for me.

As Cathy and I were walking in the mountains near Pokhara, we came across a caravan of horses and donkeys laden with general merchandise, run by Tibetan merchants, who go far into the mountains and service all of the remote villages.

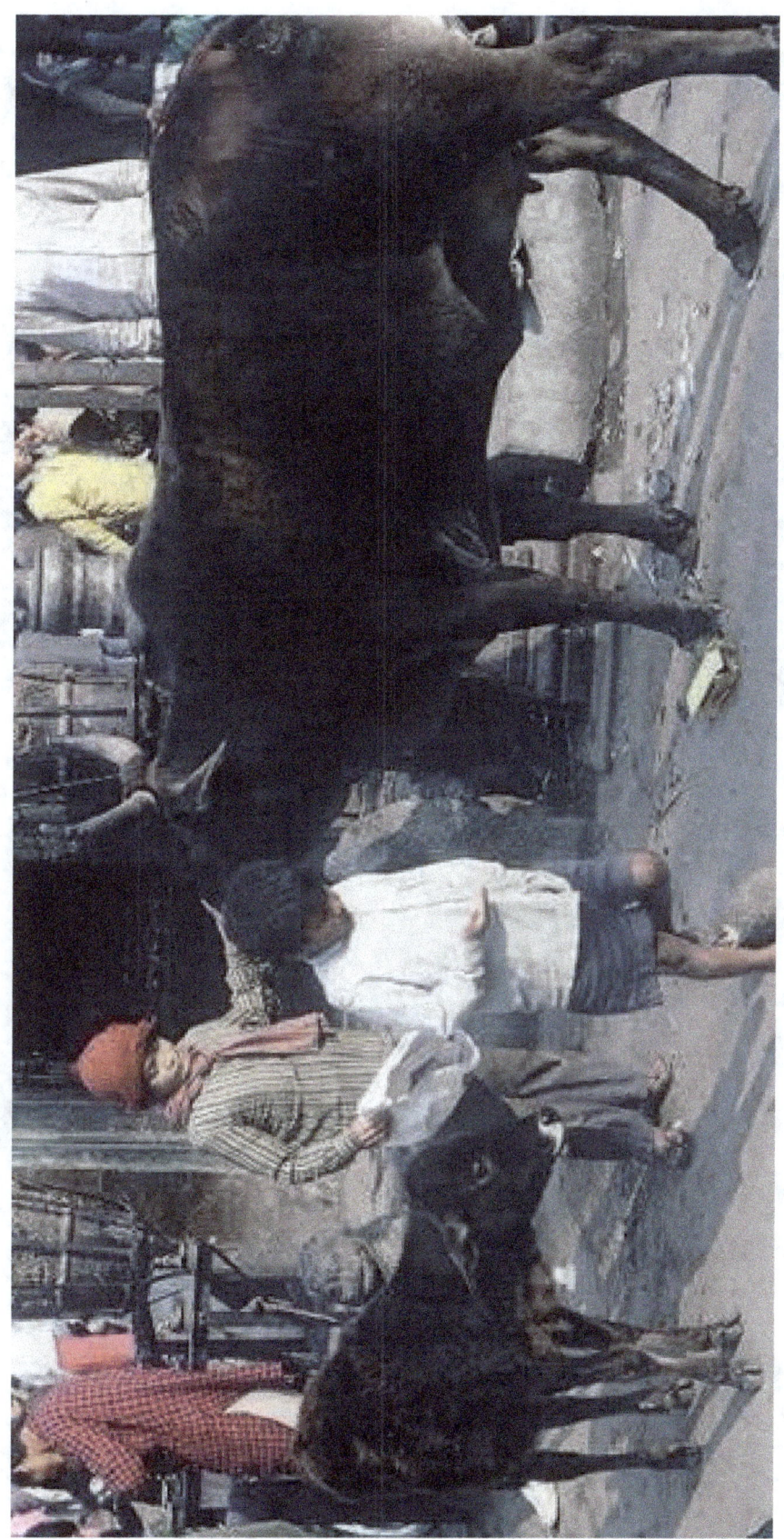

Like many Indian cities, cows wander freely through the streets of Kathmandu.

Fortune teller creating a person's astrological chart. The fortune tellers in Nepal don't depend on crystal balls but do precise calculations of exactly where and when you were born and then factor in the zodiacs and wallah, you have your fortune.

Young girls are always seen carrying their infant siblings to help their mother, who is usually in the fields harvesting the wheat.

A young woman working the threshing machine in a field outside of Kathmandu.

Porters are both male and female: here we have a mother and child that are carrying huge baskets of produce.

The public baths in Kathmandu. Outdoor baths are a necessary feature since most homes do not have indoor plumbing. Here the baths serve a dual purpose of cleaning on the lower levels and storing the wheat on the upper levels.

A young girl gathering water at the well has almost a biblical look and I can imagine her being Rebecca at the well from the Old Testament.

Religion dominates life in Nepal and this picture of a temple scene shows Nepalis of all ages coming and leaving the temple.

Men carrying a motor typifies the Indian and Nepali belief that it is cheaper to pay for the labor of many men to carry the motor then to purchase a truck to move the motor.

I went to many markets in Kathmandu and caught this young girl asleep when she should have been awake and and hawking her pottery.

This is a large house and courtyard, where the family spread their wheat to dry.

There is no social welfare system, so people like this blind man must beg for his livelihood.

I encountered this woman carrying her baby on the trail outside of Pokhara. The baby has his behind exposed and this is a practical way to avoid diapers.

Benares

Bathing in the River Ganges. (Author's photo)

Chapter Eighty: Benares - City of Joy

Print of Benares: James Prinsep 1834: The British Library (Public Domain) (CC-CCO-PD License).

Benares is one of the oldest continuously occupied cities in the world, dating back to 1800 BC. The city is the holiest of the Seven Holy Cities of Hinduism (the other Holy cities are: Ayodhya, Mathura, Hardiwar, Kanchi, Avanti, and Dvaraka; devout Hindus make a pilgrimage to all these cities since to die in one of these cities you receive "moksha" {liberation from constant cycle of rebirth}).

Mythologically, Benares was founded by Shiva, who defeated another Hindu God, Brahma. He tore off one of Brahma's five heads and carried it around as a trophy (Shiva was the first "headhunter" and a clumsy one at that: He dropped it and where it fell became the holy site of

Benares). For over three millennia, it was a Hindu theological center, even visited by the Buddha, who preached his first sermon nearby.

The Mughals were first supportive of the city, building huge temples and ghats under Emperor Akbar. Aurangzeb, the last important Mughal Emperor, was fanatically anti-Hindu, tearing down temples and putting up mosques in their place (Benares is now about 25% Muslim).

Tom and I arrived in the city, coming here from Kathmandu, which was like leaving the circles of heaven coming to the rings of fire, surrounded by the dying, the dead and the burning pyres. We walked from the train station through winding lanes, overshadowed by elaborate wood trellised balconies, dark, iron-studded doorways, and crumbling 19th-century mansions, now housing tens of Indian families and pilgrims.

Benares is famous for its open-air burning cremations. We, as Westerners, are morbidly fascinated by this Indian death ritual. There have been cremations here for over three millennia. The ritual is officiated by a priest, but it's the first-born son who performs the cremation ceremony. The actual preparation of the body, laying the corpse on wood and burning the body is done by a sub caste of Untouchables because the cremation itself is considered an unclean act. The final process in the burning is to pierce the skull of the dead to release his spirit. Then, the ashes are spread into the Ganges.

Manikansika Burning Ghat (photo by Dennis Jarvis who released image to Creative Commons: Attribution -Share Alike 2.0 Generic License {with attribution to Dennis Jarvis})

Cremation Ghat Benares (Photo by Vyacheslav Argenburg/ http://www.vascoplanet.com Creative Commons-attribution 4.0 International License)

Does the Indian find solace because the death ritual was performed correctly? Yes, I believe that the son has ensured that the father's spirit is now free. The body is just an empty vessel. The corporal body returns to the five basic elements: air, water, fire, earth, and space/atmosphere. This spirit can now be reborn into another life.

The Old Guard transports the flag-draped casket of the second Sergeant Major of the Army George W. Dunaway, who was buried with full military honors at Arlington National Cemetery. (U.S. Government Photo, Public Domain)

Then, I reflected on our own death rituals. Being in the army, you develop a bond with your fellow soldiers. As a fellow soldier told me: "Once you are in the army, you are part of a large family." Too many of that family were senselessly killed in Vietnam.

The ritual of a flag-draped coffin, the 21-gun salute, and the well-tended graves at Arlington National Cemetery. All these rituals have meaning on what it is to be an American and the sacrifices made. For our dead soldiers, this ritual may not give us solace, but it gives meaning to their sacrifice: our family has lost one of its own and he will be remembered.

Benares, away from the burning ghats, is a fascinating city: at every corner, there is a small shrine, the crumbling buildings painted with Shiva images. Every cobblestone lane is filled with shaven-haired children and wandering cows, both shitting everywhere. Mothers sitting in darkened doorways, rouging their babies' eyes with black kohl to ward off Kali, the goddess of death, because she only takes away beautiful children. There are sadhus everywhere, some pedaling rickshaws, one selling toy watches and balloons, others begging, and some constantly smoking chillums under black umbrellas. I spoke to one frail, elderly Sadhu, walking with a cane.

Sadhu I befriended in Benares.

He told me that he had given up all his worldly possessions and had been on the road for two years now. Times were tough and he wanted to work for me, doing anything. He had come to Benares to die, like so many pilgrims, so he could achieve moksha (release from the constant rebirth cycle). I bought him a chai, and he told me of his former life as a minor government clerk. His wife had died, and his children were all married; he decided it was time to devote his life to God. He still fervently believed in Shiva, but sleeping in doorways and spending his days begging for food had taken its toll; he had bad arthritis and walked with a heavy limp. I gave him a ten-rupee bill, and he thanked me profusely. I wish I could have done more for him, but there were beggars everywhere. Especially heartbreaking were the sleeping mothers lying in the street, with their malnutrition-ragged children, holding out their filthy tin cups for baksheesh.

I wandered into the Muslim quarters, passing dozens of black vested, skull-capped old Muslims, smoking water hubbly-bubblies, which were filled with a mixture of tobacco and charcoal.

This neighborhood had small, faded white mosques, outdoor cafes, vegetables and fruit displayed in pyramid-style stacks, and halal butcher shops: the flies encrusted on the slabs of bloodied goat shanks hanging on hooks. The women were clad in colorful purdahs, dragging little children as they did their daily shopping.

While I stayed in Benares, I took a short bus trip to Sarnath. This was the place where the Buddha gave his first sermon and started his mission to spread the "Eightfold Path" of enlightenment (see my chapter on Buddha's First Sermon for a more detailed explanation of the Buddhist creed), traveling all over India. The emperor Ashoka erected a large stupa at Sarnath in the 3rd century BC to commemorate the beginnings of the Buddhist religion.

Mother wearing purdah with child (Author's Photo)

Emperor Ashoka's Buddhist Stupa at Sarnath (author's photo)

Chapter Eighty-One: Hot-L Benares

View of Benares: Lieutenant Colonel Forrest 1824 (Public Domain).

Wandering around the old town near the Ganges river banks, we chanced upon a hotel that was once the proud home of a wealthy Hindu family but now is a dilapidated tourist hotel housing mostly freaks and rucksack travelers. The aged sign advertising the hotel was so weather-beaten that the E in HOTEL was almost completely faded off, hence the "HOT-L Benares." This once palatial mansion was cut up into shoebox-sized rooms. We must have lucked out because our room must have been the presidential suite: there was beautiful floral molding on the walls, and the ceiling had a detailed arabesque designed rosette in plaster, which at one time must have held a gorgeous multi-light chandelier but now was graced with a single dangling light bulb. The walls were all peeling paint and there were two rope beds, a small dresser, and a cigarette burned table with two wobbly chairs. If this were New York City, this would be called a single room occupancy

(SRO) hotel, sans the hot plate in each room. Like the SRO, the bathroom was down the hall. However, we did have a small balcony, which was closed off by a broken pane set of French doors and overlooked an alley facing other dilapidated former mansions. This was the area where the poorer Hindu families stayed, sometimes up to ten families in a single house. Death is a big business in Benares, and as we found out, only the very rich are cremated here due to the cost of the wood for the briar, the services of the Hindu Brahman priest, and the monopoly of the untouchable class which handled the dead and the cremation. The people staying in these dilapidated mansions were part of the service industry that catered to the pilgrims, sadhus, and grieving loved ones of the dead. When we weren't exploring the city, we stayed in our room smoking the legal hashish and talking, mostly about the differences between Nepal and India.

Tom was still moping over Claire while I spent my time writing in my journal and playing peekaboo with a cute little Indian girl of about three or four across the alleyway, maybe 10 feet away, in another dilapidated mansion. The little girl stayed with her mother and other siblings while the father worked, and I never saw her playing outside. However, when she saw me, she was dumbstruck: a tall, long-haired, bearded "Alien from Planet 9"- a "hippie," and she would run out into her balcony, scream "hippie," and run away. Like all children, she never tired of this game and kept repeating it over and over. I, for my part in the game, would hide behind the French doors and then spring up, yelling, "Boo!"

Although it was owned by a fat, balding Hindu, everything in the hotel was run by an energetic Nepalese boy, Parup, about 15 years old, who spoke fluent English. He collected the daily rent, took our food orders, cooked the food, and provided any tourist information we needed; a virtual one-man band, always cheerful and smiling.

The lock to our room was unique: it was a two-part mechanism where you took half the lock with you, the locking part where the key fit in, while the other part locked the door so no one could get in. But you must carry this big cumbersome half lock with you, otherwise, you will never get back into your room.

The other travelers in the hotel were like a microcosm of the whole freak experience in India. Downstairs is an American, Carl, a basket-case who had lost himself in heroin, got hepatitis from a dirty needle, and continued shooting up. He had been arrested by the Indian police, had his visa revoked, and the American Embassy was now sending him home. He had come as a regular tourist, fell in with the wrong crowd, and the cheap, easy drugs swallowed him up.

Also, downstairs is a musician, Alex, taking sitar lessons and practicing his instrument at all hours. He is a dedicated, serious student and doesn't do drugs.

On our floor is a Starfleet Academy cadet from California, Megan, who went native in costume: dressed in saris, bangles, and nose ring and in relationships, bringing home a variety of matted hair, bearded Sadhus for her "lover of the week." Also, on our floor are two French junkies: one, Jacques, is a poster child for why you shouldn't do smack: ghostly wan, sunken cheeks, and mostly immobile, except for the drool. The other one, Remy, is always scheming, with some hair-brained spiel to get money off you, like selling you shit grass when you can get a better grade from the government store at a cheaper price (marijuana is legal here and sold by the local government stores). I have let Alex, Megan, and Remy tell their own stories from the "Hot-L Benares." (To be continued)

Chapter Eighty-Two: Charon

Charon forcing sinners on his boat to Hell: Gustave Dore from his Illustration of Dante's "Inferno" 1857 Public Domain (CC-CCO-PD License).

I hired a small boat with a wizened boatman before dawn to see the sunrise on the burning ghats. Even at this early hour, the steps along the river were filled with bathers chanting "Hara Krishna, Hara Ram, Ram Ram." Away from the main temples, women were slapping clothes clean on the rocks. On the platforms overlooking the river, Sadhus were setting up their oils and aromatic spices.

The sun was a small red dot, then an ever-growing overturned bowl, and finally, a red disc burning through the river fog. The river is alive with boats - small rowboats with fishing lines draped in the blueish-brown water, slumbering chipped and sun-faded houseboats, and the white draped coffin boats carrying the dead to the burning ghats. Our boat passed white bundles drifting by in the current: young children and Sadhus are not burned and are left to sink in the river.

I heard the gongs from the Shiva Temple and the wailing of "Hara Ram" from the widows' house. This house, which fronts the river, has only widows who never remarry after their husband dies. They devote their lives to Ram (God). Twenty-four hours a day, there are women chanting and singing praises to God. We passed the monkey temple, where there were dozens of monkeys scrambling all over the steps, begging and screeching. The waterfront is very picturesque: crumbling sandstone palaces interspersed with white stucco houses, a huge Redstone Mosque, and the burning ghats.

As the morning wore on, the temples filled with pilgrims: Hindu men in their best suits, women in gold embroidered saris, holy white chalked naked Sadhus, old women in rags, begging and white clad priests wearing the Shiva symbol, a red paste-pitchfork on their forehead.

As I sweep the horizon, there are fires burning up and down the riverfront. We headed back. I felt I was a condemned sinner on the River Styx. It didn't help that my boatman was a "dead" ringer for what I had pictured Charon to be: silent, toothless, and possessing a fierce visage. My faith and deeds are being weighed on the scales of the Judgement Angel as depicted by Hans Memling's triptych "Last Judgment."

Unfortunately, I have come up short and am one of the damned. Charon, disguised as a poor Indian fisherman, is ferrying me into the burning fires of hell on the nearby shore.

As I glided to my fate, the shoreline ablaze with burning pyre hell fires, I remembered a modern-day Charon, Travis Bickle, in "Taxi Driver." His yellow Checker cab speeding through the dark Lower East Side streets, dodging the plumes of white spouting smoke manhole covers while ferrying his condemned teenage prostitute to the seedy Hell Hotel, where her devil/pimp waited impatiently.

New York City Charon, with a Checker instead of a Raft to transport the Damned. (Movie Poster: although Poster is copyright to Columbia Pictures, poster is low resolution and is used in commentary of film where words alone can not convey the reader's understanding of the film and therefore qualifies as fair use of the image under copyright laws of the United States).

Chapter Eighty-Three: Freaks, Houseboats, and Nietzsche

The water is wide
I can't cross over
And neither have
I wings to fly

Build me a boat
That can carry two
And both shall row
My love and I

There is a ship
And she sails the sea
She's loaded deep
As deep can be

But not so deep
As the love I'm in
I know not how
I sink or swim

Oh love is handsome
And love is fine
The sweetest flower
When first it's new

But love grows old
And waxes cold
And fades away
Like summer dew

Build me a boat
That can carry two
And both shall row
My love and I
And both shall row
My love and I

"The River is Wide"

17th Century Scottish Folk Song

Houseboats on the river banks of Benares (author's photo)

Tom and I were walking around the Benares waterfront; I was taking photos and Tom was studying the various potions and incense that a Sadhu was selling. From about 50' away, we were hailed by these two freaks from the roof of a houseboat parked at the shore. We went over, and they asked us if we wanted to share a chillum. We deftly climbed onboard and joined them on the roof.

The houseboat was about 25' long, one story high, with windows all around. We met Fritz and Wolfgang, two travelers from Ulm in southern Germany. I told them of my German experience in the army and that I had visited Ulm to see its beautiful Gothic cathedral. They had flown into Bombay and had been in India for about a month. I asked how it was living in a houseboat, and Wolfgang offered to show me around.

Hippies living in a houseboat on the Banares waterfront (author's photo).

The inside was a long gallery and then smaller partitioned rooms towards the back. It was an inferno inside (That's why they were sitting on the roof.), and the toilet was a septic box that had to be treated with lime daily to keep the smell down. There was no drinking water in the boat and being on the shore didn't help with the mosquitos and horse flies.

"Where do you get your water?"

Fritz answered, "The landlord gives us a large plastic jar of water every day when he collects the rent."

I had always thought that living in a houseboat (a la Amsterdam) would be fun, but this wasn't my dream house here. However, the two were friendly. One was an aspiring Buddhist and practiced yoga daily. "Benares," Wolfgang, the aspiring Buddhist, said, "is a fascinating city and we live right in the heart of it."

Tom and I had walked the back streets up and down the hills, encountering a shrine on every corner. I also told him of the monkeys roaming wild at the Monkey temple here.

Wolfgang said, "You see so many older and sick Hindus coming here to die because they'll be given an instant 'get into Heaven card' Moksha (release from the constant cycle of rebirth). Benares is a city dedicated to Shiva and he takes special care of the old and dying."

"Don't you find it a little gruesome, the constant burning of the city of the dead?"

"No, it's really a city of rebirth. When a Hindu dies, his family prepares him for the cremation ritual, which releases his Spirit to be reborn again. My father died somewhere in Russia during WW II, and we never had the sense of closure that these Hindus have here."

"So, how is your Buddhist training coming?"

"I'm basically just starting; yoga relaxes my mind and keeps me receptive to new ideas and philosophies. I hope to get further into this when I go to Sarnath Ashram, which is the site of Buddha's first sermon to his followers."

I told him about Sri Aurobindo's ideal that there is divinity in every person. "So, this Aurobindo has a theory similar to Nietzsche's "übermensch."

I wasn't totally familiar with the übermensch concept. I only knew that the Nazis had corrupted Nietzsche's teaching to fit their super-race ideology.

I asked Wolfgang to explain Nietzsche's übermensch to me. "Nietzsche believed that there would be a 'superior' man in the future. This superior man would look for the meaning of life, not in death, but in the fullness of life here and now. Nietzsche also said that the Christian God is dead.

Nazi German metal Propaganda Poster showing a typical German soldier as the "Übermensch" (Superman) 1940 (Public Domain).

"By that, he meant that the values of Christianity are no longer useful for modern man. A whole new set of values will be created by the übermensch based on love of the present world, values that are life-affirming and creative. The übermensch must be strong enough to master all of his emotions, good and bad.

"Life is suffering and the concept of the eternal recurrence (being reborn endlessly into the same body) means that the übermensch recognizes that all beings keep making the same mistakes over and over. The übermensch, by mastering his emotions through the will to power, gives him the power to self-affirm and master one's instincts.

"He can accept his faults and mistakes and develop a new set of life-affirming positive values to live life to the fullest. He also said that not everyone can be an übermensch because it takes a special kind of person: strong enough to master his emotions and at the same time be creative.

"Nietzsche thought that the two individuals closest to the übermensch ideal were Goethe and Napoleon."

Friedrich Nietzsche: "I may not be an "übermensch" but I do have a "superior" moustache" 1872.

"Wow, he sure sounds like an elitist to me and how is this übermensch going to be created?"

Wolfgang replied, "Nietzsche wasn't specific about how this ideal would come about; it was a future goal, but every man can train his mind to use the Will to Power to self-affirm and master his emotions. Nietzsche also said that since God is dead, then Man can make his own destiny free from the Christian morality."

I said, "I don't think Nietzsche went far enough. Aurobindo stressed there was divinity in every man. He can access this divinity through yoga (In Nietzsche's terms, master his emotions). Aurobindo believes that only by self-realization can you attain a level where you have mastery of your consciousness. Nietzsche stops here, but accessing the divine concept leads you to the final step, the Overmind, where you attain pure consciousness.

"You are the God now. This is the next huge step in human evolution (ape to man; man to God)."

Wolfgang thought about this and then asked me for details on Auroville, which he now wanted to visit for himself. We all had a final chillum of hash; Tom and I thanked them and got off the houseboat.

Chapter Eighty-Four: Alex's Tale (Room 1C)

From Concerto to Raga - The Transformation of a Young Musician

I grew up in a musical family; my father is a music instructor at a New York City Public High School and my mother was a former ballerina who now gives private dance lessons. From age 8, I wanted to be a classical violinist and practiced for hours every day, forsaking street stickball and friends for private lessons. My teacher was a patient middle-aged housewife who gave up a promising musical career to raise a family, now vicariously imbuing her skills with aspiring neophytes like me.

I was no child prodigy but had progressed enough to be accepted at the New York City School of Performing Arts, where I met other students who shared my passion for music. My hero at that time was David Ostriak, a classical violinist who knew all the great modern Russian composers like Prokofiev and Shostakovich, working hand-in-hand with them to create a perfect symbiosis of composer and performer. I especially admired Ostriak's dedication and courage. He performed on the frontlines in dimly lit factories, with bombs falling all around him, to bring his passion for music to enthusiastic Russian soldiers in the darkest days of the Stalingrad Siege.

I went on to the Berkeley School in Boston, where I discovered the music of Schoenberg and Berg with its non-Western musical bar notation and atonal sound. I found like-minded musicians, and we formed a string quartet performing this expressionistic music. I was especially drawn to the 2nd Violin Concerto of Allan Pettersson, a Swedish composer whose noir music reflected the horrors of the Second World War. The savage, stringent music matched my anxious mood when friends and acquaintances I knew were sent off to the brutality of the Vietnam War.

Then, one day, a college friend played me a record of an Indian composer-performer named Ravi Shankar; I was blown away by this strange music. Here was music that spoke to my soul, and I later found out that Shankar had said that you must perform not for yourself but in deep reverence for God. This is sacred music that could be innovated like jazz to create your own personal hosanna to the Lord. I ran out and bought a Ravi Shankar album and listened as though I was in a mesmerizing trance. I decided then that I would buy a sitar and get lessons. However, it wasn't that easy. Getting a sitar was impossible; I tried all of the music shops in Boston, even advertising, without any luck. Lessons were even more elusive. There was no one advertising sitar instruction, so I applied for a sabbatical and left for India about the time when George Harrison's sitar-infused "My Sweet Lord" was hitting the radio stations.

India overwhelmed me. I was both repulsed and fascinated at the same time. The poverty seems unbearable, but the spell of India possessed me: the friendly people, exotic food, and the temple music all enthralled me. The India Tourist Bureau recommended Benares as an important center of sitar music. I got the first train here from Bombay. At first, I thought this was a city of the dead. Now, I see it as a city of salvation. If you die here, you are promised by Shiva that you will be released from the cycle of reincarnation, achieving union with the divine. I bought a good second-hand sitar and found a sitar instruction school, which I enrolled in. After a few weeks of imbuing the heady atmosphere of this magical place and discussions about Hinduism with my teacher, I realized I was spiritually dead. Back home, I wanted to be the best violinist so I could perform before large audiences for money and fame. I see now that I was "looking through a glass darkly." Yes, one should strive to be the best, but you must use this violin or sitar to achieve a oneness with God. I don't know if I'll ever have the patience of a yogi to sit in one position for days, emptying my mind, but I can sing the praises of God with my instrument. I want to be a humble servant of God and the only way I know to do this is through my music.

Man playing sitar: Saubhagya Gandharv (UNSPLASH)

It took me fifteen years to develop my expertise on the violin, and now I have a new instrument that I'll have to learn from the beginning. Will I ever be as good as Ravi Shankar; I don't believe so. However, now I have a "right-minded goal," as the Hindu sages would say, or "before I saw in part, but now I see as a whole," as it is stated in the Bible. My sitar will be used in the loving service of My Lord.

Chapter Eighty-Five: Megan's Tale (Room 2D)

"The fault, dear Brutus, is not in our stars / But in ourselves, that we are underlings."

-(Julius Caesar, Act I, Scene III).

My friend Angie and I came to India on a lark. I had dropped out of college and was hanging with these far-out nature freaks. We did marijuana and spent some time in San Francisco, where I started telling fortunes with Tarot cards. Angie was into jewelry design and both of us felt that we needed to take our crafts to a higher level. The Beatles went to India, where they found spiritual gurus, and India seemed to be a cool place to really get into fortune telling, palm reading, and other spiritual divinations. However, things didn't quite work out that way. We bee-lined for Goa and spent a month on the beach there. I smoked a lot of dope and had a lot of sex, but no spiritual insight.

Angie dug the scene: sex, drugs, and rock and roll. Then she got sick, hepatitis or something like that, and she flew home for a cure because she didn't trust the Indian doctors. Now, I was alone but still digging the Indian scene. I split for Benares because this was the spiritual center of India. There, I could really get into my palmistry and Tarot and learn about astrology as a basis for predicting the future.

I really loved how the Indians dressed, especially the women with their elaborate saris. While in Goa, I watched the gypsy women working on the roads, carrying bricks and stone. They were all dressed up, wearing their finest clothes and steel nose rings. It was right then that I decided to adopt the Indian fashion and started wearing saris, complete with steel bangles, sandalwood necklaces, and a large gold nose ring. (It was no worse piercing my nose than it was piercing my ears when I was in high school back home.) I also purchased a pair of fancily designed heavy gold hanging earrings to compliment my beautiful gold thread saris and filigree gold nose ring. You can tell by my outfit that I am a walking 24-carat bejeweled Indian princess, if I do say so myself.

In Benares, I met this handsome, long-haired sadhu, Rudha, who offered to be my teacher in palm reading for a small sum of money. He would read my palm, and then we would smoke hash and make the sweetest love. Later, I met another handsome sadhu, Ashok, who promised to do my astrological chart and teach me how to tell fortunes using astrology, again for a small fee. Ashok taught me how to do an astrological chart and also taught me quite a few of the love positions from the Kama Sutra, which felt so good on a hashish high.

Tarot Reading: Derek Lee (UNSPLASH)

Ahahhh…I do love these tall, dark sadhus. They are so knowledgeable and spiritual in divining your fortune.

I just hope my daddy will keep sending me money so I can continue my "spiritual" lessons.

Chapter Eighty-Six: Remy's Tale of Woe - The French Connection (Room 2E)

Jacques and I were childhood friends. We did everything together, including smoking Moroccan hash, which is easy to come by in our hometown of Marseilles. We dropped out of high school to get stevedore jobs in the port. I drove a forklift and Jacques a delivery van. Marseilles is an exciting and exotic multi-racial city. There were Arabs from Algiers and Morocco, Africans from Dakar and Somalia, and Vietnamese, each living in their separate enclaves. The call to prayer from a broadcasting muezzin drowned out the church bells in my neighborhood. Added to this were the Muslim Albanian musclemen who worked for these French gangsters who controlled the prostitutes, bribed the cops and city officials, and dominated the hash and heroin trade for all of Europe through their "ownership" of the port.

Jacques and I started a good side business: selling Moroccan hash to our former classmates. Then the shit hit the fan: we were robbed at gunpoint by a rival drug dealer, who took all of our stash, about two thousand dollars in street value, and warned us that if he ever caught us selling in his "turf" again, he would kill us. Now, we were stuck between "a rock and a hard place." We owed the Albanian thug two thousand dollars and even if we had the money to pay him back, we still had nowhere to sell our hash. Then I remembered what my friend Sergey had told me of India: the plentiful dope, cheap living, and easy American girls. I convinced Jacques that we should go there, and we split without paying the Albanian; a week later, we were living on the beach in Goa.

Sergey was right: the dope was dirt cheap and plentiful. Right away, I was beginning to plan how we would smuggle this high-grade dope back to Marseilles and sell it at a big profit. Meanwhile, I was enjoying the scene here: getting high, laying on the beach, and finding a different American or Aussie girl each night.

These girls really loved my French-accented English. However, all they wanted to talk about was Existentialism and Camus' "The Stranger," thinking I would know all about that because I was French. I never heard of Camus or Existentialism, so I asked a fellow French freak about him, and he gave me his copy of "The Stranger," saying, "This is a classic." The book is about this Frenchman Meursault, who doesn't cry at his mother's funeral, starts a loveless sexual relationship, and, in the heat of the day on the beach, kills an Arab who had tried to kill him. He is put into jail and convicted to be guillotined, not so much for the murder, but because he didn't cry at his mother's funeral. Give me a fuckin' break!

Smoking Dope: Ahmed Zayan (UNSPLASH)

In jail, he is afraid of dying and yells at a priest, saying, "God doesn't care about us," and then accepts his fate, saying, "We all must die sometime." He rationalizes his impending death by saying, "God doesn't give a shit about us. What difference is it if he dies now or, like his mother, lives a long, meaningless life?" He is always alone and would die that way and he would accept his fate passively. What a piece of "merde." Every day in Marseilles, you see senseless killings. That dope dealer was going to kill us for taking his turf. Someone else kills his girlfriend because she cheated on him, or Meursault kills because the sun got to him, and he was afraid the Arab would knife him. Camus is saying his life or death means nothing in the grand scene of things. This guy sure wasn't my idea of a hero. I admire someone who takes control and lives life to the fullest. Jean-Paul Belmondo in "Breathless" is this kind of guy. He took what he wanted: money, cars, girls, and didn't give a shit about how they felt toward him. In the end, he is betrayed by that American bitch but decides to go out in a shooting blaze of glory. He is a man who is in charge until the end and never regrets anything. Someone should write a novel about this guy; I'm sure that would be a classic, too!

Jacques dug this scene, but hanging with these far-out French freaks got him into heroin and soon he was hooked. Just sitting and staring glassy-eyed in a drug stupor all day. I must get him out of here, but my money is all but gone. Luckily, this sheila "lent" me some Traveler's Checks, and Jacques and I split for Benares that evening.

We've been in this fleabag hotel for two weeks now, and I spent the last of our money buying low-grade hash to sell to the freaks here. The savvy freaks know that this is merde ganja, but we managed to sell all of it at a pretty good profit to the tourists. We were getting by, but then Jacques took the money for dope and we're back in the same situation as Goa. My dreams of buying a stash and smuggling it back into Europe are gone. We need every rupee just to survive.

Well, let's see how far my posturing on Camus and my sexy French accent can get me by with the steady stream of naïve American chicks that come to Benares. "je veux faire l'amour avec vous."

Chapter Eighty-Seven: "We Hardly Knew Yah, Tommy Boy."

"Happy Trails to You," Roy Rogers.

Tom and I were sitting in our room at the Hot-L Benares and planning where to go next. I was off to Delhi and the north of India, which I hadn't seen, and Tom, who had just started his journey, was going down South into the "Bible Belt" of Hinduism. I had told him about Auroville and the mastering of your consciousness and Sathya Baba. Hopefully, he could find this elusive guru before he left India. He was on a quest to discover the secrets of Hinduism, just like when he had stayed in a monastery in Japan to learn about Zen Buddhism.

Tom and I had been together for about three months in India and Nepal, and I really liked this guy. He was smart, open-minded, and knew what he wanted while I was somewhere in the clouds, loud-mouthed and headstrong, leaping into a situation before thinking about it. Yet we were best friends: we could spend hours talking about philosophy, religion, and books, and each of us was eager to explore and discover India. Most importantly, we could trust each other, not just with our possessions but with our emotions: we "bared our souls" and shared our deepest ambitions, desires, and dreams. There was an unspoken bond that we would be there for each other if we needed it. We have been through a lot together: sharing shoebox stifling rooms, enduring endless overstuffed and smelly third-class Indian rail trains, eating tasteless stall food, and even Claire who we both knew in the biblical sense. Outwardly, we were just two dopers, but inwardly, we were both passionately following our dream and supported each other to achieve it.

Traveling pairs you up with a diverse and mostly facile group, where dope is the commonality of your relationship. When you find a kindred spirit, someone you can truly share your experiences with, that person enriches your quest and gives you the moral support to realize your vision. Tom was one of these few; now, we were each going our own way, and we both felt the poorer for it.

These two Pelicans going off in different directions symbolized my relationship with Tom, each of us going our own separate ways. Photo by Oytun Babur Ozen on UNSPLASH.

North India

Taj Mahal: Lieutenant-Colonel Forrest from his book "A Picturesque Tour Along the River Ganges." 1824 (Public Domain).

Chapter Eighty-Eight: Delhi

I arrived in Delhi by train in the late afternoon. I was traveling alone and headed for a traveler's hotel in Chandni Chowk, in the heart of Old Delhi. I was in a state of bewildering amazement; this was some alternate universe. The people were the same Indians, the streets jammed with the same cars, taxis, and rickshaws, but the atmosphere was story-book Arabian Nights. Everywhere you turned, there were huge red sandstone mosques, forts, gateways, and shops with Arabic script. I was a "stranger in a strange land".

Delhi is old, but not as old as Benares, and yet you felt it had been here for thousands of years. In reality, there are seven separate Delhi's. Each time one Delhi was destroyed by conquerors, a new one sprouted up nearby. The first recorded Delhi was described in the "Mahabharata" as a city of beautiful gardens and spacious mansions. Ferozi Shah Kotla was Delhi's fifth city, and this was destroyed by Tamerlane, the Mongol conqueror, in 1398 AD. Shah Jahnabad, Delhi's seventh city, was the Mughal capital, but it was still destroyed by the Persian Nadir Shah in 1739, who stole the famed, jewel-encrusted Peacock Throne.

The current Delhi is teeming with people; the buildings are run-down and peeling, the streets filthy, and there are gordian knots of electric wiring everywhere, an electrician's nightmare. Dominating Chandni Chowk are the sandstone megaliths of Jama Masjid, India's largest mosque, and the fanciful Lahore Gate, the entrance to the gigantic Red Fort. The grandiose bazaars are more like Bagdad souks than Indian bazaars. Kinari Market has stall after stall, on both sides of the aisle, crowding out the passersby, selling gold, silver, trinkets, and brightly printed rolls of cloth.

The Red Fort was built by Shah Jahan, who also built the Taj Mahal. The fort took nine years to complete, and it became the seat of Mughal power, after they removed the government from Agra. Here, you see the wealth and majesty of Mughal rule. From huge, pillared audience halls to marble and jewel-encrusted music chambers to the women's chambers, with a marble fountain shaped like an open lotus flower, you experienced the extravagant lifestyle of India's rulers. You have the royal apartments, with their marble lattice screens, and the Diwan-i-khas, a small pavilion that was once covered in sheets of silver and studded with gemstones.

The royal baths are all marble and there are three rooms: one room emits hot vapors, the second emits scented rose water, and the third room, cold water. Lastly, the fort has its own mosque: Moti

Majid, the Pearl Mosque, which is made entirely of white marble that shines like a shimmering pearl. Gazing in wonder, I think of the money and labor required to build these edifices, and still, the country remained rich and prosperous. You could see why India was such a coveted prize, conquered by Aryans, Turks, Persians, Mughals, and finally, the British. This is a country blessed and cursed by its abundant wealth.

The Persian Nadar Shah sitting on The Peacock Throne 18th century AD. (Public Domain)

Many mosques were built on the sites of razed Hindu temples. The ornate floral Hindu columns were reused to support Muslim mosques.

I wandered for days, photographing the ruins, tombs and mosques. Emperor Humayun set the standard for garden tombs, with waterways and fountains leading to the tomb entrance.

The tomb is red sandstone, and the dome is a perfect half-circle of gleaming marble. What is most memorable about Humayun's tomb is standing in the middle of the tomb, staring up three stories to the white tomb ceiling, where all around you are gleaming white window trellised marble and feeling a sense of calm and peace, no object visible except the rectangular marble tomb. You absorb the Mughal aesthetic of beauty in its utter simplicity: nothing but you and God in this sonorous space.

Emperor Humayun's tomb Delhi.

The Quib Minar is a massive sandstone victory tower, marking the site of the first Muslim kingdom (1193). It is five stories of intricately carved red sandstone, encircled by four walking rings of wrought iron. It was also used as a minaret to call the faithful to worship at the ruined mosque next door.

This ruined mosque, Quwrivat-i-Islam, is made up of hundreds of garlanded Hindu pillars salvaged from destroyed temples (and now, karma-like, it too is destroyed). In the center of the mosque's courtyard is a fourth-century AD Hindu cast iron pillar. This is supposed to be the flagstaff of Vishnu. The metallurgy is so fine that for close to two millennia, there has been no rust on the pillar. Here, you have two faiths intertwined, each vying for God's attention, a truly Indian work of art.

The Quib Minar and the ruined mosque Quwrivat-i-Islam: Lieutenant Colonel Forrest, 1824 (Public Domain).

New Delhi

New Delhi is the crowning architectural achievement of Sir Edward Lutyens. It was started in 1911 as British India's new capital and took twenty years to complete. Its buildings are a synthesis of Western classicism and native Indian design. New Delhi is an impressive, planned city with gardens and fountains everywhere. Monumental government buildings are set in parklike squares; there are houses of worship for Christians, Hindus, and Muslims, residential blocks for government civil servants, and even a national stadium.

This was intended as the centerpiece of Britain's thousand-year empire in India (similar to Hitler's thousand-year Reich, and we all know how well that went!). Two world wars, the Great Depression, and, oh, don't forget, Indian Independence, showed the delusional folly of this dream. Well, cheer up, John Bull, the Indians are enjoying it now. The imperial reign here lasted only sixteen years (Fatehpur Sikri, the Mughal folly, lasted for fifteen years as capital of their empire). The Raj is dead. Hallelujah and good riddance!

Chapter Eighty-Nine: Partition

One day two women[a] came to King Solomon, [17] and one of them said: Your Majesty, this woman and I live in the same house. Not long ago my baby was born at home, [18] and three days later her baby was born. Nobody else was there with us. [19] One night while we were all asleep, she rolled over on her baby, and he died. [20] Then while I was still asleep, she got up and took my son out of my bed. She put him in her bed, then she put her dead baby next to me. [21] In the morning when I got up to feed my son, I saw that he was dead. But when I looked at him in the light, I knew he wasn't my son. [22] "No!" the other woman shouted. "He was your son. My baby is alive!" "The dead baby is yours," the first woman yelled. "Mine is alive!" They argued back and forth in front of Solomon, [23] until finally he said, "Both of you say this live baby is yours. [24] Someone bring me a sword." A sword was brought, and Solomon ordered, [25] "Cut the baby in half! That way each of you can have part of him." [26] "Please don't kill my son," the baby's mother screamed. "Your Majesty, I love him very much, but give him to her. Just don't kill him." The other woman shouted, "Go ahead and cut him in half. Then neither of us will have the baby."

-I Kings 3: 16-23, Revised Standard Bible

How and why did the Partition happen?

Great Britain, after World War II, was in a sorry state: massive debt, staggering unemployment, costly implementation of a universal health system, and civil unrest at home. Added to this was the cost of the empire.

Labor Prime Minister (PM) Atlee was determined to cut costs and give India freedom as soon as possible.

Gandhi and Nehru had been agitating for independence since the 1930s as part of the India National Congress Party (almost 100% Hindu).

The Muslims under Mohammed Ali Jinnah founded the Muslim League, and they were agitating for a separate state for Muslims.

The British had protected the rights of minorities by guaranteeing a number of legislative seats in the governing Indian Parliament to each minority: Muslim, Jain, Sikh, and Christian. This was the British system of divide and rule, giving no ethnic group full control of the government. An independent India would be dominated by Hindus and the Muslims would be powerless.

When World War II started, the Hindus opposed helping the British. Gandhi, Nehru, and hundreds of Indian Congress Party members were arrested and not freed until the war ended. The Muslims, however, cooperated with the British and that gave them British parliamentary backing for their movement for statehood.

In 1946, the British proposed a ten-year federation plan (each state would be loosely bound to determine their destiny over that period); this was accepted by the Muslims, but Gandhi firmly rejected it. The English Parliament voted that India would become independent in July 1948. In the meantime, communal violence between Hindus and Muslims was killing thousands of people. The country was descending into chaos and the British couldn't afford to send their army to keep the peace.

In March 1947, PM Atlee appointed a headstrong, totally incompetent Viceroy named Louis Mountbatten to finalize independence. Sentiment in Britain was divided: people like Winston Churchill favored a separate Muslim state because they saw it as a capitalist buffer against socialist India (as exemplified by the Indian Congress Party's political agenda). Both the Hindus and Muslims would not compromise in their stands and the violence was getting worse. Four thousand died in Calcutta alone in a single riot. The British had now lost control and Mountbatten exacerbated this by setting an arbitrary date of August 1947 for independence, almost a full year ahead of the date parliament decreed. This short timeframe gave neither Muslims nor Hindus time to reconcile their differences. This ultimatum ensured that there would be two separate states.

Mountbatten with Gandhi 1947.

Mountbatten was an impetuous, condescending official who knew little about India. To make matters even worse, Radcliffe, the lawyer charged with dividing India up, had out-of-date maps and census figures. So, he didn't even know where the dividing line between Hindu and Muslim communities should be, and he had never even been to India before. He arbitrarily divided villages in half, split the Punjab down the middle, and gave away the eastern portion of Bangal without knowing that the jute factories were all in Hindu Bangal and most of the jute fields in Muslim Bangal, thus ensuring economic chaos and hardships.

These two "criminals," Mountbatten and Radcliffe were so cowardly that they didn't inform Hindu or Muslim leadership of the exact partition boundaries until one day after independence!

The result was genocide on a horrific scale: two million people killed, a hundred thousand women raped, killed, and abducted, and sixteen million people displaced.

There were people in transit from one country to another for months after independence. Entire trains pulled into India from Pakistan with every passenger: men, women, and children killed and maimed. The British wouldn't send their army for the safety of these people and will forever be guilty of the genocide of these people; the rest of the world just stood by and did nothing.

Sikhs walking to India after Partition, leaving their homes in newly formed Pakistan to avoid being massacred by vengeful Muslims. 1947: Margret Bourke-White for "LIFE" Magazine.

The long-term effect of this balkanization of the Indian subcontinent resulted in regional hatred, unstable military dictatorships in West Pakistan, famines and civil unrest in East Pakistan, and the Indo-Pakistan War over Bangladesh's Independence. In India, in 1948, Gandhi was assassinated by a Hindu extremist for his failure to stop partition.

Gandhi Cremation 1948

The British were in India for over 200 years and yet they never really understood India or its religions. It was their "Dharma" to ensure that India as a whole nation would survive upon independence and here they failed miserably. The consequences of that failure resulted in a powder keg of constant conflict in the Indian subcontinent between India and Pakistan and relegated Great Britain to a second-rate power in the eyes of the world.

Chapter Ninety: Bangal Lancers, Adventurers and Novelists - The Creation of a Myth

Oh hark! the drums do beat, my love, no longer can we stay.
The bugle-horns are sounding clear, and we must march away.
We're ordered down to Portsmouth, and it's many is the weary mile.
To join the British Army on the banks of the Nile.

Oh Willie, dearest Willie, don't leave me here to mourn,
Don't make me curse and rue the day that ever I was born.
For the parting of our love would be like parting with my life.
So stay at home, my dearest love, and I will be your wife.

Oh my Nancy, dearest Nancy, sure that will never do.
The government has ordered, and we are bound to go.
The government has ordered, and the Queen she gives command.
And I am bound on oath, my love, to serve in a foreign land.

Oh, but I'll cut off my yellow hair, and I'll go along with you.
I'll dress myself in uniform, and I'll see Egypt too.
I'll march beneath your banner while fortune it do smile,
And we'll comfort one another on the banks of the Nile.

But your waist it is too slender, and your fingers they are too small.
In the sultry suns of Egypt your rosy cheeks would spoil.
Where the cannons they do rattle, when the bullets they do fly,
And the silver trumpets sound so loud to hide the dismal cries.

Oh, cursed be those cruel wars, that ever they began,
For they have robbed our country of manys the handsome men.
They've robbed us of our sweethearts while their bodies they feed the lions,
On the dry and sandy deserts which are the banks of the Nile.

"Banks of the Nile" 19th century English Folk Ballad (Public Domain)

5th Bangal Cavalry at Khurkowdah, Indian Mutiny 1857: Louis William Desanges, 1860 (Public Domain).

As I was perusing books in a second-hand English bookstore in Delhi, I came across a dog-eared book: "King of the Khyber Rifles" by Talbert Mundy. In a flash, I was nine years old back home in New Jersey, laying down in a backyard tent, reading "King of the Khyber Rifles" and thinking how exciting it must have been chasing Partha tribesman on horseback, disguising yourself to be a native, so that you could infiltrate the enemy camp, foil the impending uprising of tribes and, of course, leave with the girl that had been your arch enemy.

Serving God and Country in an exotic land, having one death-defying adventure after another and returning home a hero. Little did I know that fifteen years later, my dreams would come true. I would be serving God and Country in an exotic land: Korea, the Land of the Morning Calm. As for death-defying adventures, if you count catching VD, being chased around the room by an irate whore, wielding a butcher's knife, trying to kill me and surviving a plane crash, then yes, I had death-defying adventures. Coming home a hero was pretty much out of the picture: the anti-war demonstrators called us "Baby-killers" and "Imperialist Pawns". They should have blamed our President and Congress for sending us to that hellhole and not the poor GIs who got drafted and sent there to serve and die in a senseless war. These soldiers truly deserved a hero's welcome when they returned home.

English novelists, many of them old Indian Army hands, perpetrated the myth of the dashingly handsome and fearless soldiers-of-fortune and the myth of the heroic British soldier fighting against all odds to become a hero. C.A. Henley's "With Clive In India" tells how out-numbered British soldiers overwhelmed their Hindu and Muslim enemies and saved the Country for the Queen (well, in this case, the fight was to preserve a money-grubbing, abusive, and exploitive private company: The East India Company and the hero (Clive) was a crook, that absconded with company money and speculated in company stock to amass a fortune - but don't sweat the details). The adventuresome myth of the swashbuckling hero remained etched in the stone of popular imagination. Every young and enterprising British lad wanted to make his fame and fortune in the British Army in India (Go East, Young Man).

In America, we had the classic mythmaker of the American West: Buffalo Bill. Here, he didn't need a novelist to extol his glorious deeds; he lived on the fame of his earlier life. Buffalo Bill was an army scout (his valorous service won him the Congressional Medal of Honor), a buffalo hunter, an Indian fighter, and, above all, a showman par excellence.

His Wild West spectacles were wildly popular here in America and in Europe. He sold nostalgia: a fairy tale of calvary/Indian-battle re-enactments, with real-life participants like Sitting Bull and Annie Oakley.

Sitting Bull and Buffalo Bill in his "Wild West Show" 1885.

Buffalo Bill: Look at all those Indians over there, Sitting Bull, I told you to bring a few of your friends for a make-believe fight between the cavalry and the Indians; you're brought half of the Sioux nation!

Sitting Bull: Well, Bill, you wanted a real-life action adventure of Indians fighting soldiers and now you've got it. My Indian friends have been unemployed since The Little Bighorn and they're just itching to get into another fight with the US cavalry.

Buffalo Bill: Now, wait a minute, this wasn't in your contract! I'm supposed to be the hero here and defeat the Indians.

Sitting Bull: That's show business, Bill. Besides, after I defeat you and eat out your heart, I've got a book deal and a movie in the wings depicting this Great Indian Victory. It's been fun working with you, Bill, Sayonara Baby!

The frontier closed in 1890, according to historian William Jackson Turner; however, Buffalo Bill brought it back. He popularized the American frontier in the minds of the average American.

In America, Hollywood converted the myth into reality. I cannot think of a Western without seeing a vast, arid John Ford landscape in Monument Valley, where John Wayne, sitting high in the saddle, is chasing Indians or cattle rustlers. This is the lasting myth of the American cowboy; unless, of course, you're swayed by the power of popular mass advertising: a lone, reedy-thin cowboy in a 10-gallon Stetson and fancy leather boots, riding off into the sunset, puffing his Marlboro and coughing out his lungs, all the way down the Pecos Trail.

Similarly, the British soldier in India was glamorized by the handsome Cary Grant in "Gunga Din." The Indian Gunga Din dies, but Cary Grant lives on, ready for the next adventure: the perfect example of the brave and resolute British Army hero. Never mind that Indian Gunga Din saved the day with his bugle and died a true hero and not Bangal Lancer Cary Grant, but you must see the big picture: we need Cary Grant to deliver those immortal words: "You're a better man than I, Gunga Din."

Sir Richard Burton 1864.

The army in India did produce a "larger-than-life" genuine explorer, adventurer, and author: Sir Richard Burton. While on leave from the Indian Army, Burton masqueraded as a native barber and was the first non-Muslim Western to enter the Holy Shrine (Kaaba) of Mecca. He wrote a colorful and exciting account of adventures: "A Pilgrimage to Mecca and Medina."

He had a great facility for learning foreign languages and, while in India, kept a family of monkeys in his room because he thought he could decipher their language. Burton went on to many other adventures, including an attempt to find the source of the Nile River in Africa with fellow explorer John Speake. He was a true explorer: intensely curious, studying the people, culture, and environment of the countries he visited and then researching his findings and writing captivating, colorful, descriptive prose about his experiences. (My Hero! When I grow up, I want to be just like him!) Today, he is best remembered for his translation from the Arabic of "A Thousand and One Nights." Burton transformed innocuous children's bedtime stories into a racy "Double XX" Adults-Only version that shocked Victorian morals and sensibilities. (Oh, by the way, this Burton isn't related to Sir Richard Burton, the English actor who swept the married Elizabeth Taylor off her feet, also shocking our morals and sensibilities).

Chapter Ninety-One: One Chooses to Forget, Another Clings To Remember

India has many tribal groups that have not integrated into the mainstream Hinduism. I had mentioned the tribal people from the hills around Puri and there are other tribes from the hills around Assam that speak dozens of myriad languages: they range in population from hundreds of thousands to a few hundred villagers. What I find fascinating is that while most tribal groups cling to their identities and traditions, this "tribe" wants to forget who they are.

"White Curry"

The Anglo-Indians are a product of three hundred years of British inter-marriage with the local populace. Under the Raj, they were a privileged group: they administered and ran the Indian railroad and held government administrative positions in the British colonial government. After independence, the local Indians took over and they were without jobs. The British, of course, deserted them and refused them UK passports. They were called "half-baked bread" by the Indians; many spoke only English and didn't have any fluency in either Hindu or Urdu.

The richer ones migrated to the US and the UK, but the poorer ones had no choice but to "melt" into the local populace, often hiding their true identity. Most got away with this because they were very light-skinned; Indian males, in advertising in local newspapers for a suitable bride, always state: "must be fair complected."

I thought of our own racial prejudice. There are numerous books about light-skinned black women passing for white in our society. In pre-Civil War New Orleans, there was the famous "Quadroon Ball," where young women who were one-quarter black would debut in society for civil relationships (it was against the law for the races to inter-marry legally) or to become mistresses to rich white cotton plantation-owners and businessmen.

Many white American males proudly claim to be part native American as a mark of virility, as long as it is three or four generations removed and, of course, they don't look like a native American.

Racial prejudice runs deep in America, and this was "scientifically" proven by pseudo-sociologists who studied phrenology to prove one race's inferiority compared to the race in power. Later, accredited sociologists proved this false: there is no inherent inferiority between the races.

My favorite parade in New York City isn't the cartoon balloon-filled Macy's Thanksgiving Day Parade, nor the drunken swagger of the St. Patrick's Day Parade: it is the Puerto Rican Day Parade. Here , you see the rainbow diversity of the one million plus Puerto Ricans living in New York City. They range in color from charcoal black to milky cocoa to lily white. Yet they are all united and equal as Puerto Ricans. We, fellow Americans, could learn from this example.

Looking at photographs of Anglo-Indian families, it is hard to distinguish them from a typical British family. There was a famous Anglo-Indian Hollywood actress, Meryl Oberon, who vehemently denied being an Anglo-Indian. In today's America, the most famous Anglo-Indian is the singer Norah Jones, born of an American mother, Sue Jones, and the father is the renowned sitar virtuoso Ravi Shankar.

Nora Jones, 2010.

Perhaps in three or four generations, these integrated American and British citizens will proudly proclaim their Anglo-Indian bloodlines. However, for now, the rich class will pass for white and the poorer class for pure Hindu, and that's the way they want it.

The Tribe that Clings to Remember (The Kalash)

"Go children of the Lenape, why should Temenund stay? The Pale Faces are Masters of the Earth and the Time of the Redmen has not yet come again. My day has been too long. In the morning I saw the sons of Unimas happy and strong and yet before the night has come, have I lived to see the last warrior of the wise race of the Mohicans."

James Fenimore Cooper "The Last of the Mohicans."

The Kalash in Pakistan and India are the last remnants of Kafiristan in Afghanistan. They were spared the mass conversion of their Afghan brothers and sisters in 1892, when Kafiristan (Land of Unbelievers) became Nuristan (Land of Enlightenment) because they were across the border in Raj, India.

Three Kalash women, 2016.

The Kalash people are distinguished from their Muslim neighbors by their religion, customs, language, and fair skin. What makes them unique is that they claim to be descendants of Alexander the Great's Army. It was recorded by Alexander's biographer Arrian that he left hundreds of wounded and sick soldiers behind in the high mountains of Afghanistan when he hurriedly marched to defeat Hindu King Poros in the Punjabi plain. Alexander never returned for these troops, and the Kalash claim to be direct descendants of these soldiers. Their religion consists of many different gods, like the Macedonian Greeks. Their language is a proto-Indo-European language, similar to the ancient Greek language. Their customs, such as their dance festivals, are similar to the ancient dances of Macedonia and Thrace. The Kalish make large wood-curved horses for funerary objects: like the Greeks, they had tomb guardians; their neighboring Muslims have only simple wooden markers as gravestones. They are the only tribes' people in Pakistan to make and drink their homemade wine, which they may have learned from Alexander's soldiers. They are very fair-complected, some even having green eyes.

Rudyard Kipling wrote a short story about the Kalash and their heritage called: "The Man who Would-be King." Two British adventurers traveled to Kafiristan and set themselves up as Kings with the "magic "power of rifles, weapons never seen by the people of Kafiristan. The Kalash believed they were gods, descended from Alexander the Great; when it is discovered that they are ordinary humans, one is killed, and the other is tortured and crippled. The crippled one manages to get back to India and tells a newspaper editor (Kipling) this fantastical tale and, to prove the veracity of his claim, shows him the severed head of his companion, still crowned with a golden diadem.

Many critics wondered who Kipling used as an inspiration for his tale. The most likely candidate was an American soldier-of-fortune named Alexander Gardiner. He was six feet tall, with a flowing black beard, always in native dress, and he spoke several native dialects. He was one of the first Westerners to visit Kafiristan and wrote about the people and customs, especially the wine-drinking, which he imbibed quite heavily. His colorful, near-death escapes were the perfect model for Kipling's "The Man Who Would-be King."

Gardiner even wrote in his memoirs of two white travelers who were killed by the Kalash because they believed they were possessed of evil spirits. Gardiner thought that they were probably martyred Roman Catholic missionaries.

Gardiner married an Afghani princess and had a child; both his wife and child were killed in the constant civil wars. Broken hearted, he left for India, where he became a colonel in a Sikh

Army. After thirty years of fighting Muslims, he retired to a houseboat in Kashmir, where he died peaceably after writing his memoirs.

Colonel Alexander Gardiner: American Soldier-of-Fortune (1785-1877).

The Kalash in Pakistan now number about three thousand and are facing Muslim persecution and attacks because of their "infidel" customs and beliefs. In India, there are only about a thousand poor villagers remaining, many leaving their villages (and their culture and religion) for better opportunities in the Hindu cities. Soon, the unique culture of these "living descendants of Alexander the Great's Army" will vanish completely after twenty-three hundred years.

"All of these moments will be lost in time, like tears in the rain." The android Roy Batty's death soliloquy in the film "Blade Runner."

Chapter Ninety-Two: Frozen Infatuation - A Photograph

The girl with the story in her eyes (author's photo).

> Someone hurt her I'm so sure
> All the pain she must endure
> She can't hide it but she tries
>
> I love the girl
> With the story in her eyes".
>
> -"Girl with the Story in Her Eyes:" Safaris.

I was walking around the Chandni Chowk of Delhi and stopped in a dilapidated chai house, off the main thoroughfare for breakfast. That was when I saw her standing at the counter, buying sweet cakes.

She was small in height, 4'10'', still growing, about 16, dressed in a brownish-gray, rough wool jacket that had seen better days and khaki trousers with worn leather sandals. She had limpid, mahogany eyes, thick eyelashes, and long black hair, but it was her face that shone with a luminescent glow, bathed by the early morning sun.

She seemed lost in a private, dark reverie; I quickly snapped a photograph. My imagination ran wild: I envisioned her as an arranged child bride, a helpless victim of poor parents, eager to get her out of the house, promising her to an older, balding, fat suitor with money, who was justifiably captivated by her beauty and willing to forgo the mandatory dowry to possess her.

After photographing her, she noticed me, focusing her attention directly on me. Her expression was one of infinite sadness, infused with expectancy as if begging the question in my thoughts, "was I there to save her?" I was shell-shocked, my heart pierced by those sinking lodestones; I clicked another image, my camera an objective foil to my helpless infatuation.

The same girl as above (author's photo).

Here was a girl on the cusp of womanhood, seemingly trapped, with no one to turn to for succor. My photograph had "possessed" her soul and those supplicating eyes spoke to me, "now that you 'own' me, rescue me!" For a heart-breaking second, I would have given everything I possessed to assuage that sorrow. I should rush over, try to talk to her, but time and my reactions were frozen, dumbstruck by the spellbinding desperation of her "plea."

The second passed and she walked out, leaving me remorseful and numb. What would become of her? This child bride would have two or three kids by age 20; her fragile beauty would be lost, poverty cruelly coarsens this fleeting luminescence, leaving only a furrowed mask of her former loveliness. She would be recognizable only by her lovestruck husband, who does not see the everyday stark present, only the golden visage remembrance of youthful passion.

I left the café and the memory of that moment faded: India has a way of constantly assaulting your senses, thrusting new people, places, and loves in a never-relenting staccato beat.

I always send my 35mm film rolls back to the States; local development cost me dearly, with scratched slides and faded colorization. So, it was over a year before I viewed the slides. However, when I saw these two slides, I was again instantly mesmerized by her fragile innocence. I kept blowing up a closeup of her haunting face, changing the amount of light, adding and subtracting color, obsessed with precisely capturing her, as the sun illuminated her ethereal effervescence.

Yes, the photographs had stolen a "soul," but it was mine that was lost. Odysseus abandoned Circe, but her witchcraft spell remained forever etched in my consciousness.

"There are the moments which are not calculable and cannot be assessed in words; they live on in the solution of memory, like wonderful creatures, unique of their kind, dredged up from the floors of some unexplored ocean." Lawrence Durrell: "The Alexandria Quartet"

Chapter Ninety-Three: Agra Beyond the Taj Mahal

Agra was the Mughal capital of their empire in the sixteenth and seventeenth centuries AD. Agra fort, the seat of the Mughal government, has a magnificent reception hall, the Diwan-I-Aam, where the emperor received his public audience. Row upon row of red sandstone sculpted pillars, topped by half-moon scalloped arches, were meant to display the power and grandeur of Mughal rule. Here, the emperor sat on his "Peacock Throne" to receive the awed dignitaries.

Town and Fort of Agra: Drawing by Robert Sears, 1860 (Public Domain).

The Diwan-i-khas had a throne of marble placed on a terrace of the fort, from which the emperor could watch elephant fights directly below him. There is also a tiny gem of a mosque, decorated with precious stones and silver, used only by the emperor as his private mosque.

The double-storied, octagonal tower, Musamman Burj, is the most heart-breaking structure in the fort. Here Shah Jahan was imprisoned for the last years of his life, by his power-crazed son, Aurangzeb. Shah Jahan would gaze at the Taj through his windows but could never visit it, nor would he build his own mausoleum: a black marble copy of the white marble Taj, planned directly opposite the Taj, so they would gaze with love upon each other for all eternity.

Moreover, the artistic legacy of the Mughals lives on. In its heyday, the royal workshops produced dazzling carpets, exquisite diamond-encrusted jewelry, Qurans with beautiful calligraphy, and delicate miniature paintings, always showing the human figures in profile.

In the back streets and alleys leading off from the Friday Mosque, you still find these small craftsman workshops. These cubby-holes produce silver and gold jewelry, gold thread embroidered textiles called "zardozi", inlaid marble handicrafts, and beautifully painted Mughal miniatures. I bought one of these paintings, which looked like a genuine page from an old, illuminated manuscript. Later, talking with a knowledgeable Indian about this painting, he told me the real story. Illuminated manuscripts were paintings interspersed into fancy calligraphic Qurans to visually explain the texts. What these present-day painters do is to go to remote Muslim villages with fancy and colorful modern-day Qurans and give them to the village imans (priests). They would then buy their old Qurans that had been used for hundreds of years. Once they had bought these books, they tore out the fine calligraphic text, page by page, and painted traditional miniatures atop each page of writing, with the writing sticking out from the painting, so it would look like a two-hundred-year-old manuscript painting. Pretty slick! However, it is a beautiful, handmade painting, and I am still happy with my "counterfeit" antique purchase.

Mughal Painting (Author's painting and Photo)

Chapter Ninety-Four: Fatehpur Sikri (City of Victory)

Fatehpur Sikri is Disneyland India (sans the rides). It is a fantasy landscape of huge squares, spacious geometric gardens, bubbling fountains, mosques, mausoleum, palace, and a debating house (for discussing all of the great religions of the world).

I wandered for hours in awe of the profusion of architectural styles, shapes, and patterns of the grandiose buildings. All the buildings are made of a uniform red sandstone (with the exception of the white marble mausoleum.). This reminds me of the row upon row of city block brownstones in Brooklyn, which are also individually ornamented with gables, fanciful turrets, bay windows, and stone reliefs. (The red and pink sandstone Victorian townhouses in Brooklyn have become "brownstones" due to the harsh New York City winters).

The architecture was based on the magnificent buildings that the Mongol Tamerlane constructed in Samarkand and Bukhara in Central Asia in the 14th century AD. The Mongols (Mughals is an Indian corruption of Mongols) came from that area before they conquered India. But there are also Hindu influences in the carvings and floral decorations. Thus, it is a truly Indian style of architecture.

Fatehpur Sikri was constructed in the 1570s by Akbar, the Mughal emperor, to celebrate the birth of his son, Jahangir, and his victory over the Gujarat Kingdom. It only served as the capital of the Mughal empire for fifteen years (1570-1585) and was finally abandoned in 1601. Some say the reason for this was a lack of an adequate water supply or that the emperor just lost interest in it. Here, the buildings are in good repair and need little imagination to picture how magnificent the city must have been in its heyday.

"In Xanadu did Kubla Khan a pleasure dome build," Coleridge could have been writing his poem about Fatehpur.

You enter through a huge sandstone arched gate and come upon the main square, where the palace mosque and mausoleum are. Instead of Mickey and Goofy greeting you, there are herds of goats and hundreds of crows and vultures.

In the main square is a beautiful white marble tomb of a Sufi mystic, Salim Chishi, who influenced Akbar with his religious teachings.

Buland Darwaza gate to Jami Masjid mosque, Fatehpur Sikiri, India.

Akbar was a great warrior who expanded his empire, but he was also a seeker. He wanted to know which religion was the "true" religion. He built a special building, the Ibadat Khana, the debating house, where every week, he would assemble mystics, theologians, and sadhus to have them expound on their faith and then discuss the main points of their faith in comparison with the other religious leaders' beliefs.

He concluded that all faiths were valid means for accessing God. Then, he took a further step by taking the best tenets of each faith, creating a court religion, which he and his close circle of advisers and nobles adopted. This syncretic religion is really more of a moralistic philosophy than a sacred faith. This "religion" died when he did, but it showed the great tolerance he displayed towards all faiths in his realm.

Fatehpur is truly a fairytale at dusk, when the red sandstone turns to black and the fantastic turrets, onion domes, and witches' hats of the buildings stand out like a huge ruin of a medieval castle, overlooking a barren plain, waiting for the pomp and ceremony of an emperor that would never return.

Mughal Emperor Akbar holding religious discussions with representatives of various religions in the Ibadat Khana pavilion in Fatehpur Sikri (The two black clothed individuals at left of painting are Jesuit priests. (18th century, artist unknown) (Public Domain).

But Fatehpur was a failure even in Akbar's own lifetime. I believe that this was because it was a private, selfish dream; a dream for the rich only: the emperor and his court. It didn't involve the ordinary people in everyday life that make a city alive. The parallel to this is Brasilia, the capital of Brazil. This is a new city, constructed with futuristic architecture, broad avenues, and huge fountains, but it is cold and sterile. There is no "street life:" it is a city for the automobile, not for the walker. Brasilia was built in the geographic heart of the country, but it only attracted the politicians to live there. They did their government business and returned to Rio de Janeiro on the weekends.

America, too, had its planned cities, but here they were built for the people. Levittown, on Long Island and Pennsylvania, was built for the returning World War II soldiers who wanted to escape the noise, filth, and congestion of New York City. They wanted a house that was their own, one that had a small patch of grass in front and a backyard for children to play in. Robert Moses, the premier builder of bridges and superhighways, gave the common man access to the open spaces of former farms on Long Island. Ambitious builders gave them planned communities with schools, hospitals, shopping centers, and even beaches (Jones Beach Park).

They built mile after mile of cookie-cutter tract houses, complete with a yard and a garage for the automobile they needed to get to New York City to work. These weren't beautifully designed homes; they were small boxes, one or two story high, but they filled the need, and the government-sponsored cheap loans so that these veterans could own their own piece of the American dream.

Levittown in Pennsylvania 1959. (Public Domain, photo was never copyright.)

I was brought up in one of the little box houses in New Jersey, but my parents thought it was a dream come true. You had families raising their children in a safe, friendly, clean environment, and I always had other kids around to play and ride my bike with.

These communities thrived because ordinary people created their own lively cities based on their dreams for a better life, not on the foolhardy extravagances of the idle rich.

Fatehpur Sikri at dusk (author's photo).

Chapter Ninety-Five: The Freak Buys a Sitar

"Buy you a guitar and put it in tune

You'll be a rockin' and a rollin' soon

[Chorus]

Impressin' the girls, hittin' hot licks, yah, they dig me"

-"All American Boy:" Bobby Bare

As I walked around the narrow alleyways of Agra, I came across a small shop that made and sold Indian musical instruments. In the window was a beautiful sitar. My first thought was, "How much is that doggie in the window, the one with the long neck and shiny brown body?" I had heard records of Ravi Shankar, the famed Calcutta sitar master, in the States and was fascinated by the exotic sounds the sitar made. I had also listened to classical Indian sitar music and wondered if I could ever play this instrument.

Woman playing sitar, 1900 (Public Domain).

So, I entered the shop and prepared for the traditional souk hard sell; I picked out a beautiful sitar, inlaid with white bone decorations. The base was a large natural gourd, handsomely shellacked to a glossy gleam. What started at $200 US, I finally got down to $95 US. I chose a soft velvet material case because it would be easier and lighter to transport. They tuned the sitar for me and played it, so I could hear the sound, comparing it to a cheaper instrument. I said to myself, "this is all Greek to me," but I felt my sitar had a crisper, more resonant sound than the other instrument. I bought it and walked out, knowing that I really had bought the doggie in the window. Now I had to protect my baby from the mass of passengers with their massive bags, struggling to get a seat next to me on Third Class Indian rail. I arrived at Delhi Main Station and immediately checked the sitar into the whole baggage area; I had saved the sitar this time and hopefully, I would be able to do the same later.

Indian Classical Music

Indian classical music is a totally different sound from European music. It is hard to follow or find a melodic line and the beat line has no regularity; so how do you understand this music?

The two foundational elements in Indian music are: raga and tala. Raga forms the melodic structure, note intonation, relative deviation (spacing of notes) and the order of notes. Tala keeps the time cycle (time between beats) and determines the framework of the beat.

The raga uses a given set of notes and is a mode between tune and scale. These notes are ordered in melodies, with various musical motifs and a certain sequencing of moving from one note to the next. The space (time interval) between notes is more important than the actual note itself because this spacing determines the sentiment, atmosphere, and mood of the raga.

The tala is the framework of beats, not a steady repeating accent pattern, but a hierarchical arrangement of beats, depending on the feeling or mood you're portraying in the raga. The best definition of this is as follows: the raga gives the performer a wide range of ordered notes. This creates a melody that expresses a feeling or mood, while the tala provides a framework for rhythmic improvisation using time (space between beats, which enhances the mood of the song).

A typical Indian ensemble consists of a tabla (drum) that keeps the rhythm. Then you have a stringed instrument called a tempura, which plays a constant harmonic drone; this gives the sitar player a point of reference and also provides the background that supports and sustains the particular melody. He can then improvise, by spacing his notes, to achieve the mood he's creating in this raga piece.

Indian music started as a series of notes that enabled singers to chant the poems of the Rig Veda. Since there wasn't a written language, the Vedas were sung: intonation, spacing, and rhythm were essential to convey the message of the Vedas. When the Vedas were finally transcribed, the words and meaning were the same as when it was first chanted several millennia ago.

Teacher teaching young Brahman youths the proper intonation, beat, spacing and pronunciation in Veda Chanting. This type of instruction has been practiced in the same manner for over three thousand years.

Jaipur

A royal Rajput procession, mural at the fort at Jodhpur, Rajasthan, India. (18th century)

Chapter Ninety-Six: Jaipur - "Pretty In Pink"

> Pretty in pink
>
> Isn't she?
>
> Pretty in pink
>
> Isn't she?
>
> -"Pretty in Pink" The Psychedelic Furs

There aren't very many men who have multiple fields of excellence spanning such diverse disciplines as science, art, statesmanship, and war. In the West, we have Leonardo da Vinci, who was both a great artist and a remarkable prescient scientist. In India, Sawi Jai Singh II was one of those we call a Renaissance Man.

Sawai Jai Singh II 1725 AD. Unknown artist, British Museum.
(Public Domain)

He was a renowned military leader, so skilled in war tactics that the Mughal Emperor Aurangzeb called him "a man and a quarter," even superior to his legendary father Singh I for his victories over the Maratha kingdom (Here is an example of a Hindu king in service to the Mughal (Muslim) Emperor battling a Hindu kingdom). He was also a skilled administrator and humanitarian. He convinced the Mughal emperor to abolish the odious poll tax for Hindus, ensuring civil content and serving as an economic stimulus to increase the economic prosperity of the country.

In the field of urban planning, Singh II created a whole new city: Jaipur, in 1728 AD. Jaipur is a jewel, built almost entirely out of red sandstone, which is burnished pink in the morning sun and golden bronze in the afternoon sun. Jaipur is a walled city with seven majestic stone gates, enclosing a geometric grid of streets and squares. Off the main avenues are the small artisan shops producing silver jewelry, pottery, and other handicrafts. Behind these shops, he built the spacious mansions (Havelins), originally owned by rich merchants but now housing schools and offices. There are nine large block grids based on the nine divisions of the Quranic universe. He also allocated spaces for vast bazaars, mosques, and schools.

However, Singh II's signature achievement is the Jantar Manta, a park of astronomical observatories. Singh II was keenly interested in astronomy and the astronomical park he built contains huge sundials that measure accurate local time; round open structures to measure celestials' arcs; and instruments to calculate the start and finish of monsoons.

There are nineteen masonry structures in this stargazer's theme park that resemble from above a giant's kiddy park. The Samrat Yantra is the world's largest sundial and could have been Led Zeppelin's inspiration for "Stairway to Heaven," a long triangle set on its side with steps to the top seventy-five feet high.

There are round metal hoops, Chakra Yantra with a brass tube intercepting the circle to calculate angles of heavenly bodies from the Equator. Two circular Stonehenge structures, Ram Yantra determine celestial arcs from the horizon to the zenith of the Heaven, as well as showing the altitude of the sun. The most fantastic structure is the Rashivalaya Yantra, which consists of twelve huge LEGO pieces: a cross between an abstract work of art and a skateboarder's practice arena to calculate heavenly bodies' arcs. Each of the twelve pieces of this puzzle points to a different zodiac constellation to assist the court astrologers' horoscopes. All of these instruments were intended for the human eye to divine the mysteries of celestial Heaven.

Samrat Yantra: Lead Zeppelin meets de Chirico. The Stairway to Heaven in a surrealistic cityscape.

Singh II left a legacy that was soon surpassed by telescopes and astrolabes, but he will always be remembered as a seeker, a dreamer who sought to order the seeming chaos of the universe.

Chapter Ninety-Seven: Upward Mobility in the caste system - The Rajputs

Rajputs in 1868: New York Public Library Photo (Public Domain)

The Rajput first appeared as a distinctive group in the 7th century AD. Many scholars think they came from many different places: Huns and Turkmans from Central Asia, various tribal groups and other ethnic cattle-raising groups in the area of northern India (present-day Rajasthan). These warriors were fierce and carved out kingdoms throughout Pakistan, India Rajasthan, and throughout the Ganges valley. These warriors were from all different classes and social groups. Once they gained power, they bribed Brahmins to write genealogies showing that they were ancestors of the original Kshatriyas (warrior) caste. (Brahmin to Warrior: "So you want me to create a genealogy chart that shows you are an original Kshatriya and trace your lineage back to the Vedic age? No problem! That'll be 100 rupees. For another 50 rupees, I can make your Vedic "ancestor" a chariot driver for Prince Arjuna, famed hero of the "Mahabharata"). They fought each other and were only loyal to their clan, not to a greater Rajput social or political grouping. This is similar to the Germanic tribes in the 4th and 5th centuries AD in Europe, which developed into full-blown feudalism and prevented the formation of nationalist states. In India, it also prevented the formation of a single Rajput empire. Once these mostly illiterate warriors took over a province, they became a social class, a ruling and landowner group that legitimized a fictional noble descent. The Mughal army offered another way to achieve mobility in the caste system. Once these casteless soldiers had served and received land or wealth for their service, they "married up" by taking a wife from a poor Hindu warrior family and then making it their own ancestry and caste. These soldiers also changed their dress, manners, and customs to adhere to the ancient Kshatriya caste rules. Unfortunately, in their quest to be recognized as Kshatriyas, they rigorously enforced the "suttee," the self-immolation of widows after their husband's death.

When the Muslim armies descended on India in the 10th century AD, the Rajputs fought and defeated the first wave. Here, you had swashbuckling, sword-wielding mortal kombat contests between Hindu and Muslim cavalry, charging each other on Arabian steeds. This was very similar to European knight combat, without the clunky armor. However, the Delhi sultanate was very powerful and defeated all the separate, disunited Rajput kingdoms throughout the Ganges Valley.

The Mughals, however, could not conquer northern India Rajasthan, home of the majority of the Rajput warriors. When the Mughals came to power, they first fought the Rajputs, but then allied with them through a series of marriages, where princely noble Rajput Hindus sent their daughters to marry Mughal princes and nobles. Emperor Shah Jahan, builder of the Taj Mahal, had a Rajput mother. These marriage alliances freed up the Mughals to continue their consolidation of the Mughal Indian Empire and gave them valiant Hindu warriors for their armies (the "marriage treaties" required the vassal Hindu kingdoms to supply troops for the Mughal armies, many times being forced to fight other Hindu kingdoms in their service to the emperor) and it confirmed the warrior status of the princely nobles that had entered into these marital arrangements.

However, many of the Rajput kings continued to fight the Mughals. They built a string of fortresses in Rajasthan like the one above, the Amber Fort outside of Jaipur. I visited Amber Fort, which is just about 8 miles from Jaipur and what was fascinating about this structure was that it was more of a luxurious palace than a fort. Constructed of red sandstone and marble (note the pink glow of the red sandstone) with beautifully furnished interior apartments, audience halls, courtyards, gardens, and places of worship, Amber Fort is a synthesis of Hindu and Mughal

Amber Fort: Watercolor by William Simpson 1860 (Public Domain).

architecture.

In the middle to the late 18th century, the Mughal power declined, and the Rajasthan kings rode out from their forts, declared independence from their marriage alliances, defeated the Mughal armies, and consolidated their regimes under their own rule. One, the king of Mewar would never let his children marry into the Muslim nobility. He continued fighting and was the only Rajput Kingdom that never succumbed to nominal Mughal "vassal" rule and became a national folk hero for his bravery and warrior skills.

Maharana Pratap, Ruler of Mewar (present day Udaipur) who successfully fought off the Mughal Empire. to keep his Kingdom free. Painting by Surendra Singh Shaktawat 2023.

The Rajput class is a prime example of how the nominally rigid caste system was elastic enough to create a whole new social class and incorporate and legitimize this casteless group into the existing Kshatriyas caste structure.

Chapter Ninety-Eight: Mahavira and the Jains

(NO, THIS ISN'T AN INDIAN DOO WOP GROUP)

The main assembly hall of Dilwara Jain Temple. (GNU Version 1.2, free to use photo with no restrictions)

After sight-seeing in the "pink" town (Jaipur), I went back to my tourist hotel. There were no freaks at this place, only small Indian businessmen, salesmen and a few families. After dinner, I was reading in the lounge and there was one other person sitting nearby, reading a newspaper. I went over and started a conversation. It turns out that he was Jain and I asked him about his religion. I knew almost nothing about it, except they believed in not killing anything and were usually rich merchants.

"Jainism is an old religion, founded by the Twenty-fourth Tirthankara, Mahavira, in the sixth Century BC. He is not a God, like Buddha, who was also born in the sixth century BC, but is a spiritual guide, to assist man in the journey of the soul from one body to the next body.

Mahavira giving half his clothing to a begging Brahmin.

"All Jains adhere to four cardinal beliefs: nonviolence, many-sidedness (multiple viewpoints for every action), no attachments (to worldly possessions), and lastly, asceticism. A practicing

Jain makes five vows, which amplify these cardinal tenets of the religion: nonviolence to every living creature, speak the truth, do not steal, celibacy (chastity, if unmarried and faithfulness to your marital partner, when married), and non-possessiveness."

I interrupted him, "But most Jains are extraordinarily rich. How do they justify their riches, with their belief in 'non-attachment and non-possessiveness'?"

"It's true, there are many wealthy Jains, and many served in high-ranking posts in the Hindu-Rajput kingdoms. However, this was only to secure the well-being of our people and save us from the Muslims, who were killing us indiscriminately. We needed this Rajput protection because we Jains would not offer any resistance to the blood-thirsty Muslims. Also, as a way of penance for our wealth, we started many charities and built beautiful temples to offer devotion to our founder Mahavira and help our more unfortunate human beings."

"Then how are you different from Hinduism?" I asked.

"We, like the Hindus, believe in universal religious toleration and in the rebirth of the soul after death. However, our conception of the soul is different from the Hindus. The Hindu soul passes directly to either a higher or lower state, depending on whether you were good or bad in your earthly life. Jains also believe in karma. If you were bad, you will be reborn in the lower caste status, but each rebirth gets a different soul: A soul, so-to-speak, tailor-made for that individual. We, like many Hindus, are pious vegetarians. We also practice meditation, but our emphasis is to use this mediation to conquer worldly attachments for non-possessiveness, not for enlightenment as the Buddhists preach. We are a peace-loving people who work to transform the individual for the betterment of all mankind."

I thanked him for his explanation of Jainism. He told me I should visit Mt. Abu and see how they venerate Mahavira there. I told him I had to get back to Delhi in two days and unfortunately, didn't have the time. He then advised me to see Sanganer, about one-half hour by bus from Jaipur. There is a small but exquisitely carved Jain temple there, dating to the eleventh century AD.

I followed his advice and got a local bus to Sanganer, a gem of a craft city. Here they make woodblock-printed cotton cloth, and hand-painted blue pottery and tiles. When I arrived, I asked an Indian where the Jain temple was located; he directed me to the old walled part of the city. Sanghijl temple was small, but intricately carved, especially the stone pillars of the Assembly Hall. There was a fascinating bronze statue of Mahavira, sitting Buddha-like, with a crown of cobras:

on the statue's chest was a small mandala with a cross in the middle of it. It was like the "bleeding-heart" figures of Jesus you see in Roman Catholic churches back home. No one could explain the symbolism and it seemed out of place. But the Jains preached universal toleration of all religions, so it could have had some Christian significance after all. The most beautiful thing about the statue was Mahavira's serene countenance of inner peace: the bronze eyes stared directly at you, as if it understood you, and offered solace and forgiveness.

Mahavira meditating in the Lotus position.

Chapter Ninety-Nine: Hawa Mahal - Palace of the Winds

Hawa Mahal: Jaipur (1799 AD).

The most famous building in the "Pink City" of Jaipur is the Hawa Mahal, the "Palace of the Winds." This building is one of my personal favorites of all the architecturally built monuments (as opposed to stone-carved temples and caves) in India. It was built by Maharaja Sawai Pratap Singh in 1799 and designed by the architect Lal Chand Ustad, who designed it to resemble a honeycomb: a mass of semi-octagonal bays and 953 stone latticed windows.

This grandiose building is really the back of the palace and is constructed of pink sandstone. What makes it truly marvelous is that it is a beautiful synthesis of Hindu and Mughal architecture. The Hindu influences are seen in the fluted pillars and floral decorations, while the Mughal architecture is represented by the filigree stone on the windows and the semi-octagonal bays, which imitate the honeycomb ceiling interiors of mosques and mausoleums in Iraq and Persia.

The name "Palace of the Winds" refers to the cool breezes that waft through the small lattice windows and keep the inhabitants comfortable during the hot Indian summers. It was here that the ladies of the court were able to observe life below in all its splendor and yet not be seen from the street level.

Detail of main facade showing the semi-octagonal bays.

Besides the glorious architecture, the building is a chameleon: the sunlight transforms the color of the sandstone. The picture at the top of the page shows the Hawa Mahal in the early morning light, where the brownish-pink sandstone shines out in all its pristine purity. When I was in Jaipur, I took a similar photo of the facade in the late afternoon and here the sun's rays burnished it into luminescent bronzed gold.

Honeycomb dome in the Mausoleum of Zunirrud Khatun: Baghdad, Iraq 11th century AD.

Hava Mahal in the afternoon: the sandstone shines a luminescent gold in the late afternoon sun (author's photograph).

Chapter Hundred: Lakshmi's Prayer

> Oh hard is the fortune of all women kind
> They're always controlled, they're always confined
> Controlled by their parents until they are brides
> Then slaves to their husbands for the rest of their lives
> Oh I am a poor girl, my fortune is sad
> I have always been courted by the wagoner's lad
> He courted me daily both by night and by day
> And now he is loaded and going away
> Your parents don't like me because I am poor
> They say I'm not worthy of entering your door
> I work for my living, my money's my own
> And if they don't like me they can leave me alone
> Your horses are hungry, go feed them some hay
> Come sit down beside me as long as you may
> My horses ain't hungry, they won't eat your hay
> So fare thee well darling, I'll be on my way
> Your wagon needs greasing, your whip's for to mend
> Come sit down beside me as long as you can
> My wagon is greasy, my whip's in my hand
> So fare thee well, darling, no longer to stand
> -"Wagoner's Lad": 19th century Appalachian Folk Song (Public Domain)

"Hear me, Lord Shiva, I am Lakshmi, your humble servant and tomorrow I will die. I am 17 years old, and I have lived in the Hawa Mahal of my father all my life. I am the proud third daughter of the king and have never left the palace rooms and courtyards. I sit with my sisters at the stone filigree window, feeling the cool summer breezes, hidden and apart from the outside world, while looking down at life below, a life that I will never be a part of ever. I see mothers with laughing children, men selling sweet melons, merchants displaying fine gold jewelry and colorful religious festivals that pass right under my eyes. I am curious about the world out there, but I will always remain an outsider, never taking part in any of the joys of life and now even this life will be gone. I must say goodbye to my beloved sisters and brothers and family that I will never see again.

"Tomorrow, I shall be reborn: a third or fourth wife to a Mughal Prince in Delhi in an arranged marriage. I must publicly stop worshipping you, Shiva, and adopt Islam as my new faith. This is a cruel faith, worshipping a vengeful god who seeks only to destroy my people. However, I will always love you and try to follow your guidance. It is my Dharma that I must sacrifice my life to my hated enemy, killer of many Hindus, for the good of the kingdom. Like Arjuna in the "Bhagavad Gita," I need your counsel and advice to help me make the right decisions. Once I arrive at the Mughal palace, I will never leave that place. I will be alone, never having the company nor friendships that I have now. I will be in service to my hated Lord husband, who will do as he wishes to me. My happiness must be sacrificed for the good of the kingdom and I do this willingly. Hopefully, I will be reborn to a better, fuller life after I die.

Oh, Shiva, give me the strength to help me fulfill my destiny. I will never abandon you, even though I must outwardly profess my allegiance to Allah and follow strange customs and rituals of the new religion. I can look forward to a life of luxury, many servants, and anything that I desire; however, I beseech you to help me with my loneliness and to overcome my doubts. And above all, to guide and give me succor to fulfill my duties and be the exemplary wife, reflecting great honor and praise on my father and our kingdom, which will now have the peace it justly deserves".

Nur Jahan, Empress Consort to Mughal Emperor Jahangir (1577-1645) Watercolor by unknown artist 1725 (Public Domain).

Nur Jahan was the power behind the Mughal throne and effectively ran and controlled the Mughal kingdom because her husband, Jahangir, was incapacitated for most of his reign due to his opium addiction and frequent illnesses.

Chapter A Hundred and One: People of India

A typical middle-class family with a child who has Betty Davis eyes. With all the poverty in India we forget that there is a middle-class larger than the population of Great Britain.

A tribal group or landless tenant farmers that come to Calcutta looking for work.

A child gathering manure in old Delhi. She has straw on her head, which she will use to mix with the droppings of manure that will eventually be made into cakes for cooking fuel.

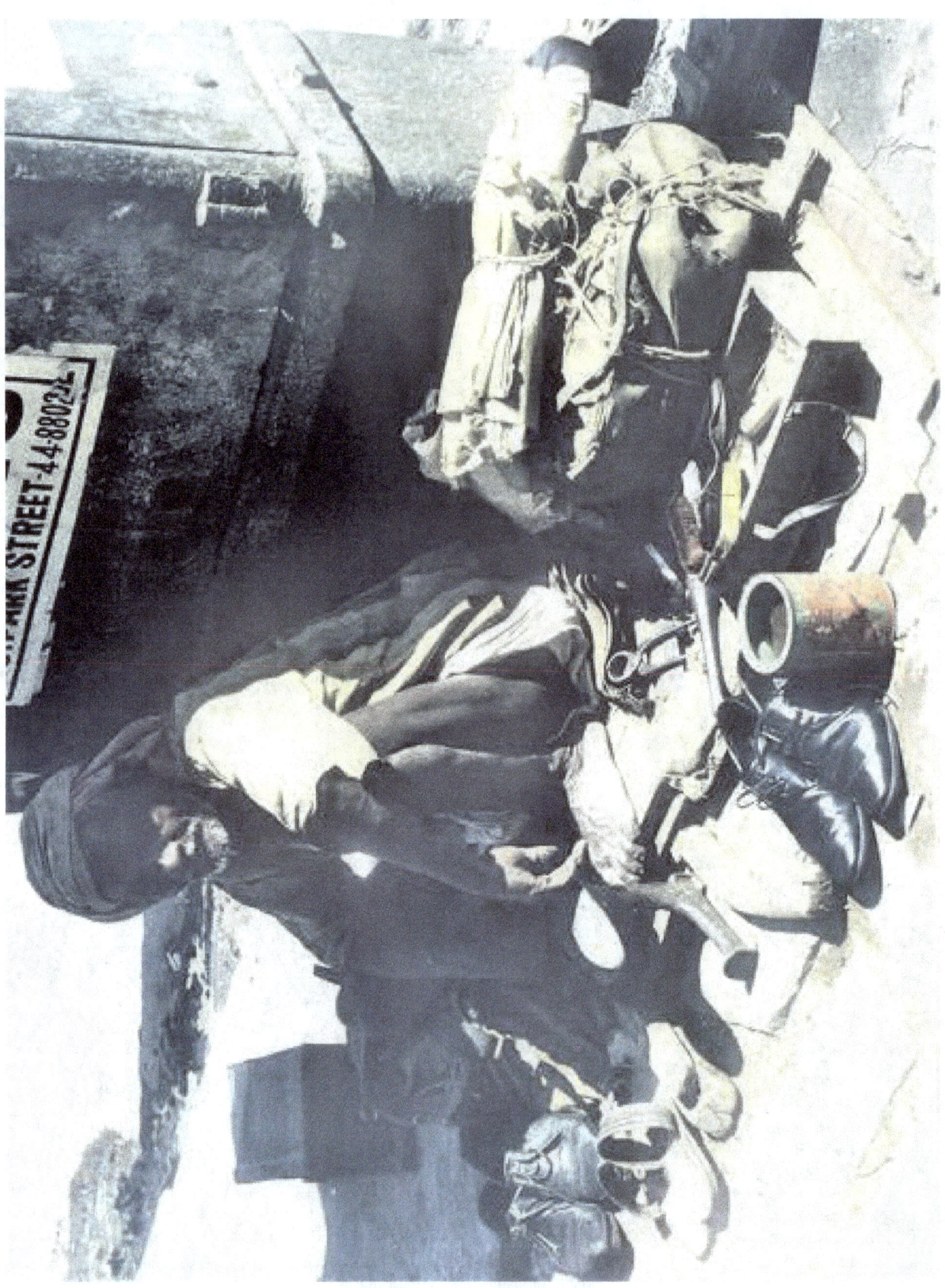

There are so many people who cannot afford a shop, so they do all their work on the street. Here is a Shoe repair service on the streets of Calcutta.

Although India is mostly a land of farmers, many people make a living from the sea as these fishermen, who are pushing their boat out to start their fishing day in Puri.

Old woman selling potions on Banares waterfront.

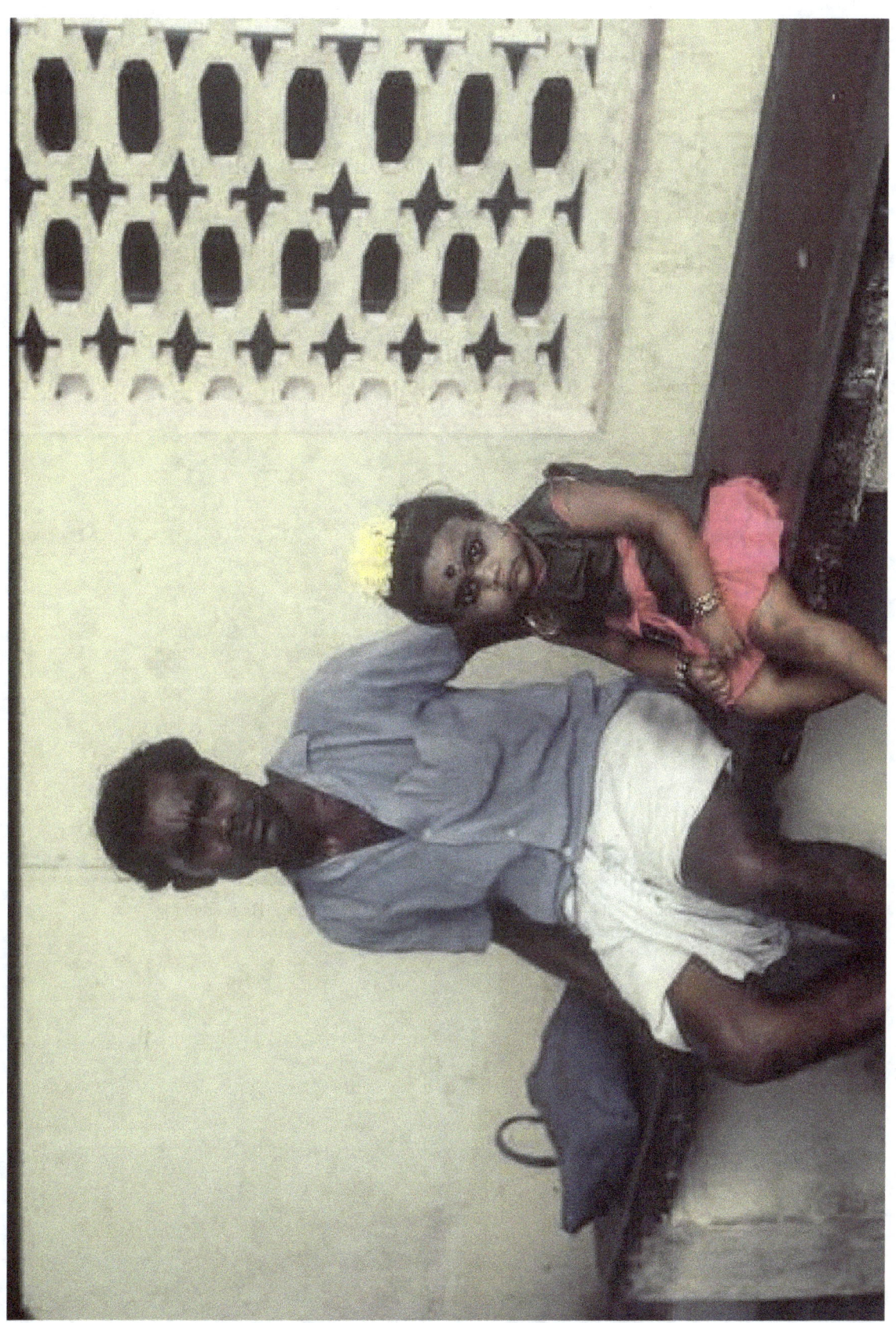

A father and daughter in a train station near Madras in South India.

A Hindu man smoking and holding his daughter outside of Khajuraho. He is smoking a water pipe with a mixture of tobacco and charcoal; the water cools the harsh smoke.

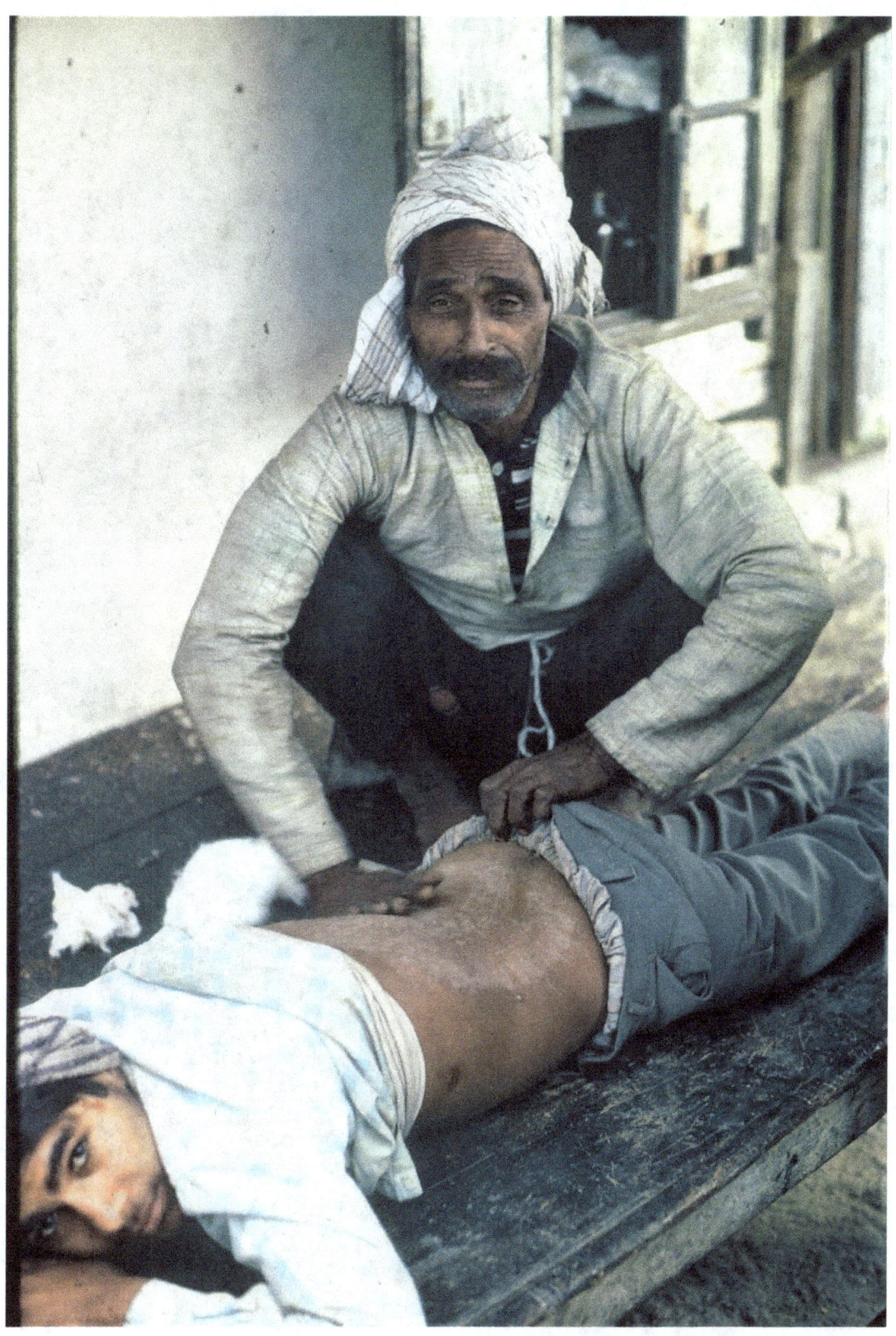
In India everything is done either in the streets or in small storefronts, where you can see what you pay for. Here is a healer applying a soothing salve outside of Bombay.

Merchant holding daughter in their storefront store outside of Allahabad

A Sadhu giving his blessing for a few rupees in the temple city of Madurai.

An untouchable sweeper cleaning the ghat steps in Benares.

A Muslim jeweler in old Delhi.

An angry Barber who doesn't want to be disturbed while he's shaving the head of this customer in Madurai.

A Hindu priest reading the sacred scriptures in Khajuraho.

An old woman selling flowers in the temple city of Srirangam.

A scribe in Benares. Scribes do a thriving business, since many of their customers are illiterate.

An ordinary Hindu on the streets of Benares.

A Beedi maker (a cheap Indian cigarette) in the South of India.

A Sadhu on a platform on the waterfront in Benares.

A gypsy mother and child in the countryside of Goa.

Women gossiping at the Village water well, South India.

Wandering Indian hobo looking for work near Khajuraho.

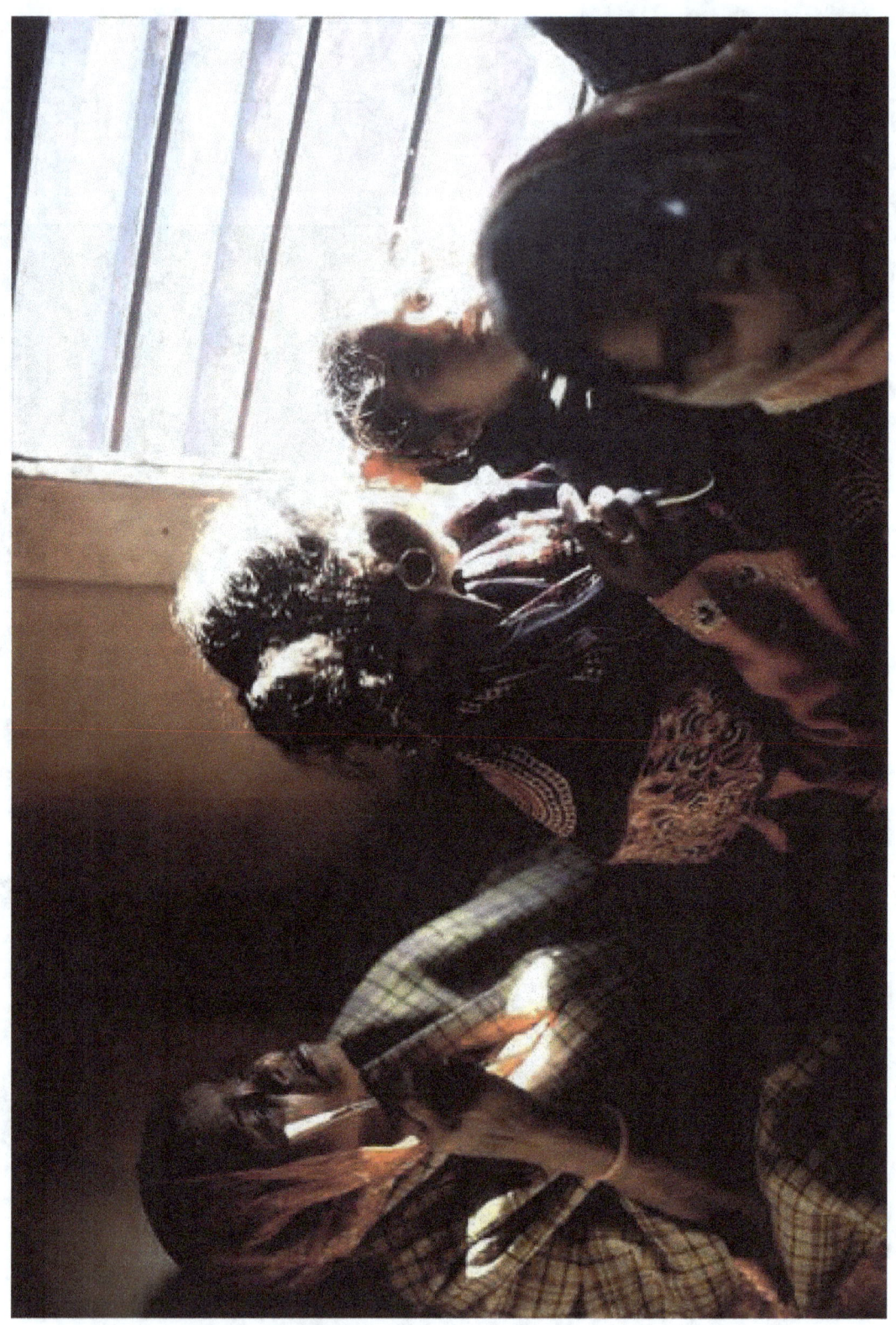
Three generations of Hindu women riding 3rd Class Train, South India.

The Parting Glass

"But since it fell unto my lot

That I should rise and you should not

I gently rise and softly call

Good night and joy be to you all"

"The Parting Glass"

18th century Scottish Aire

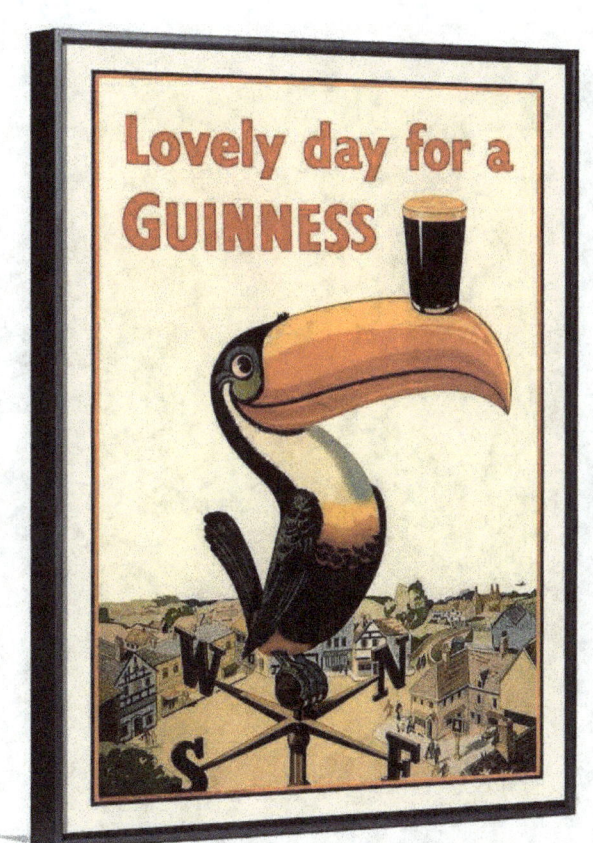

Guinness poster of the 1930s (Public Domain).

Chapter A Hundred and Two: The Last Day in Asia

"I got my mind on eternity

Some kind of ecstasy got a hold on me."

-"Wonder Where The Lions Are": Bruce Cockburn

Arrival of an imperial procession of the emperor Farrukh Siyar - at Delhi's "world-revealing" Masjid Mosque. Author unknown 1719 , Louvre Paris. (Public Domain)

This was my final day in Asia after almost three years. I spent it wandering around the Chandni Chowk, absorbing the sights, smells, sounds, and mystical spells of India one last time.

India is the most fascinating country I've ever experienced. The endless variety of people, languages, customs and religions, the sunbaked vistas of beauty and ugliness, the exotic foods, the joy of discovery, and the endless frustration.

I remembered the paradises that I had lived in and never wanted to leave: unspoiled golden sand beaches, breathtaking Himalayan mountainscapes, and green mansions of forests and jungles. I experienced the yin and yang of extremes: the yin of radiant glowing dusk skies so clear that the Milky Way broke through nightly, mornings crisp and calm as the dew leaves the fields, sunny days on lapis lazuli ocean beaches; the yang of crowded smog-filled cities, the draught of dusty planes, the flooded monsoon waterways, the overwhelming concentration of garish neon and electric billboards that blotted out the night and the enervating heat that sucked all of the energy out of every pore of your body.

Yet what really mattered on my "road less traveled" were the people that I encountered along the way. I arrived in Asia as a soldier with a fixed concept of duty, honor, and responsibility. I met soldiers of a similar vein and other soldiers who made me expand my horizons to see the many-sidedness of every issue and event. I lived half of my time immersed in a subculture that was joyful, frightening, giving, greedy, callous, and ultimately humane. What started as a pleasurable "one-night stand" in the pleasure dome became an obsessive manic indulgence in the circles of the "Inferno." I emerged with a poignant understanding of the hopes and dreams, the foibles and falseness, and the innocence and irony of what it takes to survive in the real world and still retain one's basic humanity.

On my long voyage home, I left the soldier behind and became a sojourner. A siddhartha discovering ancient philosophies and religions that made me question my Christian values and Western lifestyle. I met serious acolytes, deeply involved students, religious sadhus, lost-generation expatriates, authoritative monks, stoned-out freaks, and lonely, questioning individuals seeking a solution to life's basic questions. What they all had was passion; a willingness to sacrifice everything to achieve nirvana, Taoist acceptance of the Cosmos, supra-consciousness, Christ's message of love, the inward peace of devoting yourself to your fellow man or any other goal that gives life meaning. I, too, felt the psychic energy of the different spiritual communities and experienced the bone-weariness of fighting impossible odds to help a few families stay alive, while millions more starved and still there was no answer. The selfless devotion of Major Gardiner or Mother Teresa or the nameless Seventh-Day Adventist doctors was beyond me. I was too weak and selfish to live that life, but it affirmed my moral beliefs that one can make a difference: one person helping one other person.

Along the way, I over-indulged in drugs, some to numb the senses, others to find instant access to new doors of perception, to see the awe and beauty of life like a child sees it. To become a part of the greater whole, to be aware of the everyday wonders that surround us. I shared this experience with steadfast friends: a complete openness of my inner thoughts to another person.

I was bewitched by "La Belle Dame Sans Merci "sorceresses, looking to others to fulfill me. I took many lovers, some for pure carnal pleasure, others hoping to realize that magical moment when you are both in cinque physically, intellectually and even spiritually; you are as one person and now are somehow fulfilled. You don't need anything else. You feel that hole in your heart is healed, and you've found life's answer in a girl by your side or in a close friend who becomes a long-lost brother to you. For that brief moment, you're totally submerged in the epiphany of your love.

Life on the road is hard and you're always going one way and she or he another. Relationships mesh and then are rent asunder in a matter of days, weeks or months and you realize that you have been bewitched and must move on to find a different solution to your emptiness.

I have spoken with many of the people of each of the countries I've visited. Some like the Ibans and the Balinese were sure of their goals and content in their non-Western lifestyle. Others like the middle-class Indians were working toward the Indian dream or others in ashrams the negation of dreams. Many believing in the present system as the best hope to find fulfillment in life. I empathize with their aspirations: taking what I could use from them in discovering answers to my own doubts and questions.

I sat back and tried to analyze and reflect, to keep my mind open to all of these different experiences; the answer isn't an earthly paradise nor drugs, a loving person, or even a compelling vision of the godhead. I realized that you must put all of this into a blender and transform it into something usable for the "Bildungsroman" of my life.

Somehow, I came full circle: I arrived three years ago with a sense of duty and responsibility and now these values were reasserting their power over me. Before, I was a naive American: culturally bound by Christian moral values and Civic Patriotism; I felt that I had all of the answers etched in stone, black or white, but going through the "Valley of the Shadow of Doubt" here, I realized these values needed to be reexamined and found they still have validity, but for totally different and more complex reasons.

What I believe now is that we are part of the TAO, the flow of the universe. We must swim with the current, let it take us wherever it wants. God is in everything ("Let the Force Be With You") and of everything like Spinoza's pantheism. But even more importantly, I believe in the divinity of man, that we can access extraordinary power through self-control and analysis and become one with God.

Like Prince Arjuna in the Bhagavad Gita, you must fulfill your dharma (duty), but don't take pleasure or boast about what you have to do. With this responsibility comes a new awareness that we must understand to selflessly practice love toward our fellow man.

"When I was a child I spake as a child. I understood as child. I thought as a child. But when I became a man, I put away childish things. For now I see in a glass (mirror) darkly. But then face to face. Now I know in part; but then shall I know even so as I am known. And now these three remain: Faith Hope and Charity (Love) but the greatest is Charity."

First Corinthians, Chapter 20, Verses 12-14 - King James Bible, The New Testament

These experiences were my "trial by fire," and I hope I conveyed to the reader how important these discoveries were in understanding myself. However, you should get out on your own: explore and embrace your physical, mental, and spiritual self to discover who you really are (One size does not fit everyone!).

Now that you've had the pep talk huddle, get out there on the field and win this one for the "Gipper." "Boom chicha rah, boom chicha rah, boom, sis, boom, bah, Roosevelt High School Rah! Rah! Rah!" And never forget the immortal words of Doctor Emilio Lizardo in "The Adventures of Buckaroo Banzai," "Laugh-a-while you can, Monkey-Boy".

HIPPIE-KI-YAY!

Chapter A Hundred and Three: Flash Gordon's Worst Fear

"Flash Gordon Conquers the Universe," 1940. (Public Domain)

Dale: What is it, Flash? What are you afraid of? Is it Ming's soldiers ready to attack us?

Flash Gordon: Dale, I've never been so frightened in all my life! Do you see that small, stooped-over, bespeckled, middle-aged man in a gray rumpled suit sitting on a park bench over there? That's Bosworth Crawdaddy, the notorious book reviewer for the New York Chronicle. I had sent him a copy of my "Stoner to Seeker: 1970s Asian Hippie Trail," and it looks like he's reading it now. Wait, he seems to be tearing out the pages of my book, screaming and cursing. Dale, if I get a bad review, there goes the movie contract and so much for our dream of a house in the suburbs, the manicured green lawn with a white picket fence, and our 2.5 kids.

Dale: (Aside: Sighs despondently, Why ooh Why am I always stuck with the losers? I should have married Ming!) Don't worry, Flash. There'll be other things that you can do if he does give you a bad review.

Flash Gordon: I guess you're right, Dale; there's always "American Idol." I've been rehearsing a deeply soulful rendition of "Does Your Chewing Gum Lose Its Flavor on the Bedpost Overnight," and it's a surefire winner!

Narrator: Well, boys and girls, now that you too have finished the book (Atta Boy! and Atta Girl!), you can come to Flash's rescue by writing a glowing, inspiring, and praiseworthy review ("This book is the best thing to come around since packaged sliced bread.") to encourage him for further adventures.

Bibliography

A quirky, opinionated, and annotated bibliography.

"And now you know the rest of the story," Paul Harvey, American radio political commentator.

Paul Harvey.

This bibliography will be different from your standard bibliography in that I try to reference material relevant to the 1970s and 1980s, the time frame that I spent on the Indian subcontinent. The exception to this would be some of the photography books I recommend that show how the society and culture of India, Nepal, and Bangladesh are "timeless". This is also true for biographies which start in the '60s and '70s or earlier and follow the lifespan of the subjects.

For a must-see introduction to the culture, lifestyle, history and society of this fascinating country, I recommend two documentaries. The first is Louie Malle's "Phantom India." Malle arrived in India from France with a ragtime group of photographers and moviemakers. He wandered all around India, into the small villages and into the slums of the big city and spoke with numerous Indian politicians, religious leaders, journalists and average Indians in his idiosyncratic and poetic panorama of what India was in the late 1960s. Malle is looking at India from the viewpoint of a Western foreigner, trying to understand the people, religion, and culture of this strange, fascinating, and bewildering alien civilization, and at the same time romanticizing it as a simpler, more honest way of life as compared with the "decadent" bourgeois society that he came from.

The second documentary is Michael Woods' "The Story of India." Here he traces India from the very beginning when the first homo sapiens left Africa and settled in India. There are still ethnic tribes in the hills of central India that have preserved their language and lifestyle from this first migration wave into India. He then explores the Indus Valley civilization, the cradle of India, the Aryan invasions, and the art, religion, and society of that time. He continues the story through the Muslim invasion of India, the Mughal period and the European conquest of India. He is English and reflects on England's 400-year history in India, first as a trading company and then as the jewel in the crown of the British Empire.

The above two documentaries show India from a Western point of view. What I would recommend to you is to see how the Indians look at the West and that would be the movie "Hara Krishna, Hara Ram." This dates back to 1971, but it is available on Amazon and on YouTube. Here, you can see how the Indians look at Westerners, particularly hippies. They are seen as dope-smoking, evil corruptors, especially of virtuous Indian women. I have watched the movie and found it hilarious with its broad stereotyping of hippies. However, this movie was seen by millions of uneducated Indians, and many actually believed it to be true. This was particularly disturbing to women travelers who were groped, assaulted and called names because the average Indian thought that all hippie women were whores, especially if they were unaccompanied and traveling on a budget.

As a general book introduction to India, my favorite is "India" by the Touring Club Italiano, 1985, the author Antonio Monroy and photographers Martinelli and Meazza. Here, you have history, religion, culture, art, geography, and customs combined with beautiful photography to give a true picture of this fascinating country. I believe it is out of print now, but it is a must-have if you want to understand India. The book can probably be found on eBay or Amazon.

For current information on a particular country, I am a great believer in travel guides and heartily recommend "The Lonely Planet" guides on each of the countries I traveled to. These are "meat and potatoes" (hold the potatoes) main course books, chock full of historical, political and social references, as well as describing all the must-see (and the not so must see) attractions, usually with a wry sense of humor. The best cultural guides are the "Blue Guides" series, which go into excruciating detail on the monuments and ancient cities, with detailed maps and planned itineraries. The last two series of travel books, "Insight" and "DK" Guides, give you a photograph, drawing or old print of the temple or shrine they are describing in words (somehow, I thought the Taj Mahal would be bigger). For in-depth history and culture of a country, I have a cherished Eleventh edition of the Encyclopedia Britannica (1911) (Frederick Jackson Turner did the part on American history, John Muir on the scenic beauty of the American wilderness, and Bertrand Russell and T.H. Huxley did articles on philosophy). I must also mention my constant, faithful companion that I carried throughout my wanderings (like Alexander the Great with his well-worn copy of the "Iliad"): "Golden's Guide to Asia." This little red book was my perennial inspiration (and many times my pillow) on my journey and still has an enduring influence on me and occupies first place on my bookshelf.

As far as the songs I cite at the beginning of many of my chapters, they can all be listened to on YouTube. This is also true of the videos showing the dance, musicians, and religious practices and chanting of the Hindu priests. I implore you also to listen to Ravi Shankar, Nusrat Fateh Ali Khan, and Bollywood film scores to understand the musical heritage and current popular culture.

As for the photographs, drawings, prints, and cultural artifacts that I have embedded in my journal, some are my own, but the majority were found on Wikimedia Commons, which gives legal justification for Creative Commons Share Alike and public domain for usage. I also use UNSPLASH, which has free photographs to use copyright free if you are a member. For the other images, I have done my best to get "creative common" fair usage, citing the author or organization that holds the copyright and proper licensing agreements. If I missed any attribution, I sincerely apologize to the owner of the image that I used. There is a complete illustration index with all licensing approvals.

I have not included any cookbooks or recipes on the food I have described because any exotic dish preparation can be found in easy-to-follow steps on food channels or YouTube videos.

I have annotated with my two-cent comments on many of the books, magazines, newspapers, and videos that I have read on a particular topic or important issue that merits further investigation. I further divided the bibliography by book chapter, giving in-depth studies on my select issues.

Enough of this: all of the above sounds better given by a fast-talking lawyer rapidly going through the disclaimers (in three-part harmony). "The Really Big Shew Must Go On."

Books on India by Non-Freak Travelers

Traveling by rail: "The Great Railway Bazaar" 1973, Paul Theroux. You have to get used to Theroux's style of writing, which is dry and unsympathetic, but there are gems of observation which make it worthwhile.

Traveling by road: "Days and Nights on the Grand Trunk Road: Calcutta to Khyber" 1997, Anthony Weller. Conquerors, religious monks, robbers and truck drivers have all used this 3000-year-old road and Weller, a poet, captures the history and rhythm of movement magnificently.

Traveling by boat: "A Picturesque Tour Along The Rivers Ganges and Jumna in India 1826, Lieutenant Colonel Forrest. The early impressions of the Ganges reflect a timeless portrait, but it is the 24 color drawings that are really fascinating.

Traveling as a soldier: "The Devil Drives: A Life of Sir Richard Burton 1984, Fawn Brodie. The India part shows how startlingly original Burton was, and the rest of his life was extraordinary. However, the last part of his life was tragic. The British government didn't know how to handle him and sent him off to exile in South America.

Traveling as "A Stranger in His Own Land": "India: A Million Mutinies Now" 1991, V.S. Naipaul. Naipaul was an Indian raised in Trinidad and his book is all about the ordinary Indian: civil servants, gangsters, businessmen, farmers and women in a man's society- all written from an outsider's point of view, depicting their struggles and worldviews. He wrote this from his experiences traveling around India in the early 1960s- a must for understanding the caste system, the politics, religions and how India survives because of and in spite of all of the above

Traveling as a seeker of blue sheep, white leopards and spiritual guidance: "The Snow Leopard" 1972 Peter Matthiessen. A moving story of one man examining his life and goals high in the mountains of Nepal (Spoiler: he never really sees the snow leopard because, in his words, he was not ready to see it).

Traveling to understand the real India: "The City of Joy" 1984, Dominique Lapierre. To understand what India "is" for over half the population, this is a must-read, very different from the Patrick Swayze movie. This is a tough love song for my favorite big city in India: Calcutta.

These are my personal favorite written books, but I could have added at least a dozen more. However, now I would like to discuss photography books that show all of India. I will cite particular photography books on specific subjects below in my chapter bibliography.

Attention! The following is a paid political endorsement, and I approved this message:

"Stoner to Seeker Volume One: Bangladesh and Nepal" and "Volume Two: India" by Gordon Schwerzmann. When I started this project, my original thought was to have a written journal accompanied by my photographs. I have done this with the Far East in my first volume, "Soldier to Sojourner," and in my second book, "Sojourner to Stoner", where I have one book of text and one of photography. I look at this as an Oreo cookie: the hard chocolate sides are my photographs, while the white cream is my textbook. It is very hard to separate them and get the full flavor of this literary and pictorial delight, so I entreat you to look up my photography books and give them a whirl. "Thank you very much," to quote a famous American who, unfortunately, has left the building permanently.

"India" by Steve McCurry. McCurry is a National Geographic Magazine Staff Photographer, and this is a large format book showing some of his best work. McCurry is famous for his portrait of a startlingly hauntingly beautiful young Afghan girl with green eyes, which has become as recognizable as the Mona Lisa.

"Workers" and "Exodus" by Sebastiao Salgado: These books have extensive parts on India, but all the photographs are poetry-in-motion. Salgado is the greatest living photographer and one of my personal favorites.

"India" by Andres Bitesnich 2009: This Austrian photographer has captured the grit as well as the poetic in his memorable, mostly B&W images.

"India through the Lens 1840-1911", editor Vidya Deheja, 2001. This is a collection of old sepia black and white photos taken mostly by British soldiers and administrators and shows India during the time frame described. This is a fascinating time capsule which shows how the British were really intrigued by India and traveled all over the country photographing its wonders.

"A Day in the Life of India" 1996 Michael Tobias and Raghu Rai, this is one of a series of "A Day in the Life" of various countries in the world, and it is one of the better ones, showing the colorfulness and timelessness of India and it's fascinating people.

If I missed any of your favorite written books or photography books, please let me know and I will personally look them up. I'm always searching for books that tell the story of the real India. I can be reached at gordonroyschwerzmann@gmail.com.

Chapter One: Calcutta

"Calcutta" by Geoffrey Moorhouse 1972. This is the city of despair that I encountered in my travels, written by an Englishman who also reflects on what the city was when it was the jewel of the Indian Empire.

Calcutta: "Chitpur Road Neighborhoods" Peter Bialobrzeski. Chitpur Road was the 5th Ave. of Calcutta and all the mansions of the rich were there. They're still there but in various states of decay as the photographs show: a fascinating view of how great Calcutta was and the present-day squalid reality.

"Home and the World: A View of Calcutta 2014," Laura McPhee. Here, you have lyric and dreamlike interior views of the crumbling mansions of Calcutta, now home to dozens of Indian families and businesses. The effect of the photographs is like a dream, which weaves in and out of reality.

"Calcutta: Some Kind of Beauty," Fionn Reilly. Here is lower depths Calcutta: the life on the streets, the struggle to exist-documented in heart-wrenching, haunting images that will stay with you forever.

Mother Teresa: "Come and See," Linda Schaefer 2003. This photographer went to work for Sister Teresa, helping the sick and dying and eventually gained the confidence of the frail Albanian nun. Once this happened, Schaefer was able to document Teresa's mission works in luminous photographs.

Chapter Three: Women in Indian society

"White Mughals: Love and Betrayal in 18th century India," William Dalrymple. Heart-moving account of doomed romance: a British East India company man falls for Mughal Princess. Reading this book will tell you a lot about how women were treated in India before the modern era. Dalrymple is one of the best and my favorite writer on India and I will reference his books in other chapters.

Chapter Five: Black Hole of Calcutta

"The Anarchy: The Relentless Rise of the (British) East India Company" 2022, William Dalrymple. This book shows the greedy, power-grubbing and corrupt British East India Company, which came to rule almost all of India and why they had constant wars with the local Indian rulers, one of which resulted in the infamous "Black Hole of Calcutta".

Chapter Seven: Tagore

"Essential Tagore," Editor: Fakral Alam 2014. Rather than recommending a biography, I am recommending his creativity in total: his poetry, songs, letters, novels, travel writing, plays, and short stories, as well as some of his artworks, are all in this one book. Rabindranath Tagore was truly a Renaissance man.

Chapter Eight: Dance, Dance, Dance: you can watch many of the Indian classical dances on YouTube, and I would recommend watching a dance spectacular Bollywood production to see what the average Indian enjoys in a song and dance movie.

Chapter Fourteen: Sufism

"Essential Sufism": editor James Fadiman. A collection of fables, poems, and prayers which show all aspects of Sufism for the beginning student of this Islamic mystical wisdom. However, I'm not sure it really explains what Sufism is, but if you can understand and appreciate this collection, it's a great introduction to this mystical faith. To really understand Sufism, I believe you need a teacher to guide you in your beliefs, which involves self-examination of your consciousness to unite with Allah.

Chapter Seventeen: "Ibn Battuta: The Travels," Edited by Tim McIntosh Smith. This is an abridged version and very readable and I would recommend it if you are interested in this world-famous traveler.

Chapter Eighteen: Shipbreaking 101

"Breaking Ships" Roland Buerk, 2002. Burke is a South Asian correspondent for the BBC, stationed in Dhaka, Bangladesh, and as far as I know, wrote the first book, and in my opinion, the best book on shipbreaking. It is a people book and the characters stay with you, all their hardships and despair.

Chapter Nineteen: Furdo's Story

After I had left Bangladesh, the newly formed government and the government of West Pakistan developed a formal agreement that would repatriate the Biharis in these refugee camps. By 2002, 170,000 Baharis had been repatriated back to Pakistan. This was primarily the literate classes: civil servants, lawyers, well-to-do industrialists, shop owners and army personnel. This would have included Furdo's extended family since they were all highly educated and worked white-collar jobs. There were over 300,000 Biharis who chose to be repatriated but were rejected by Pakistan because they could not afford to provide for these illiterate, mostly farming refugees, given their poor economic status following the war. Later, in the early 2000s, West Pakistan also could not repatriate these Biharis since they were overwhelmed with support for approximately one million Afghan refugees that flocked to Pakistan after the American invasion of Afghanistan.

In 2002, West Pakistan President Pervez Musharraf publicly stated that the remaining refugees were the responsibility of Bangladesh to take care of. The leverage he used was that there were at least 1.5 million illegal Bangali refugees in West Pakistan, and they would be deported to Bangladesh if the new government insisted on repatriating the remaining 300,000 Baharis.

In 2008, the Dhaka High Court granted citizenship to Baharis, who were minors at the time of independence, and everyone born after 1971 was granted citizenship and the right to vote. However, today, there are still approximately 116 camps throughout Bangladesh, housing anywhere from 250,000 to 300,000 Biharis.

In 2008, the UN studied a Bahari camp, "Geneva Camp" in Dhaka, where there were 25,000 Biharis, the majority living in squalor, 10 people living in one room, one outdoor public toilet shared by 65 people and only 5% of that camp were literate.

Baharis are allowed to work outside the camps, and many have become truck drivers, rickshaw operators, garment factory workers, auto mechanics and small business owners. The children attend the local Bangali schools but are often bullied and harassed when their schoolmates find out they are Bahari. The older people have difficulty because they do not speak Bangali, only Urdu, and they have very little access to public facilities like the law courts, schools and even manual labor jobs that require a knowledge of the Bangali language. The older generation still dreams of returning to Pakistan. The younger people often drop out of school because of financial hardships, the girls because of childhood marriages and many of the young students still have to look after younger siblings because their parents are either working or incapacitated. In recent years, 2020 to 2022, many of the working class Biharis lost their jobs due to the COVID-19 epidemic.

OBAT HELPERS, a US nonprofit charity out of Indianapolis, Indiana, published a book in June of 2022: "Challenges and Prospects of Bahari Camp Residents in Bangladesh" (OBAT HELPERS Press). OBAT has been working in the camps, providing K2 education, scholarships for promising Bahari students, job training programs and health care. The book they published outlines how the Bangali government could help the Bahari camps by improving abysmal sanitation, providing adequate public water supply and mandating universal public education, especially for women. However, Bangladesh is one of the poorest countries, and they can barely provide for their own Bangali citizens, let alone the Biharis.

Women have been working outside of the camps, but due to childhood marriages and overcrowded living conditions, there has been a rise in domestic violence against women in the camps.

With the younger generation gaining citizenship and attending the local schools, there is hope that the camps will eventually be dissolved, and the Baharis will finally be integrated into Bangladesh society once the older generation passes.

Chapter Twenty-Three: Khajuraho and the Kama Sutra

For Khajuraho, you need color photography and diagrams or drawings for the Kama Sutra. You have your choice of many options; I will try and give you the cheaper ones that will give you a great introduction to both subjects.

"Khajuraho" by Desai Davangana is a good introduction with detailed photos of the 23 Temple complex and "Kama Sutra: The Book of Sex Positions" by Sadie Cayman gives you 50 explicit drawings on how to increase your love-making pleasure (Be sure to take notes- you will be tested on this!).

Chapters Twenty-Four: Mahabharata & Chapter Twenty-Five: Ramayana

"The Illustrated Mahabharata and Ramayana" by DK, the travel guide publisher, are the easiest to get through these dense (now abridged) epics, so you enjoy these classics and you don't have to slough through them as a strenuous duty with the older stilted translations.

Chapter Twenty-Seven: Kailasha and the Ellora Temples

Since this is my favorite structure as well as sculpture in all of India, I feel you should splurge and that means "Ellora" by Gilles Beguin. This is an expensive large format book, and the text and photography are informative and gorgeous.

Chapter Twenty-Eight: Waiting For Godot: Indian Style

Sathya Sai Baba was a highly influential and beloved guru and it was unfortunate that I never got to see him. However, you can read about him in the book "Satya Sai Baba" by Peggy Mason and Ron Laing. This is the best book available in English on this Indian holy man.

Chapter Thirty: Bombay

"Bombay", a Time-Life series book of the "Great Cities of the World", will give you a good introduction to the city near the time that I visited it.

For the red-light district: "Falkland Road" by Mary Ellen Mark offers a sympathetic portrayal of the prostitutes and the photography is revealing and heart-wrenching.

For the Indian circus: "Indian Circus" by Mary Ellen Mark is the best exposition of this popular entertainment, which may soon disappear due to movies and the Internet.

Chapter Thirty-Three: West Meets East

"Gandharan Art of North India" 1968 by Madeleine Hallade. This scholarly monogram on Gandharan art has not become outdated and I love this book: large format, informative and insightful text and copious full-page illustrations.

Chapter Thirty-Six: Ajanta

"Ajanta Caves" by Bennoy Behl shows the paintings as well as the rock-cut temples in majestic color photographs. I also own this book, and it constantly reminds me of the splendor of these magnificent ceiling paintings.

Chapter Thirty-Seven: Why Buddhism Died in India

The classic "Journey to the West" called "Monkey: a Folk Novel of China" by Arthur Waley (translator) is still the best version of this popular tale and this is the one you should read.

Chapter Thirty-Eight: The Magic Bus

"The Hippie Trail: A History" 2017, Sharif Genie and Brian Ireland. This is the best and most detailed chronicle of that wild and crazy time when hundreds of thousands of Europeans and Americans left London for Goa and Kathmandu on buses, Bedford trucks, Volkswagen minibuses or just hitch-hiked. The authors interview the travelers, the overland "Magic Bus" companies' drivers and many of the locals along the way. It was a magical time and like "The Odyssey," the thrill was overcoming all the obstacles to get to the Oz of Kathmandu.

There is a video on YouTube called "Road to Kathmandu" produced by Exodus Travels, a "magic bus" company out of UK and it's dated 1975, lasting about an hour. Here, the vehicle is a converted Bedford truck, and you get the truck driver giving his views of the countries they passed through and why young people are on the bus. It is also very informative, with local photography of the people and places of the countries that the bus went through to get to Kathmandu. The old video shots of medieval Nepal made me want to dig out my old rucksack and get back on the road again!

Chapter Thirty-Nine: Goa: Freak Paradise

Goa was the pot of gold at the end of the hippie rainbow trail. Here, people stayed for years; the attraction was free lodging, cheap drugs, free love and rock'n'roll.

To get a flavor of that time, "Apocalyptic Tribes, Smugglers and Freaks" by Richard Ehrlich interviews over five hundred freaks, seekers and dopers to relate their true experiences. This is "Bits and Pieces" history, but it is accurate and informative of the Goa and Kathmandu hippie scene.

"Eight Finger Eddie" by Earthman tells the story of the first and one of the last hippies to remain in Goa. A fascinating story of a man who lived without responsibilities and yet was the father figure for all the young freaks in Goa.

"Once Upon a time in Goa" by Terry Ternoff deals with the music scene of Goa. Ternoff started bands and played with others for years in Goa. The electronic music raga rock featuring loud drum music and repetitive staccato guitar has become famous throughout the world and a major influence on international dance music.

In my journal, I have used extensive photographs from the Facebook website "I Love Goa" by Vikram Jain. Here, you can see the wild abandonment, the music, parties and the drug scene. These photos are invaluable documents which really tell the story of Goa and why it attracted so many freaks. The photographs should be collected in a book which would tell the story of Goa's hippies much better than any written chronicle, just like the movie and photos of Woodstock remain imprinted in our imagination rather than any written history of that event.

There is a YouTube video done by an Australian: "Goa Reunion", who was the son of a hippie couple and raised in Goa as a small child. He became a filmmaker, and his project was to bring all of the freaks, hippies, and druggies back to Goa for a reunion after 40 years. This is a fascinating documentary as these now middle-aged, established people talk about how they were when they were young and what attracted them to Goa. A final amusing note on this video is that when they were hippies, they hated technology, television and all of the modern electronics; however, they were only able to get together now by connecting through the Internet, Facebook, where they found out about friends and lovers from that era.

There is also a YouTube video that I purchased called "Last Hippie Standing," made in 2001 by Marcus Robbin. This features extensive interviews with Goa Gill, one of the last hippies who has been in Goa for about 30 years. He has now turned to the Hindu religion for spiritual solace but looks back at his life when Goa was sex, drugs, and rock'n'roll.

Chapter Forty-One: Lusiades

"Lusiades": Oxford Classic Series,1998. This is a new translation, easy to read and the translator kept the poetic eight stanza format of the original Portuguese poem.

Chapter Forty-Three: Albuquerque and Chapter 44: Old Goa

"Conquerors: How Portugal Forged The First Global Empire" Roger Crowley. Crowley's book is a good layman's overview of the Empire.

"Encompassing the Globe: Portugal and the World in the 16th and 17th Centuries" 2007, Editor: Jay Levenson, Arthur Sackler Museum Book Catalogue of the excellent Smithsonian Exhibition of 2007. The full breadth of the Portuguese experience in Asia is magnificently presented in this profusely illustrated "coffee table" book. There is also a second book, which is only a detailed bibliography, which gives you everything you need to know to become a full-fledged Portuguese scholar.

Chapter Forty-Eight: Traveling on India Roads

"Travels in Arabia Deserta" Charles M. Doughty 1888. One of the greatest travel books of all time. If you love the majestic and sonorous, albeit archaic, language of the King James Bible, you'll love Doughty's writing style.

Chapter Fifty-Three: Dawning of A New Age

"Madam Blavatsky: The Mother of Modern Spirituality" 2012, Gary Lachman.

Spiritual prophet, flower child, or fraud- any of these descriptions would be true for Madame Blavatsky at different times in her life. She was, however, instrumental in introducing and popularizing Eastern religious thought to the West. As co-founder of the Theosophical Society, she had a loyal following which numbered in the thousands in the late 19th century.

As far as being a fraud with her Secret Masters, one critic stated that Madame Blavatsky invented the Ancient Masters, who explained the mysteries of the universe, because she felt that, as a woman, no one would listen to her. They would listen to great male authorities like the "Hidden Masters."

After she became a Buddhist, she preached love and brotherhood of man and would fit right in at Woodstock. With the decline of the Theosophical Society, she is fading into obscurity, but all of the new-age people with their tarot cards, crystal balls, and vague ideas of the brotherhood of all people should rightly credit her as the Mother of their movement.

Chapter Fifty-Six: Jesus as the First Freak

"The Unknown Life of Jesus Christ" Nicholas Notovitch 1894. This can best be appreciated as a "historical novel."

"The Gospel of Mary" Unknown author, 2nd century A.D. I have interpreted this from an Eastern or Buddhist viewpoint- you can find a translation of the Gospel on YouTube (it is only 5 or 6 pages for the extant Gospel) and offers myriad interpretations. It is the only Gospel written by a woman and the Gospel itself shows the difficulty that Mary, as a woman in 2nd century AD Palestine, had trying to convince the male disciples of Jesus of the truth of her revelation. The fascinating thing about this gospel is that Christianity could have followed an entirely different path to salvation if Mary's words were heeded: Salvation by introspection and self-examination of the mind as opposed to salvation through the sacrifice of the crucifixion and death and resurrection of Jesus Christ.

Chapter Fifty-Nine: Sri Aurobindo, The Mother and Auroville

Sri Aurobindo: For a great introduction to the life and philosophy of Sri Aurobindo, I would recommend the classic "The Adventure of Consciousness" by Satprem, which was originally published in 1970. The author was very close to the Mother and presented Aurobindo's religious philosophy in a readable and understandable manner.

"The Essential Aurobindo: Writings of Sri Aurobindo," 2001, edited by Robert McDermott. This book selects the best of the thousands of pages that Aurobindo wrote and is invaluable for its discussion of Eastern as well as Western philosophy. The spiritual philosophy elucidates how "integral yoga" will advance evolution into the spiritual state where man becomes God.

Auroville: In my time in Auroville, I spoke only with Westerners about what they wanted to achieve in Auroville. However, more than half the colony at that time were Indians who also belonged to the Aurobindo Ashram. Akish Kapoor grew up there and wrote two books. The first "Dream and Reality," a collection of interviews with the early pioneers of Auroville, including the viewpoints of many Indian residents, letting them speak on what they believe Auroville is and how they can further their spiritual enlightenment by working and living there.

The second book, "Better To Have Gone," tells the story of an early Western Auroville family and how their blind faith resulted in their tragic deaths. The surprising twist is that both Kapur and his future wife were raised in Auroville (the wife was the orphaned daughter of the doomed couple) and did not know each other (there were only about 500 residents there at that time in the 1970s and 1980s), found each other in college in the US, married, and returned to live in Auroville. The book also deals with Kapur's spiritual journey from being raised in Auroville, moving to the States and yet missing the spiritual nourishment of this utopian community and finally returning to live there with his family. I highly recommend this book to understand why Auroville is so fascinating and continues to grow while other utopian communities have withered and died.

As far as videos on Auroville are concerned, I would not recommend any! They emphasize the ecological or artistic community and don't deal with the spiritual life of the inhabitants, nor do they understand the true purpose of living in this utopian community.

Chapters Seventy-One: The Ideal of Kathmandu

"Seven Years in Tibet" Heinrich Harrar. This is one of my favorite books of all time and chronicles a way of life that is now mostly destroyed by the Communist Chinese takeover of Tibet.

Chapter Seventy-Two: Kathmandu: The Promised Land

"Far Out: Countercultural Seekers and the Tourist Encounter in Nepal" 2017, Mark Liechly. This book is by far the best explanation of why Kathmandu was such a magnet for hippies, mountaineers and general tourists. It goes into detail on the history of the hippie experience there and how it affected themselves and the Nepalese people. It brought back sweet memories of my time there.

"A Season in Heaven: True Tales from the Road to Kathmandu" 1998 David Tomory. This book was written by a freak who interviews various travelers, freaks and seekers on the road to drugs, enlightenment and freedom. A majority of the stories are heavily concerned with drugs, but there are insightful and spiritual stories which show how multifaceted the hippie experience in Nepal and India was in the 1970s.

"Ten Years on the Hippie Trail" 2013, Ananda Brady. This book was written by an early traveler on the Asian hippie trail who ended up living in Kathmandu, studying jewelry design from a Nepalese goldsmith. Later, he converted to Hinduism and continues to travel to India as his spiritual center.

"Portraits of Nepal" and "The Little Book of Nepal" Julian Bond. This freelance photographer has been photographing the Himalayas and Southeast Asia for over a decade. The two books that I recommended are better viewed on Kindle for your computer than the paperback versions. Here are the real people of Nepal in closeup, unvarnished realism, as well as the medieval cities and majestic mountains.

Chapter Seventy-Three: We Are More Than Cuckoo Clocks, Cheese and Chocolate

"Nepal" by Toni Hagen. This is a pioneering book: a combination of geography, anthropology, ecology, sociology, botany, and cultural study of Nepal and its people. It is still invaluable today and has not, for the most part, been outdated. As I said in my chapter on him, he became great friends with the Dalai Lama for his work with the Tibetan refugees and this may be his lasting legacy.

Chapter Seventy-Eight: Benares: City of Joy

Benares has to be seen; it cannot be described in words. That is why I recommend two photo books.

The first is a glossy color coffee table book, "Banares" by Henry Wilson 1999 which captures the dynamic and realistic way of life and death that takes place daily in Benares.

The second book, "Kashi: The Breath of the Labyrinth," 2020, Giada Baiocco (Book is in Italian). This is a poetic and dreamlike photographic depiction of life and death and what it means in the philosophical sense in these beautifully haunting B&W photographs. (Kashi is the Hindu name for Benares.)

Chapter Eighty-One: Freaks, Houseboats and Nietzsche

"What Nietzsche Really Said" Robert Sullivan and Kathleen Higgins, 2001. This book is easy to read and clearly untangles a lot of Nietzsche's own muddled thinking. It is especially good at deciphering the "God is Dead" and the "Ubermensch" theories that Nietzsche developed. A good introduction before reading his revolutionary philosophic books.

Chapter Eight-Six: Delhi

"City of Djinns: A Year in Delhi" 2003, William Dalrymple. The book has history, myth, a ghost story and a cast of thousands: the famous and forgotten, the living and dead. There are seven

Delhi's (Eight, if you include New Delhi). It discusses the old craftsmen, eunuchs, businessmen, politicians and the strained interaction of Hindus and Muslims in this Jambalaya Stew of India. Dalrymple is the best Western interpreter of Indian life and history today; his books are lively and scholarly, and he is not afraid to show the foibles and follies of his fellow countrymen in the country they ruled for four hundred years.

"Delhi, Agra and Fatehpur Sikri": "The Lonely Planet Travel Guide." These North Indian cities are fascinating because of their Mughal architecture and history. The Guide gives detailed historical background and where to see the mosques, forts, museums, and back street craft shops, as well as walking tours of these fascinating cities.

Chapter Eight-Seven: Partition

"Partition" Barney White-Spunner, 2018. This is written from a British point of view on the Partition, and it shamelessly exonerates the British army (he was a former British general) for not stopping the ethnic bloodshed. White-Spunner has an interesting observation that India would have remained united if the British had granted independence to India after the 1919 riots and Salt Tax demonstrations; Muslims and Hindus could work together at that time and an independent India would have given the rights to all religious groups. The book is well researched and does not spare the British on their ultimate failure to prevent Partition.

"Midnight Furies: The Deadly Legacy of Indian Partition" by Nishad Hajari 2020 is written from an Indian point of view and it concerns the personalities and conflicts between the leader of the Muslims, Mohammed Ali Jinnah and the Hindu leader Jawaharlal Nehru. The author even suggests that if there had been different leaders in place, Partition could have been avoided. The book, however, does not consider the extreme religious animosity between Hindus and Muslims, which had been kept in check by the British Army, nor the savage race riots in the large cities of India, which have been going on for years and, unfortunately, became more frequent and bloodier once Britain announced India's independence. This also is well-researched and reads much better than the Spunner book.

I have mixed feelings about Partition. I initially totally blamed the British, but after doing a lot of research, I concluded the only thing the British could have prevented would have been the wholesale ethnic cleansing. There seemed to be so much hate between the Hindus and Muslims and the present form of the Indian government, which had the British "divide and conquer" representation in the National Assembly, giving each nationality and religion a representation ensured that the Muslims would have no representation in an independent united India. However, I still believe that if there had been more time before independence, difficulties could have been worked out and the country would be united today. The real question is whether a united India would have become like Yugoslavia after Tito, breaking down into various ethnic groups and religions or a Switzerland where different nationalities and religions can live together under one roof.

Chapter Eighty-Eight: Bangal Lancers

"King of the Khyber Rifles" by Talbert Mundy follows the tradition of H. Ryder Haggard's "King Solomon's Mines" and "She." This was the heyday of the British Empire and these heroic soldiers, soldiers of fortune, explorers and adventurers were the equivalent of our western "rugged individuals": cowboys, cavalrymen and outlaws. Legends die hard; "Gunga Din" is still the best British army adventurer story, but they are still making these patriotic movies, the latest being "Zulu" and "The Four Feathers," which all deal with heroic defenders of the British Empire against the local natives.

Chapter Eighty-Nine: One Chooses To Forget, The Other Clings To Remember

Today, there are only about 4000 Kalash left that practice their old ways and religion: 3000 in Pakistan and less than 1000 in India. Their religion is an animistic, pre-Hindu, Vedic religion, worshipping Nature gods. Who are these isolated people? There have been numerous scientists that have done DNA testing and while none verified the Kalash belief that they are descended from Alexander the Great's troops, the scientists have found West Eurasian DNA and the language group is Indo-Iranian, similar to the Indo-European tribes that settled in Greece millenniums ago. They have become a tourist attraction and are a protected minority of the Pakistani government, although that has not stopped the Taliban from attacking Kalash villages and killing many of the people because of their "infidel" beliefs. Unlike most Muslims, they drink wine, which they brew, and are known for their intermingling of men and women prior to marriage. There is a YouTube video of their distinctive dress and dance ceremonies, celebrating the harvest and other nature gods. They have an interesting divorce custom. When a wife wants to divorce her husband and marry a new man, this new man is responsible for paying twice the dowry to the husband that the wife brought with her to the original marriage. "Do Think Twice, It's Alright" to paraphrase Bob Dylan.

Chapter Ninety-Six: Mahavira and the Jains

"The Heart of Jainism" Sinclair Stevenson 1915. This is the Classic book on Jainism: its history, beliefs, practices, influences and what makes this religion so special. This book has been out of print, but it's constantly being brought back because it's the best in its field. I highly recommend it if you want to learn something more about the Jains.

Chapter Hundred: Flash Gordon's Worst Fear

"Flash Gordon" and "Flash Gordon Conquers the Universe" are free to watch on YouTube. Each movie serial has 12 episodes and lasts about three and ½ hours. I remember seeing a few serial episodes at my local theater but was never able to watch an entire movie until I found an old VHS tape of the entire "Flash Gordon" movie in a local thrift store. Flash Gordon is a true "American" hero, not a comic book superhero with supernatural powers. A word of advice: don't buy the German television production of "Flash Gordon" made in the 1960s (Scheisse!) and avoid, like the plague, the 1970s American movie "Flash Gordon". Stand up for your rights as a red-blooded American: you want the authentic cheesecake acting, the wire-operated spaceships, the paper mâché monsters, and the cliff-hanging episodes. I could find no better hero to emulate (well, maybe Groucho Marx), and don't forget the stirring musical theme from Franz Liszt's "Preludes" every time Emperor Ming the Merciless enters the scene.

Illustration Credits

Introduction

Map of British India 1909, public domain in country of origin where the copyright term is author's life plus 100 years or fewer. This is also in the public domain of US because copyright was taken out before 1927 and not renewed.

"The Scream' by Edvard Munch: This is a faithful reproduction of a two-dimensional public domain work of art. Public domain in country of origin where the copyright term is author's life plus 100 years or fewer. This is also in the public domain of US because copyright was taken out before 1927 and not renewed. This photographic reproduction is therefore also considered in the public domain of United States/source: https://www.pubhist.com.

The Front Cover

Left: man in tee-shirt smoking: Domediocre, Unsplash

Center: stairway to heaven: Johannes Plenio, Unsplash

Right: man in yoga position: Christian Buehner, Unsplash

Calcutta Header

Public domain. This file is of Calcutta was taken by a federal employee, Clyde Waddell, as part of his official duties. As a work of the US Federal government, it is in the public domain.

Chapter One: Calcutta

Lieutenant Colonel Forrest from his book: "A Picturesque Tour of the Rivers Ganges and Jumna, India" 1824. This is a faithful reproduction of a two-dimensional public domain work of art. Public domain in the country of origin where the copyright term is the author's life plus 100 years or fewer. This is also in the public domain of US because copyright was taken out before 1927 and not renewed. This photographic reproduction is therefore also considered in the public domain of United States/source: https://www.pubhist.com.

Salvation Army Ceylonese Colonel: public domain in country of origin (Ceylon) public domain in the US first published prior to 1927 copyright expired and was not renewed.

Chapter Three: Women in Indian Society

Suttee: This is a faithful reproduction of a two-dimensional public domain work of art. Public domain in the country of origin where the copyright term is the author's life plus 100 years or fewer. This is also in the public domain of US because copyright was taken out before 1927 and not renewed. This photographic reproduction is therefore also considered in the public domain of United States/source: https://www.pubhist.com.

Chapter Four: Great Bangal Famine of 1943

Starving Mother and Child 1943 and Starved Child with His Dog: Public domain in country of origin (India). Public domain in the US. First published prior to 1943 copyright expired and was not renewed.

Chapter Five: The Black Hole of Calcutta

Fort Williams Print and Prison Guards. This is a faithful reproduction of a two-dimensional public domain work of art. Public domain in country of origin where the copyright term is author's life plus 100 years or fewer. This is also in the public domain of US because copyright was taken out before 1927 and not renewed. This photographic reproduction is therefore also considered in the public domain of United States/source: https://www.pubhist.com.

Chapter Six: US Aid on a Personal Basis

US Marines: this file was taken by a federal employee, Sgt Ian Ferro, as part of his official duties. As a work of the US federal government, it is in the public domain.

Chapter Seven: Tagore

Tagore: Public domain in country of origin (India). Public domain in the US. First published prior to 1943 copyright expired and was not renewed.

Chapter Eight: Dance

Village Dancers: This is a faithful reproduction of a two-dimensional public domain work of art. Public domain in country of origin (India) where the copyright term is author's life plus 100 years or fewer. This is also in the public domain of US because copyright was taken out before 1927 and not renewed. This photographic reproduction is therefore also considered in the public domain of United States.

Dancing Girl/ Cosmic Dancer: This is a faithful reproduction of a two-dimensional public domain works of art. Public domain in country of origin where the copyright term is author's life plus 100 years or fewer. This is also in the public domain of US because copyright was taken out before 1927 and not renewed. This photographic reproduction is therefore also considered in the public domain of United States.

18 Arm Shiva: Author Jean-Pierre Dalbera released photograph to creative commons attribution share alike 2.5 generic license, free to copy, distribute and transmit the work without restrictions with attribution of owner.

Indian Dancer: Author Sarah Welch released photo to creative commons attribution-share alike 4.0 international license free to use with attribution.

Mahua Mukherjee released photo of herself dancing to creative commons attribution share alike 2.5 generic license, free to copy, distribute and transmit the work without restrictions with attribution of owner.

Bollywood Dancers: Photo provided by Tasneem Mandviwala at amalgame.co. UK: This qualifies as fair use under United States copyright because it illustrates subject where there is no free image to do the same. It is of low resolution and the use does not affect the commercial value of the subject in question.

Flying Down to Rio: Public domain movie poster has no copyright and is now in the public domain.

Chapter Nine: Freak Goes to Movies

Satyajit Ray: Dinu Alam, New York, released photo to creative commons attribution-share alike 4.0 international license, free to use with attribution.

Columbia Record Album Cover: This qualifies as fair use under United States copyright because it illustrates subject where there is no free image to do the same. It is of low resolution and the use does not affect the commercial value of the subject in question.

Chapter Ten: Ravi Shankar

Ravi: Owner markgoff2972 released photograph to creative commons attribution share alike 4.0 international license, free to copy, distribute and transmit the work without restrictions with attribution of owner.

Chapter Eleven: You Can See the Forest for the Tree

Book Cover: This is a book cover. This qualifies as fair use under United States copyright because it illustrates subject where there is no free image to do the same. It is of low resolution and the use does not affect the commercial value of the subject in question.

Trunks of Great Tree: Author Aritr Mukcherjee released photograph to creative commons attribution share alike 2.5 generic license, free to copy, distribute and transmit the work without restrictions with attribution of owner.

Tree Overview: Author Biswarup Ganguly released photograph to creative commons attribution share alike 4.0 international license, free to copy, distribute and transmit the work without restrictions with attribution of owner.

Bangladesh Header

Woman Reclining: This is a faithful reproduction of a two-dimensional public domain work of art. Public domain in country of origin where the copyright term is author's life plus 100 years or fewer. This is also in the public domain of US because copyright was taken out before 1927 and not renewed. This photographic reproduction is therefore also considered in the public domain of United States.

Chapter Twelve: Bangladesh

Dacca Painting: This is a faithful reproduction of a two-dimensional public domain work of art. Public domain in country of origin where the copyright term is author's life plus 100 years or fewer. This is also in the public domain of US because copyright was taken out before 1927 and not renewed. This photographic reproduction is therefore also considered in the public domain of United States.

Chapter Thirteen: Bangladesh II

Buddhist Ruin: ASI monument photo released to CC-ATTRIB-SA-3.0 by Author Pratapurya.

Domed Mosque: Watercolor painting by Sita Ram 1817. This is a faithful reproduction of a two-dimensional public domain work of art. Public domain in country of origin where the copyright term is author's life plus 100 years or fewer. This is also in the public domain of US because copyright was taken out before 1927 and not renewed. This photographic reproduction is therefore also considered in the public domain of United States.

Shah Jalal: Persian miniature painting: This is a faithful reproduction of a two-dimensional public domain work of art. Public domain in country of origin where the copyright term is author's life plus 100 years or fewer. This is also in the public domain of US because copyright was taken out before 1927 and not renewed. This photographic reproduction is therefore also considered in the public domain of United States.

Chapter Fourteen: Sufism

Sufi Mystic: Persian painting. This is a faithful reproduction of a two-dimensional public domain work of art. Public domain in country of origin where the copyright term is author's life plus 100 years or fewer. This is also in the public domain of US because copyright was taken out before 1927 and not renewed. This photographic reproduction is therefore also considered in the public domain of United States.

Chapter Fifteen: A Simple Tale of Faith

Sufi Teaching: Persian painting. This is a faithful reproduction of a two-dimensional public domain work of art. Public domain in country of origin where the copyright term is author's life plus 100 years or fewer. This is also in the public domain of US because copyright was taken out before 1927 and not renewed. This photographic reproduction is therefore also considered in the public domain of United States.

Chapter Sixteen: Nusrat Fateh Ali Khan

Nusrat in Concert: Unknown photographer, taken in 1967 at Albert Hall, London, image is copyright free and in the public domain.

Chapter Seventeen: Ibn Battuta

Ibn Battuta Engraving: This is a faithful reproduction of a two-dimensional public domain work of art. Public domain in country of origin where the copyright term is author's life plus 100 years or fewer. This is also in the public domain of US because copyright was taken out before 1927 and not renewed. This photographic reproduction is therefore also considered in the public domain of United States.

Chapter Eighteen: Ship Breaking 101

Men Pulling Sheets of Steel: Stephane Grueso released photo to CC-ATTRIB-SA-2.0 license with attribution of author.

Man Cutting with Blow Torch: Nasquib Hossain released image to CC-ATTRIB-SA-2.0 license with attribution of author.

Chapter Nineteen: Furdos' Story

Liberation War Painting: Public domain. Photographed by Armas J. at Bangaldesh National Museum. This work is ineligible for copyright because it is situated in a public space (museum).

Chapter Twenty: Hinduism Demystified

Aryans Entering India: Hutchinson's "History Of Nations" 1910 public domain: copyright not renewed in country of origin (UK) and public domain in USA because copyright was before 1927 and not renewed.

Great Bath: Photo by Saqib Qayyum: The copyright owner CQUEST released photograph to creative commons attribution share alike 2.5 generic license, free to copy, distribute and transmit the work without restrictions with attribution of Author Saqib Qayyum.

Pashupati Seal: Photo: Columbia Education. This is a faithful reproduction of a two-dimensional public domain work of art. Public domain in country of origin where the copyright term is author's life plus 100 years or fewer. This is also in the public domain of US because copyright was taken out before 1927 and not renewed. This photographic reproduction is therefore also considered in the public domain of United States.

Krishna in chariot (unknown author) copyright 1932 not renewed in country of origin (India). This is a faithful reproduction of a two-dimensional public domain work of art. Public domain in country of origin where the copyright term is author's life plus 100 years or fewer. This is also in the public domain of US because copyright was taken out and not renewed. This photographic reproduction is therefore also considered in the public domain of United States.

Chapter Twenty-One: How the Caste System Began

Sadhu with Monkeys: Public domain. Library of Congress Carpenter Collection 1900.

Chapter Twenty-Three: Khajuraho

Closeup of Kandariya Mahadeva Temple: Photographer China Crisis released photo to Creative Commons-Attribution: share-alike 3.0 license free to use with attribution of author.

Erotic Sculpture: Sankara Subramanian released photo to CC-ATTRIB-2.0 license, free to use with attribution of author.

Ruin of Temple: Patty Ho released photo to CC-ATTRIB-SA-2.0 license, free to use with attribution of author.

Chapter Twenty-Four: Mahabharata

18th century manuscript. This is a faithful reproduction of a two-dimensional public domain work of art. Public domain in country of origin where the copyright term is author's life plus 100 years or fewer. This is also in the public domain of US because copyright was taken out before

1927 and not renewed. This photographic reproduction is therefore also considered in the public domain of United States. License PD-ART.

Chapter Twenty-Five: Ramayana

Rama and Sita in Exile: Old illustration from 1930s Author Taj Kumar book depot released print to public domain with no restrictions. Creative COMMONS CCO-1.0 universal public domain license.

Cambodian Dancers: Photo by Francis Decoly 1922. This is a faithful reproduction of a two-dimensional public domain work of art. Public domain in country of origin where the copyright term is author's life plus 100 years or fewer. This is also in the public domain of US because copyright was taken out before 1927 and not renewed. This photographic reproduction is therefore also considered in the public domain of United States.

Indian manuscript "Battle of Lanka" painting at the British Library by Sahibdin 1650 AD. This is a faithful reproduction of a two-dimensional public domain work of art. Public domain in country of origin where the copyright term is author's life plus 100 years or fewer. This is also in the public domain of US because copyright was taken out before 1927 and not renewed. This photographic reproduction is therefore also considered in the public domain of United States. License PD-ART.

Chapter Twenty-Six: Ramayana

Hollywood Adaptation: Painting of author of Ramayana, Valmiki, unknown author and date (18th century AD). This is a faithful reproduction of a two-dimensional public domain work of art. Public domain in country of origin where the copyright term is author's life plus 100 years or fewer. This is also in the public domain of US because copyright was taken out before 1927 and not renewed. This photographic reproduction is therefore also considered in the public domain of United States. License PD-ART.

Sita with Thorn: Indian painting 18th century AD Metropolitan Museum of Art, New York. This is a faithful reproduction of a two-dimensional public domain work of art. Public domain in country of origin where the copyright term is author's life plus 100 years or fewer. This is also in the public domain of US because copyright was taken out before 1927 and not renewed. This photographic reproduction is therefore also considered in the public domain of United States. License PD-ART.

Manuscript painting from "Mewar Ramayana" at the British Library. This is a faithful reproduction of a two-dimensional public domain work of art. Public domain in country of origin where the copyright term is author's life plus 100 years or fewer. This is also in the public domain of US because copyright was taken out before 1927 and not renewed. This photographic reproduction is therefore also considered in the public domain of United States.

Chapter Twenty-Seven: Kailasha Temple

Fergusson Drawing: This is a faithful reproduction of a two-dimensional public domain work of art. Public domain in country of origin where the copyright term is author's life plus 100 years or fewer. This is also in the public domain of US because copyright was taken out before 1927 and not renewed. This photographic reproduction is therefore also considered in the public domain of United States.

Kailasha Overview: Imgur: Creative Commons: attribution- share alike 3.0 license free to use with attribution or Verul.png released photo to Creative Commons. Attribution: share-alike 4.0 license, free to use with attribution of author.

Ramayana Stone Panel: g41m8 released photo to Creative Commons attribution-share alike 4.0 international license: free to use with attribution of author, Akshay Prakash.

Elephant Base: Akshay Prakash released photo to Creative Commons attribution-share alike 4.0 international license: free to use with attribution of author, Akshay Prakash.

Lotus Top with Lions: Y. Shishido released photo to Creative Commons attribution-share alike 4.0 international license: free to use with attribution of author.

Chapter Twenty-Eight: Waiting for Godot

Sathya Baba Postage Stamp: This is a government of India copyright work, but under national data sharing and accessibility policy of government of India. This file is available, royalty free, for all commercial and non-commercial uses.

Shirdi Baba Photo: Author unknown. This is a faithful reproduction of a two-dimensional public domain work of art. Public domain in country of origin where the copyright term is author's life plus 100 years or fewer. This is also in the public domain of US because copyright was taken out before 1927 and not renewed. This photographic reproduction is therefore also considered in the public domain of United States.

Chapter Twenty-Nine: Rachel

Wally by Egon Schiele 1912. This is a faithful reproduction of a two-dimensional public domain work of art. Public domain in country of origin where the copyright term is author's life plus 100 years or fewer. This is also in the public domain of US because copyright was taken out before 1927 and not renewed. This photographic reproduction is therefore also considered in the public domain of United States.

Bombay Header

Bombay Fort Scene: This is a faithful reproduction of a two-dimensional public domain work of art. Public domain in country of origin where the copyright term is author's life plus 100 years or fewer. This is also in the public domain of US because copyright was taken out before 1927 and not renewed. This photographic reproduction is therefore also considered in the public domain of United States.

Chapter Thirty: Bombay: Quiet Days

Ganesh Statue: Author Vijay Bandari released image to Creative Commons attribution share alike 2.9 generic license. Free to copy and share with attribution of author, Vijay Bandari.

American GI with Prostitutes: Photo by Clyde Waddell 1945. This file is of India was taken by a federal employee, Clyde Waddell, as part of his official duties. As a work of the US federal government, it is in the public domain.

Gateway of India: Author Jawahar Soneji released photo to Creative Commons attribution: share-alike international 4.0 license, free to use with attribution of author, Jawahar Soneji.

Old Print of Elephanta Caves: This is a faithful reproduction of a two-dimensional public domain work of art. Public domain in country of origin where the copyright term is author's life plus 100 years or fewer. This is also in the public domain of US because copyright was taken out before 1927 and not renewed. This photographic reproduction is therefore also considered in the public domain of United States.

Three Headed Shiva: Ronakshaw released photo to Creative Commons: attribution- share alike 4.0 international license. Free to use with attribution of Author Ronakshaw.

Circus Photo: Author Vivek Prakash released photo to CC-ATTRIB-SA-3.0 license with attribution of author.

Chapter Thirty-One: Parsi

19th Century Mica Illustration. This is in the collection of the Walters Museum. There is no copyright on this collection and it is in the public domain.

19th Century Wood Engraving of Parsi. This is a faithful reproduction of a two-dimensional public domain work of art. Public domain in country of origin where the copyright term is author's life plus 100 years or fewer. This is also in the public domain of US because copyright was taken out before 1927 and not renewed. This photographic reproduction is therefore also considered in the public domain of United States.

Tower of Silence: Drawing by Frederic Penfield from his book "Ceylon, India, China And Japan" 1907, copyright expired, now in public domain.

Chapter Thirty-Two: How to Marry a Millionaire

Newspaper Want Ads: Although image is believed to be copyrighted, it qualifies under US Fair usage for the following reasons: This qualifies as fair use under United States copyright because it illustrates subject where there is no free image to do the same. It is of low resolution and the use does not affect the commercial value of the subject in question.

Buddhisim in India Header

Sutra Painting 700 BC: Public domain. This is a faithful reproduction of a two-dimensional public domain work of art. Public domain in country of origin where the copyright term is author's life plus 100 years or fewer. This is also in the public domain of US because copyright was taken out before 1927 and not renewed. This photographic reproduction is therefore also considered in the public domain of United States. US license: PD-ART.

Chapter Thirty-Four: Sanchi

Sanchi Stupa with Gateway: Author Biswarup Ganguly released photo to GNU free doc. License version 1.2 free to use with attribution.

Griffin: Author Arnold Belten released photo to Creative Commons CCO-1.0 universal public domain with no restrictions.

Tree Spirit Yakshi: Author Nagarjun released image to Creative Commons attribution share alike 2.0 generic license, free to use with attribution of Nagarjun.

Eve: 11th century AD sculpture by Gilbertus. This is a faithful reproduction of a two-dimensional public domain work of art. Public domain in country of origin where the copyright term is author's life plus 100 years or fewer. This is also in the public domain of US because copyright was taken out before 1927 and not renewed. This photographic reproduction is therefore also considered in the public domain of United States.

Chapter Thirty-Five: Buddha's First Sermon

Afghan Buddha: Photographer Merek Gawecki 2012 released image to GNU free documentation license, version 1.2, free to use with attribution of author.

Gandharan Buddha: Author Daderot released photo to Creative Commons CCO-1.0 universal public domain with no restrictions.

Chapter Thirty-Six: Ajanta

Caves Frontal View: Author Soman released photo to GNU free document license 1.2, free to use with attribution of Author Soman.

Hugo van der Goes Painting: This is a faithful reproduction of a two-dimensional public domain work of art. Public domain in country of origin where the copyright term is author's life plus 100 years or fewer. This is also in the public domain of US because copyright was taken out before 1927 and not renewed. This photographic reproduction is therefore also considered in the public domain of United States.

Fergusson Print: This is a faithful reproduction of a two-dimensional public domain work of art. Public domain in country of origin where the copyright term is author's life plus 100 years or fewer. This is also in the public domain of US because copyright was taken out before 1927 and not renewed. This photographic reproduction is therefore also considered in the public domain of United States.

Vajrapani Fresco: Author Sadai (Thailand) released photo to Creative Commons attribution: share-alike 2.0 generic license, free to use with attribution of author, Sadai.

Chapter Thirty-Seven: Why Buddhism Died in India

Ashoka Sculpture: This is a faithful reproduction of a two-dimensional public domain work of art. Public domain in country of origin where the copyright term is author's life plus 100 years or fewer. This is also in the public domain of US because copyright was taken out before 1927 and not renewed. This photographic reproduction is therefore also considered in the public domain of United States.

Xuan Zang: Tokyo Museum. This is a faithful reproduction of a two-dimensional public domain work of art. Public domain in country of origin where the copyright term is author's life plus 100 years or fewer. This is also in the public domain of US because copyright was taken out before 1927 and not renewed. This photographic reproduction is therefore also considered in the public domain of United States.

Painting of "Journey To The West": Author Rolf Muller released photo to GNU free documentation license, version 1.2 with attribution of author.

Pilgrim's Progress: This is a faithful reproduction of a two-dimensional public domain work of art. Public domain in country of origin where the copyright term is author's life plus 100 years or fewer. This is also in the public domain of US because copyright was taken out before 1927 and not renewed. This photographic reproduction is therefore also considered in the public domain of United States.

Muslims Killing Priests: Hutchinson's "History of Nations" 1910 public domain: copyright not renewed in country of origin (UK) and public domain in USA because copyright was before 1927 and not renewed.

Goa Header

Photo from Facebook site "I Love Goa" posted by Vikash Jain. Unknown photographer and date. Photo is not copyright (as far as can be determined). It qualifies under US Fair usage for the following reasons: this qualifies as fair use under United States copyright because it illustrates subject where there is no free image to do the same. It is of low resolution and the use does not affect the commercial value of the subject in question.

Chapter Thirty-Eight: The Magic Bus

Kesey Bus: Author R. Carlsberg released photo to Creative Commons share-alike 4.0 international license free to use and copy with attribution of author, R. Carlsberg.

Smokers in Peshawar: Photo by Eddie Woods is not copyright (as far as can be determined) and it qualifies under US Fair usage for the following reasons: this qualifies as fair use under United States copyright because it illustrates subject where there is no free image to do the same. It is of low resolution and the use does not affect the commercial value of the subject in question.

Chapter Thirty-Nine: Freak paradise

"Garden of Earthly Delights" Public domain. This is a faithful reproduction of a two-dimensional public domain work of art. Public domain in country of origin where the copyright term is author's life plus 100 years or fewer. This is also in the public domain of US because copyright was taken out before 1927 and not renewed. This photographic reproduction is therefore also considered in the public domain of United States. US license: PD-ART.

Neal Cassady: GRAWLIN released photo to CC- attribution: share- alike 4.0 international license, free to use with attribution of author.

VW Van: Author Lifturn released photo to public domain free to use and copy, no license required.

Photos from Facebook site "I Love Goa" posted by Vikash Jain. Unknown photographers and dates. The photos are not copyright (as far as can be determined) and if the author is known, full credit is given. It qualifies under US Fair usage for the following reasons: this qualifies as fair use under United States copyright because it illustrates subject where there is no free image to do the same. It is of low resolution and the use does not affect the commercial value of the subject in question.

"Burning Bush" painting by Sebastian Bourdon 17th century: Hermitage Museum public domain. This is a faithful reproduction of a two-dimensional public domain work of art. Public domain in country of origin where the copyright term is author's life plus 100 years or fewer. This is also in the public domain of US because copyright was taken out before 1927 and not renewed. This photographic reproduction is therefore also considered in the public domain of United States. US license: PD-ART.

Chapter Forty: Lover Shot Down

Portrait of Maude Abrantes: Hecht Museum, Israel: Public domain. This is a faithful reproduction of a two-dimensional public domain work of art. Public domain in country of origin where the copyright term is author's life plus 100 years or fewer. This is also in the public domain of US because copyright was taken out before 1927 and not renewed. This photographic reproduction is therefore also considered in the public domain of United States. US license: PD-ART.

Chapter Forty-One: Lusiades

Portrait of Camoes: Public domain. This is a faithful reproduction of a two-dimensional public domain work of art. Public domain in country of origin where the copyright term is author's life plus 100 years or fewer. This is also in the public domain of US because copyright was taken out before 1927 and not renewed. This photographic reproduction is therefore also considered in the public domain of United States. US license: PD-ART.

Vasco da Gama's Ship: Public domain. This is a faithful reproduction of a two-dimensional public domain work of art. Public domain in country of origin where the copyright term is author's life plus 100 years or fewer. This is also in the public domain of US because copyright was taken out before 1927 and not renewed. This photographic reproduction is therefore also considered in the public domain of United States. US license: PD-ART.

Tilework: Isle of Love: Photographer Maragoto released image to CC-ATTRIB-SA-3.0 license with attribution.

Chapter Forty-Four: Trish and Old Goa

Old Goa Print and Map of Old Goa: Public domain. This is a faithful reproduction of a two-dimensional public domain work of art. Public domain in country of origin where the copyright term is author's life plus 100 years or fewer. This is also in the public domain of US because copyright was taken out before 1927 and not renewed. This photographic reproduction is therefore also considered in the public domain of United States. US license: PD-ART.

Inquisition Print: Welcome Images: Creative Commons-attribution 4.0 international license, free to use with attribution.

Ruin of St Augustine: Vyacheslav Argenburg released photo to GNU free documentation, version 1.2 free to use with attribution of author.

Chapter Forty-Seven: Dawn

Pre-Raphaelite Painting: Public domain. This is a faithful reproduction of a two-dimensional public domain work of art. Public domain in country of origin where the copyright term is author's life plus 100 years or fewer. This is also in the public domain of US because copyright was taken out before 1927 and not renewed. This photographic reproduction is therefore also considered in the public domain of United States. US license: PD-ART.

Chapter Forty-Eight: Life on Indian Roads

Doughty: photographer unknown from his book "Wanderings In Arabia" 1908 public domain, out of copyright in UK and USA.

Chapter Fifty: Hindu Concept of Time

Fair Use for Salvador Dali: This qualifies as fair use under United States copyright because it illustrates subject where there is no free image to do the same. It is of low resolution and the use does not affect the commercial value of the subject in question.

Chapter Fifty-Three: Dawning of a New Age

Helene Blavatsky 1877: Unknown photographer. This is a faithful reproduction of a two-dimensional public domain work of art. Public domain in country of origin where the copyright term is author's life plus 100 years or fewer. This is also in the public domain of US because copyright was taken out before 1927 and not renewed. This photographic reproduction is therefore also considered in the public domain of United States.

Chapter Fifty-Four: Srirangam Temple Complex

Srirangam Temple Complex 1870 (unknown photographer, owned by Leiden Univ. (The Netherlands), free usage for all, no license required.

Horses: Author Jean-Pierre Dalbera 2014 released image to Creative Commons- attribution 2.0 generic license, free to use with attribution of author.

Chapter Fifty-Five: Beedis

Women Making Beedis: Author released photo to public domain with no restrictions, CC-1.0 p.d. license.

Two Beedis Packages: Author Bhuri released photo to GNU free documentation, version 1.2 license, free with attribution of author.

Chapter Fifty-Six: Jesus as the First Freak

Hemis Buddhist Monastery: Michael Bramwell released photo to Creative Commons- attribution 2.0 license, free to use with attribution of author.

Images of Jesus: Wikimedia commons: public domain, no license required.

Chapter Fifty-Seven: From Idol to Figurehead

Postage Stamp of MGR: This is a government of India copyright work, but under national data sharing and accessibility policy of government of India this file is available, royalty free, for all commercial and non-commercial uses.

Auroville Header

Photos of the Mother and Sri Aurobindo are in the public domain: the photographs are in the public domain of India (as of 1966) and in US because it was published outside US and not published in US within 30 days. It was first published before 1964 with no copyright renewal.

Chapter Fifty-Nine: Sri Aurobindo, the Mother, and Auroville

Sri Aurobindo: Public domain in India and US, no copyright in either country.

The Mother Postage Stamp: This is a government of India copyright work, but under national data sharing and accessibility policy of government of India this file is available, royalty free, for all commercial and non-commercial uses.

Tapestry: This is a faithful reproduction of a two-dimensional public domain work of art. Public domain in country of origin where the copyright term is author's life plus 100 years or fewer. This is also in the public domain of US because copyright was taken out before 1927 and not renewed. This photographic reproduction is therefore also considered in the public domain of United States/ Creative Commons 2.0 public domain license.

Chapter Sixty-One: A Man of Constant Sorrow

George Tooker: Self-portrait. This qualifies as fair use under United States copyright because it illustrates subject where there is no free image to do the same. It is of low resolution and the use does not affect the commercial value of the subject in question.

Chapter Sixty-Two: A Walk of Song, Love, and Death

Saint Ursala: This is a faithful reproduction of a two-dimensional public domain work of art. Public domain in country of origin where the copyright term is author's life plus 100 years or fewer. This is also in the public domain of US because copyright was taken out before 1927 and not renewed. This photographic reproduction is therefore also considered in the public domain of United States. License: Creative Commons 2.0 share alike.

Chapter Sixty-Three: Ray II

"Childhood's End": this image is a book cover: This qualifies as fair use under United States copyright because it illustrates subject where there is no free image to do the same. It is of low resolution and the use does not affect the commercial value of the subject in question.

Chapter Sixty-Four: Jacob's Ladder

Luther Bible and Delacroix Painting: This is a faithful reproduction of a two-dimensional public domain work of art. Public domain in country of origin where the copyright term is author's life plus 100 years or fewer. This is also in the public domain of US because copyright was taken out before 1927 and not renewed. This photographic reproduction is therefore also considered in the public domain of United States. License: Creative Commons 2.0 share alike.

Lucian Freud Painting: This qualifies as fair use under United States copyright because it illustrates subject where there is no free image to do the same. It is of low resolution and the use does not affect the commercial value of the subject in question.

Chapter Sixty-Seven: Puri

Bondo Girl: Author Yves Picq released photo to GNU free documentation, version 1.2 free to use with attribution of author.

Lord Jagannath: Author Soft Dynamite released photo to Creative Commons -attribution: share-alike 3.0 free use with attribution of author.

Three Chariots: Author G-U-Tolkiehn released photo to GNU free documentation, version 1.2 free to use with attribution of author.

Chapter Sixty-Eight: Magic and Mystery in Stone

Stone Wheel/Sundial: Subhrajyoti07 released photo to Creative Commons-attribution: share-alike 4.0 international license, free to use with attribution of author.

Surya Sculpture: Jayantanth released photo to Creative Commons-attribution: share-alike 3.0 free use with attribution of author.

Chapter Sixty-Nine: Reise Mit Kinder

Photo of Hippies with their Children: Photos from Facebook site "I Love Goa" posted by Vikash Jain. Unknown photographers and dates. The photos are not copyrighted (as far as can be determined) and if the author is known, full credit is given. It qualifies under US Fair usage for the following reasons: this qualifies as fair use under United States copyright because it illustrates subject where there is no free image to do the same. It is of low resolution and the use does not affect the commercial value of the subject in question.

Chapter Seventy-One: Ideal of Kathmandu

Buddhist Altar: This qualifies as fair use under United States copyright because it illustrates subject where there is no free image to do the same. It is of low resolution and the use does not affect the commercial value of the subject in question.

Chapter Eighty-One: Freaks, Houseboats, and Nietzsche

Nazi Soldier: Ernest Ludwig Kretschmann created Nazi propaganda poster. Copyright has expired and work is in the public domain (CC-PD license).

Nietzsche photo taken by Frederich Hartmann 1875. This is a faithful reproduction of a two-dimensional public domain work of art. Public domain in country of origin where the copyright term is author's life plus 100 years or fewer. This is also in the public domain of US because copyright was taken out before 1927 and not renewed. This photographic reproduction is therefore also considered in the public domain of United States. License: Creative Commons 2.0 share alike.

Chapter Eighty-Six: Delhi

Humayun's Tomb Delhi: Author Eatch released photo to Creative Commons-attribution 4.0 license, free to use with attribution of author.

Chapter Eighty-Seven: Partition

Bouke-White Photograph: This qualifies as fair use under United States copyright because it illustrates subject where there is no free image to do the same. It is of low resolution and the use does not affect the commercial value of the subject in question.

Chapter Eighty-Eight: Bangal Lancers

Buffalo Bill: William Nolman and Sons photograph from Montreal, Canada. Copyright was not renewed in Canada is now public domain there. It is also public domain in US since copyright expired and first publication was before 1928, photo is in the Library of Congress (CC-PD license).

Sir Richard Burton: Photograph by Rischgitz/Stringer public domain in US since copyright expired and was published before 1928 (CC-PD license).

Chapter Eighty-Nine: One Tries to Forget

Nora Jones: Photographer Jamie Anna released photo to public domain, no license required.

Kalasha Girls: Tahsin A. Shah, 2016 released photo to Creative Commons: attribution-share-alike 4.0 international license, free to use with attribution of author.

Alexander Gardner: Photo from his memoir book, copyright expired and was not renewed, now is public domain in US (CC-PD license).

Chapter Ninety-Two: Fatehpur Sikri

Fatehpur Gate: Marcin Bialek 2010 released photo to GNU free documentation license, ver.1.2, free to use with attribution of author.

Chapter Ninety-Three: The Freak Buys a Sitar

Veda Chanting: Photo from "Real Bharat" web page. Author Ramakhishnan wrote an article with photos on culture in India 2016. This qualifies as fair use under United States copyright because it illustrates subject where there is no free image to do the same. It is of low resolution and the use does not affect the commercial value of the subject in question.

Chapter Ninety-Four: Jaipur

Samrat Yantra: Photographer Rialfer 2010 released photo to GNU free documentation license, ver. 1.2, free to use with attribution of author.

Chapter Ninety-Six: Mahavira and the Jains

Mahavira Giving Half His Cloak to Begger: Painter Samyakta 2255 released painting to Creative Commons-attribution: share-alike 4.0 license, free to use with attribution of author.

Jain Statue: Dayodaya 2001 released photo to Creative Commons-attribution: share-alike 3.0 license, free to use with attribution of author.

Chapter Ninety-Seven: Palace of the Winds

Morning Frontal View and Closeup of Façade: Chainwit released photos (two) to Creative Commons-attribution: share-alike 4.0 international license, ver.1.2 free to use with attribution of author.

Mausoleum of Zunirrad Khatun: Hussain Muttar released photo to Creative Commons-attribution: share-alike 4.0 international license, ver. 1.2, free to use with attribution of author.

Chapter Hundred: Flash Gordon's Worst Fear

"Flash Gordon Conquers the Universe" 1940 copyright expired and was not renewed. The film is now in the public domain.

About the Author

I am a first-generation American, born of immigrant Norwegian and Swiss parents. I was the first in my family to attend college (Lafayette College) on a Reserve Officer Training Corps scholarship and a second-generation soldier (my father served in the US Army during World War II). I served three years in the army and close to two years traveling in Asia. I grew up in the 1960s, the high noon of the American Empire, and see myself as a child of both Woodstock and Vietnam.

The patriotic idealism of the Peace Corps in the Kennedy years dissipated in the societal division and carnage of a senseless war. Yet my generation believed that everything was possible. We could remake America to be that visionary "Shining City on the Hill" our forefathers had envisioned. The peace, love, and music of Woodstock seemed to be a harbinger of a new age of swords into ploughshares.

It is this optimism that inspired my book. It is also my "Bildungsroman," a young man trying to understand the world and himself. I have an insatiable sense of curiosity and wonder about the world and this zeitgeist is what I strive to convey in my journal and photographs.

About the Book: Stoner to Seeker - 1970s Asian Hippie Trail

I arrived in India as a stoned freak. India was the pot of gold at the end of the hippie rainbow trail that stretched from London to Goa and Kathmandu. We were the "Freak Nation," everything was possible, we could change ourselves and society with love and understanding.

India bewitches you with its beauty: technicolor deserts, pristine beaches, majestic mountains, and lush verdant jungles; this is the Yin of India. The Yang, the other India, is grinding poverty, overcrowded chaotic cities, and resigned acceptance of your place in society.

However, it was the people I met along the way that changed me. Indians opened me to new revelations on religion and what is really important: an alternative way of life to our Western culture and materialism. The Nepalis were blissfully living in a Medieval society, where religion was a daily part of life, while the Bangladesh students were struggling to make "A Brave New World" out of the horror and chaos of the Independence War. The freaks, religious seekers, and lovers along the way were guideposts on my "Pilgrim's Progress" to understand what I really wanted out of life.

Join me on my magic carpet ride, to paraphrase Proust, "In Search of Glorious Time."

www.ingramcontent.com/pod-product-compliance
Lightning Source LLC
Chambersburg PA
CBHW081612100526
44590CB00021B/3415